Shojo Beat

La Corda d'Oro

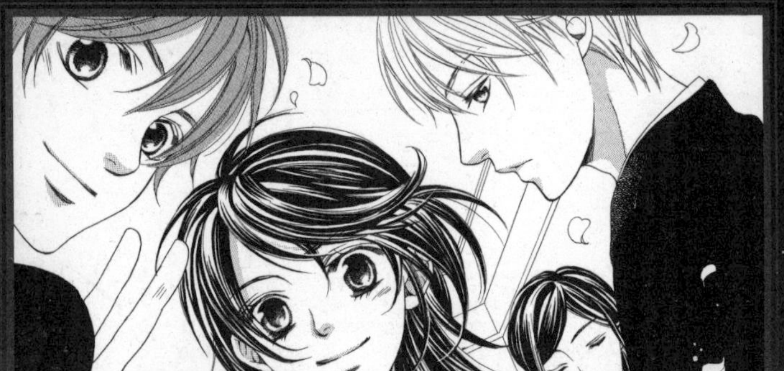

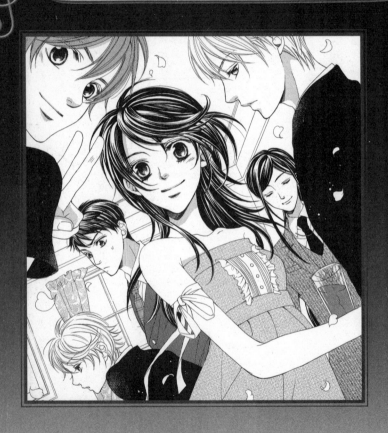

7

Story & Art by Yuki Kure

Kahoko Hino
(General Education School, 2nd year)

The heroine. She knows nothing about music, but she still finds herself participating in the music competition equipped with a magic violin.

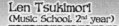

Len Tsukimori
(Music School, 2nd year)

A violin major and a cold perfectionist from a musical family of unquestionable talent.

Ryotaro Tsuchiura
(General Education, 2nd year)

A member of the soccer team who seems to be looking after Kahoko as a fellow Gen Ed student.

Keiichi Shimizu
(Music school, 1st year)

A student of the cello who walks to the beat of his own drum and is often lost in the world of music. He is also often asleep.

Kazuki Hihara
(Music school, 3rd year)

An energetic and friendly trumpet major and a fan of anything fun.

Azuma Yunoki
(Music school, 3rd year)

A flute major and the son of a graceful and kind traditional flower arrangement master. He even has a dedicated fan club called the "Yunoki Guard."

Hiroto Kanazawa
(Music teacher)

The contest coordinator, whose lazy demeanor suggests he is avoiding any hassle.

Story

Our story is set at Seiso Academy, which is split into the General Education School and the Music School. Kahoko, a Gen Ed student, encounters a music fairy named Lili, who gives her a magic violin that anyone can play. Suddenly, Kahoko finds herself in the school's music competition, with good-looking, quirky Music School students as her fellow contestants! Kahoko comes to accept her daunting task and finds herself enjoying music. The Second Selection tests the emotions of all the participants, especially Kazuki, who realizes he's drawn to Kahoko. Now the Third Selection is about to begin. But Kahoko is torn between her newfound love of music and her guilt over competing with a magic violin...

Previously ...

Kahoko begins to feel guilty about relying on magic. Meanwhile, Len catches on that the only violin Kahoko can play is her own! The roller coaster of the Third Selection is about to begin!

The music fairy Lili, who got Kahoko caught up in this affair. ↓

IF YOU DON'T HAVE AN ANSWER...
...I CAN'T ACCEPT YOU AS A FELLOW MUSICIAN.
I...
THE SECRET OF THE VIOLIN!

La Corda d'Oro

CONTENTS
Volume 7

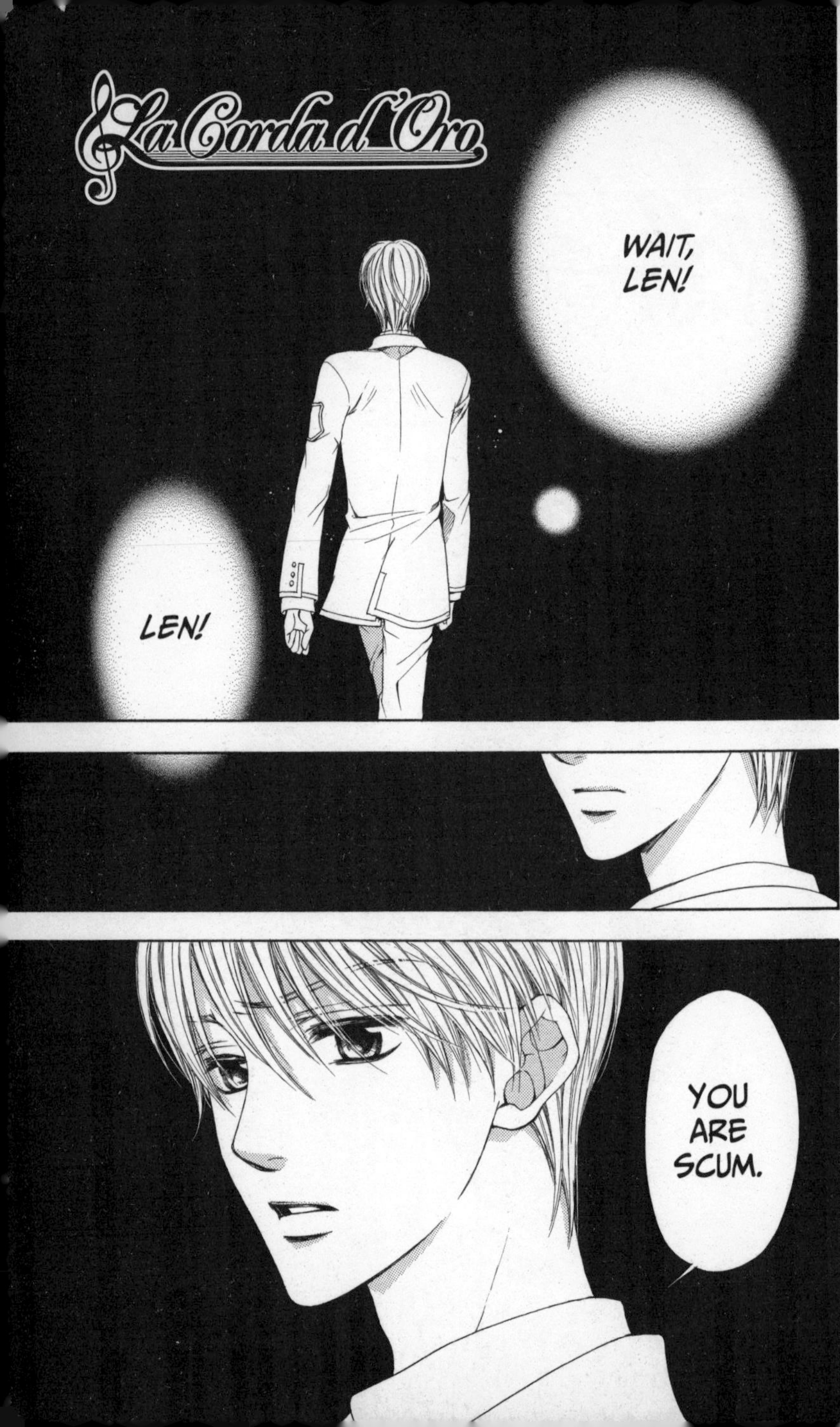
La Corda d'Oro
WAIT, LEN!
LEN!
YOU ARE SCUM.

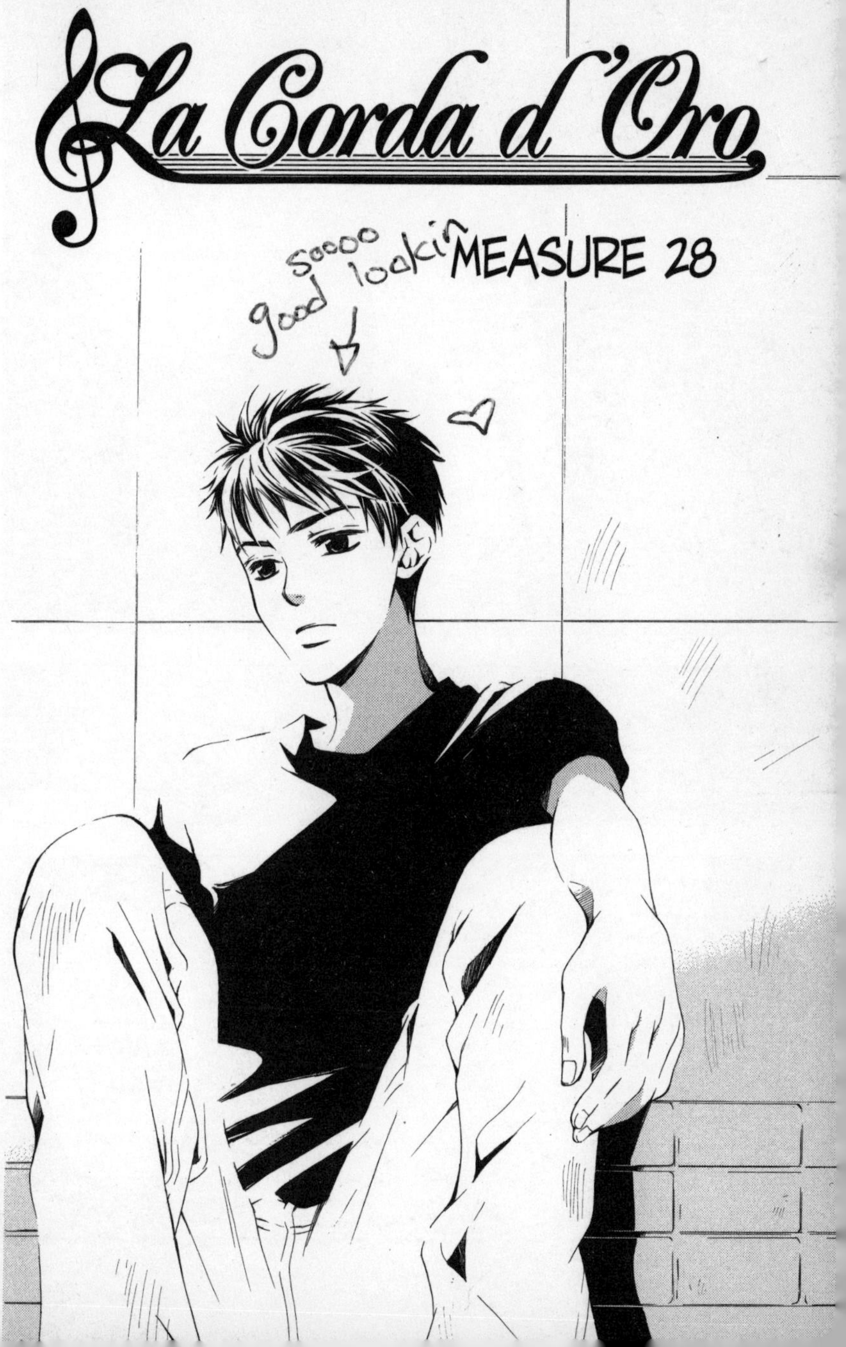
La Corda d'Oro
MEASURE 28
soooo good lookin

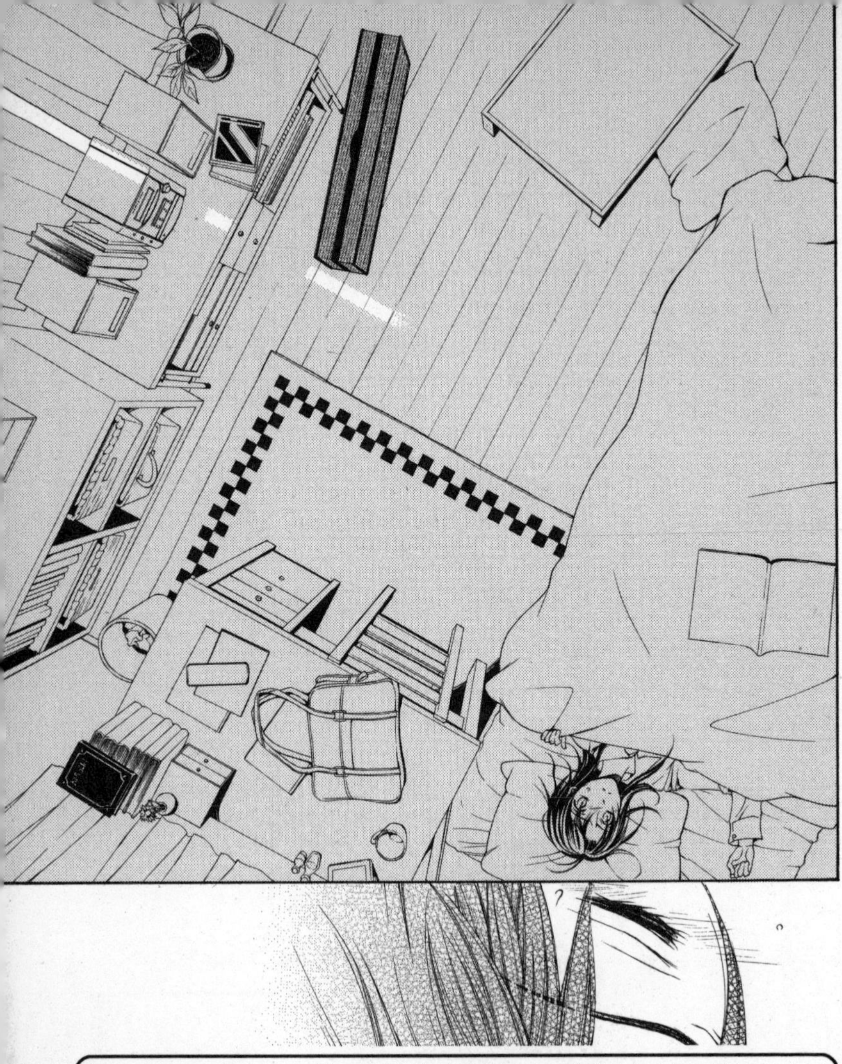

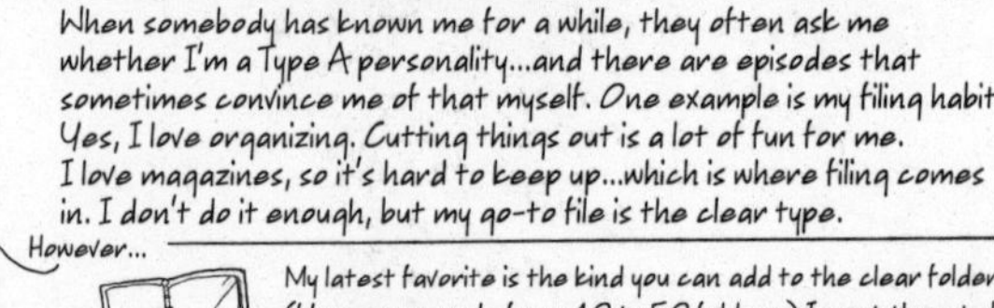

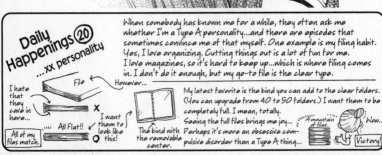

Daily Happenings 20 ...xx personality

When somebody has known me for a while, they often ask me whether I'm a Type A personality...and there are episodes that sometimes convince me of that myself. One example is my filing habit. Yes, I love organizing. Cutting things out is a lot of fun for me. I love magazines, so it's hard to keep up...which is where filing comes in. I don't do it enough, but my go-to file is the clear type.

File

However...

I hate that they cave in here...

All Flat!!

All of my files match.

I want them to look like this!

The kind with the removable center.

My latest favorite is the kind you can add to the clear folders. (You can upgrade from 40 to 50 folders.) I want them to be completely full. I mean, totally.
Seeing the full files brings me joy... Perhaps it's more an obsessive compulsive disorder than a Type A thing...

A mountain of files.

Wow...

Victory!

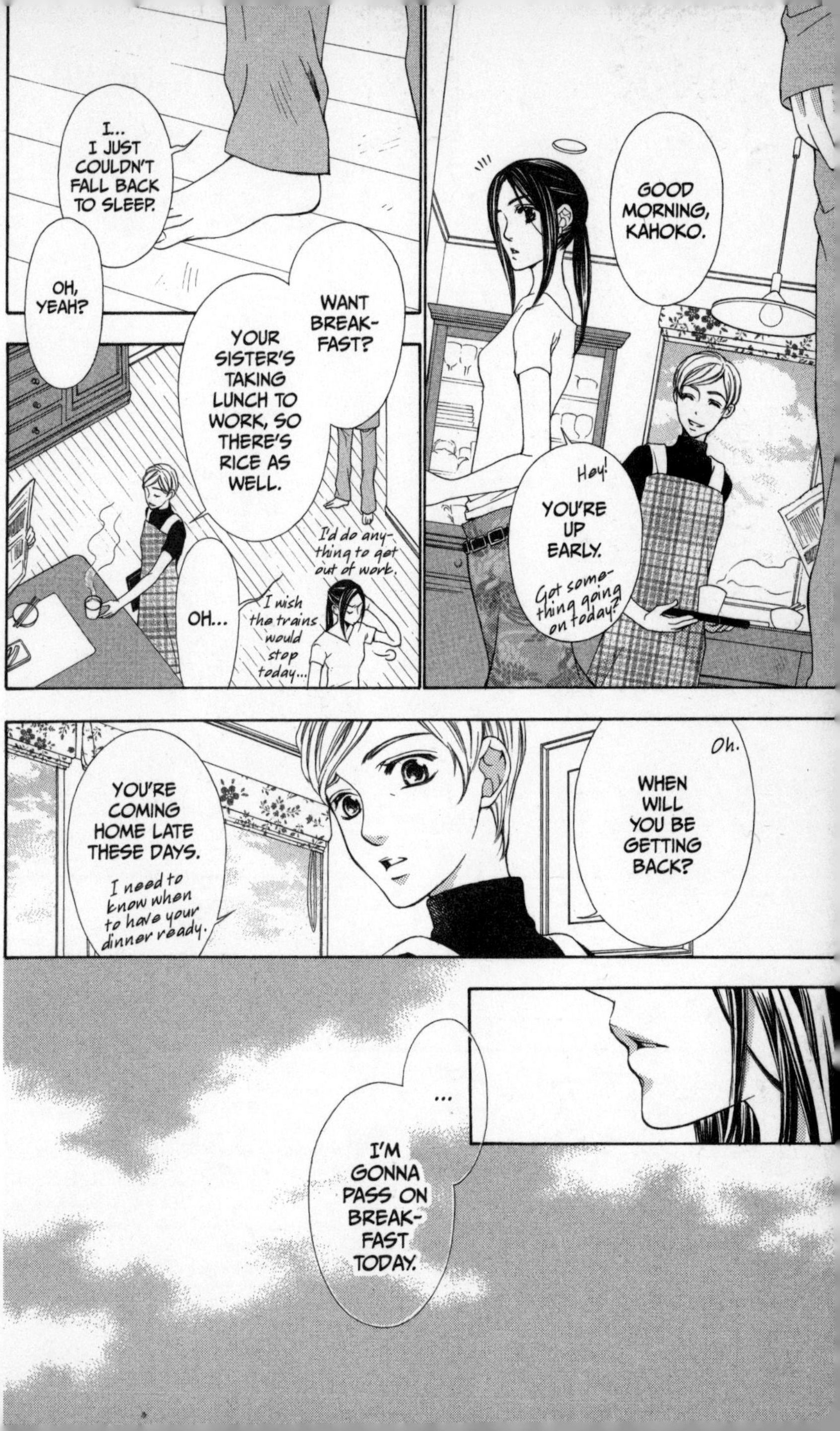
GOOD MORNING, KAHOKO.
Hey!
YOU'RE UP EARLY.
Got something going on today?
I... I JUST COULDN'T FALL BACK TO SLEEP.
OH, YEAH?
WANT BREAKFAST?
YOUR SISTER'S TAKING LUNCH TO WORK, SO THERE'S RICE AS WELL.
I'd do anything to get out of work.
I wish the trains would stop today...
OH...
Oh.
WHEN WILL YOU BE GETTING BACK?
YOU'RE COMING HOME LATE THESE DAYS.
I need to know when to have your dinner ready.
...
I'M GONNA PASS ON BREAKFAST TODAY.

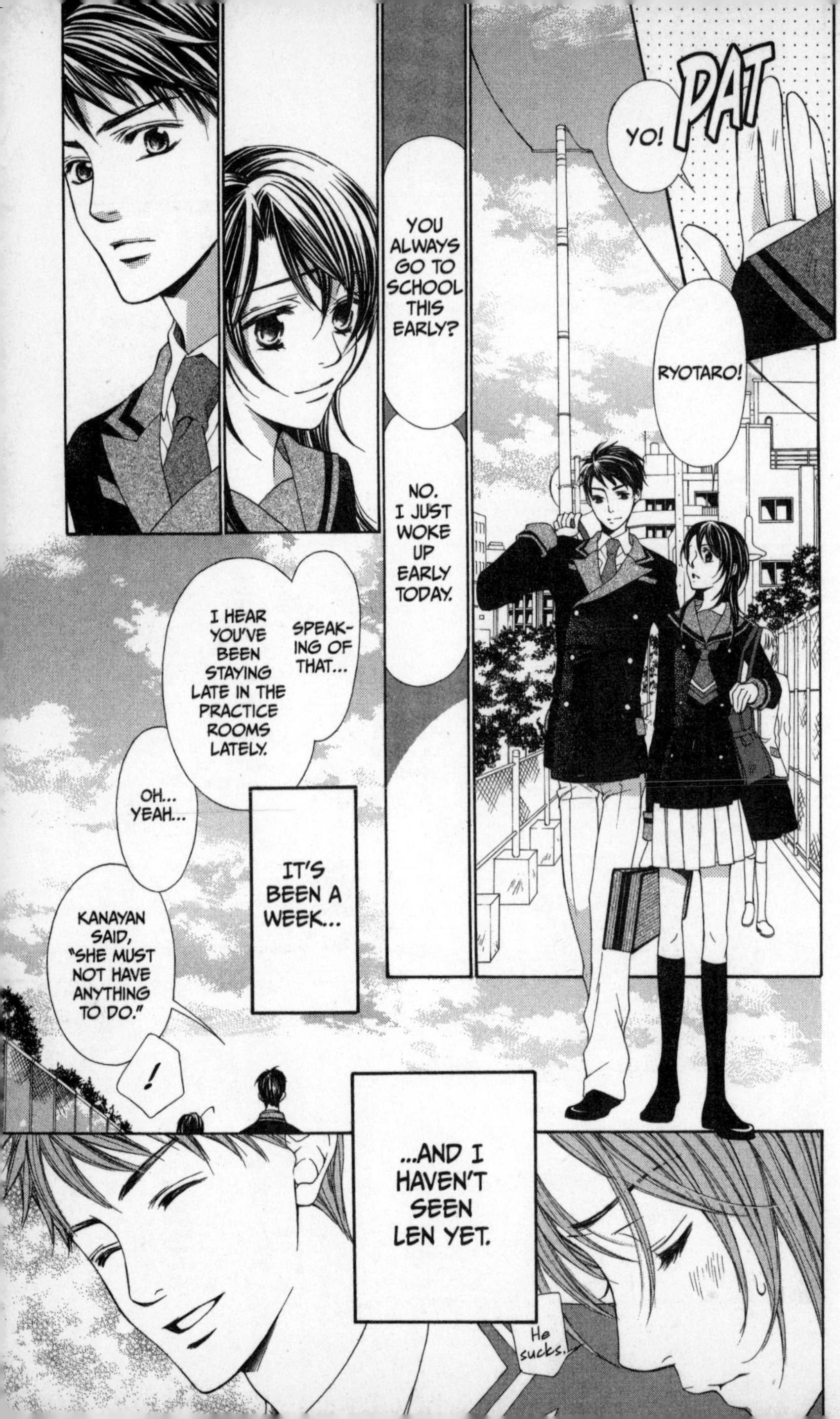
PAT
YO!
RYOTARO!
YOU ALWAYS GO TO SCHOOL THIS EARLY?
NO. I JUST WOKE UP EARLY TODAY.
SPEAK-ING OF THAT...
I HEAR YOU'VE BEEN STAYING LATE IN THE PRACTICE ROOMS LATELY.
IT'S BEEN A WEEK...
OH... YEAH...
KANAYAN SAID, "SHE MUST NOT HAVE ANYTHING TO DO."
!
...AND I HAVEN'T SEEN LEN YET.
He sucks.

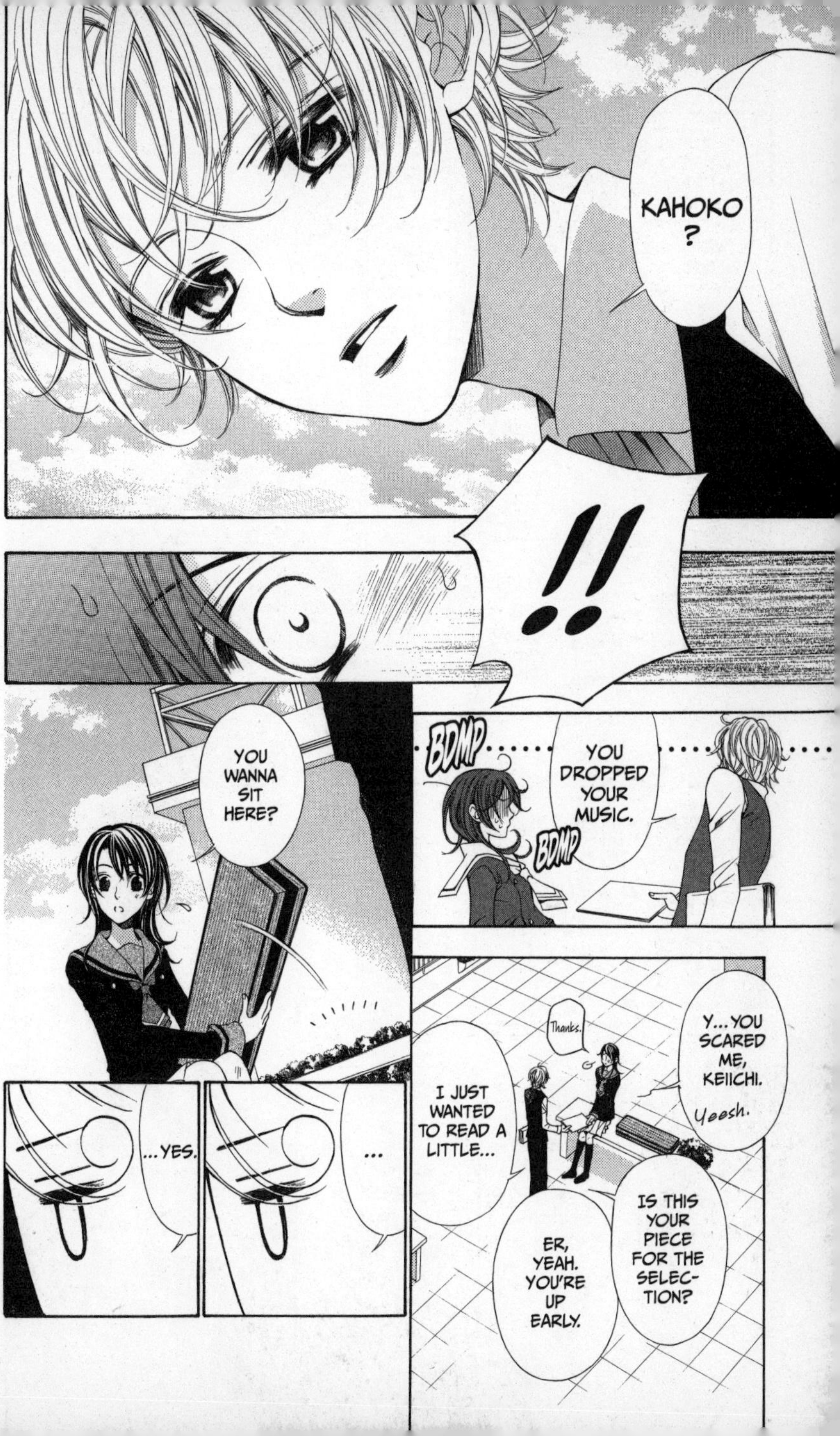
KAHOKO ?
!!
BDMP
YOU DROPPED YOUR MUSIC.
BDMP
Y...YOU SCARED ME, KEIICHI.
Yeesh.
Thanks.
I JUST WANTED TO READ A LITTLE...
IS THIS YOUR PIECE FOR THE SELECTION?
ER, YEAH. YOU'RE UP EARLY.
YOU WANNA SIT HERE?
...
...YES.

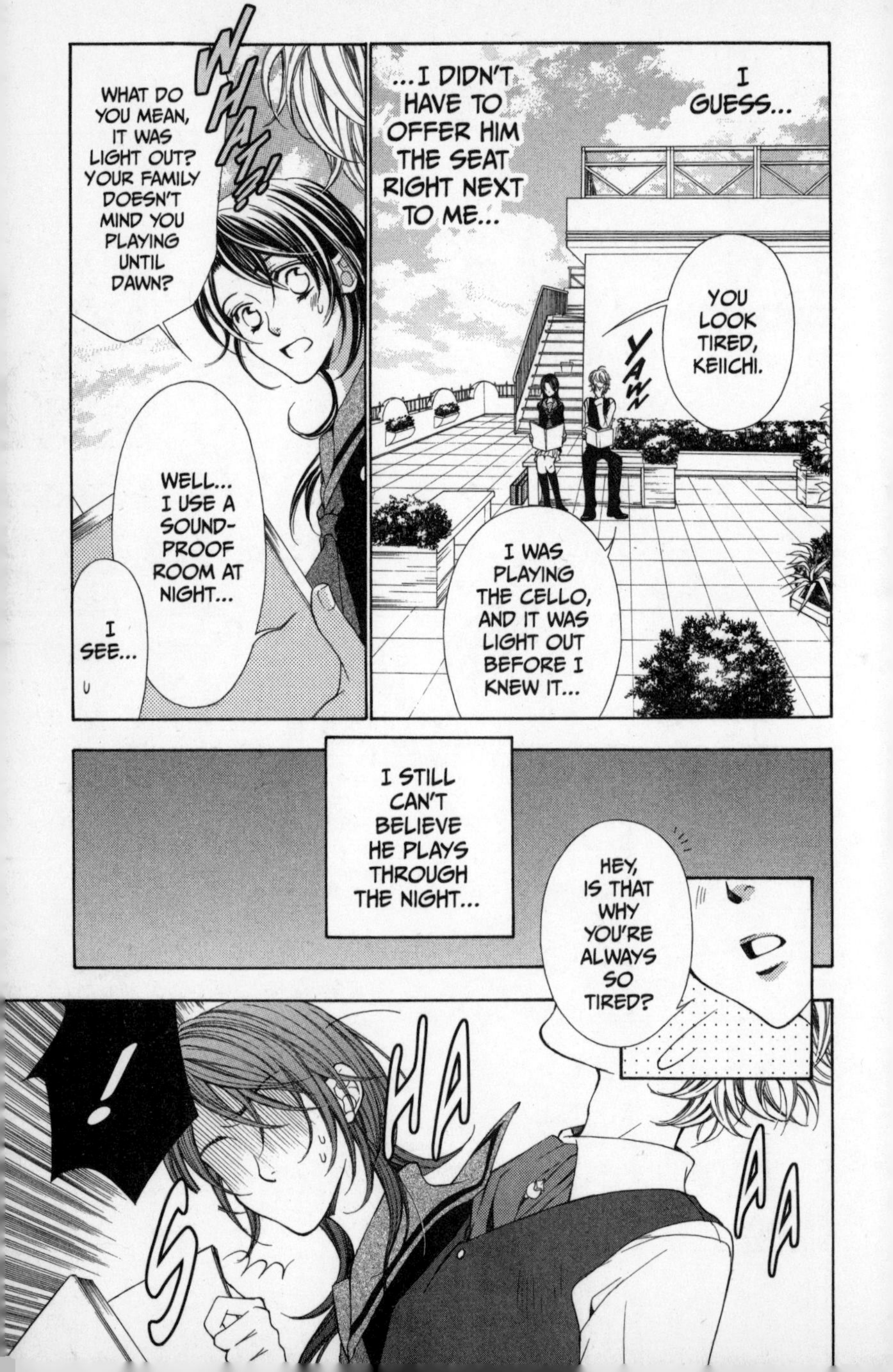
I GUESS...
...I DIDN'T HAVE TO OFFER HIM THE SEAT RIGHT NEXT TO ME...
YOU LOOK TIRED, KEIICHI.
YAWN
I WAS PLAYING THE CELLO, AND IT WAS LIGHT OUT BEFORE I KNEW IT...
WHAP!
WHAT DO YOU MEAN, IT WAS LIGHT OUT? YOUR FAMILY DOESN'T MIND YOU PLAYING UNTIL DAWN?
WELL... I USE A SOUND-PROOF ROOM AT NIGHT...
I SEE...
I STILL CAN'T BELIEVE HE PLAYS THROUGH THE NIGHT...
HEY, IS THAT WHY YOU'RE ALWAYS SO TIRED?
HA
AAA
!
S

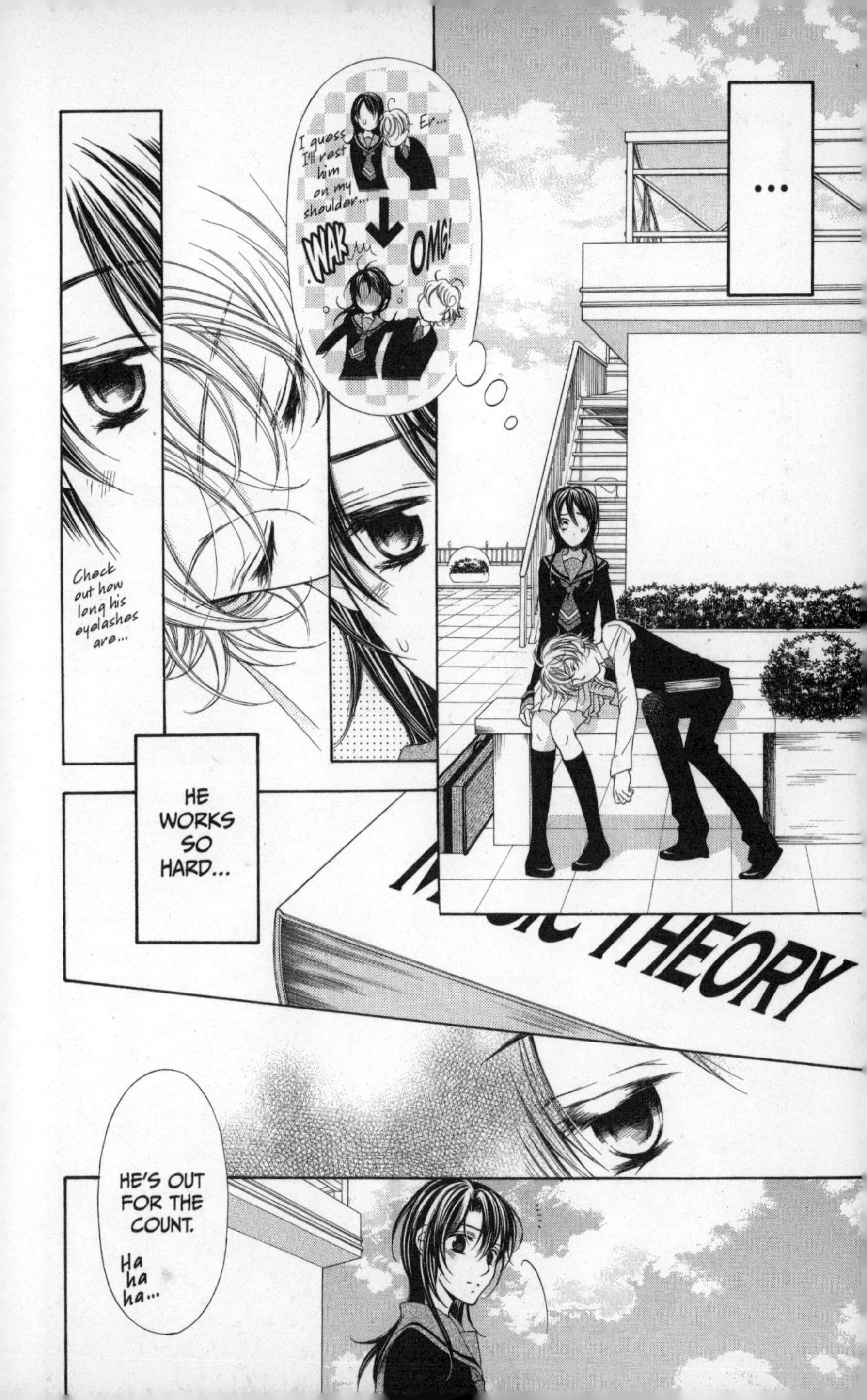
...
Er...
I guess I'll rest him on my shoulder...
WAK
OMG!
Check out how long his eyelashes are...
HE WORKS SO HARD...
THEORY
HE'S OUT FOR THE COUNT.
Ha ha ha...

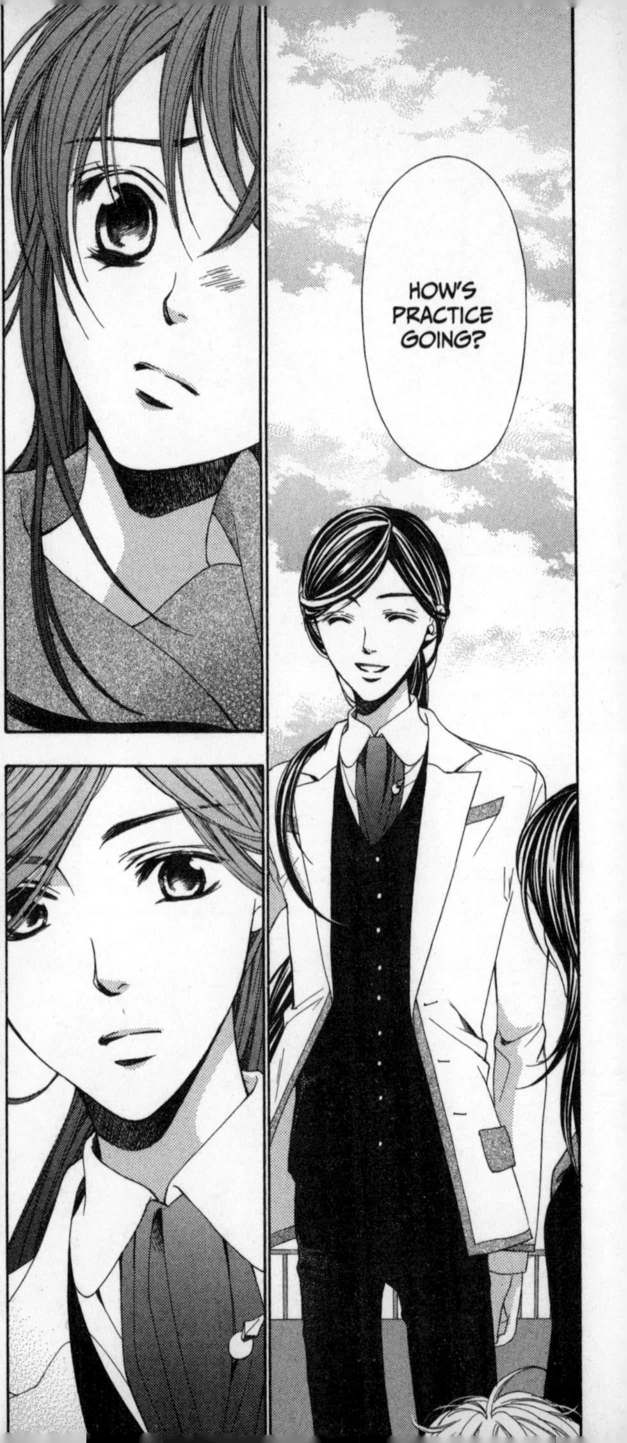
HOW'S PRACTICE GOING?

ONE

Hello. ★
Thank you so much for purchasing volume 7 of *La Corda*.
This is Yuki.
The cover illustration for this volume is the five boys. I've continued the theme of casual clothes from volume 6. Azuma's wearing pink.
I figured he'd be able to pull it off. LOL. Maybe even Keiichi would look okay, but pink is definitely not for Ryotaro or Len.
And anything goes for Kazuki.
I actually like drawing clothes for the guys more than I do for the girls. I must say, though, Azuma is always a problem for me. I had him wear a T-shirt this time, but the question remains whether he even owns one...
Probably some high-end, tailored kind...
Yep, sounds about right.

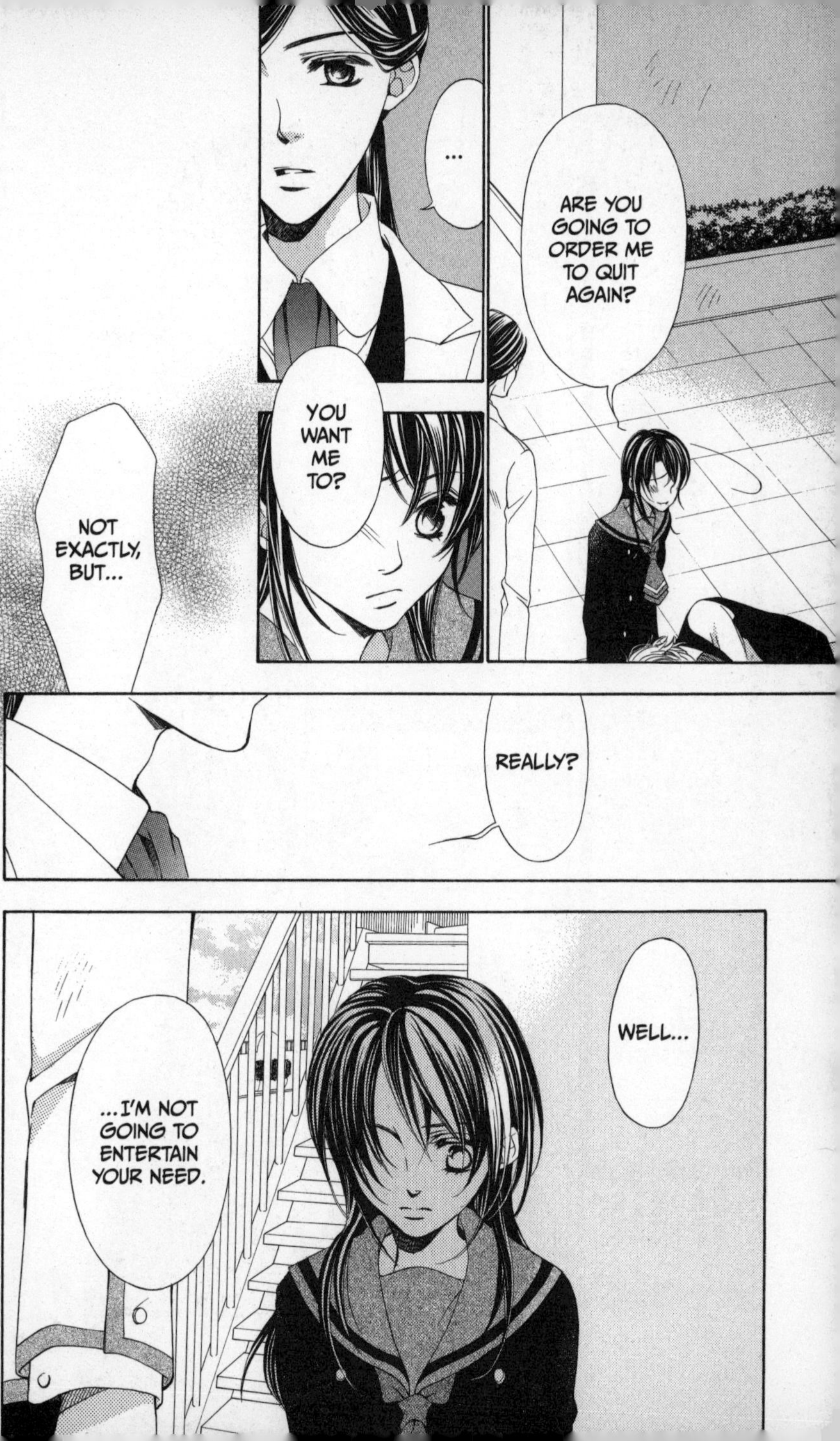
ARE YOU GOING TO ORDER ME TO QUIT AGAIN?
...
YOU WANT ME TO?
NOT EXACTLY, BUT...
REALLY?
WELL...
...I'M NOT GOING TO ENTERTAIN YOUR NEED.

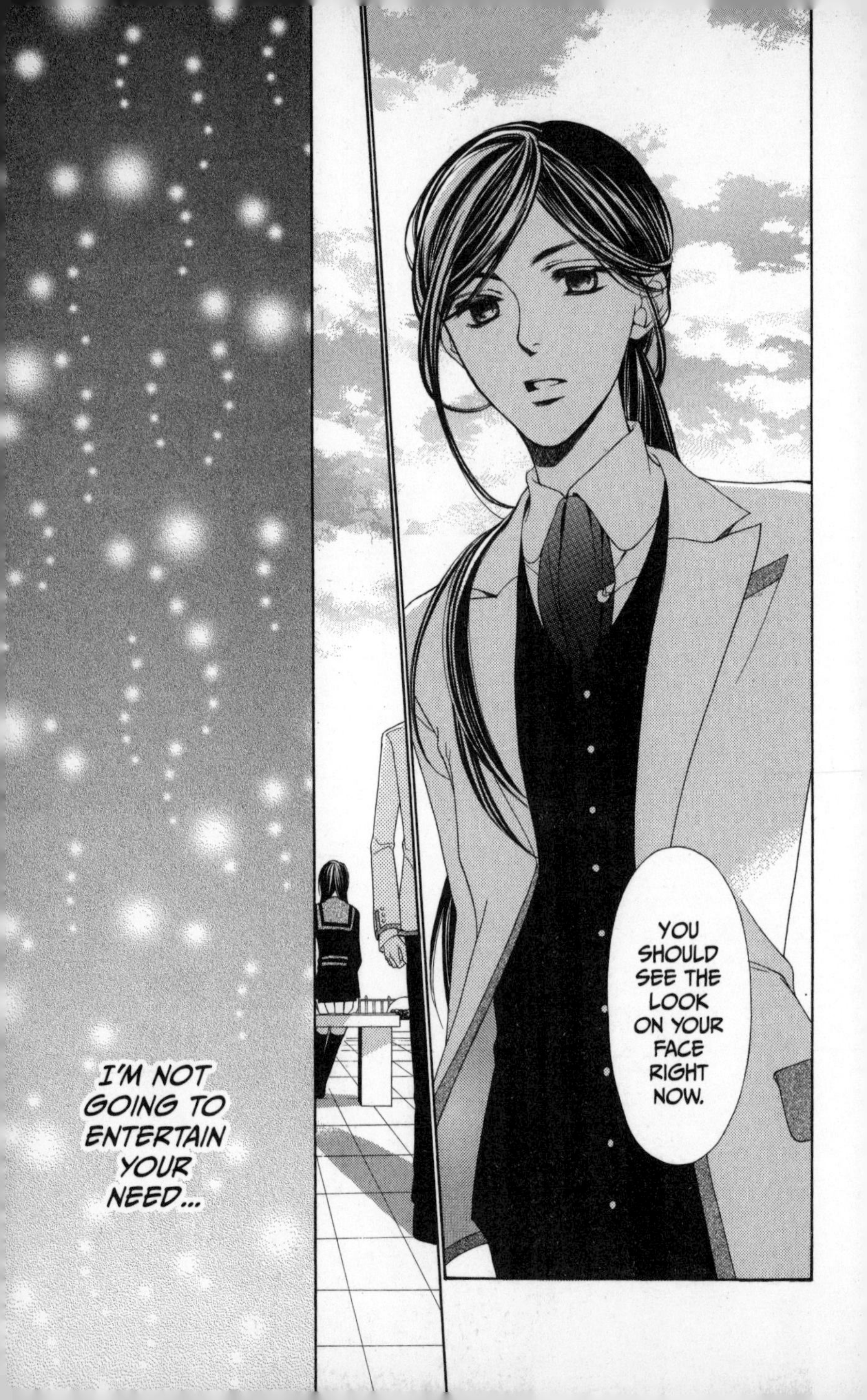
YOU SHOULD SEE THE LOOK ON YOUR FACE RIGHT NOW.
I'M NOT GOING TO ENTERTAIN YOUR NEED...

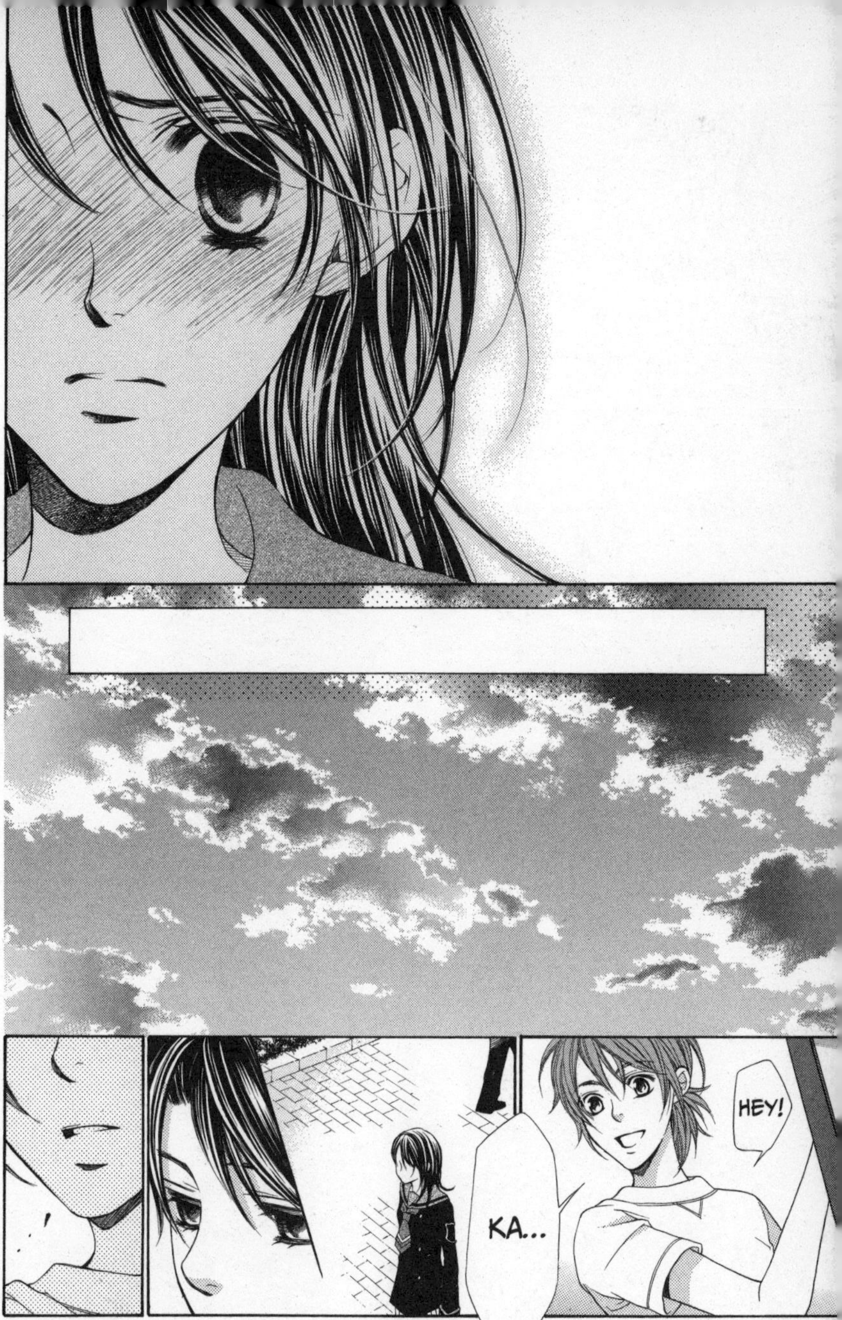
HEY!
KA...

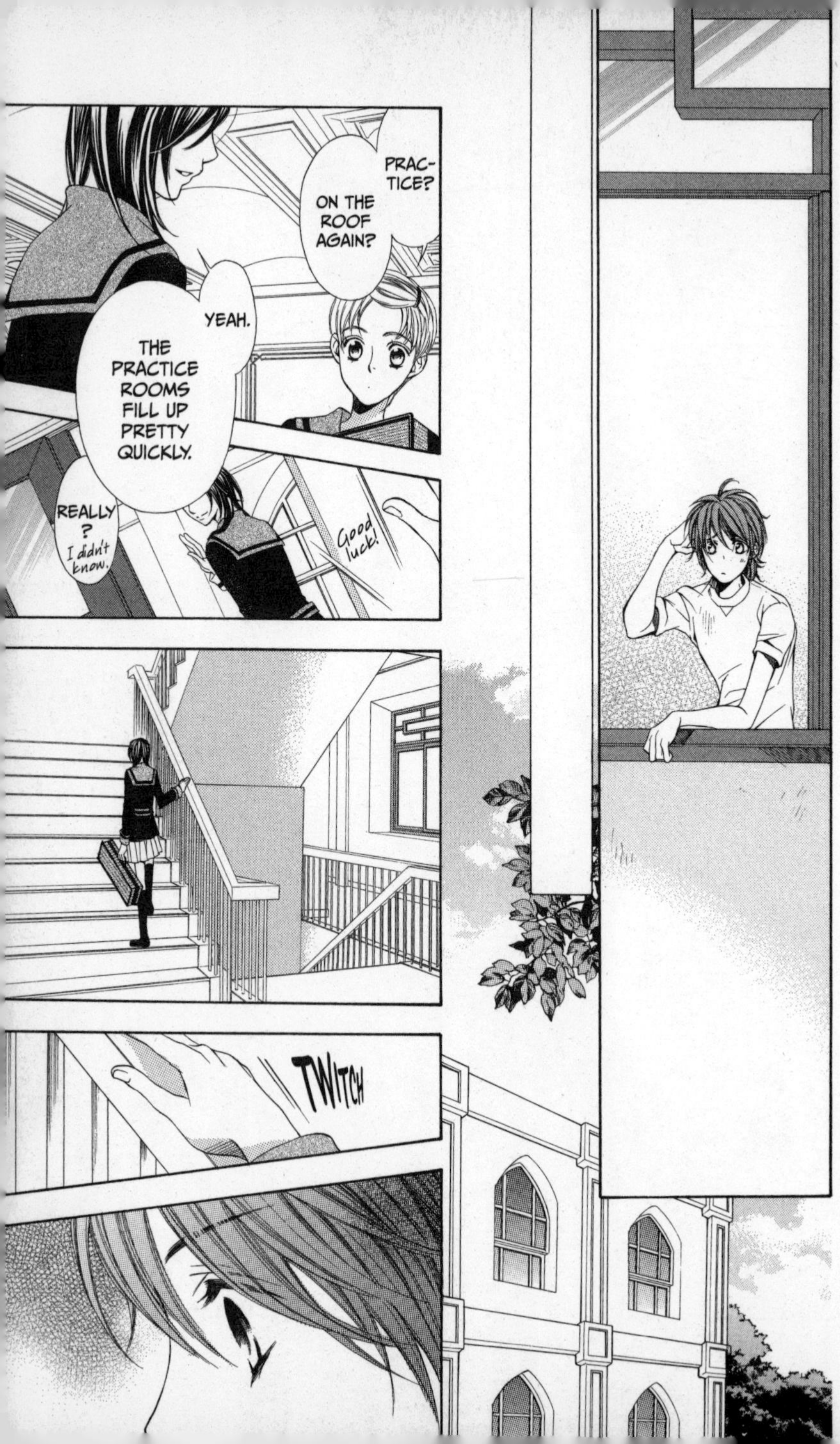

PRAC-TICE? ON THE ROOF AGAIN?
YEAH. THE PRACTICE ROOMS FILL UP PRETTY QUICKLY.
REALLY? I didn't know.
Good luck!
TWITCH

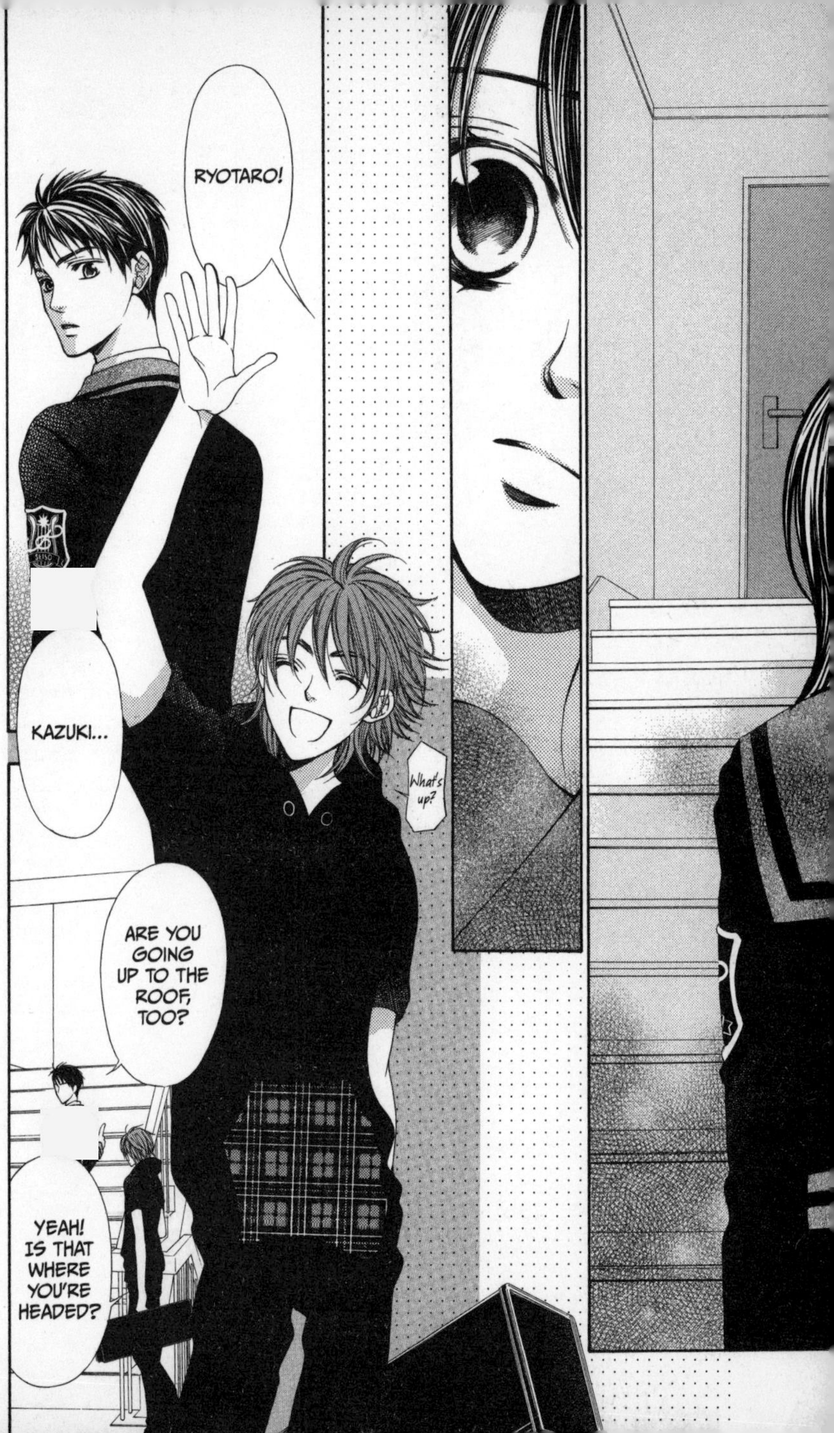
RYOTARO!
KAZUKI...
What's up?
ARE YOU GOING UP TO THE ROOF, TOO?
YEAH! IS THAT WHERE YOU'RE HEADED?

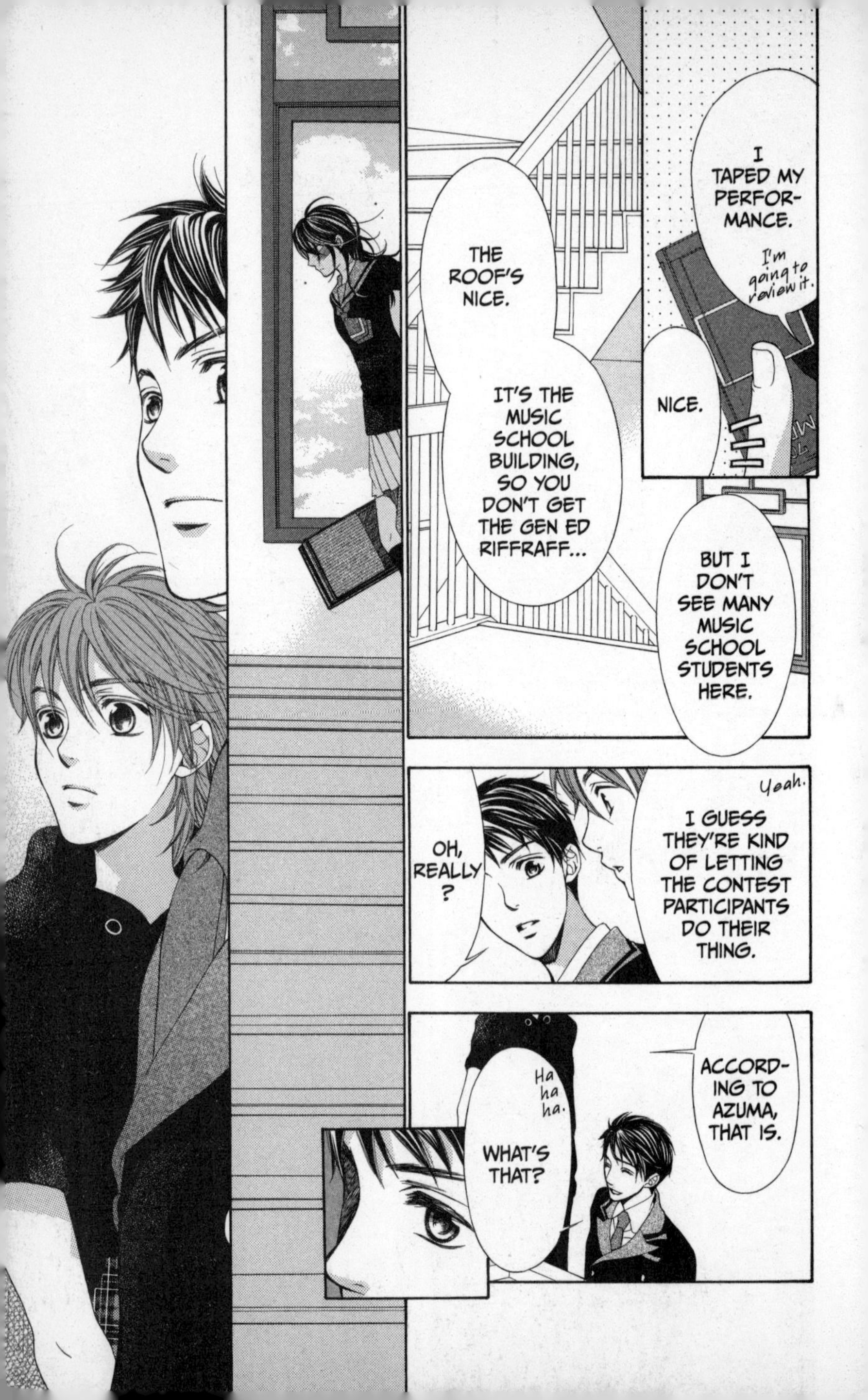
I TAPED MY PERFORMANCE.
I'm going to review it.
NICE.
THE ROOF'S NICE.
IT'S THE MUSIC SCHOOL BUILDING, SO YOU DON'T GET THE GEN ED RIFFRAFF...
BUT I DON'T SEE MANY MUSIC SCHOOL STUDENTS HERE.
Yeah.
I GUESS THEY'RE KIND OF LETTING THE CONTEST PARTICIPANTS DO THEIR THING.
OH, REALLY?
ACCORDING TO AZUMA, THAT IS.
Ha ha ha.
WHAT'S THAT?

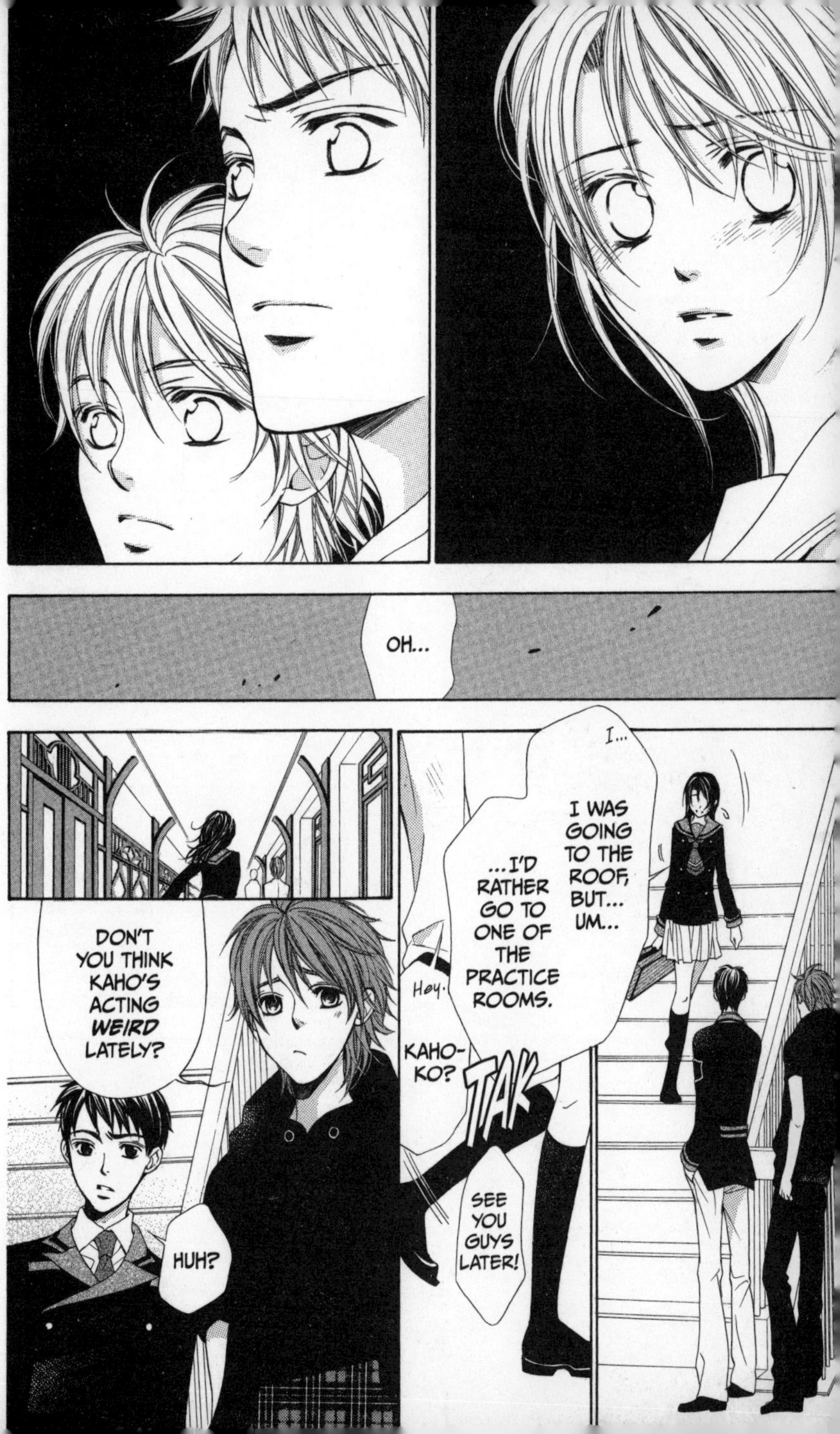
OH...
I...
I WAS GOING TO THE ROOF, BUT... UM...
...I'D RATHER GO TO ONE OF THE PRACTICE ROOMS.
Hey.
KAHO-KO?
TAK
SEE YOU GUYS LATER!
DON'T YOU THINK KAHO'S ACTING *WEIRD* LATELY?
HUH?

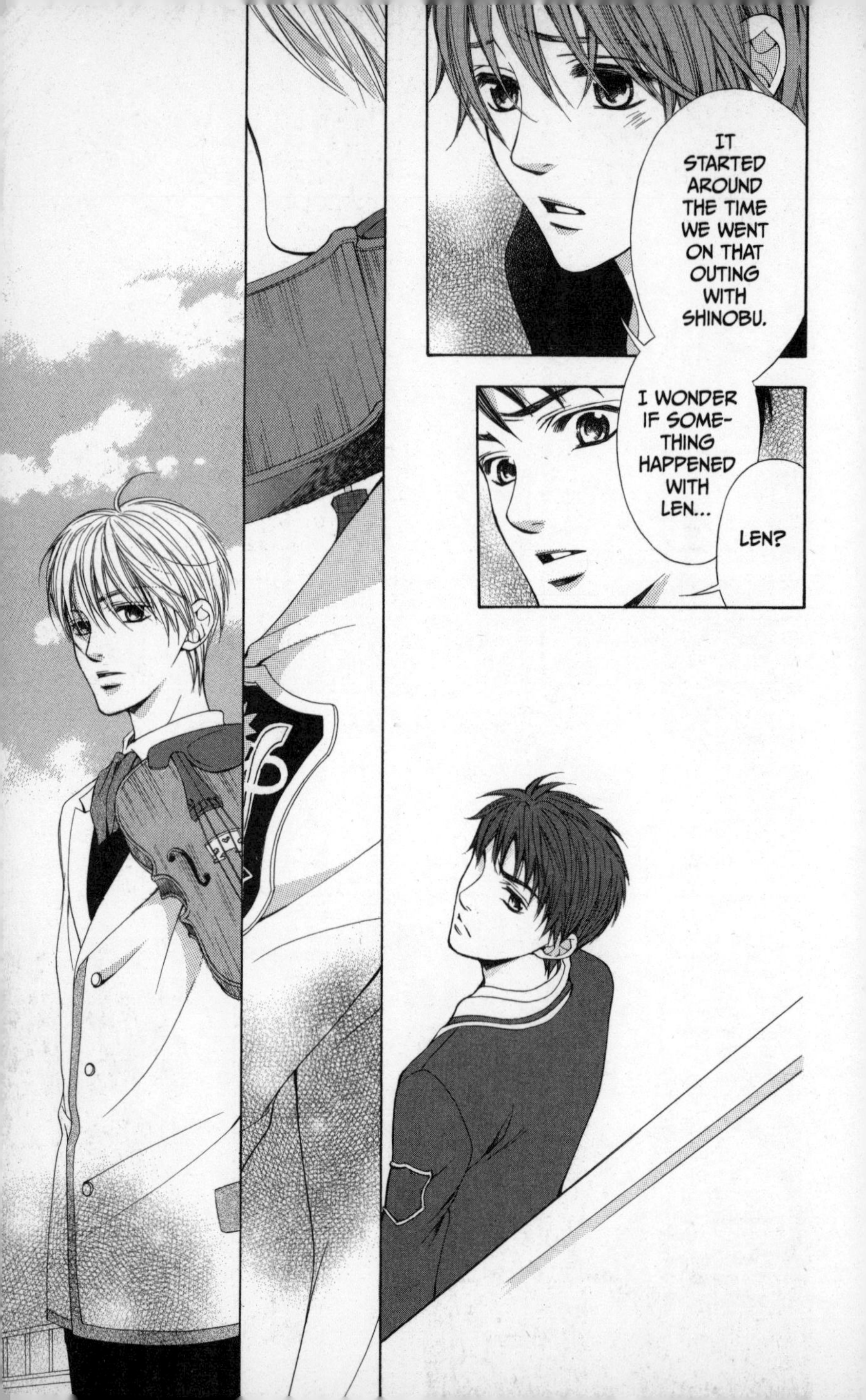
IT STARTED AROUND THE TIME WE WENT ON THAT OUTING WITH SHINOBU.
I WONDER IF SOMETHING HAPPENED WITH LEN...
LEN?

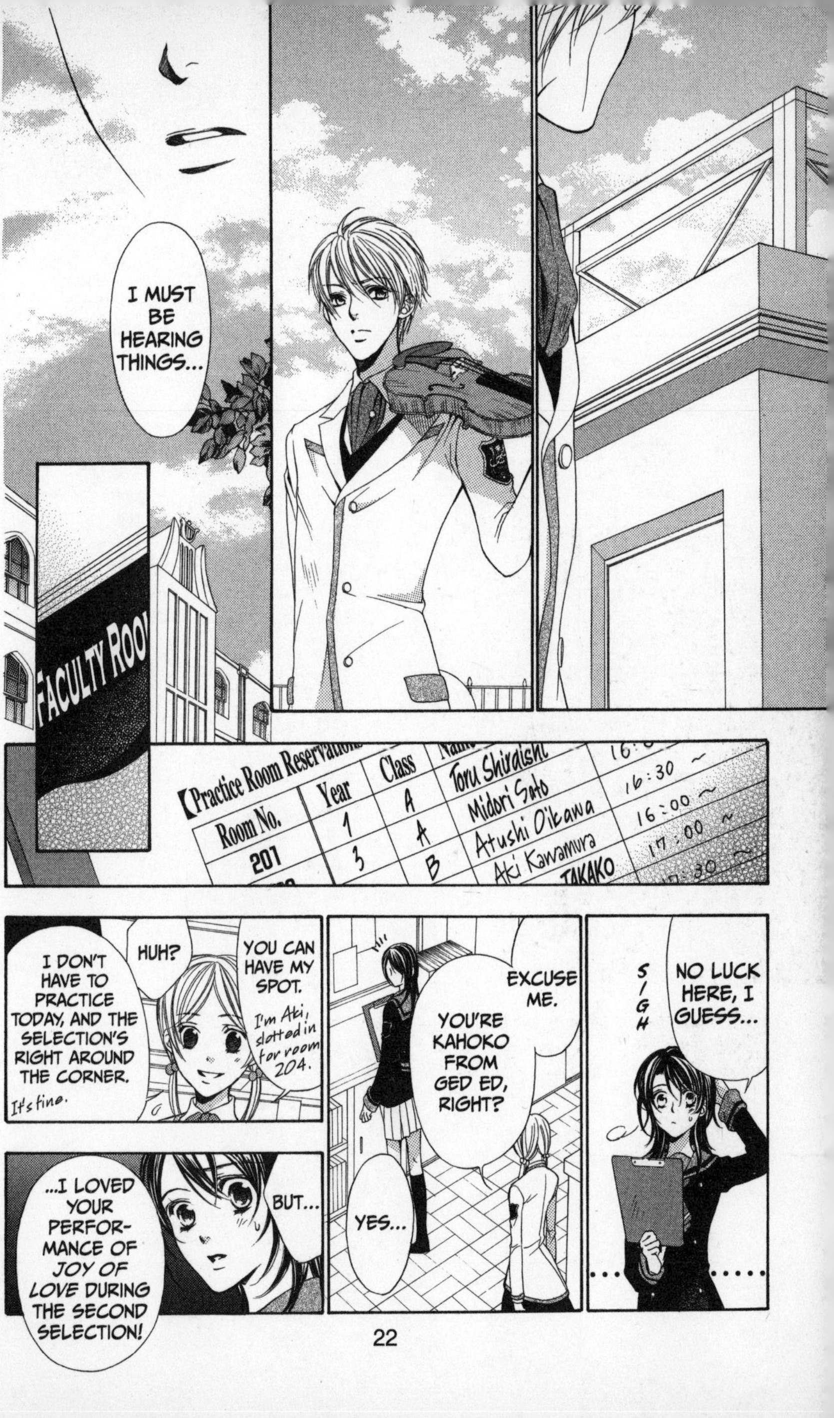
I MUST BE HEARING THINGS...
FACULTY ROO
【Practice Room Reservation
Room No.
Year
Class
201
1
3
A
A
B
Toru Shiraishi
Midori Sato
Atushi Oikawa
Aki Kawamura
TAKAKO
16:30 ~
16:00 ~
17:00 ~
SIGH
NO LUCK HERE, I GUESS...
......
EXCUSE ME.
YOU'RE KAHOKO FROM GED ED, RIGHT?
YES...
YOU CAN HAVE MY SPOT.
I'm Aki, slotted in for room 204.
HUH?
I DON'T HAVE TO PRACTICE TODAY, AND THE SELECTION'S RIGHT AROUND THE CORNER.
It's fine.
BUT...
...I LOVED YOUR PERFORMANCE OF JOY OF LOVE DURING THE SECOND SELECTION!

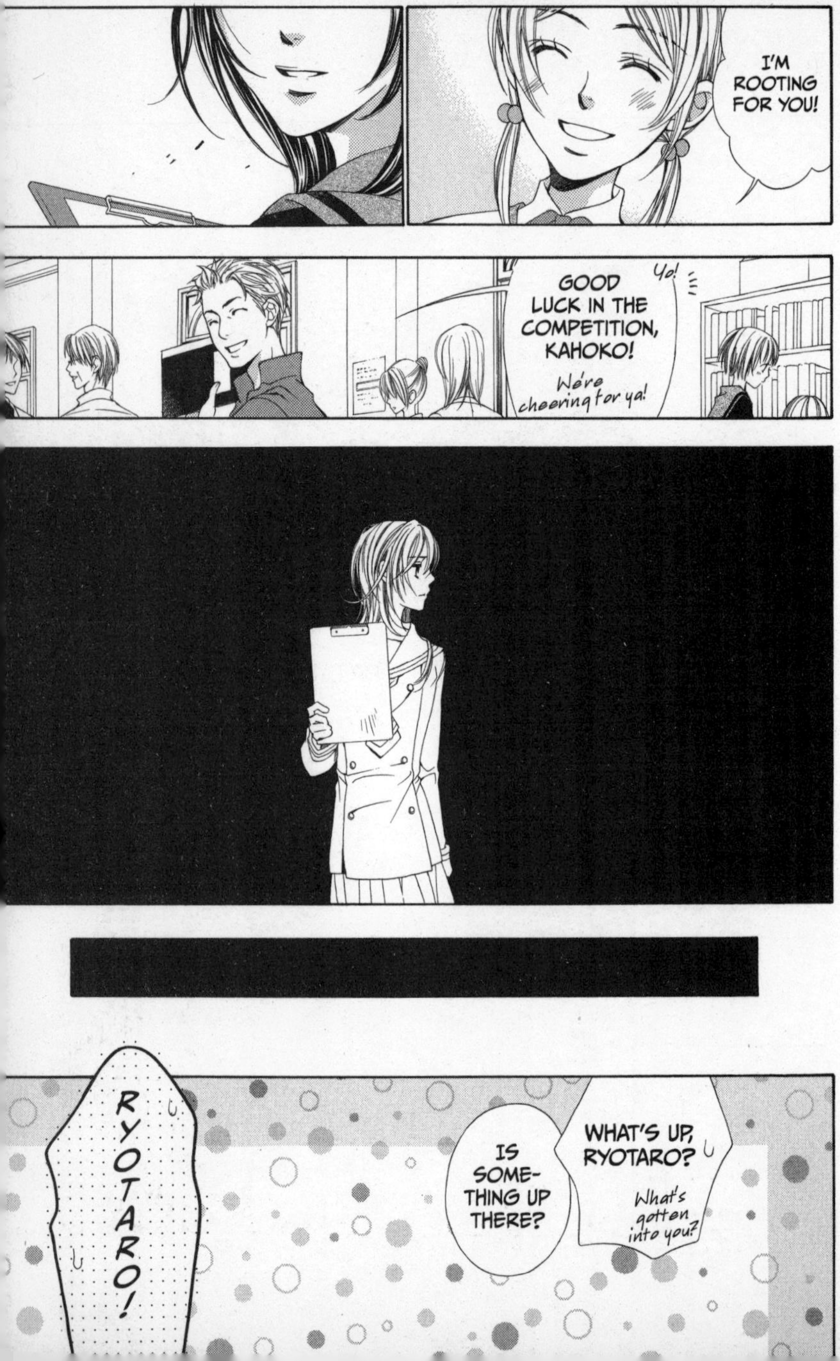
I'M ROOTING FOR YOU!
Yo!
GOOD LUCK IN THE COMPETITION, KAHOKO!
We're cheering for ya!
WHAT'S UP, RYOTARO?
What's gotten into you?
IS SOME-THING UP THERE?
RYOTARO!

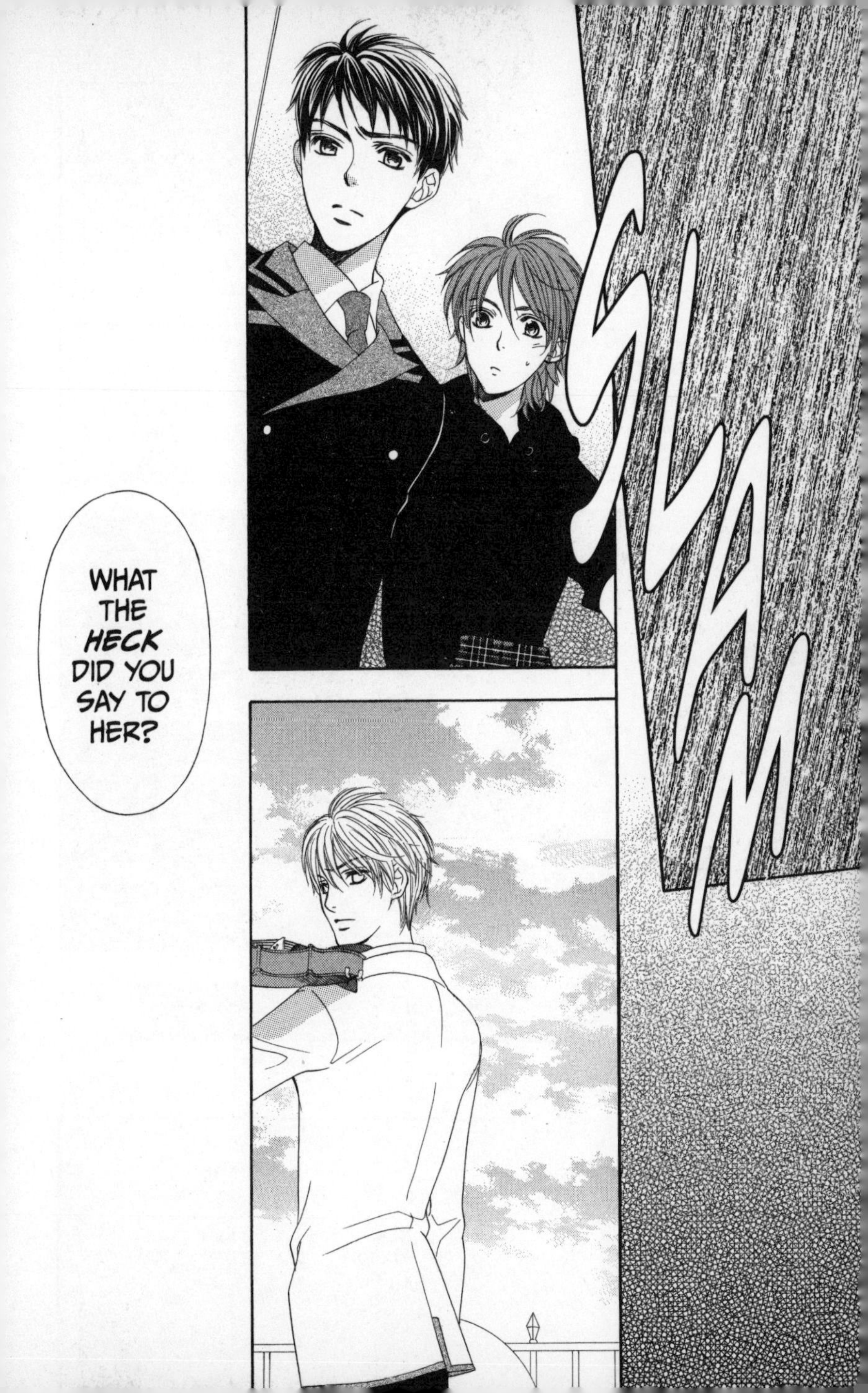
SLAM
WHAT THE *HECK* DID YOU SAY TO HER?

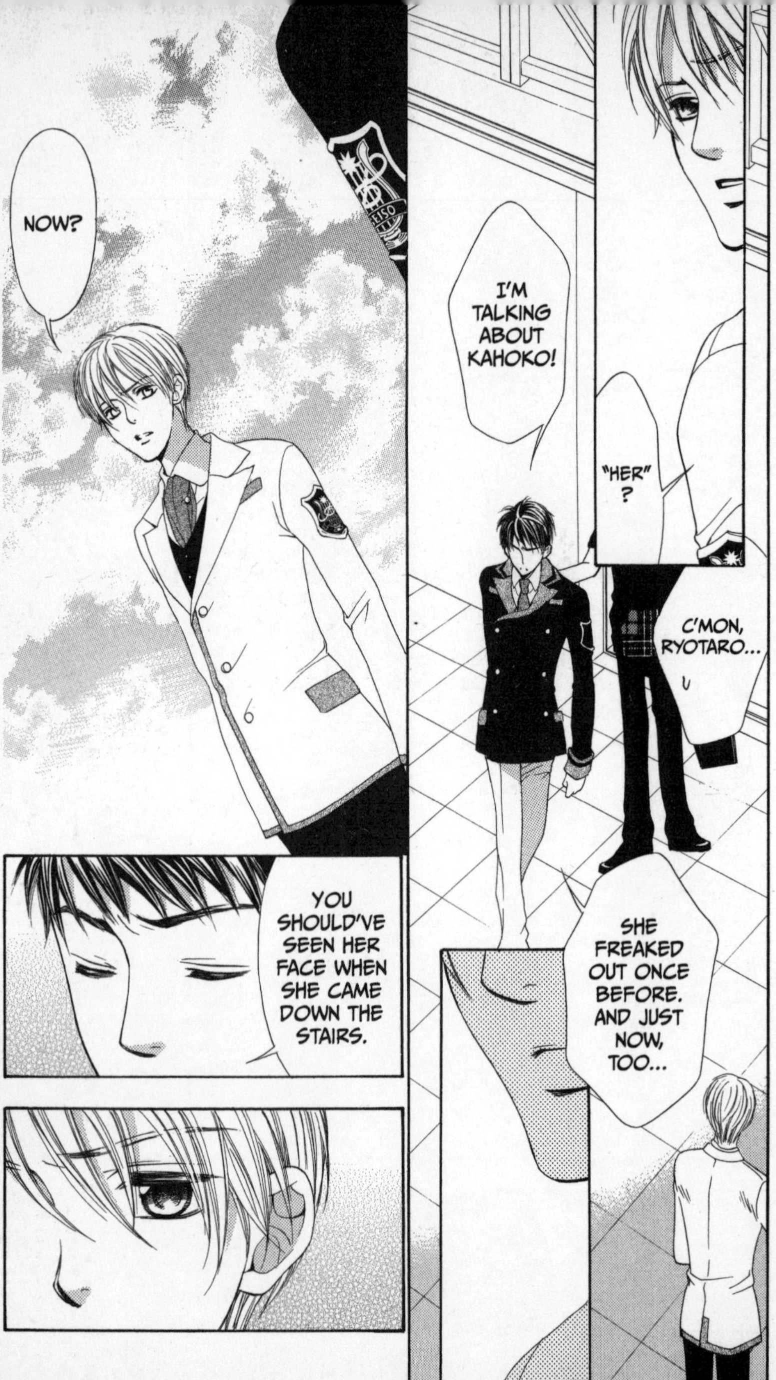
"HER" ?
I'M TALKING ABOUT KAHOKO!
C'MON, RYOTARO...
SHE FREAKED OUT ONCE BEFORE. AND JUST NOW, TOO...
NOW?
YOU SHOULD'VE SEEN HER FACE WHEN SHE CAME DOWN THE STAIRS.

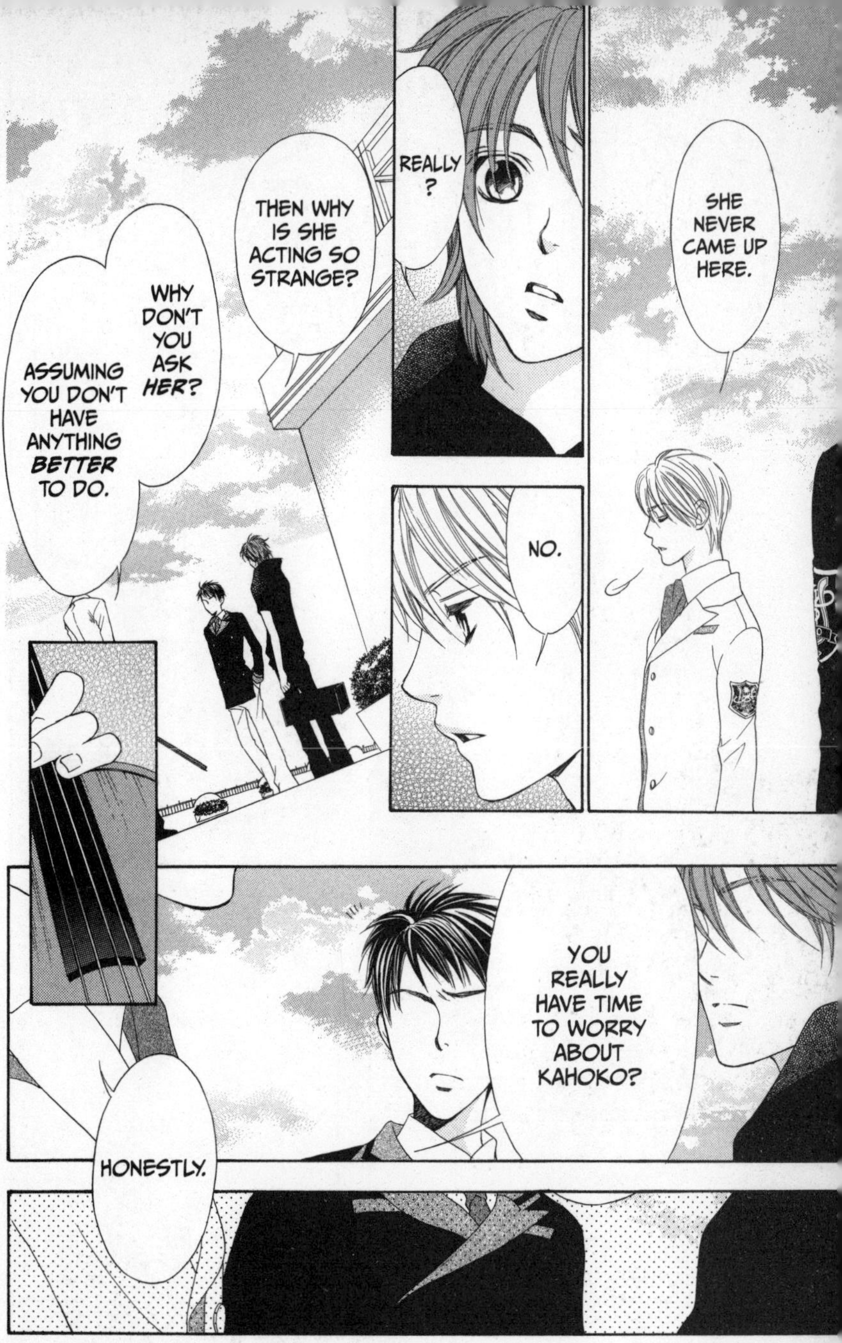

SHE NEVER CAME UP HERE.
REALLY?
NO.
THEN WHY IS SHE ACTING SO STRANGE?
WHY DON'T YOU ASK *HER*?
ASSUMING YOU DON'T HAVE ANYTHING *BETTER* TO DO.
YOU REALLY HAVE TIME TO WORRY ABOUT KAHOKO?
HONESTLY.

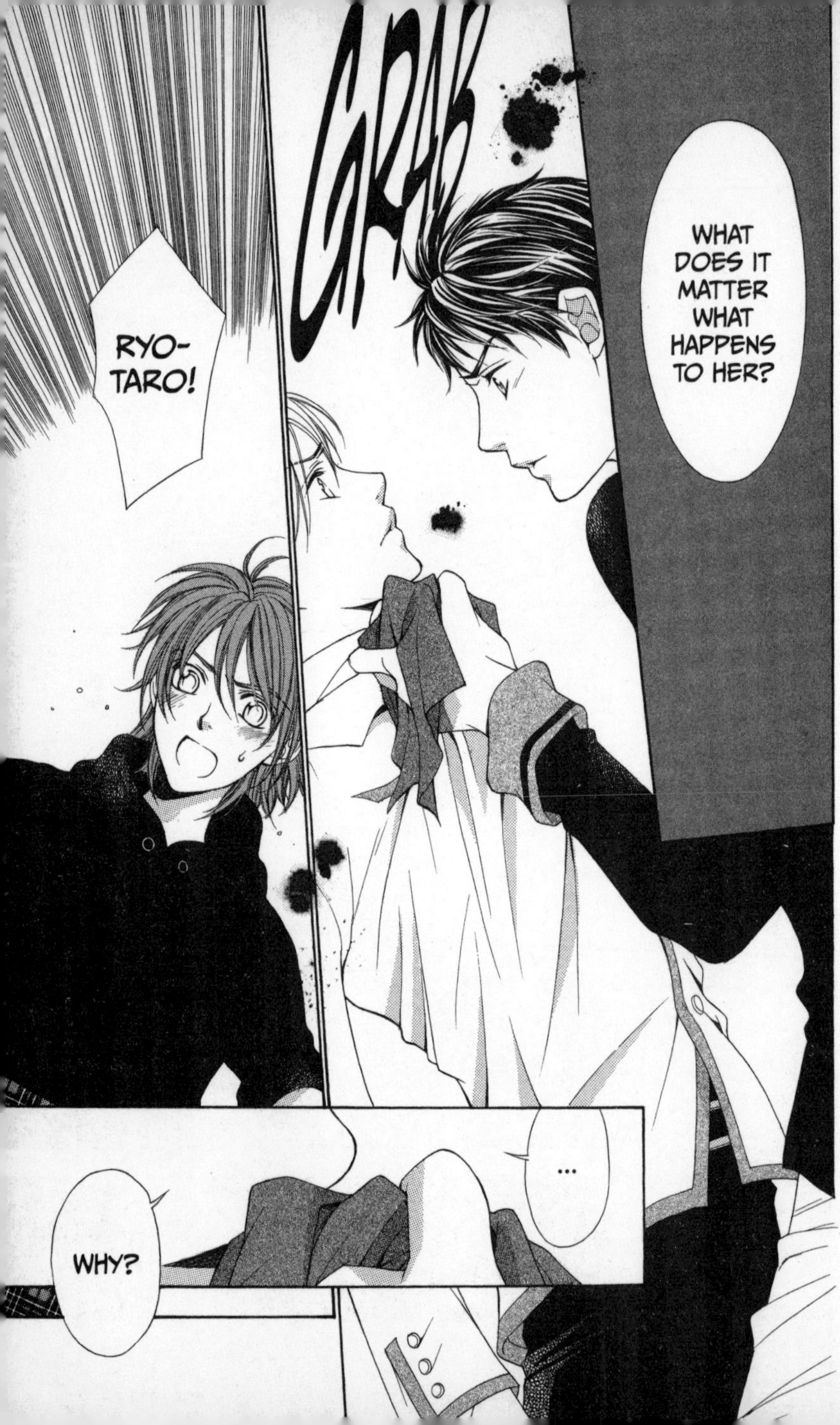
WHAT DOES IT MATTER WHAT HAPPENS TO HER?
GRAB
RYO-TARO!
...
WHY?

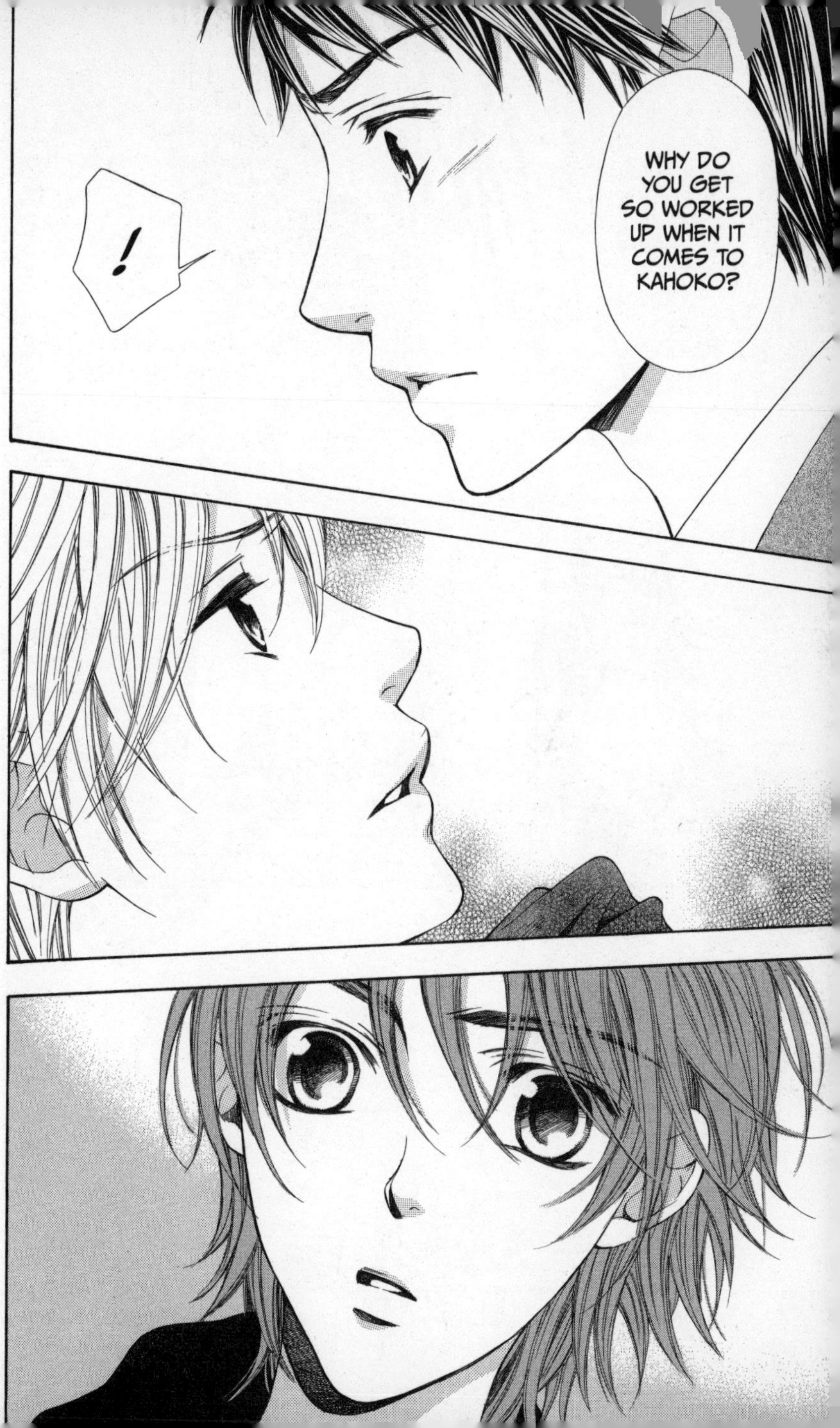
WHY DO YOU GET SO WORKED UP WHEN IT COMES TO KAHOKO?
!

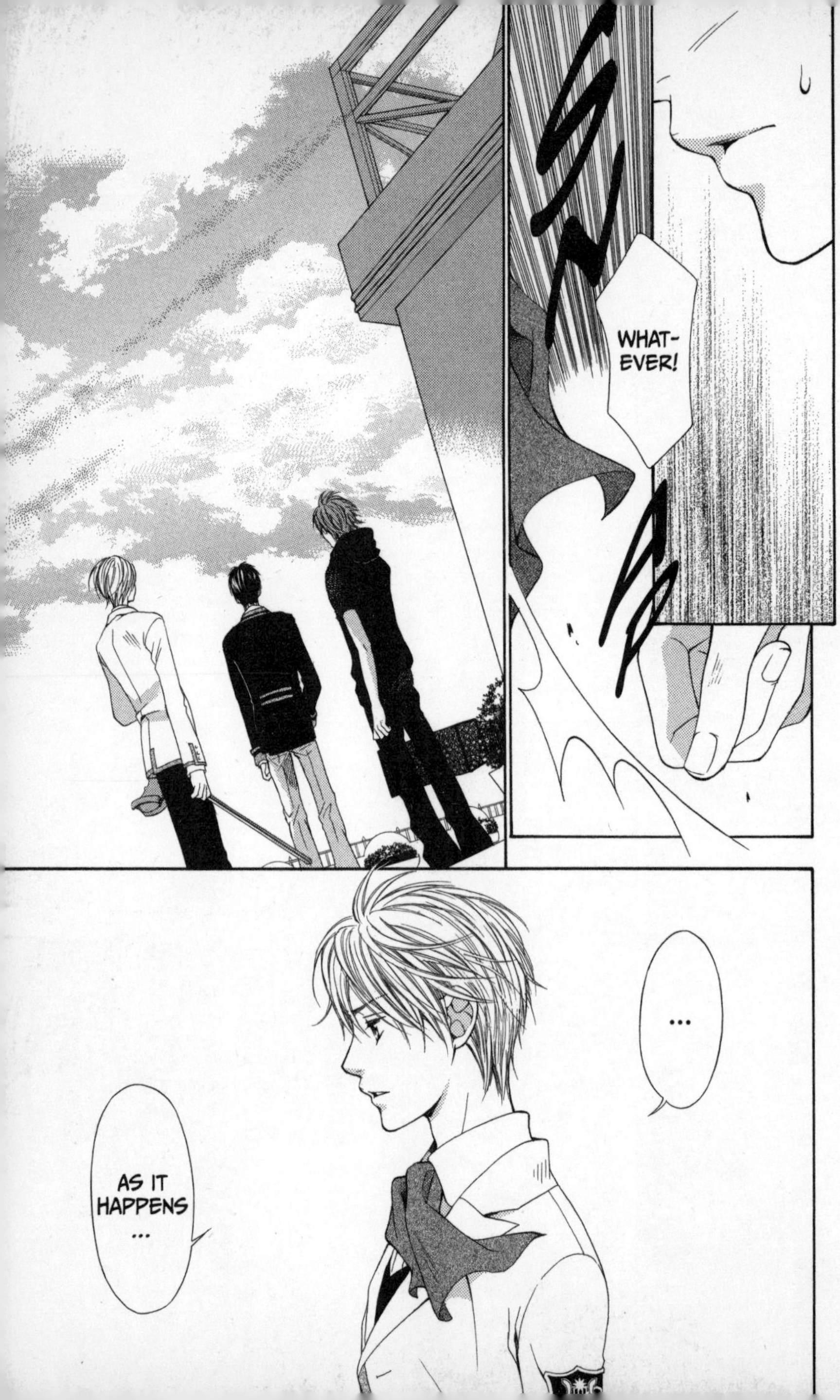
WHAT-EVER!
...
AS IT HAPPENS ...

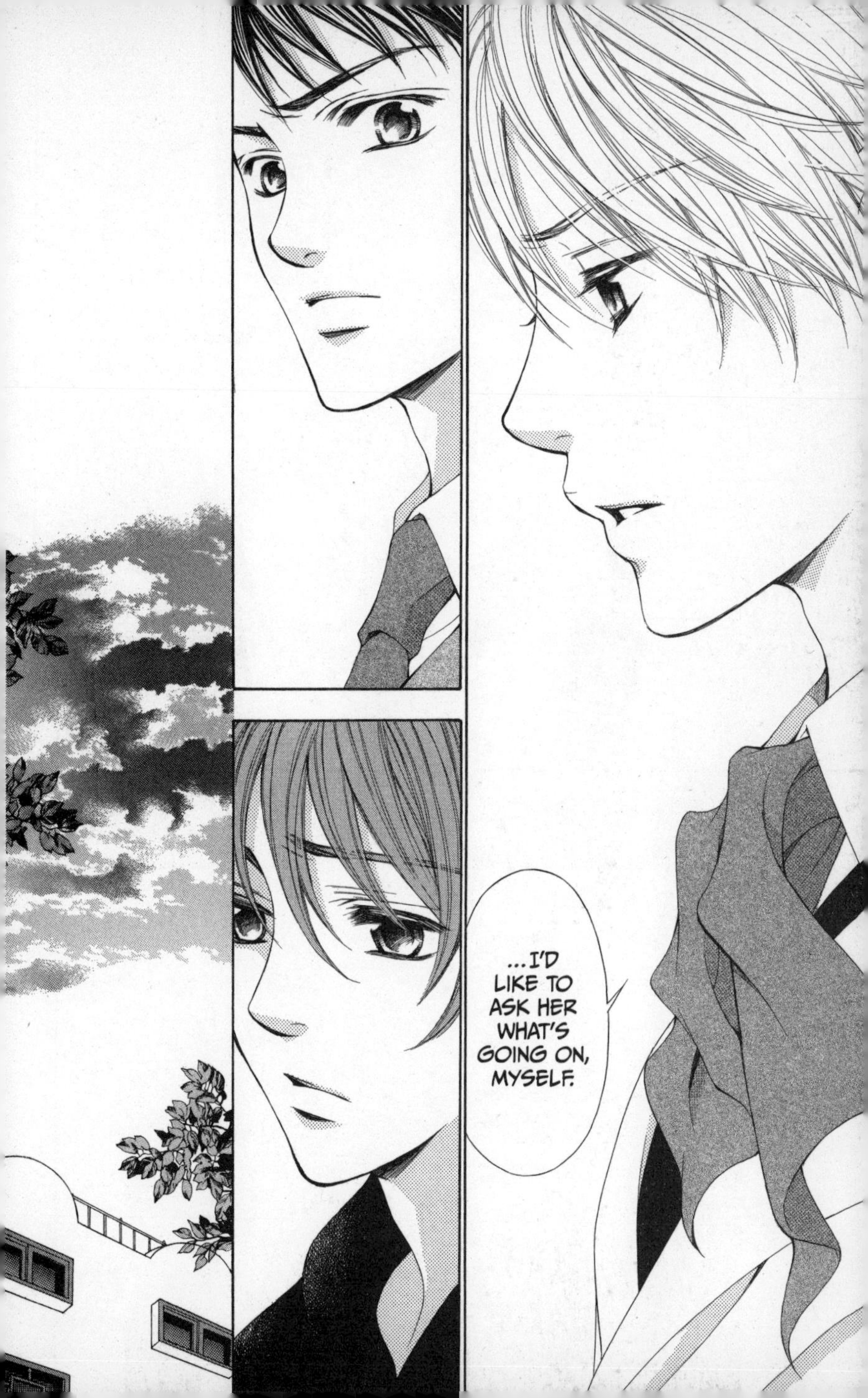
...I'D LIKE TO ASK HER WHAT'S GOING ON, MYSELF.

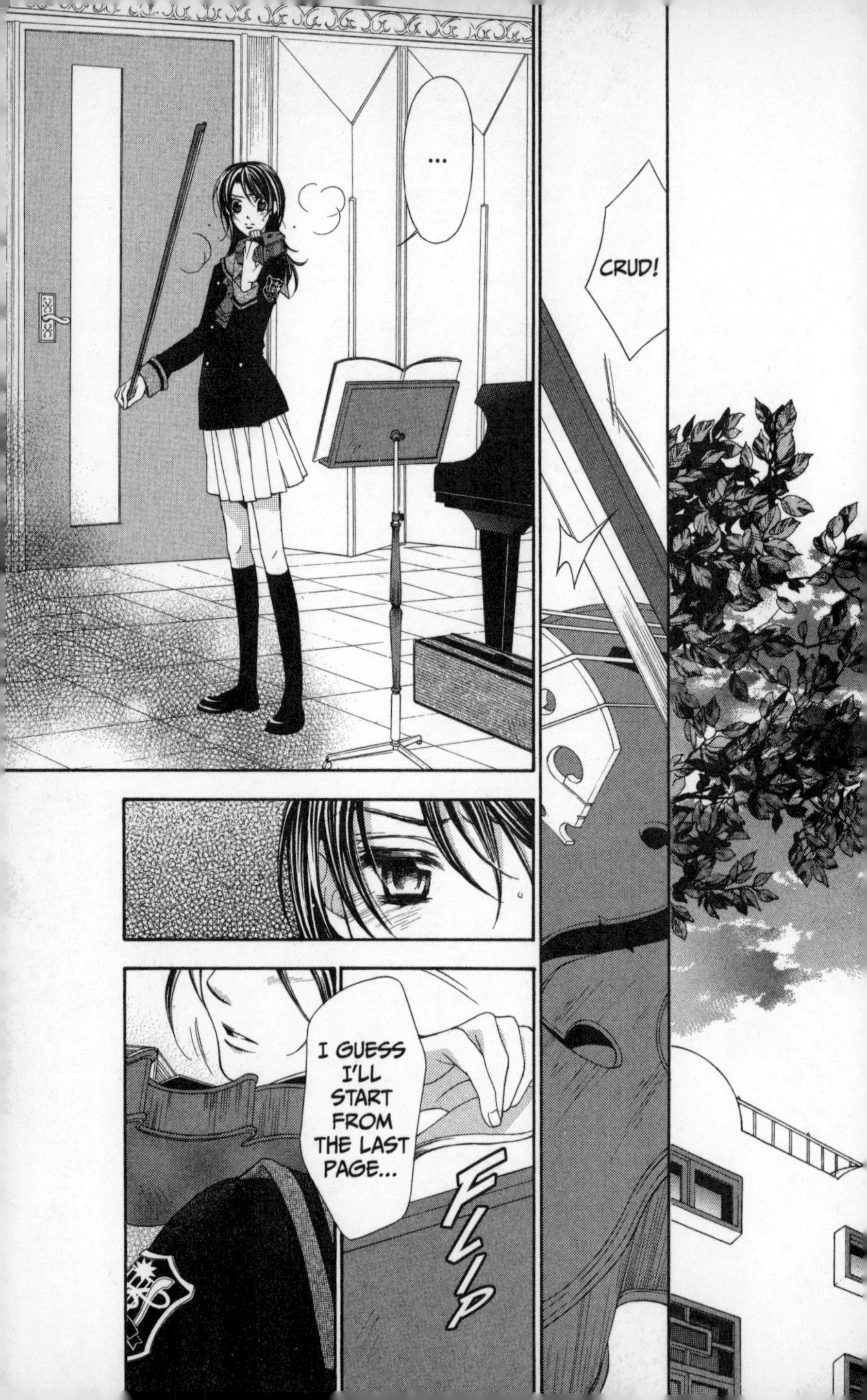
CRUD!
...
I GUESS I'LL START FROM THE LAST PAGE...
FLIP

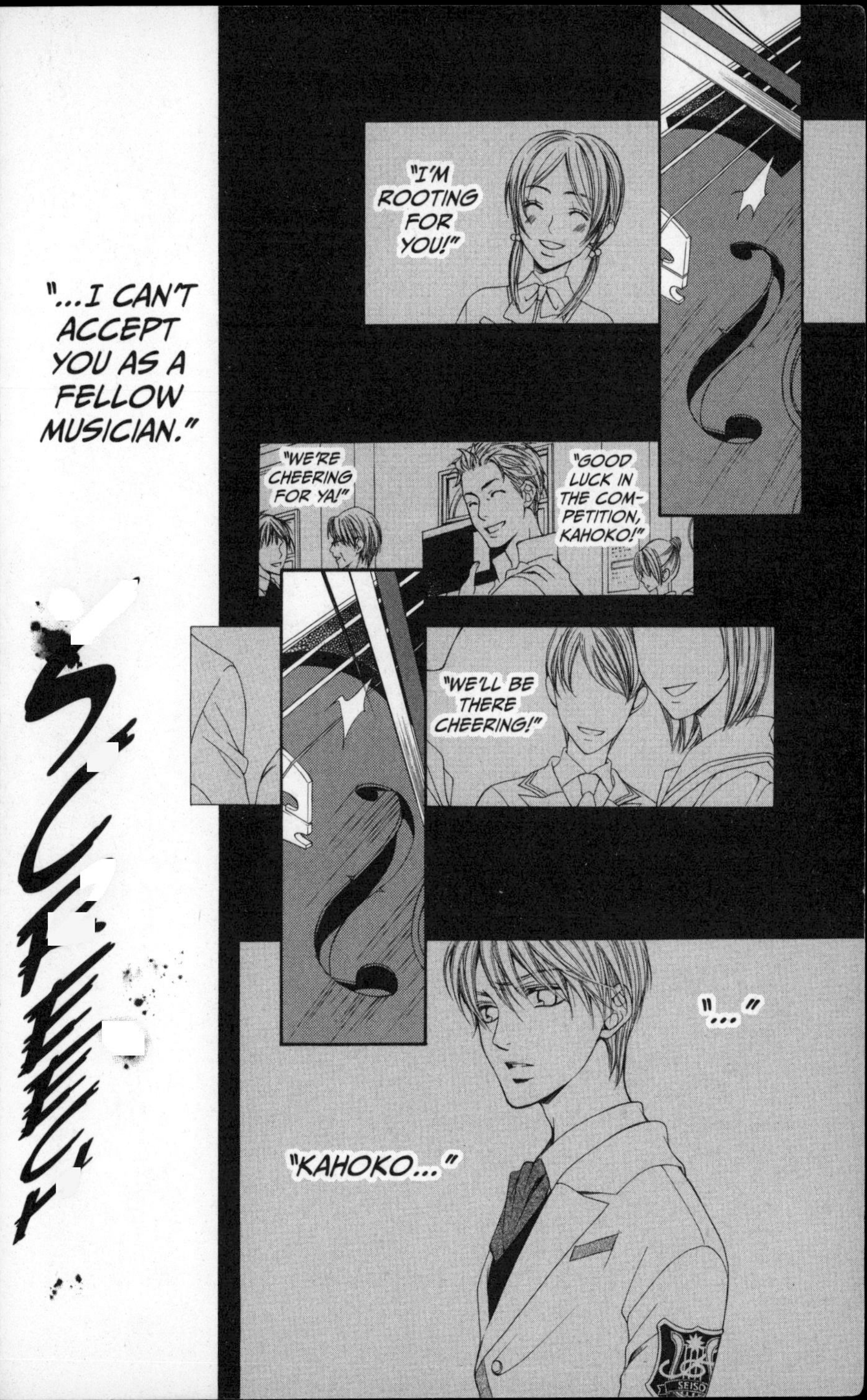
"I'M ROOTING FOR YOU!"
"GOOD LUCK IN THE COMPETITION, KAHOKO!"
"WE'RE CHEERING FOR YA!"
"WE'LL BE THERE CHEERING!"
"..."
"KAHOKO..."
"...I CAN'T ACCEPT YOU AS A FELLOW MUSICIAN."

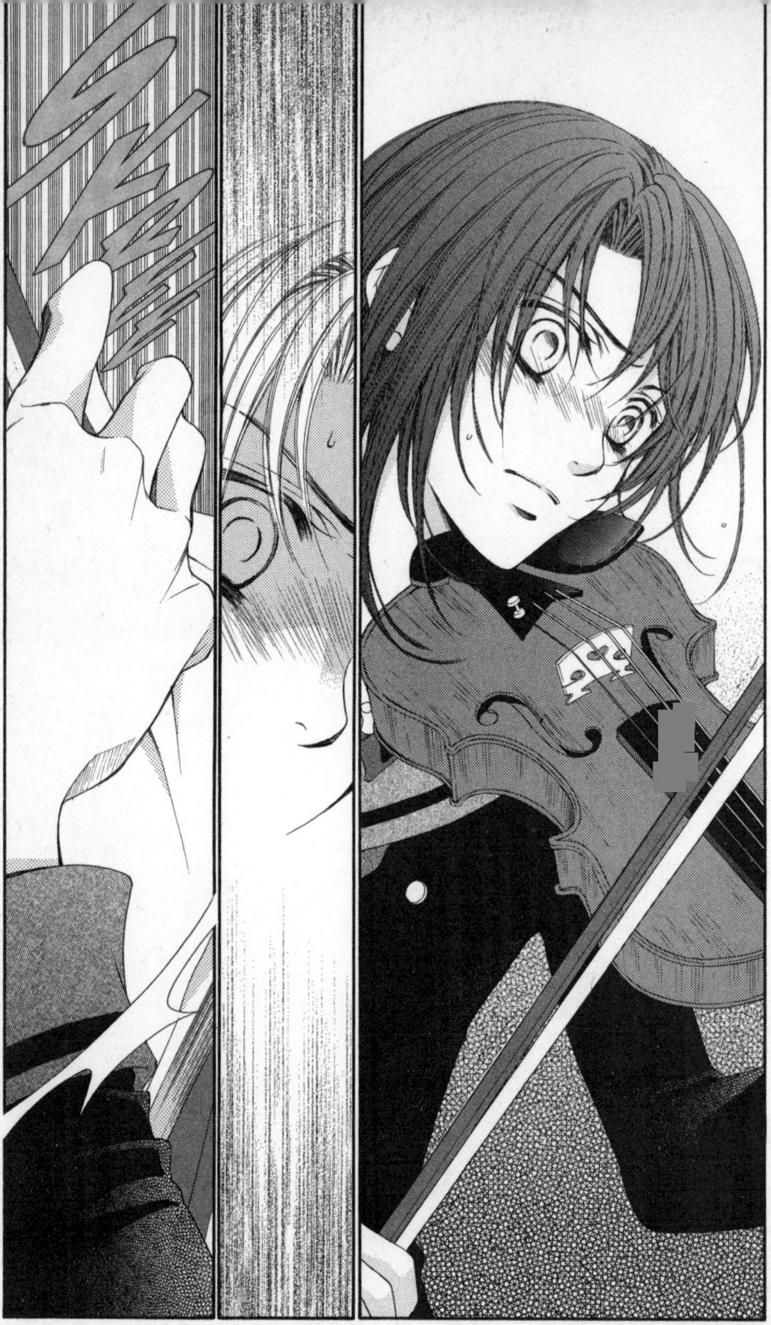
SWEEEE

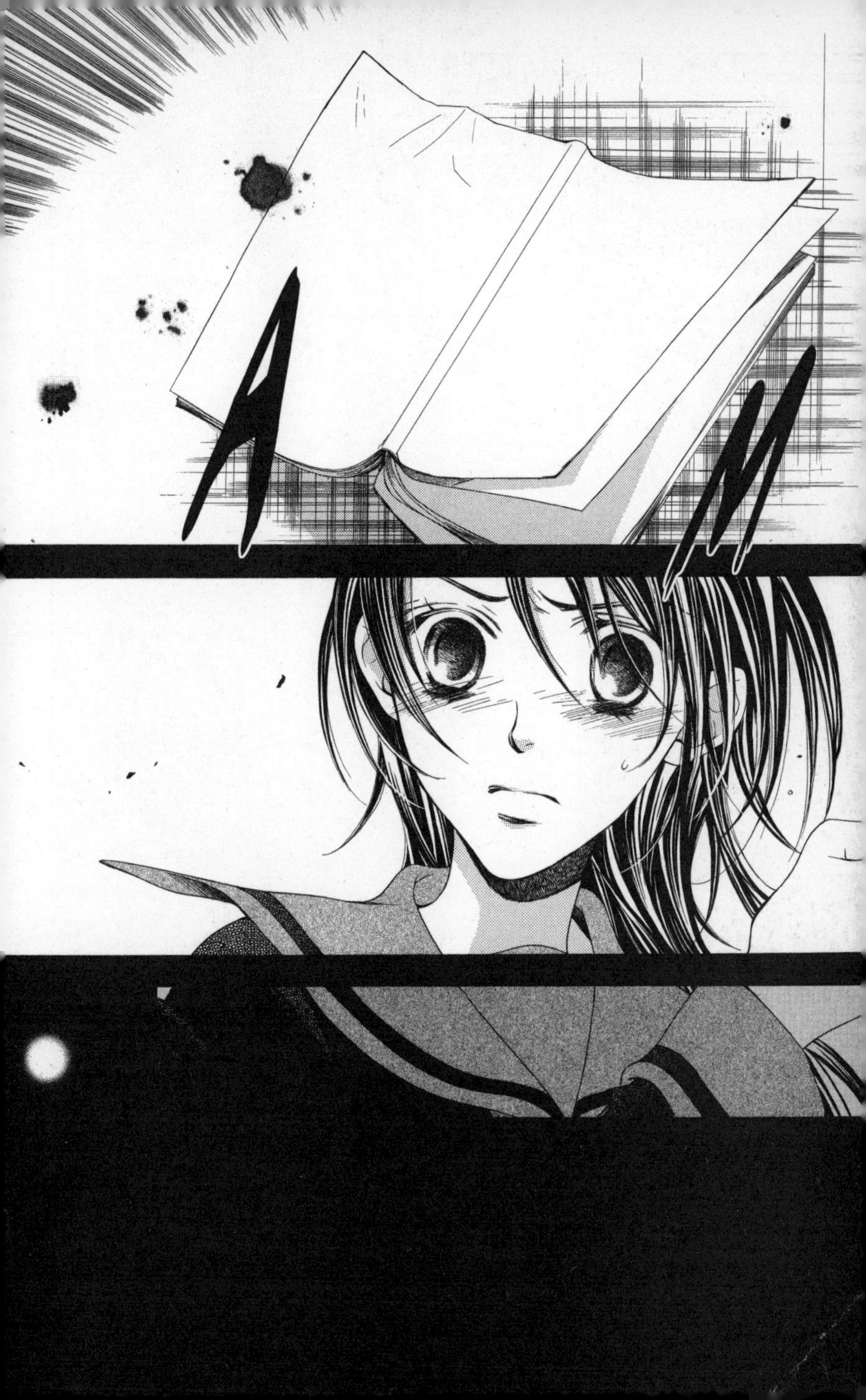

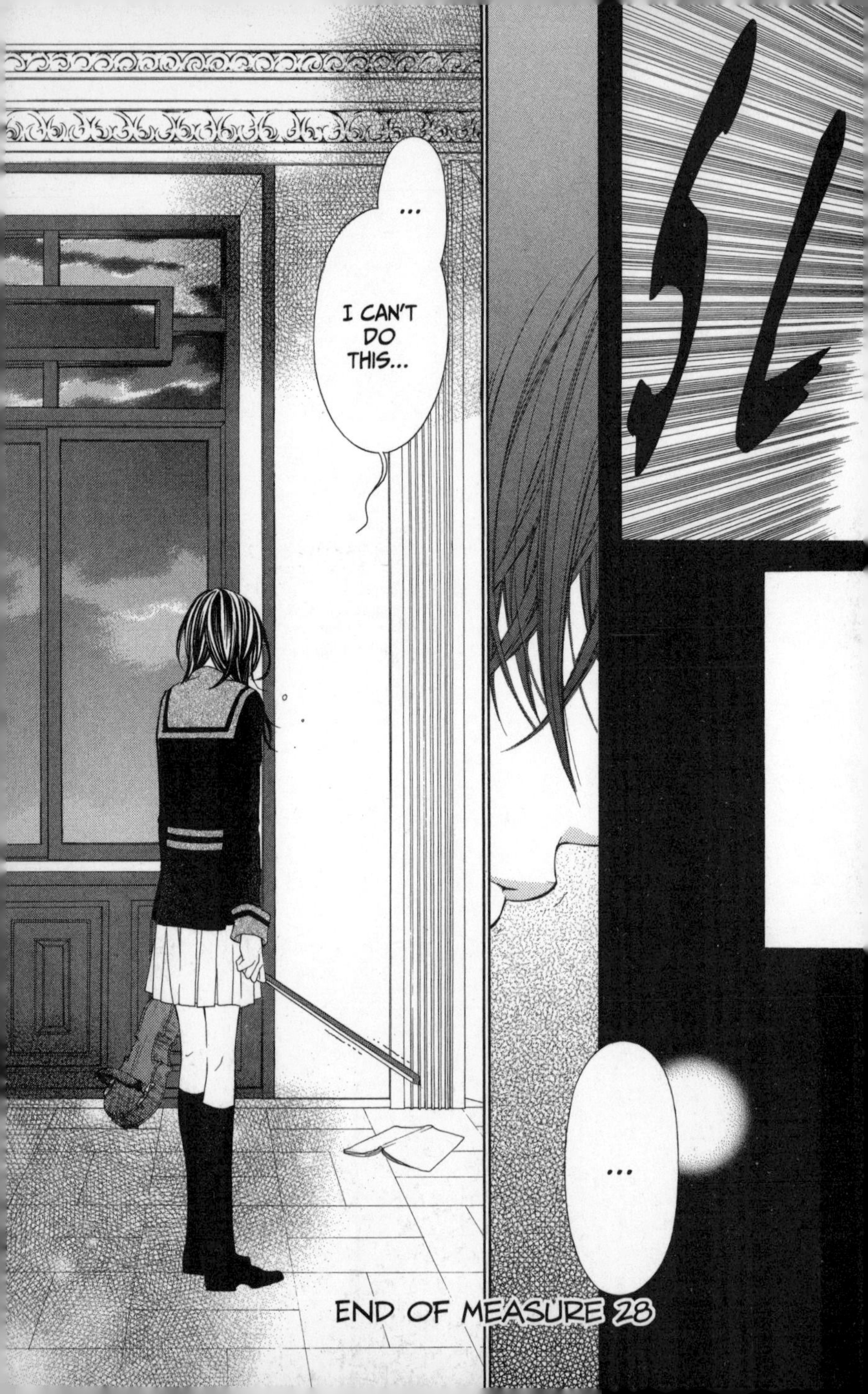
...
...
I CAN'T DO THIS...
END OF MEASURE 28

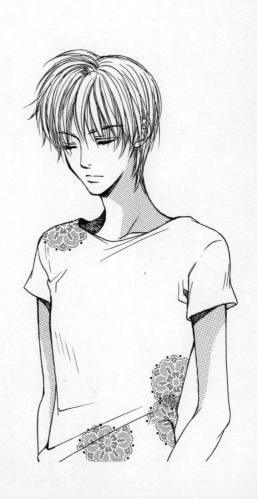

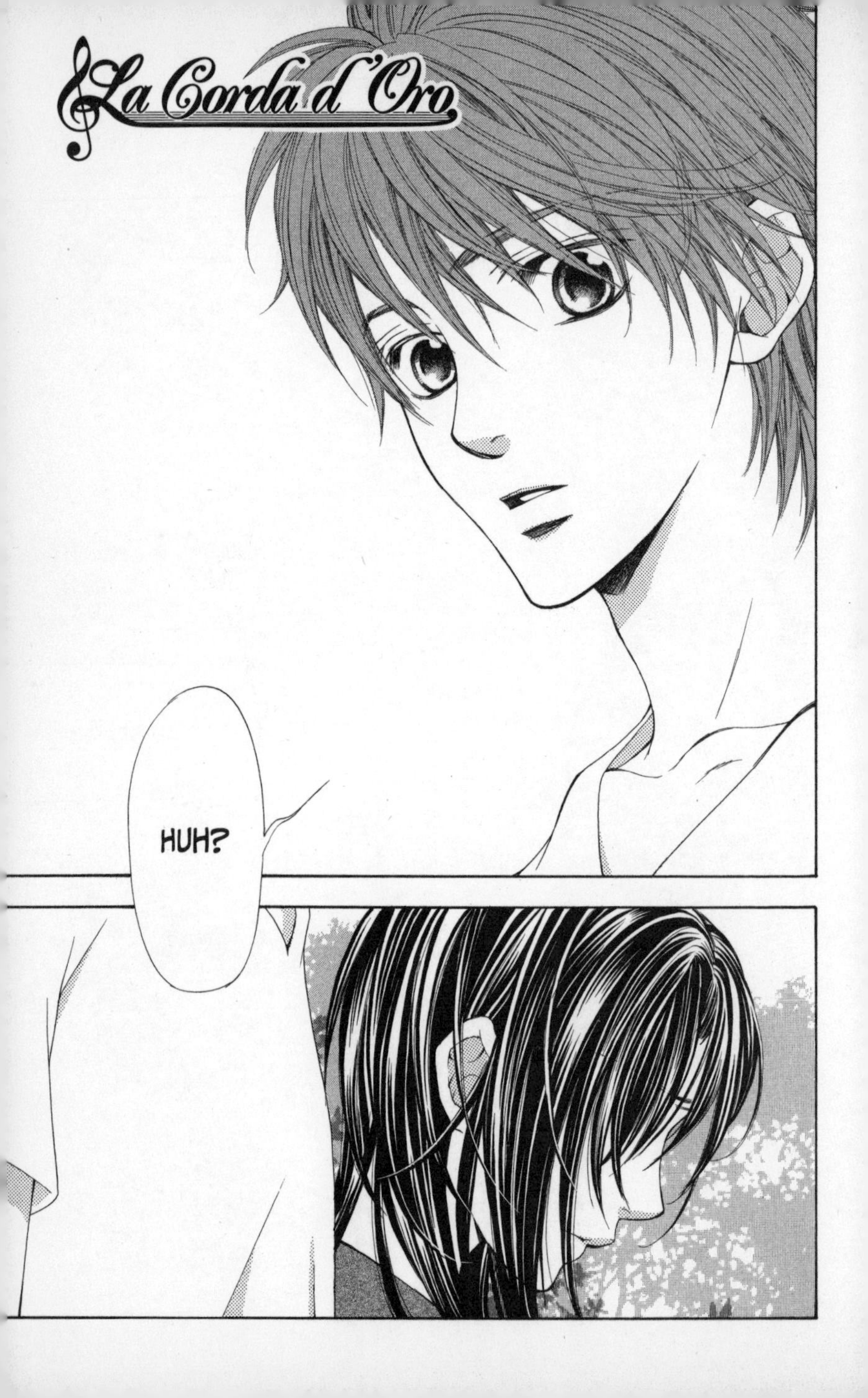
La Corda d'Oro
HUH?

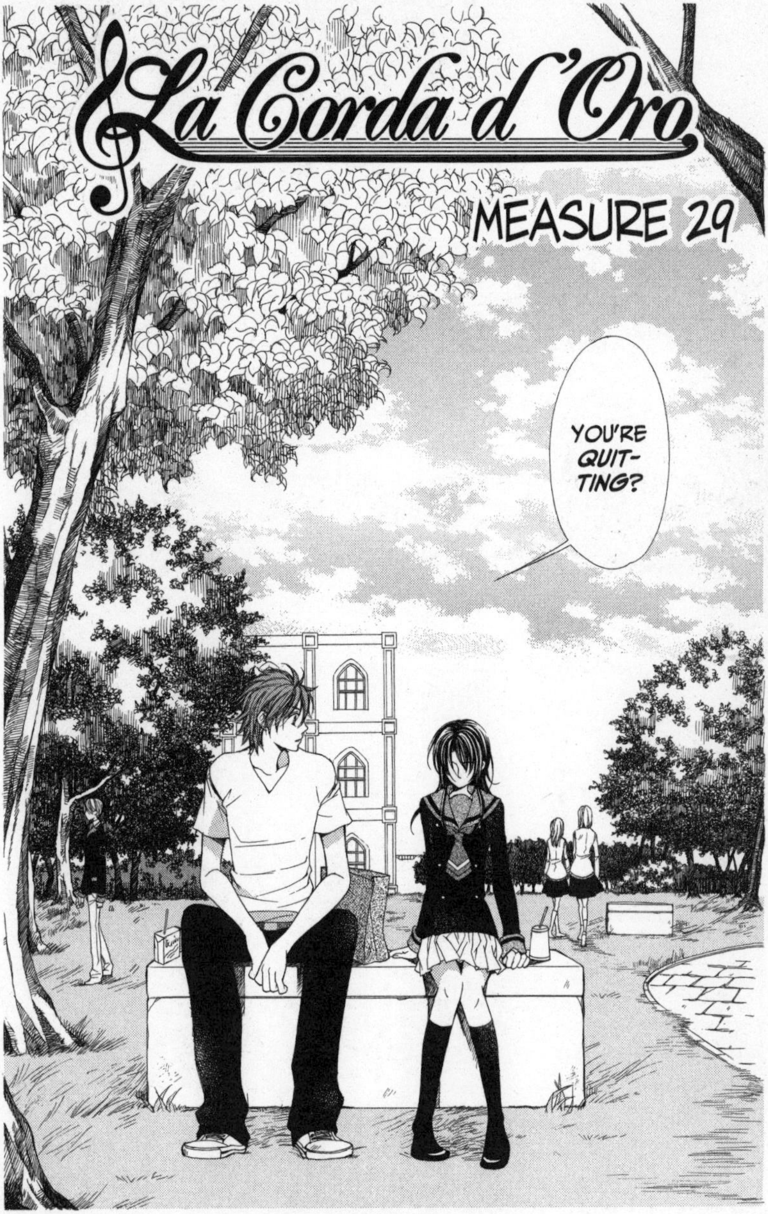
La Corda d'Oro
MEASURE 29
YOU'RE QUIT-TING?

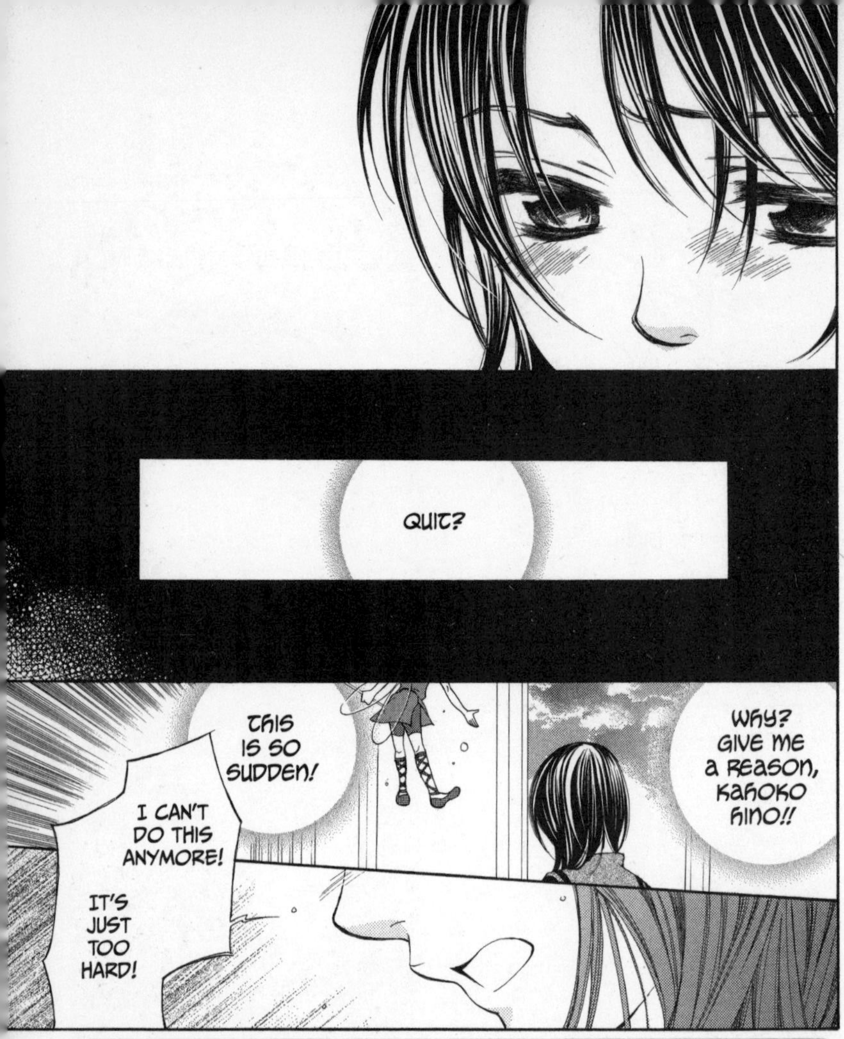
QUIT?
WHY? GIVE ME A REASON, KAHOKO HINO!!
THIS IS SO SUDDEN!
I CAN'T DO THIS ANYMORE!
IT'S JUST TOO HARD!

Daily Happenings ㉑ Quite the blow...

One of the people who helps me during script production, Tsubasa Shiino, brought a brain-stimulation game for me to play. The result...

My brain age was 80...

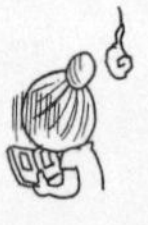

This is not something one should do while writing a script!!

That's my story and I'm sticking to it! It was pretty depressing, though.

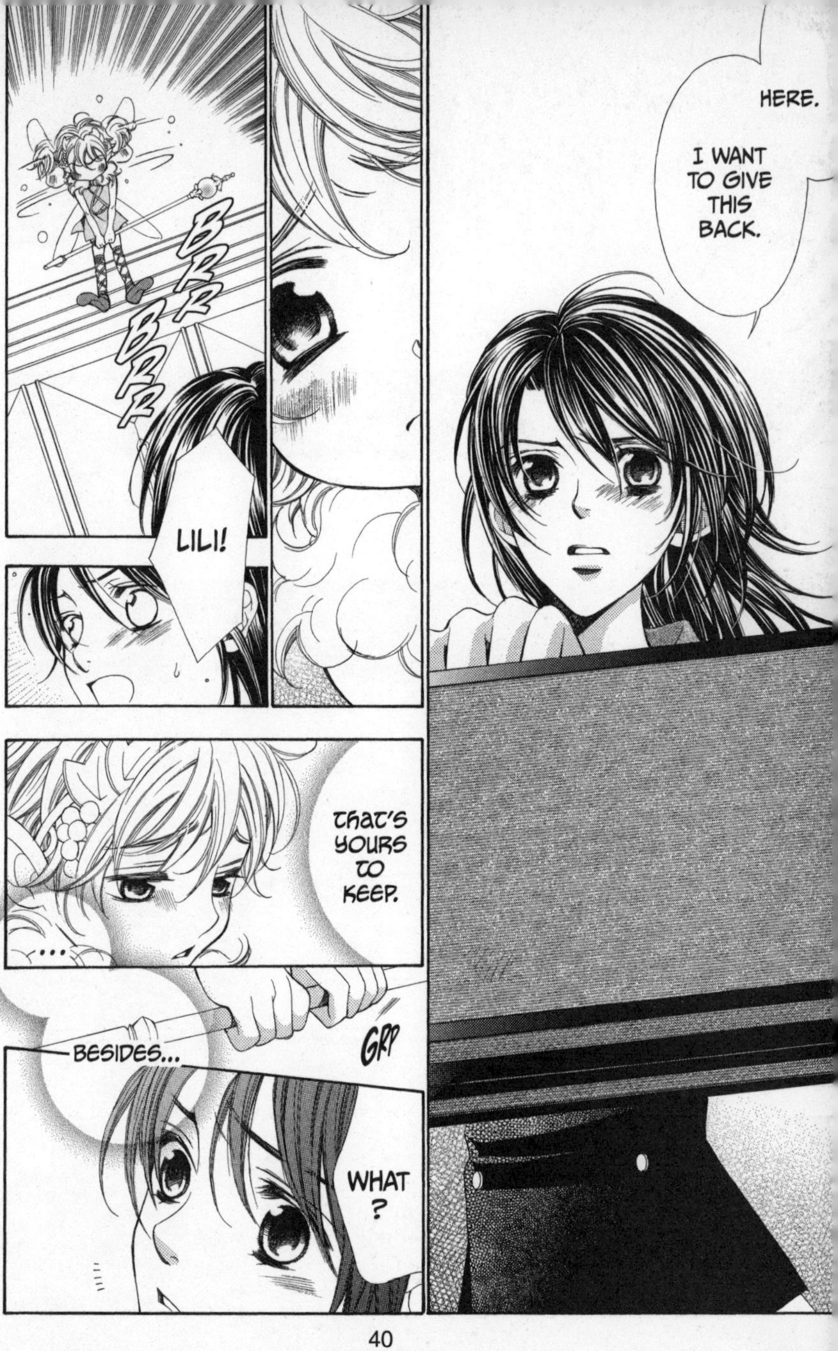
HERE.
I WANT TO GIVE THIS BACK.
BRR BRR BRR
LILI!
THAT'S YOURS TO KEEP.
...
GRP
BESIDES...
WHAT?

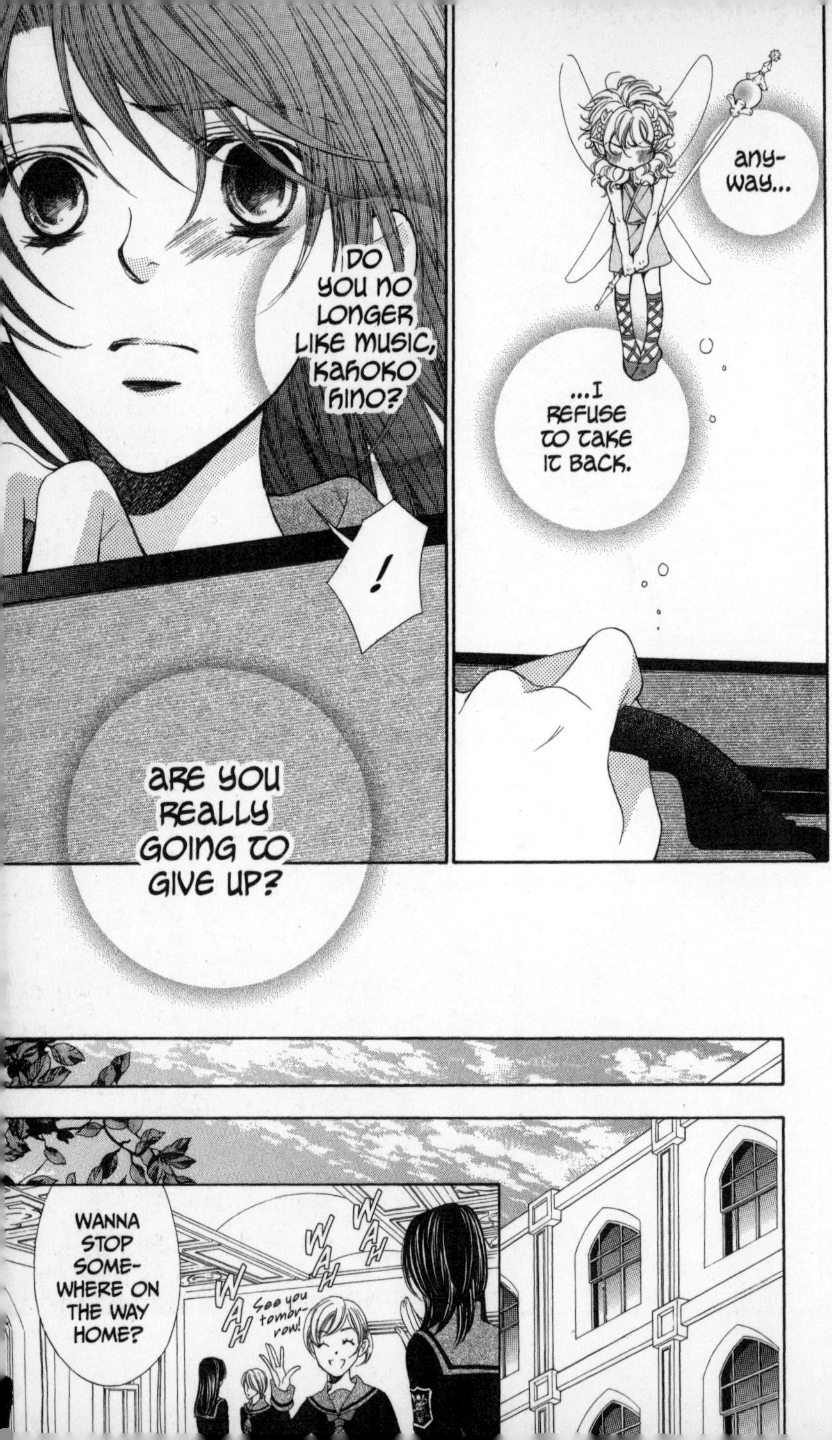
any-way...
...I REFUSE TO TAKE IT BACK.
DO YOU NO LONGER LIKE MUSIC, KAHOKO HINO?
!
ARE YOU REALLY GOING TO GIVE UP?
WAH WAH
WANNA STOP SOME-WHERE ON THE WAY HOME?
WAH
WAH
See you tomor-row!

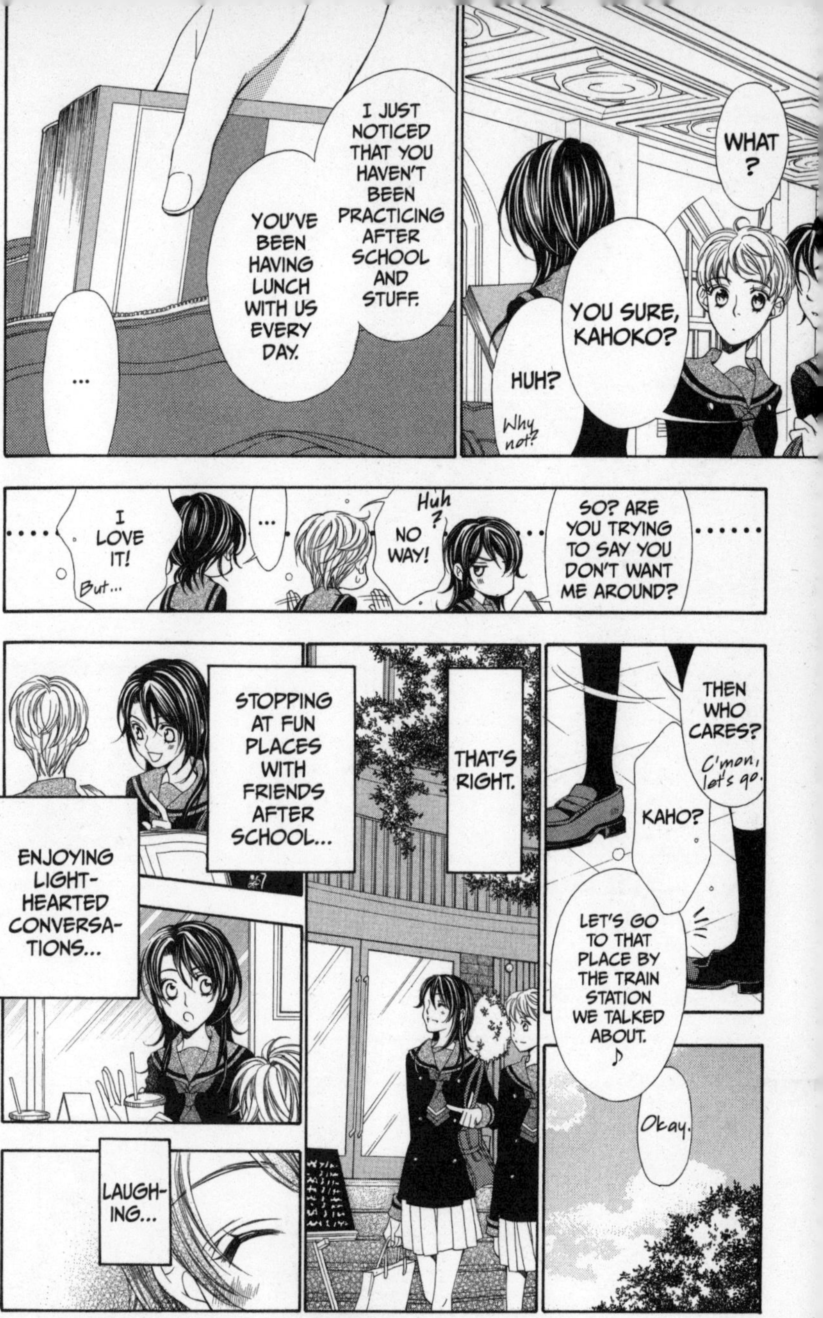
WHAT?
YOU SURE, KAHOKO?
HUH?
Why not?
I JUST NOTICED THAT YOU HAVEN'T BEEN PRACTICING AFTER SCHOOL AND STUFF.
YOU'VE BEEN HAVING LUNCH WITH US EVERY DAY.
...
SO? ARE YOU TRYING TO SAY YOU DON'T WANT ME AROUND?
Huh?
NO WAY!
...
I LOVE IT!
But...
THEN WHO CARES?
C'mon, let's go.
KAHO?
LET'S GO TO THAT PLACE BY THE TRAIN STATION WE TALKED ABOUT. ♪
Okay.
THAT'S RIGHT.
STOPPING AT FUN PLACES WITH FRIENDS AFTER SCHOOL...
ENJOYING LIGHT-HEARTED CONVERSATIONS...
LAUGHING...

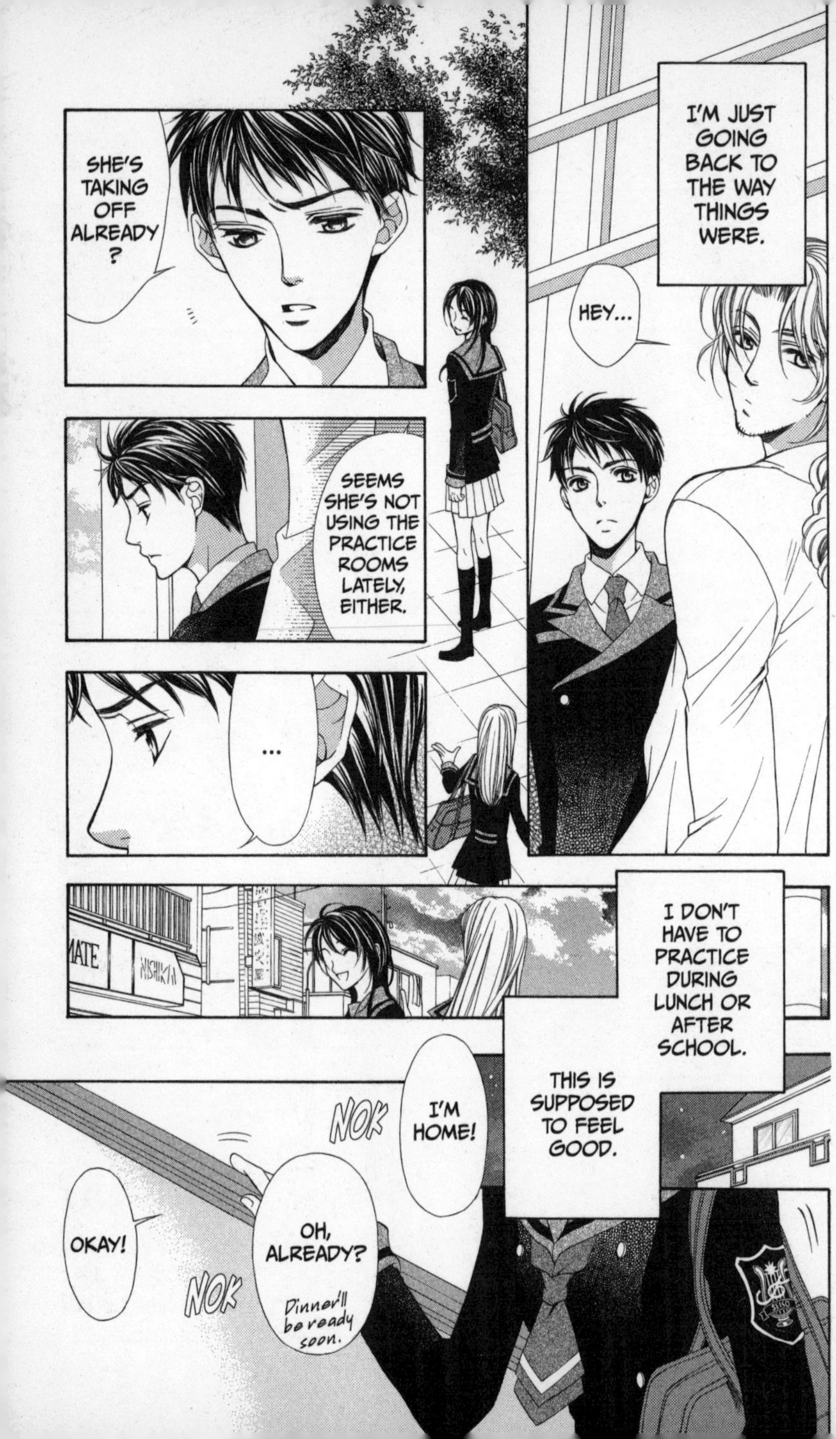
I'M JUST GOING BACK TO THE WAY THINGS WERE.
HEY...
SHE'S TAKING OFF ALREADY?
SEEMS SHE'S NOT USING THE PRACTICE ROOMS LATELY, EITHER.
...
I DON'T HAVE TO PRACTICE DURING LUNCH OR AFTER SCHOOL.
MATE
NISHIKI
THIS IS SUPPOSED TO FEEL GOOD.
NOK
I'M HOME!
OH, ALREADY?
Dinner'll be ready soon.
OKAY!
NOK

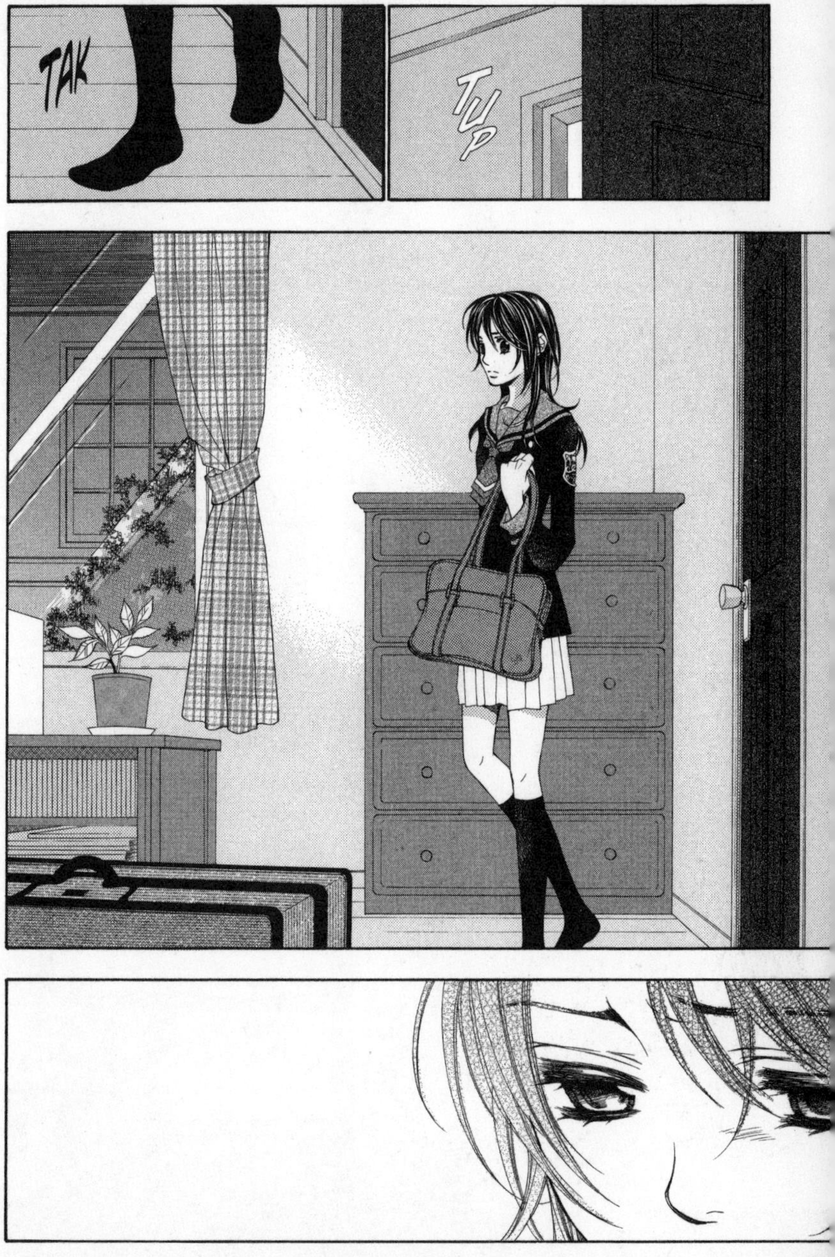
TUP
TAK

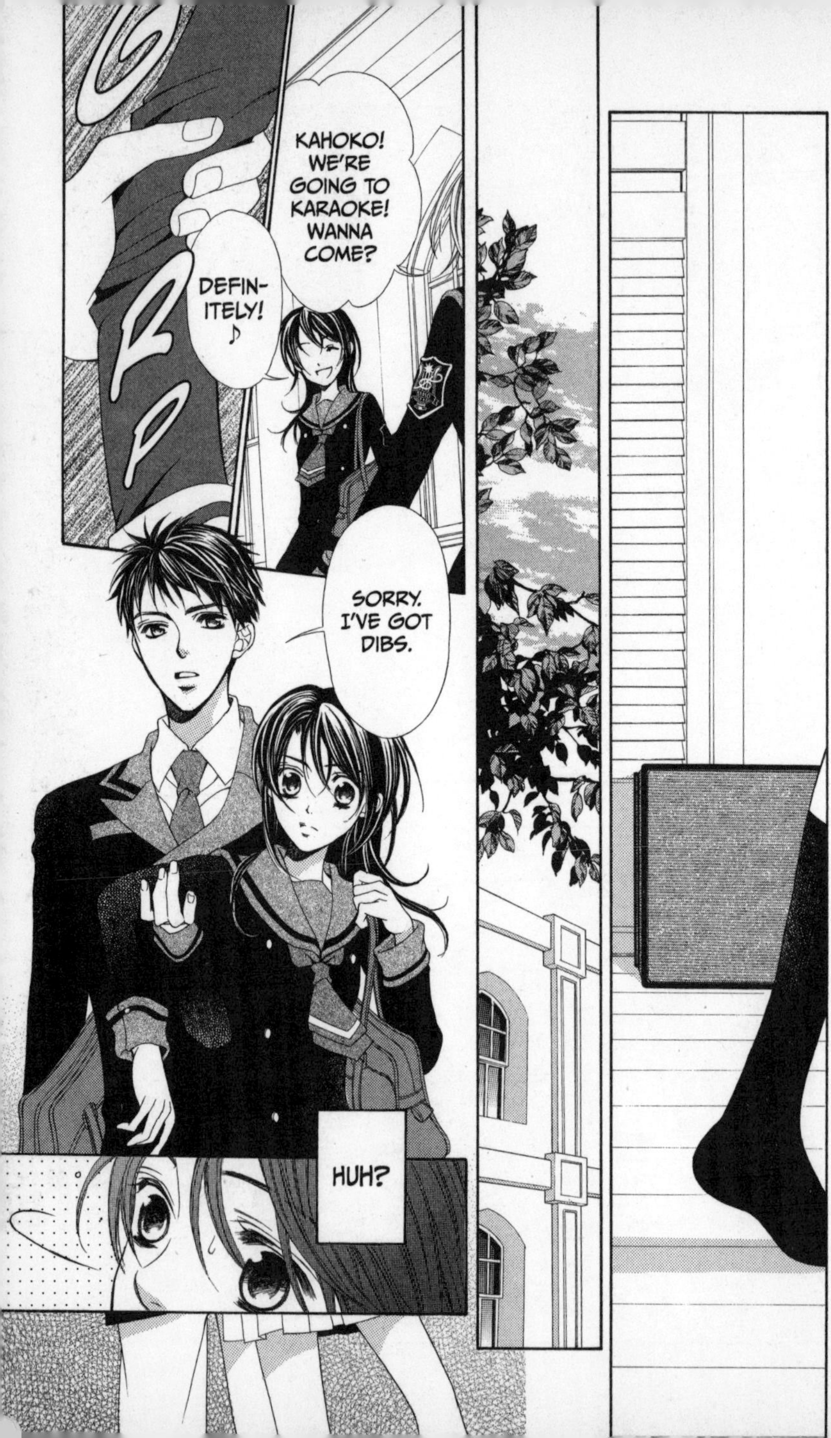
KAHOKO! WE'RE GOING TO KARAOKE! WANNA COME?
DEFIN-ITELY! ♪
SORRY. I'VE GOT DIBS.
HUH?

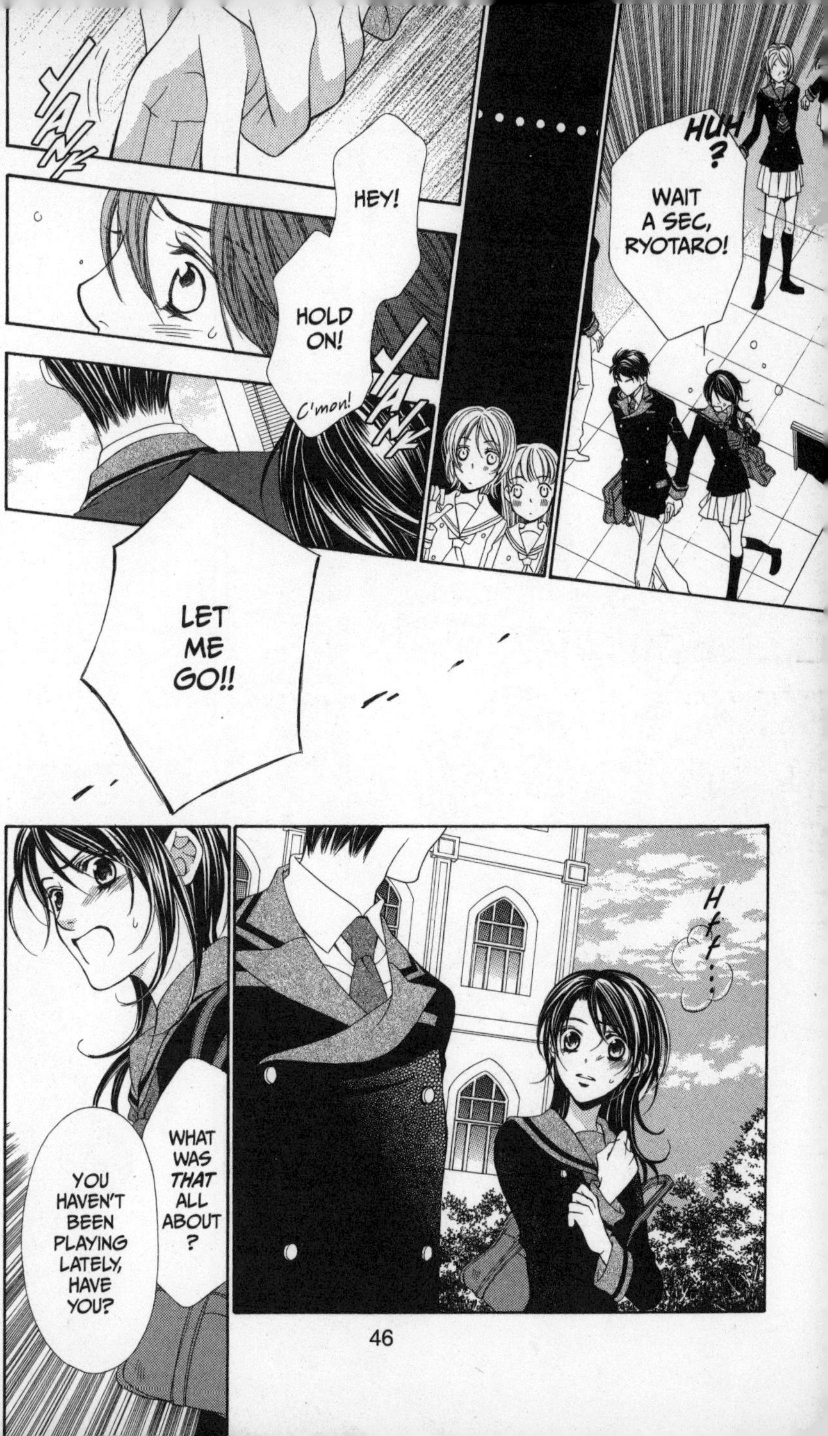
HUH?
WAIT A SEC, RYOTARO!
YANK
HEY! HOLD ON!
C'mon!
YANK
LET ME GO!!
Hff...
WHAT WAS THAT ALL ABOUT?
YOU HAVEN'T BEEN PLAYING LATELY, HAVE YOU?

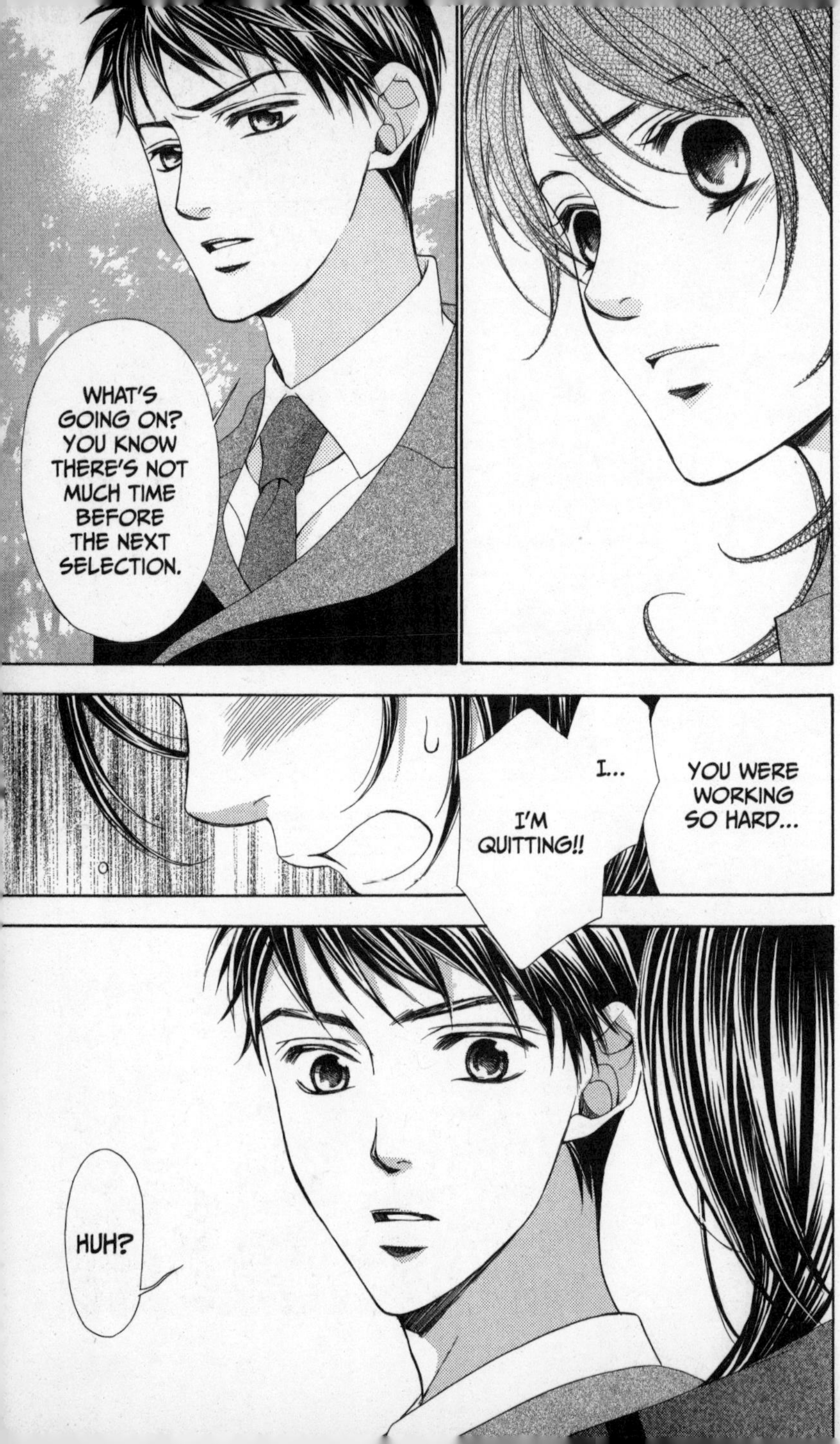
WHAT'S GOING ON? YOU KNOW THERE'S NOT MUCH TIME BEFORE THE NEXT SELECTION.
YOU WERE WORKING SO HARD...
I...
I'M QUITTING!!
HUH?

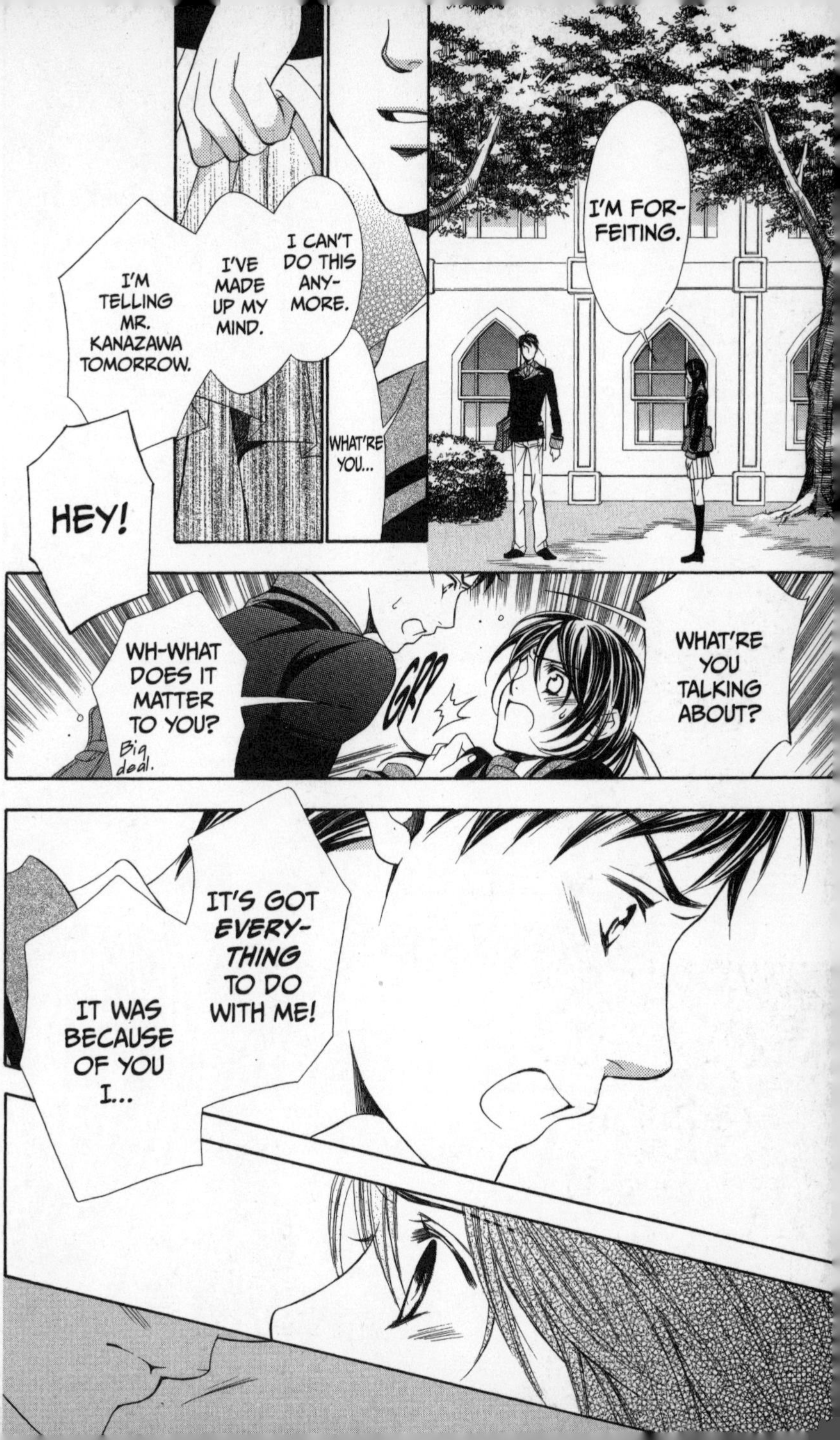
I'M FOR-FEITING.
WHAT'RE YOU...
I CAN'T DO THIS ANY-MORE.
I'VE MADE UP MY MIND.
I'M TELLING MR. KANAZAWA TOMORROW.
HEY!
WHAT'RE YOU TALKING ABOUT?
GRP
WH-WHAT DOES IT MATTER TO YOU?
Big deal.
IT'S GOT EVERY-THING TO DO WITH ME!
IT WAS BECAUSE OF YOU I...

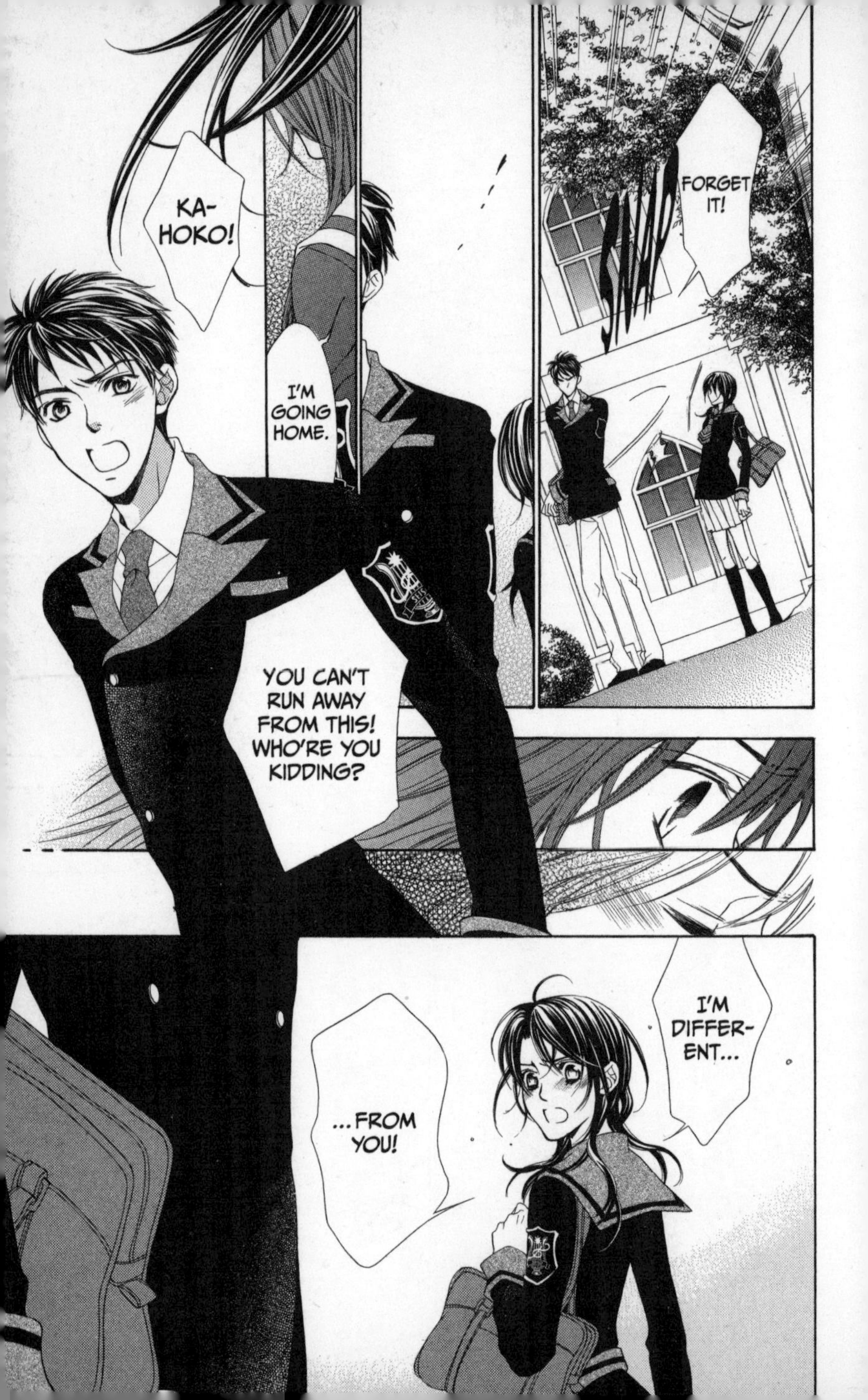
FORGET IT!
SNAP
I'M GOING HOME.
KA-HOKO!
YOU CAN'T RUN AWAY FROM THIS! WHO'RE YOU KIDDING?
I'M DIFFER-ENT...
...FROM YOU!

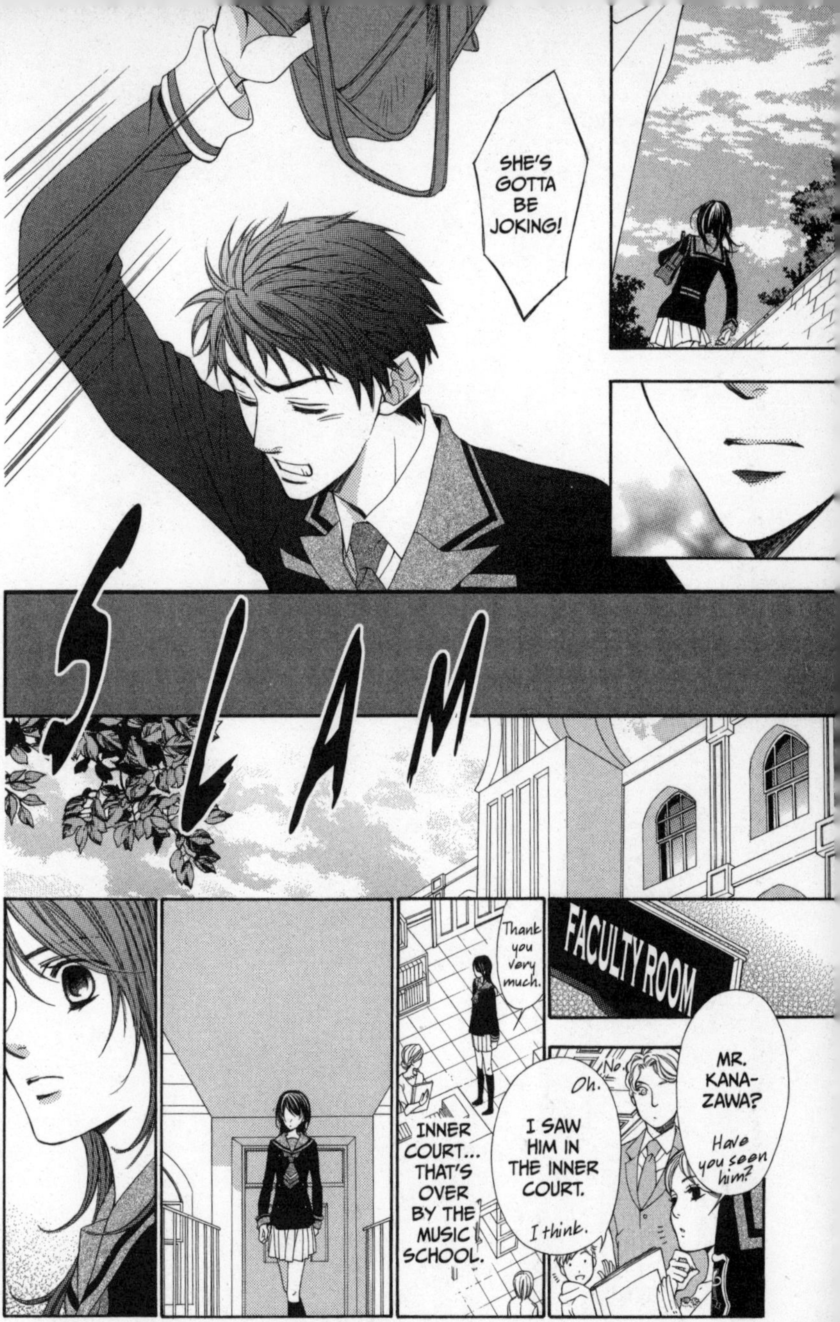
SHE'S GOTTA BE JOKING!
SLAM
FACULTY ROOM
MR. KANA-ZAWA?
Have you seen him?
No.
Oh.
I SAW HIM IN THE INNER COURT.
I think.
Thank you very much.
INNER COURT... THAT'S OVER BY THE MUSIC SCHOOL.

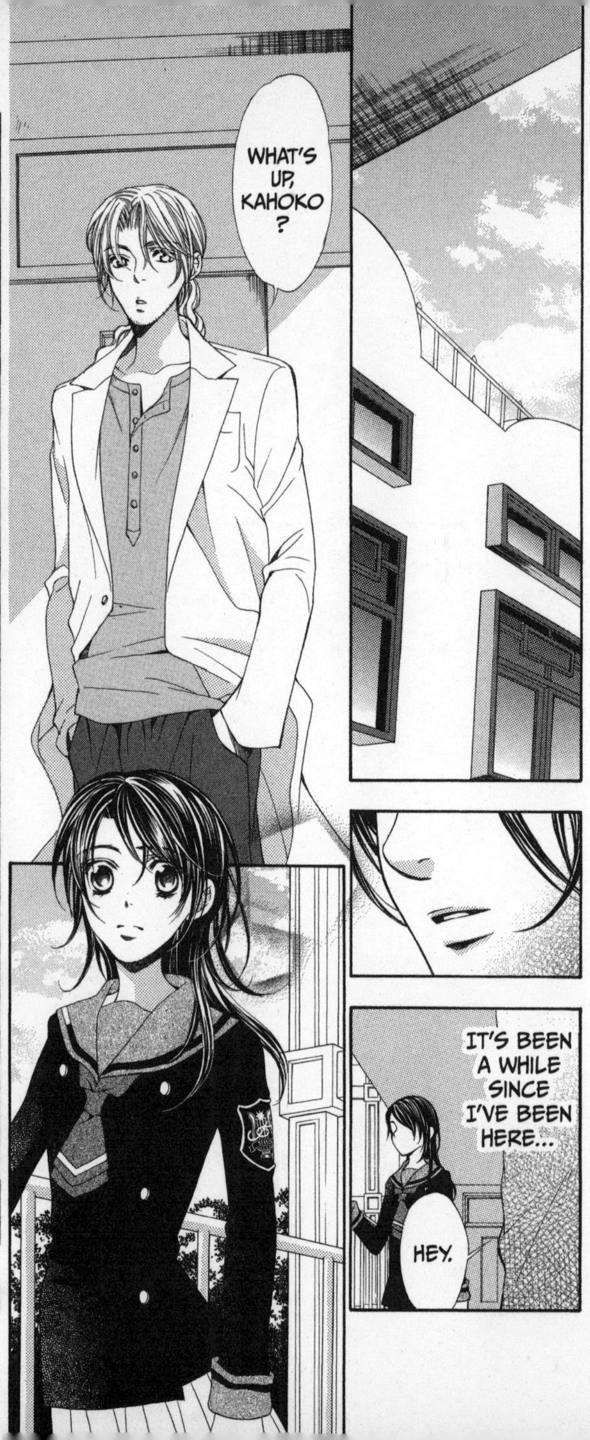
IT'S BEEN A WHILE SINCE I'VE BEEN HERE...
HEY.
WHAT'S UP, KAHOKO?

TWO

♥

I'm actually writing this in the middle of summer. The rainy season is long past and it's super hot.

However, this manga is scheduled to go on sale in Japan in October. And the anime has probably already started...
When I first heard about the anime, I was shocked. I was only involved in key visuals and illustrations, but it's been really interesting to see all the people involved.
"I see. This is how anime is produced..."
I feel over-whelmed all the time. It makes me realize what a total amateur I am...
I'm completely out of touch...
Yikes.

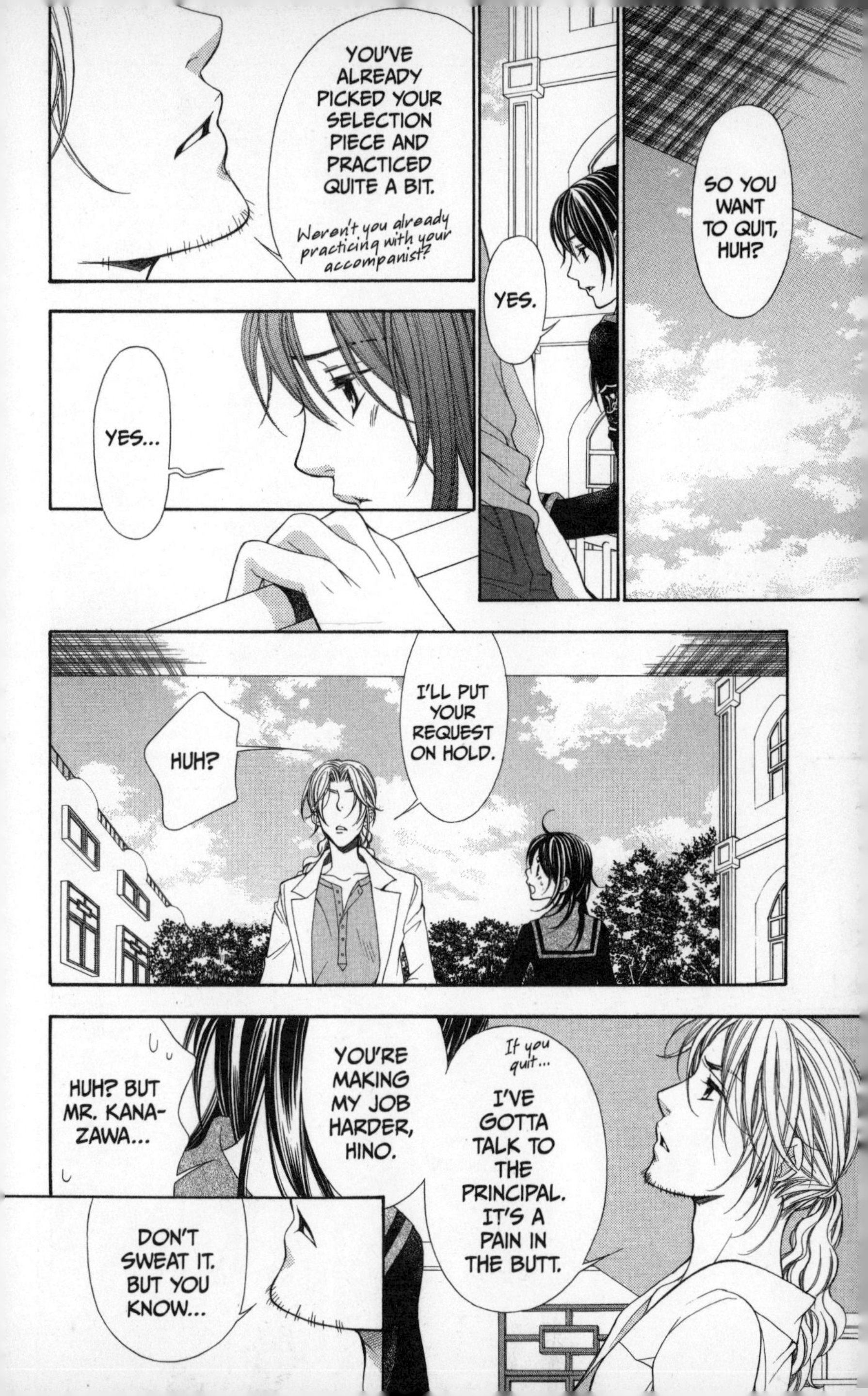
SO YOU WANT TO QUIT, HUH?
YES.
YOU'VE ALREADY PICKED YOUR SELECTION PIECE AND PRACTICED QUITE A BIT.
Weren't you already practicing with your accompanist?
YES...
I'LL PUT YOUR REQUEST ON HOLD.
HUH?
If you quit...
I'VE GOTTA TALK TO THE PRINCIPAL. IT'S A PAIN IN THE BUTT.
YOU'RE MAKING MY JOB HARDER, HINO.
HUH? BUT MR. KANA-ZAWA...
DON'T SWEAT IT. BUT YOU KNOW...

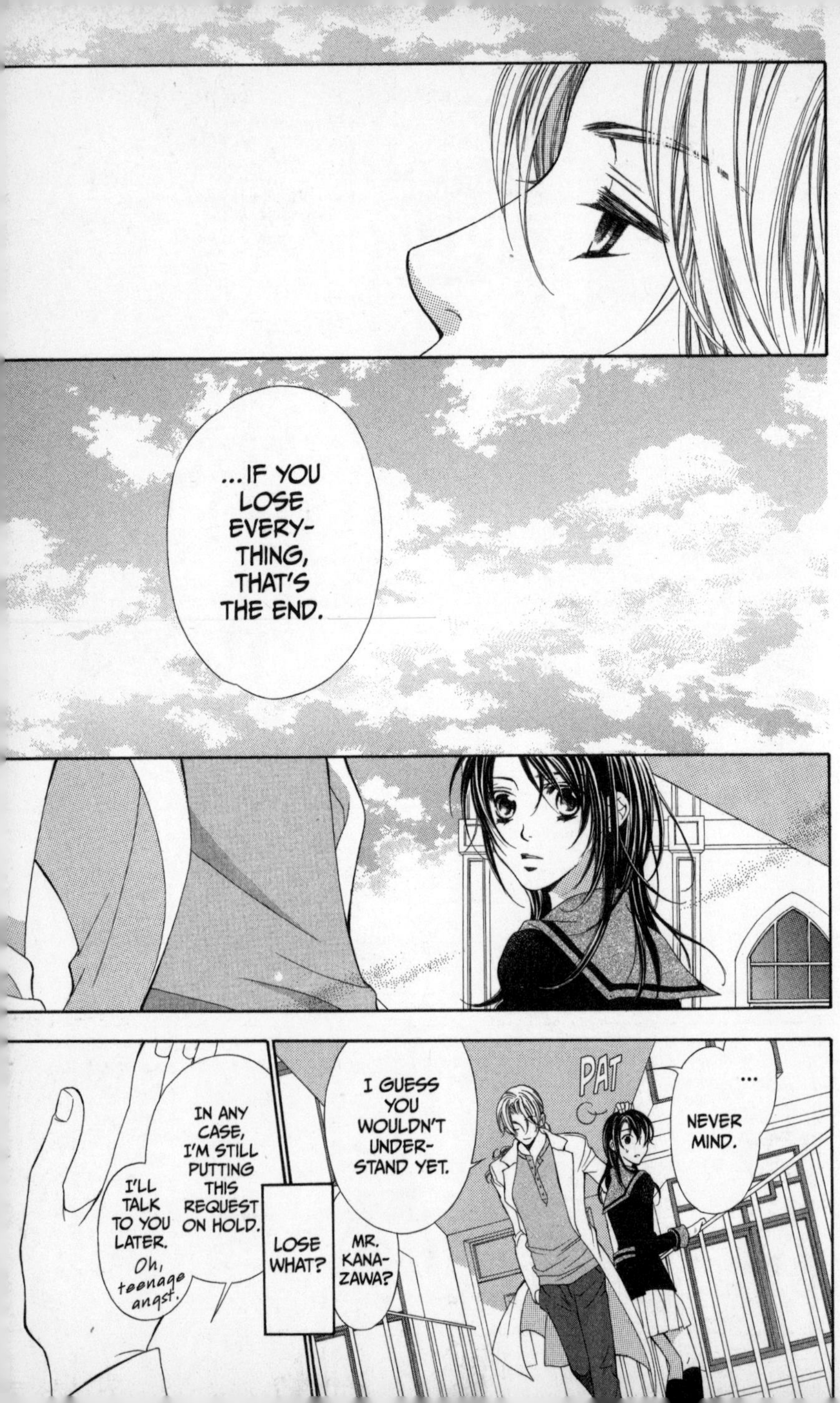
...IF YOU LOSE EVERYTHING, THAT'S THE END.
...
NEVER MIND.
PAT
I GUESS YOU WOULDN'T UNDERSTAND YET.
MR. KANAZAWA?
LOSE WHAT?
IN ANY CASE, I'M STILL PUTTING THIS REQUEST ON HOLD.
I'LL TALK TO YOU LATER.
Oh, teenage angst.

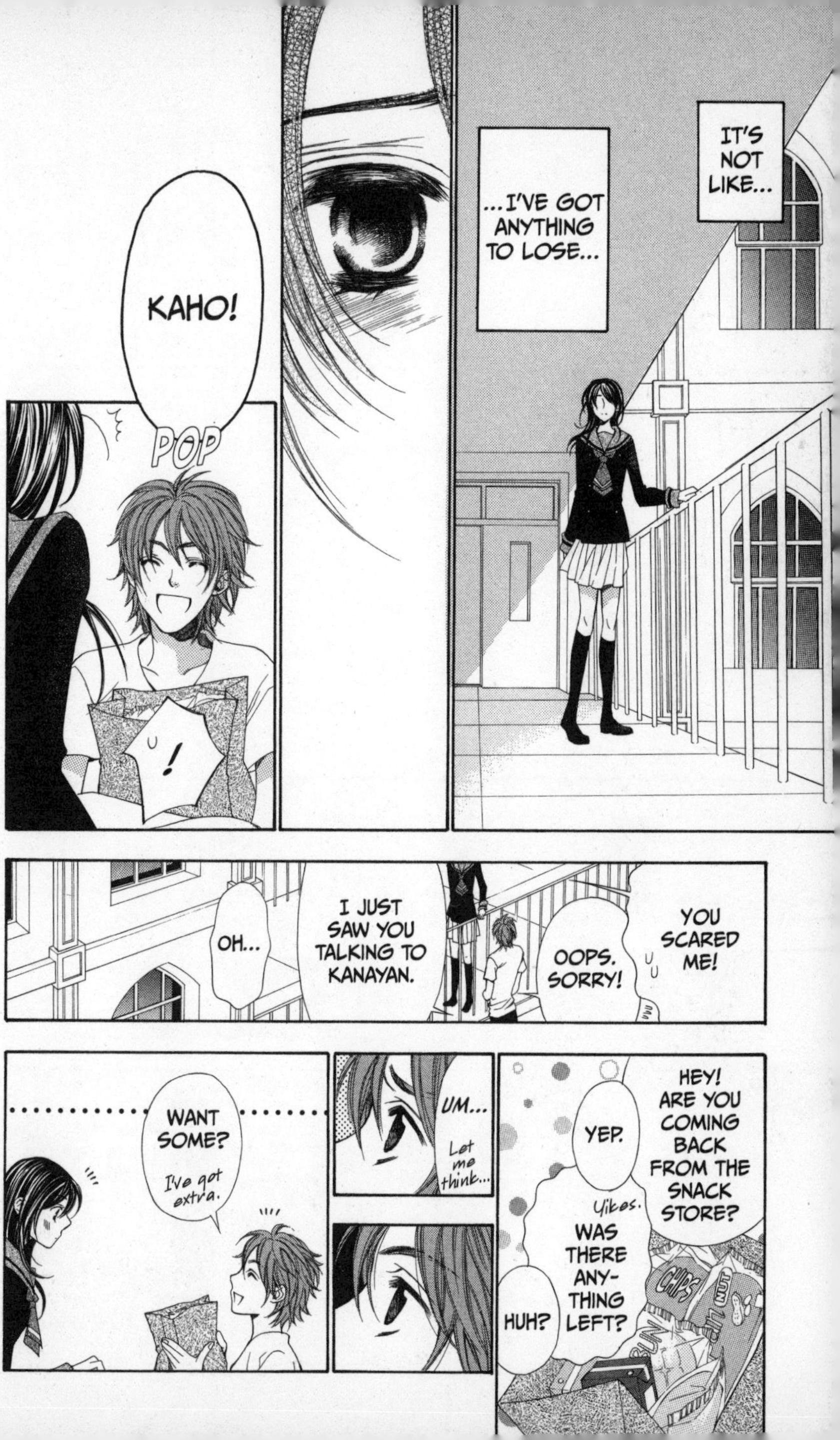
IT'S NOT LIKE...
...I'VE GOT ANYTHING TO LOSE...
KAHO!
POP
!
YOU SCARED ME!
OOPS. SORRY!
I JUST SAW YOU TALKING TO KANAYAN.
OH...
HEY! ARE YOU COMING BACK FROM THE SNACK STORE?
YEP.
Yikes.
WAS THERE ANYTHING LEFT?
HUH?
CHIPS
UM...
Let me think...
WANT SOME?
I've got extra.

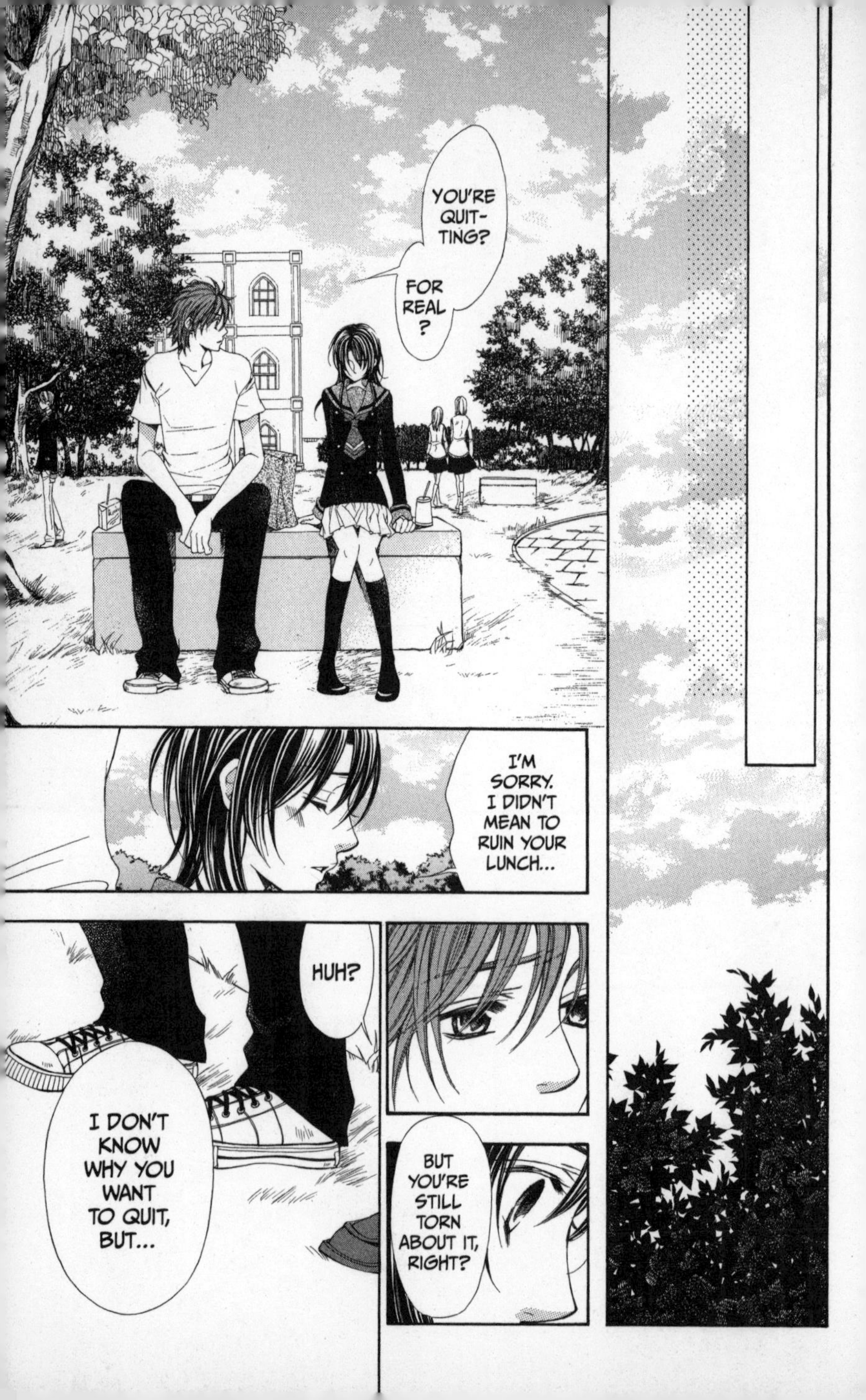
YOU'RE QUIT-TING?
FOR REAL?
I'M SORRY. I DIDN'T MEAN TO RUIN YOUR LUNCH...
BUT YOU'RE STILL TORN ABOUT IT, RIGHT?
HUH?
I DON'T KNOW WHY YOU WANT TO QUIT, BUT...

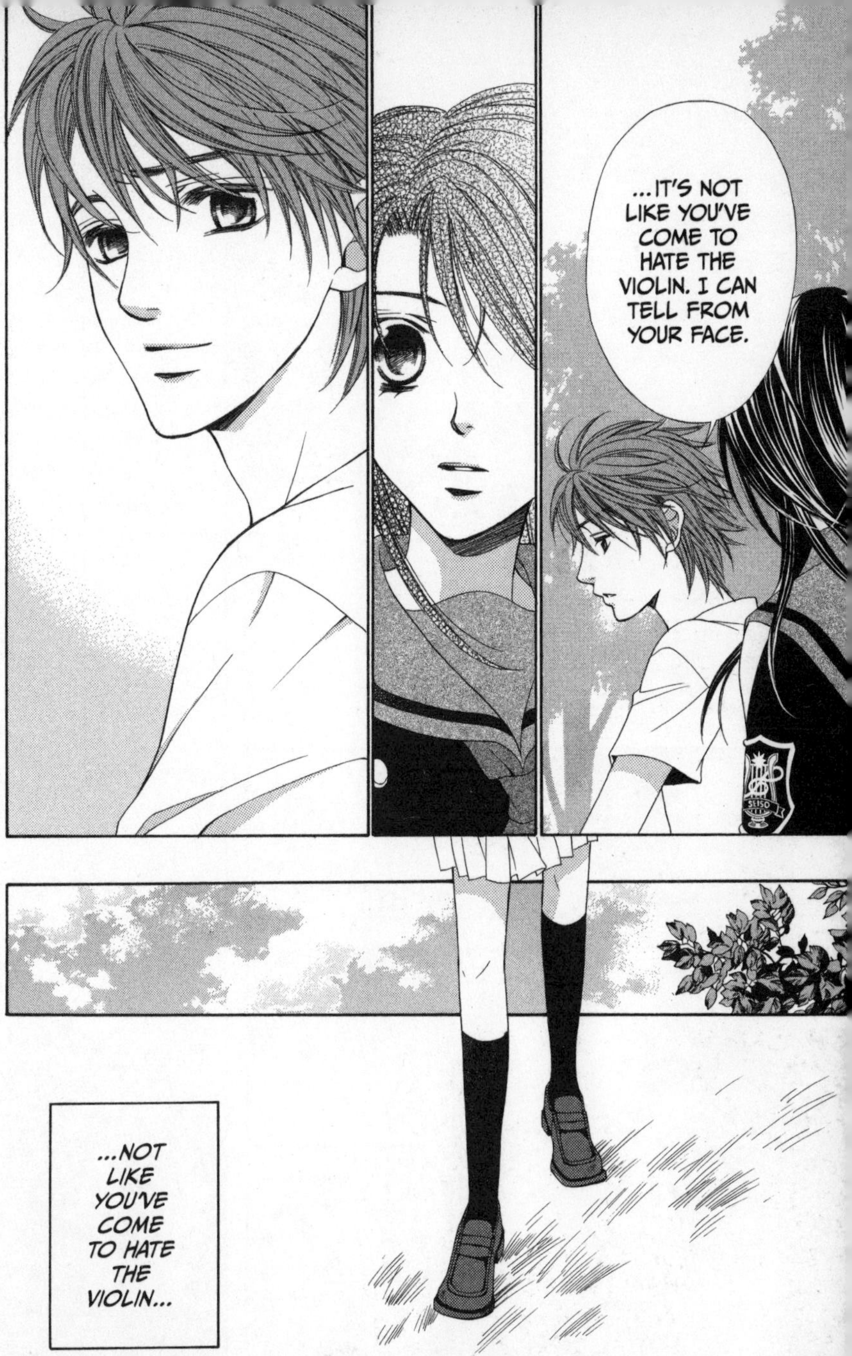
...IT'S NOT LIKE YOU'VE COME TO HATE THE VIOLIN. I CAN TELL FROM YOUR FACE.
...NOT LIKE YOU'VE COME TO HATE THE VIOLIN...

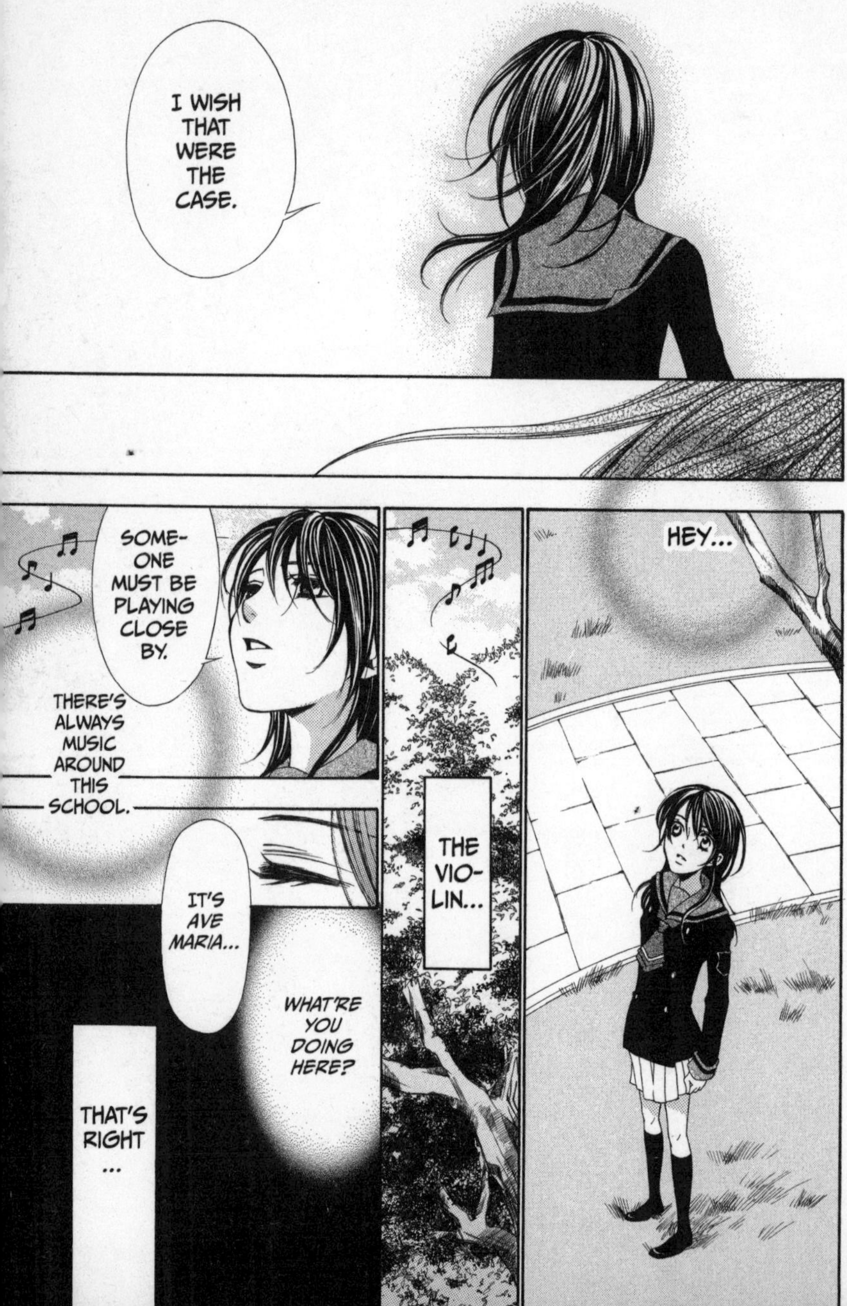
I WISH THAT WERE THE CASE.
HEY...
THE VIO-LIN...
SOME-ONE MUST BE PLAYING CLOSE BY.
THERE'S ALWAYS MUSIC AROUND THIS SCHOOL.
IT'S AVE MARIA...
WHAT'RE YOU DOING HERE?
THAT'S RIGHT ...

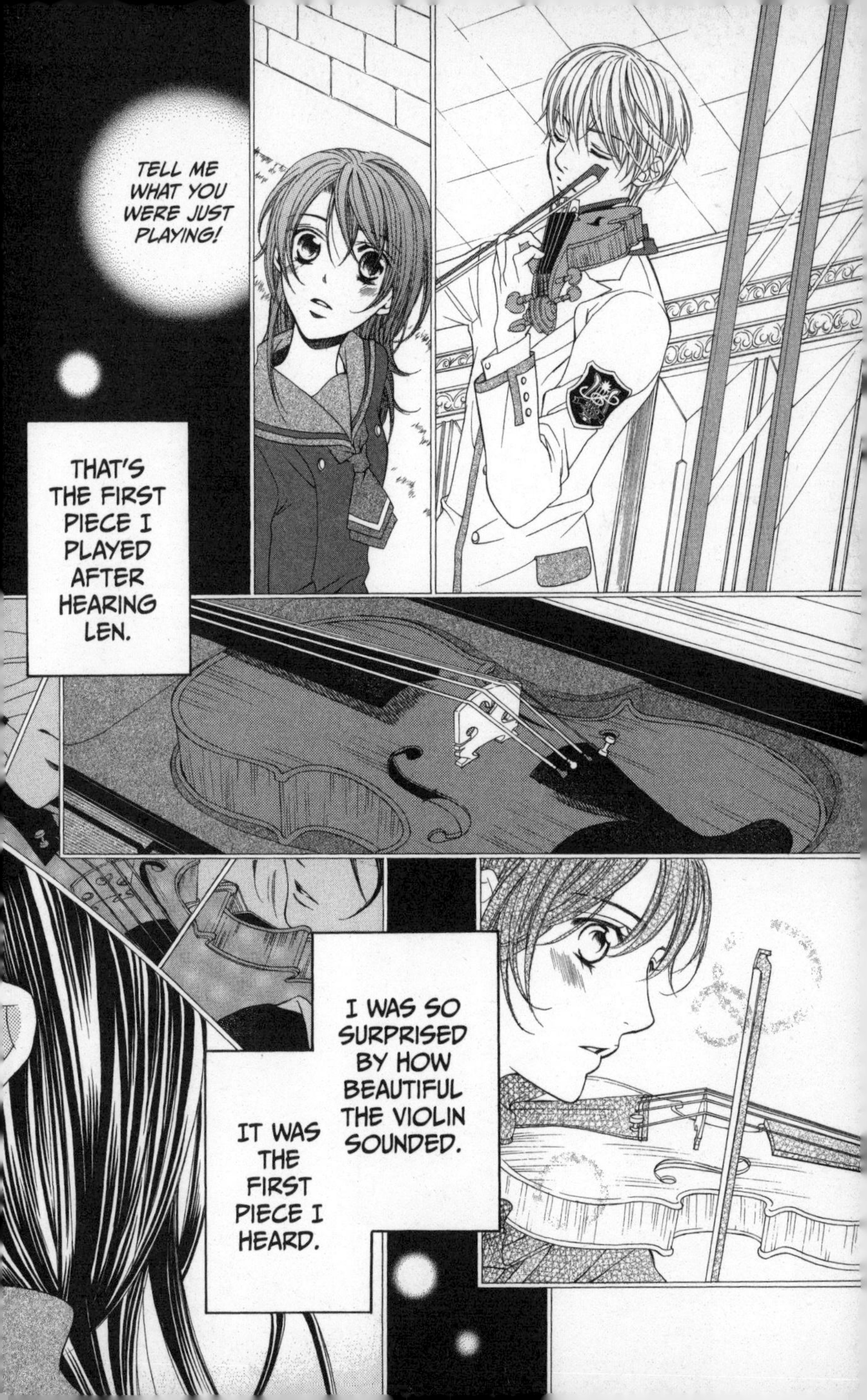
TELL ME WHAT YOU WERE JUST PLAYING!
THAT'S THE FIRST PIECE I PLAYED AFTER HEARING LEN.
I WAS SO SURPRISED BY HOW BEAUTIFUL THE VIOLIN SOUNDED.
IT WAS THE FIRST PIECE I HEARD.

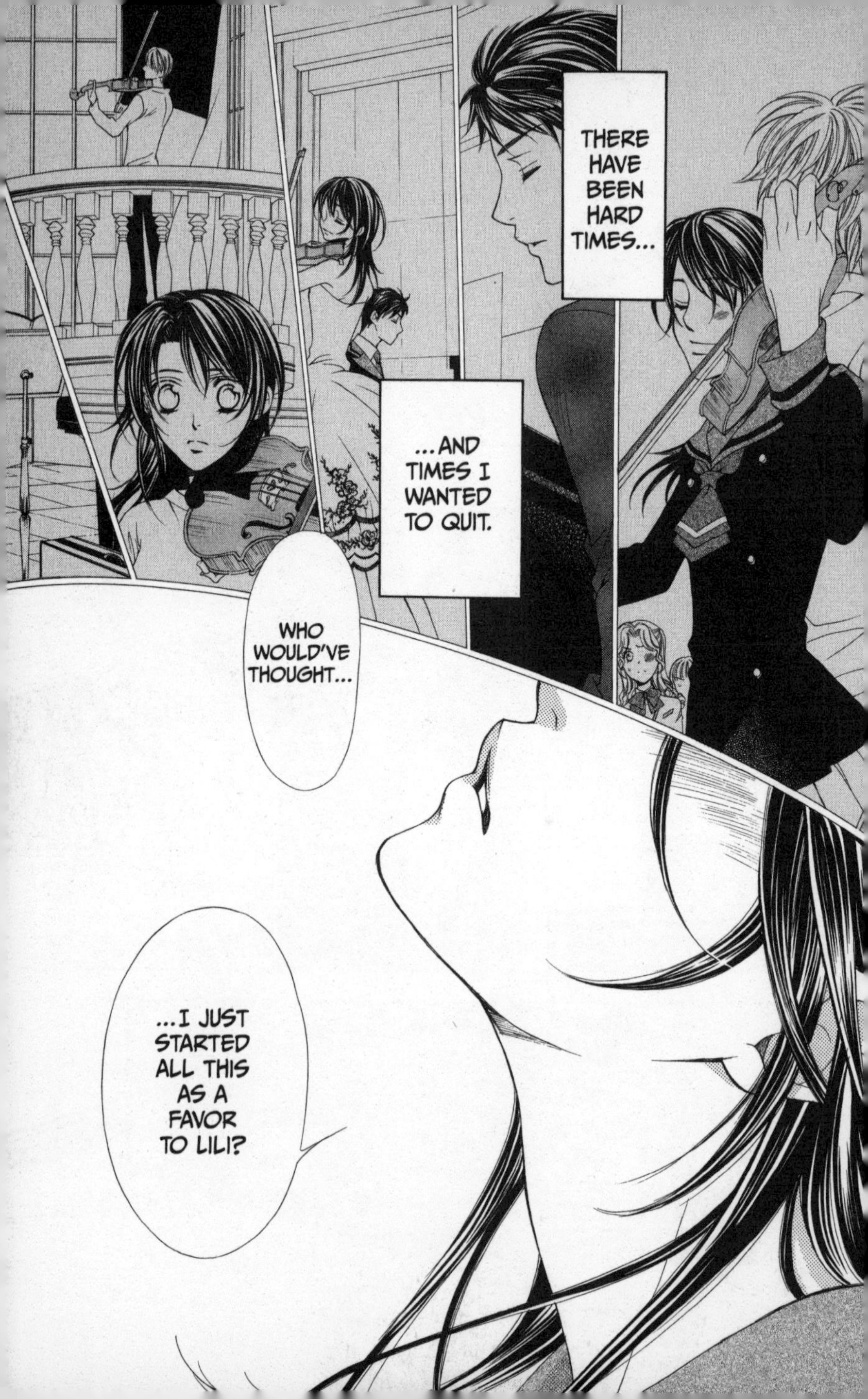
THERE HAVE BEEN HARD TIMES...
...AND TIMES I WANTED TO QUIT.
WHO WOULD'VE THOUGHT...
...I JUST STARTED ALL THIS AS A FAVOR TO LILI?

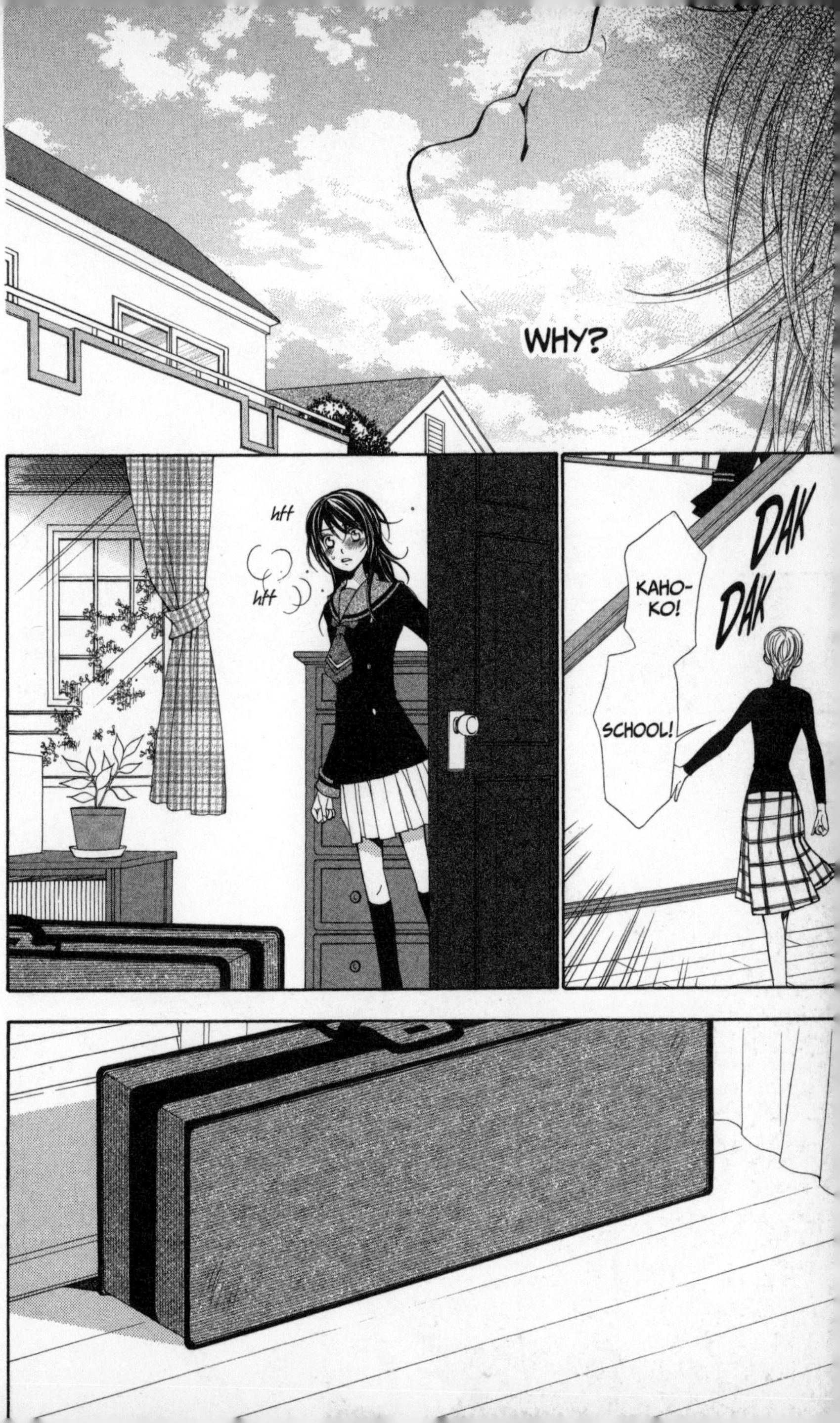
WHY?
DAK
DAK
KAHO-
KO!
SCHOOL!
hff
hff

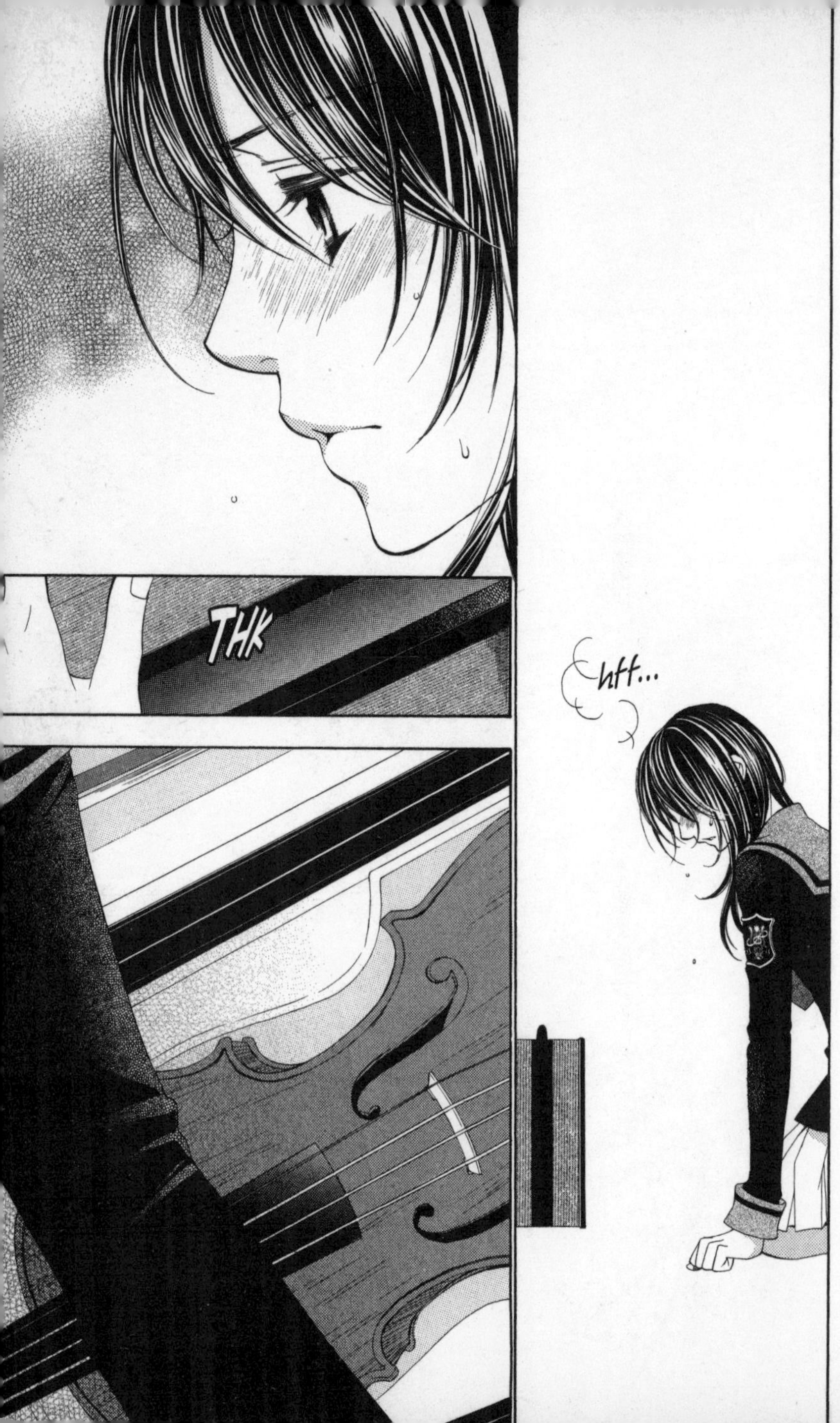
hff...
THK

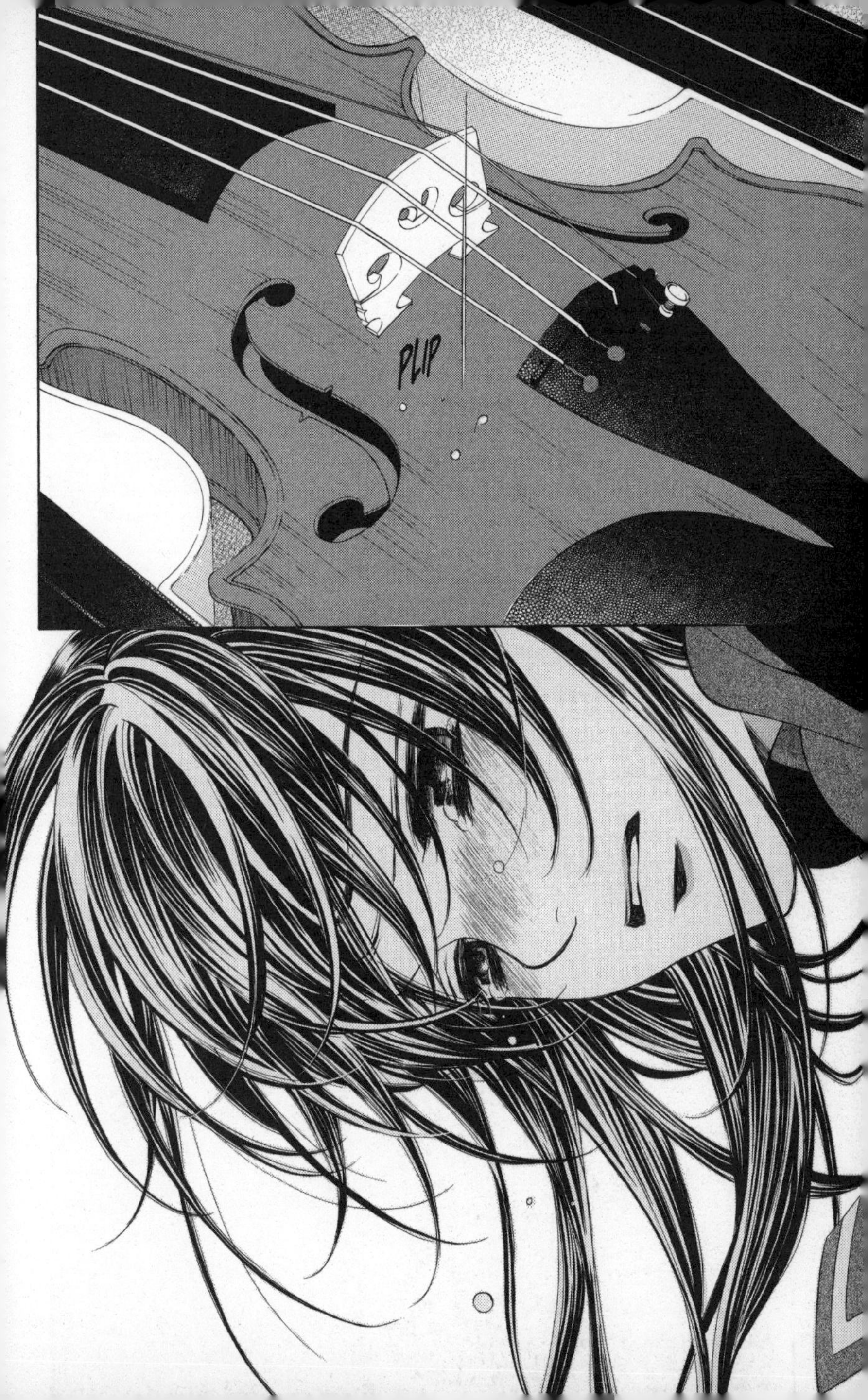
PLIP

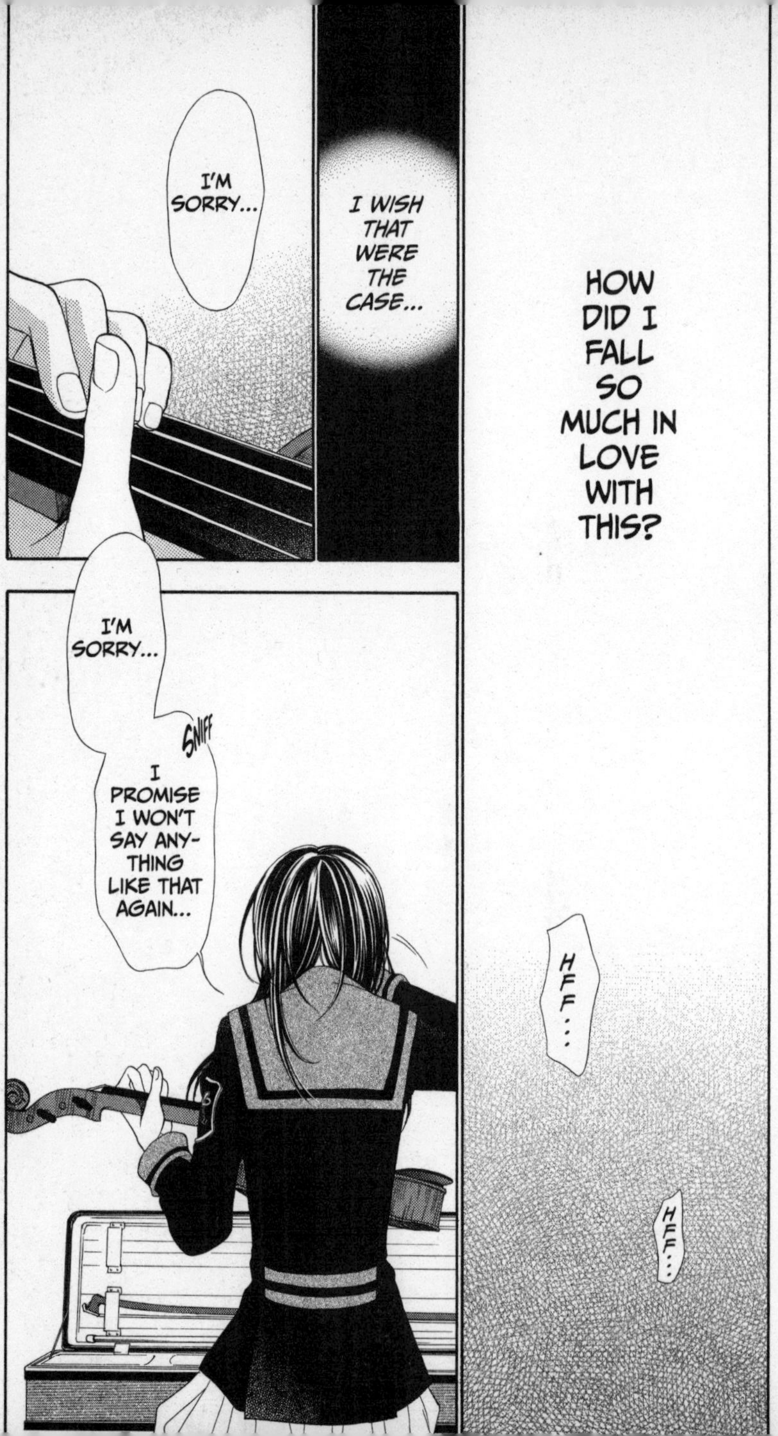
HOW DID I FALL SO MUCH IN LOVE WITH THIS?
HFF...
HFF...
I WISH THAT WERE THE CASE...
I'M SORRY...
I'M SORRY...
SNIFF
I PROMISE I WON'T SAY ANY-THING LIKE THAT AGAIN...

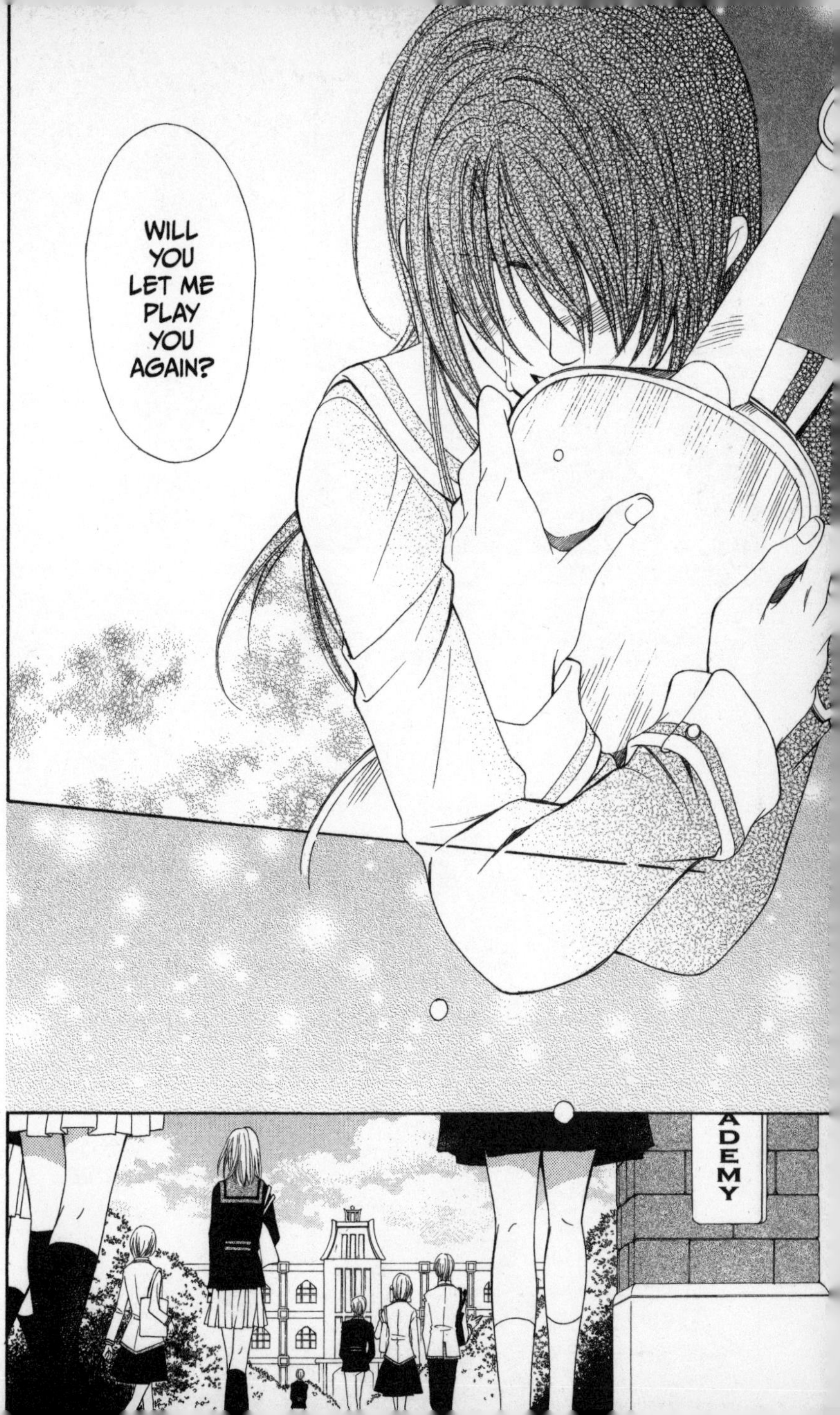
WILL YOU LET ME PLAY YOU AGAIN?
ADEMY

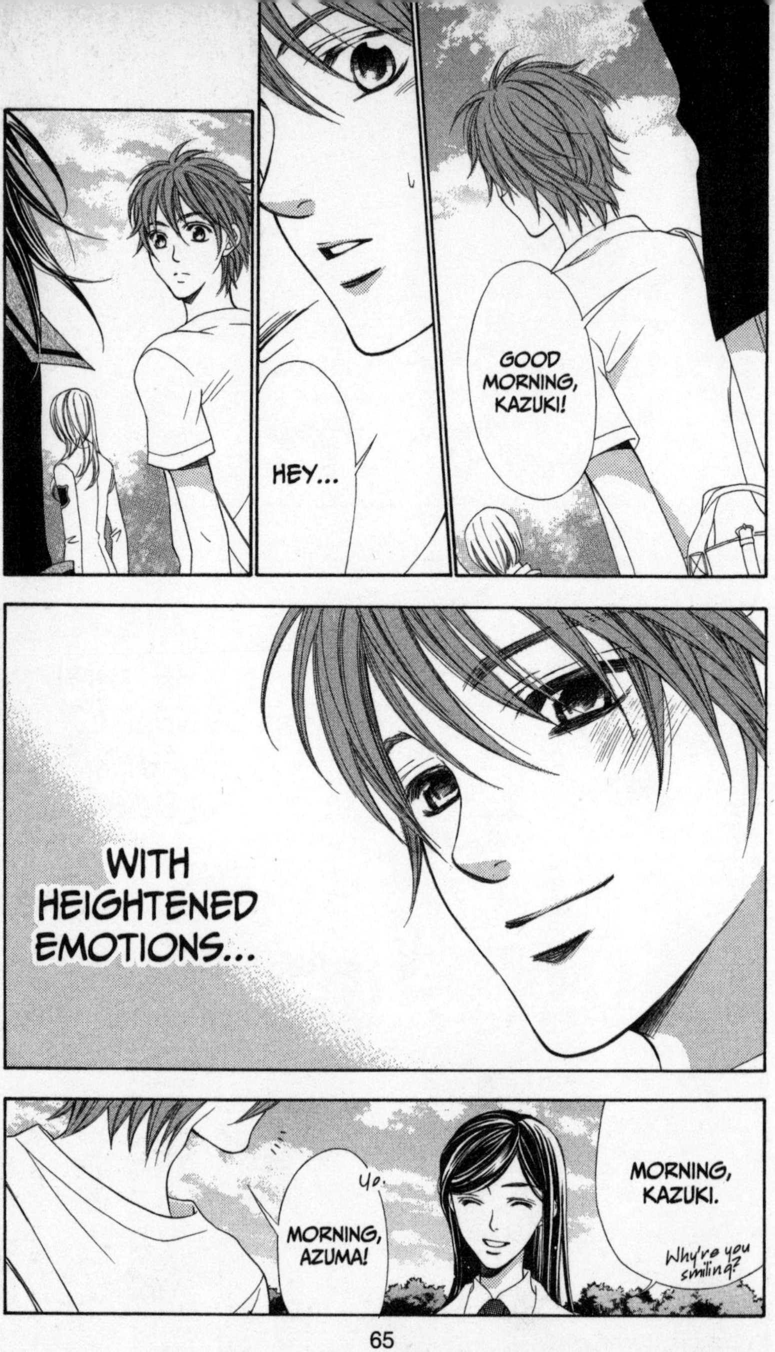
GOOD MORNING, KAZUKI!
HEY...
WITH HEIGHTENED EMOTIONS...
MORNING, KAZUKI.
Why're you smiling?
MORNING, AZUMA!
Yo.

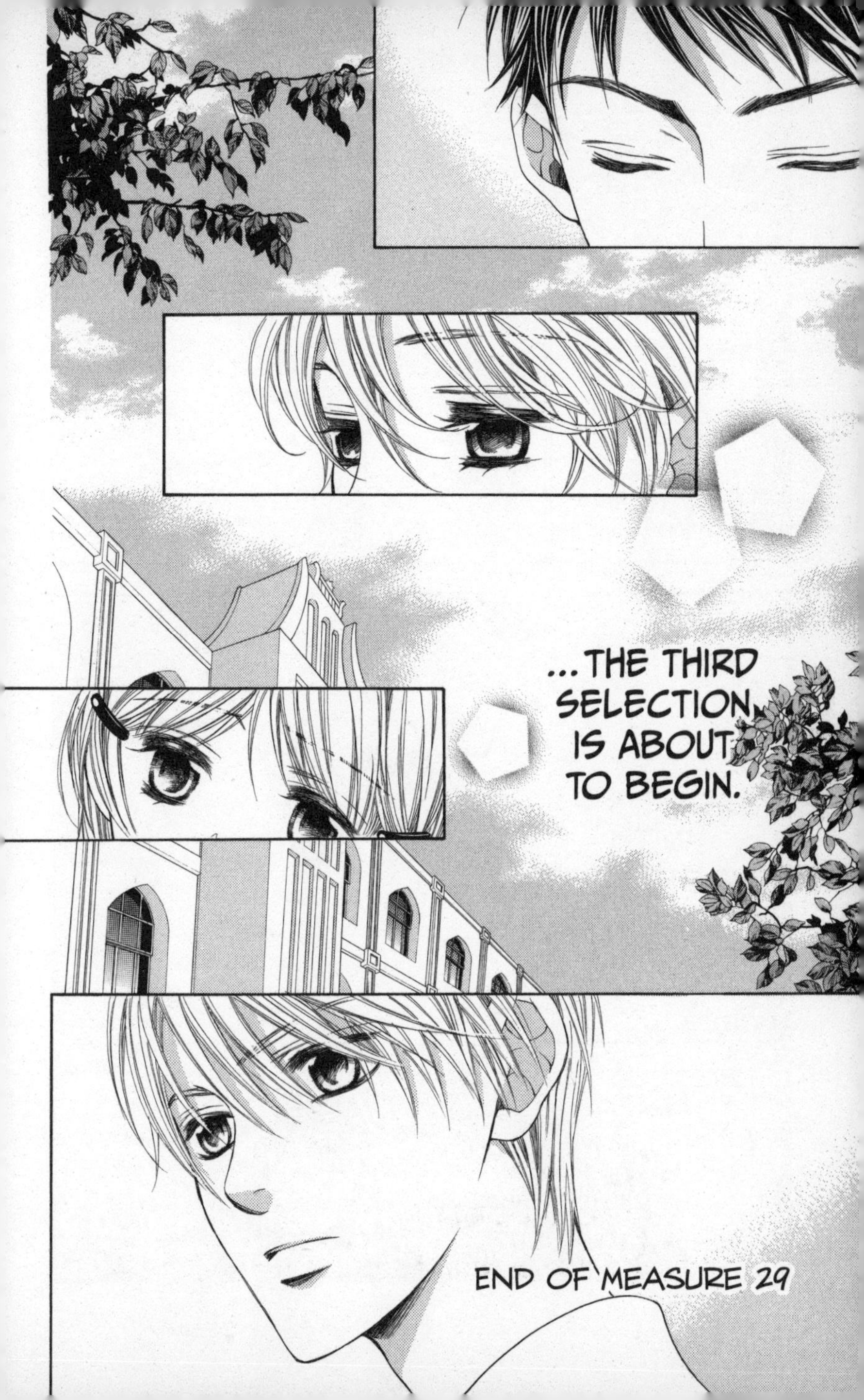
...THE THIRD SELECTION IS ABOUT TO BEGIN.
END OF MEASURE 29

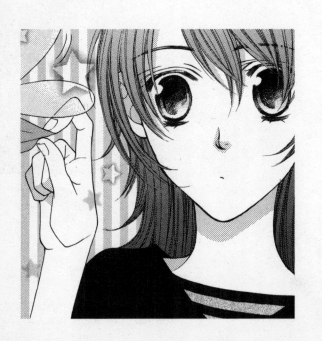

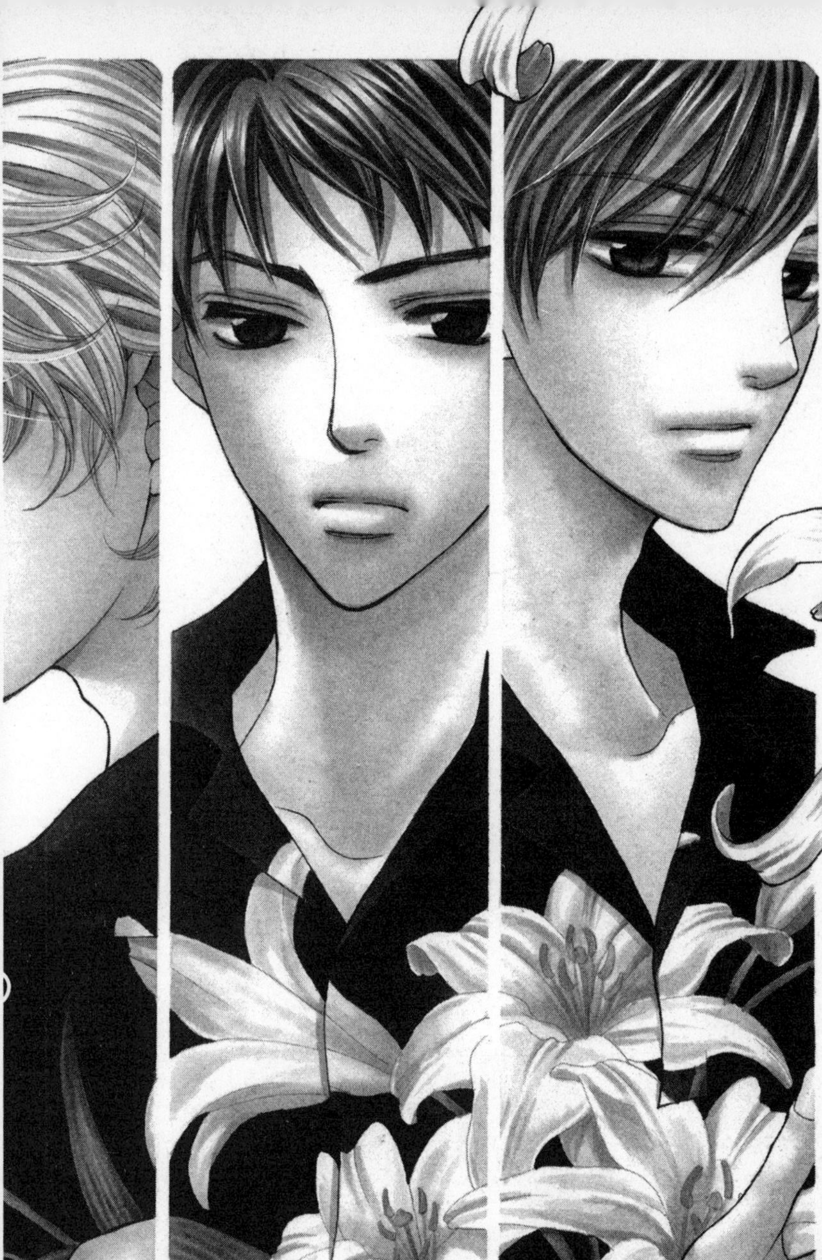

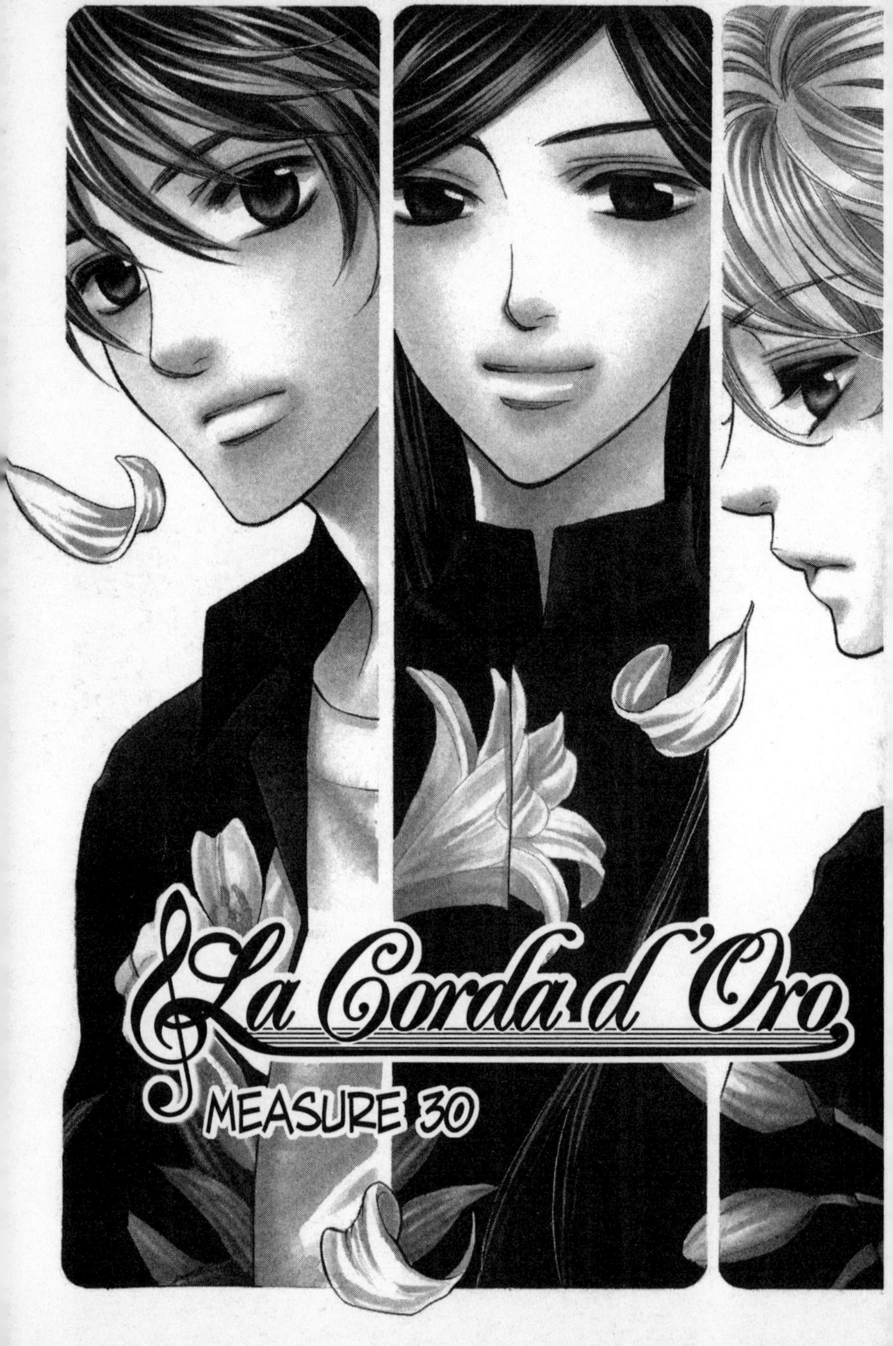
La Corda d'Oro
MEASURE 30

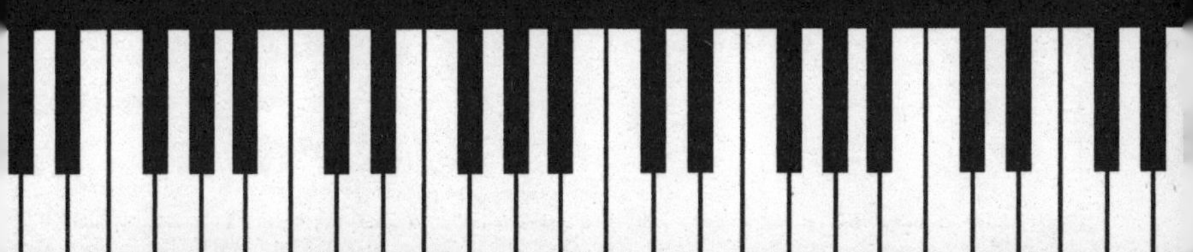

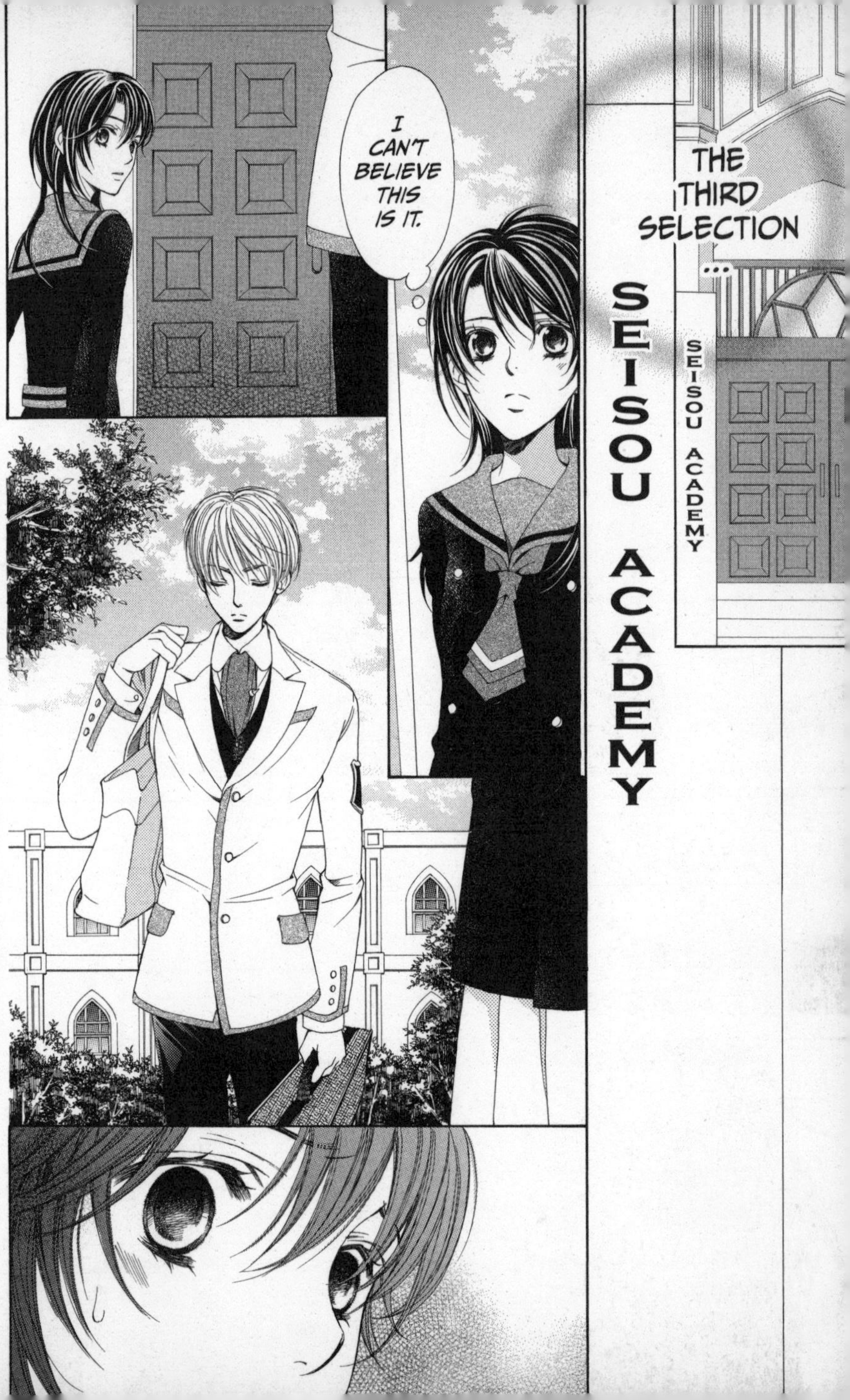
THE THIRD SELECTION...
SEISOU ACADEMY
SEISOU ACADEMY
I CAN'T BELIEVE THIS IS IT.

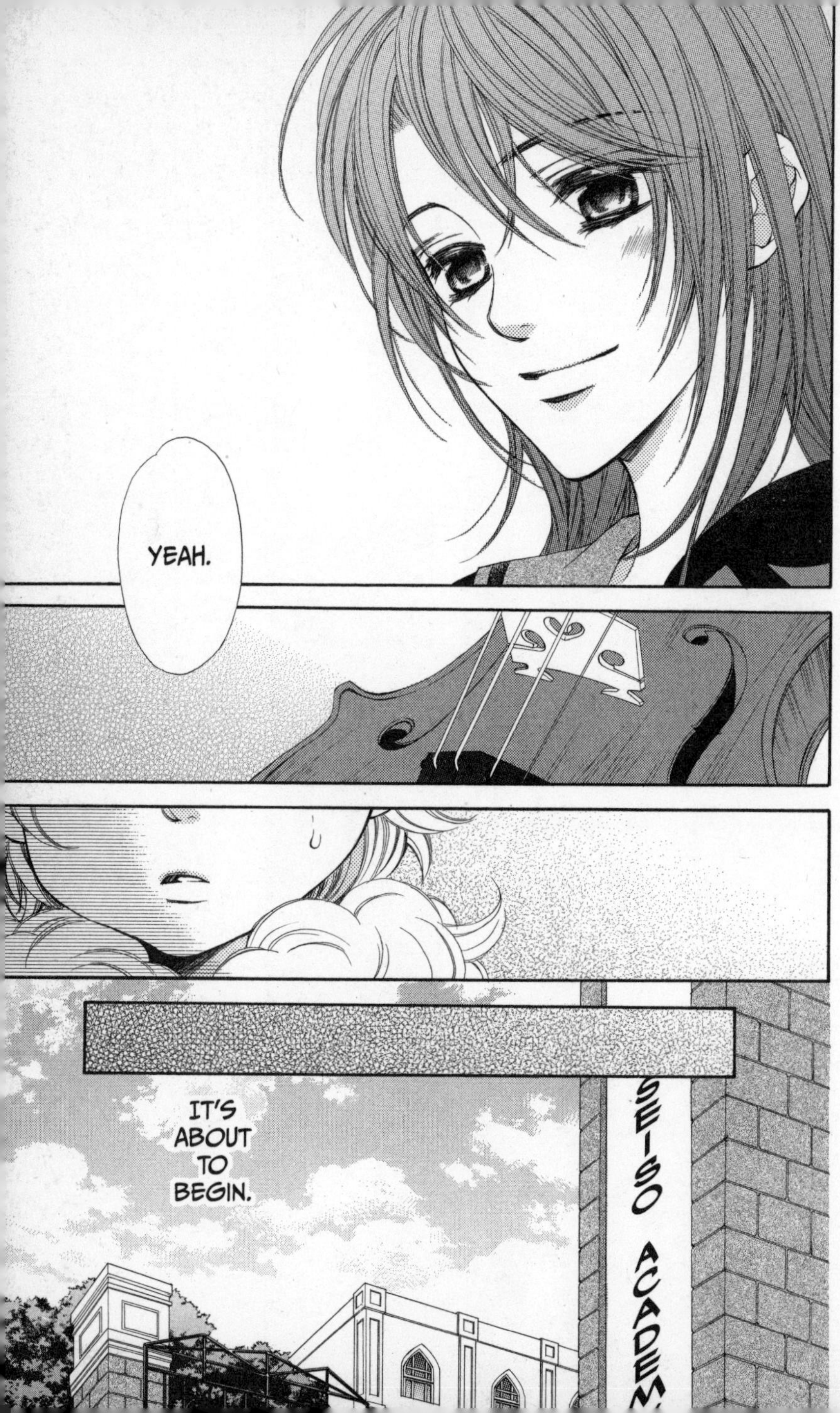
YEAH.
IT'S ABOUT TO BEGIN.
SEISO ACADEM

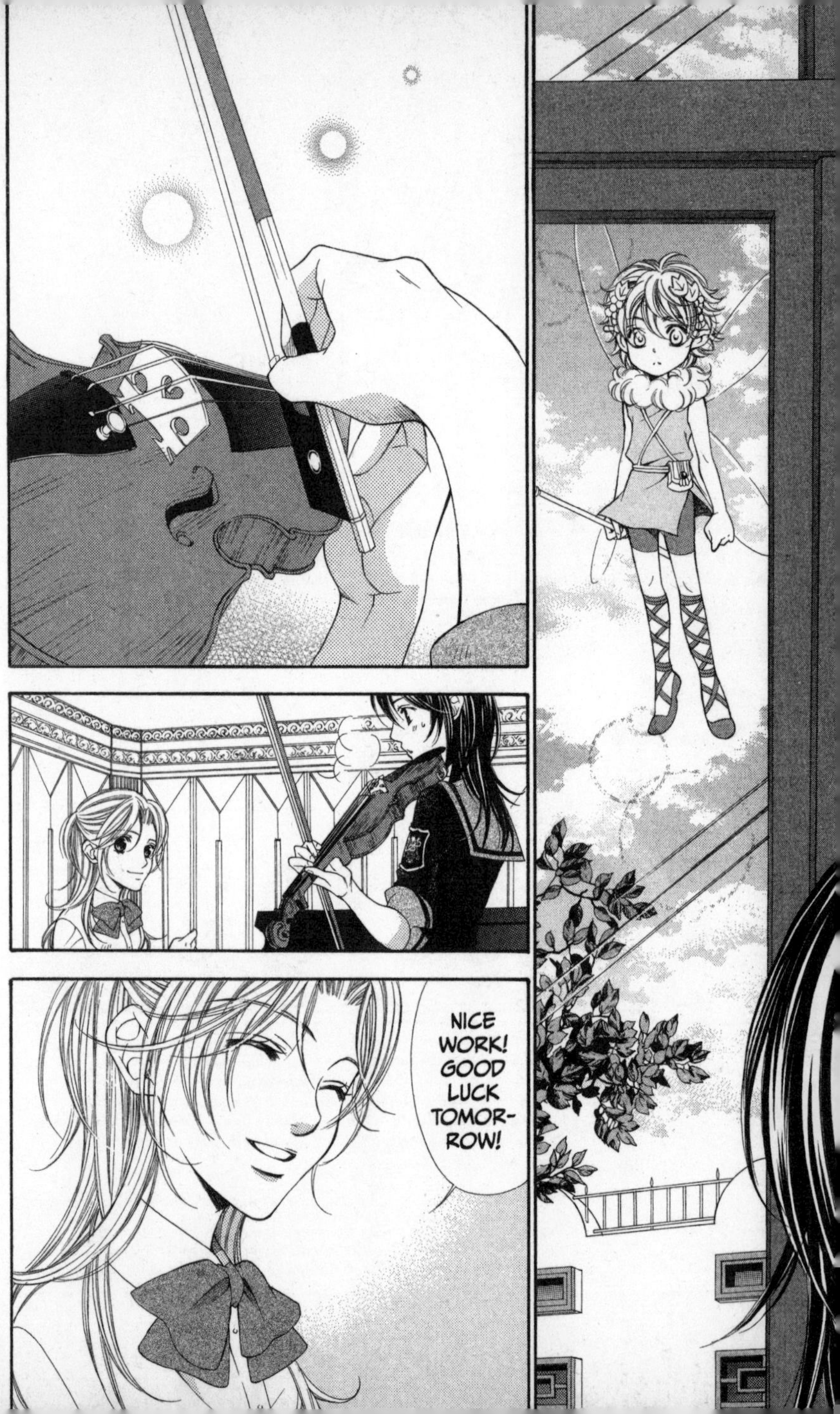
NICE WORK! GOOD LUCK TOMORROW!

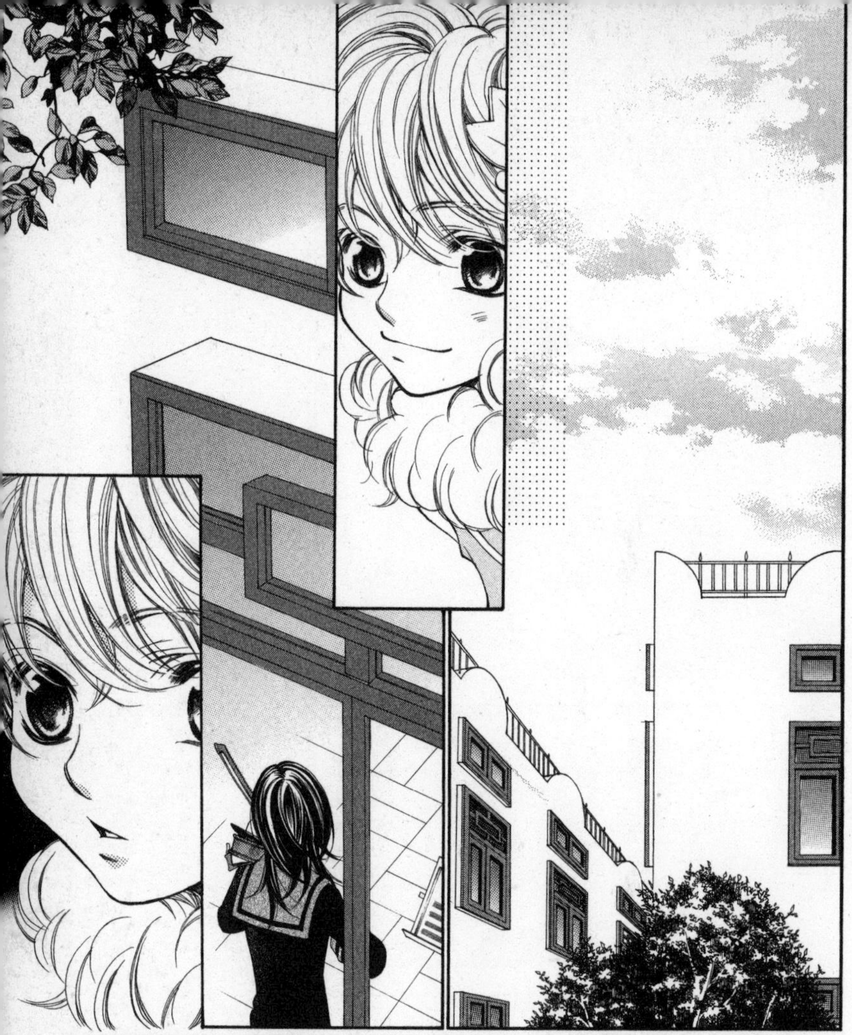

Daily Happenings 22
The workplace...

I've got four people who help me out. At any given time, there are one to three assistants at my house. Some of them have been published, some have already debuted, but we're all about the same age and we're all very close. However...The youngest of the bunch, Natsun (the leader of our clan despite her tender age), went to Kamakura and got a T-shirt from one of the temples. It's the kind with kanji lettering that's popular with foreign tourists. I've got it in a different color, so...

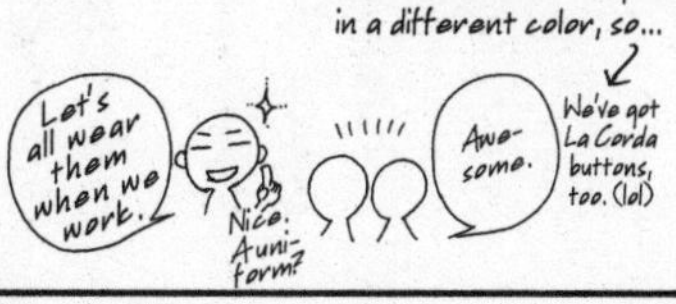
Let's all wear them when we work.
Nice. A uniform?
Awesome.
We've got La Corda buttons, too. (lol)

Our degree of closeness is at times questionable...

It's a small room, and everybody works well together. It's a good team environment. Thanks, everybody!!

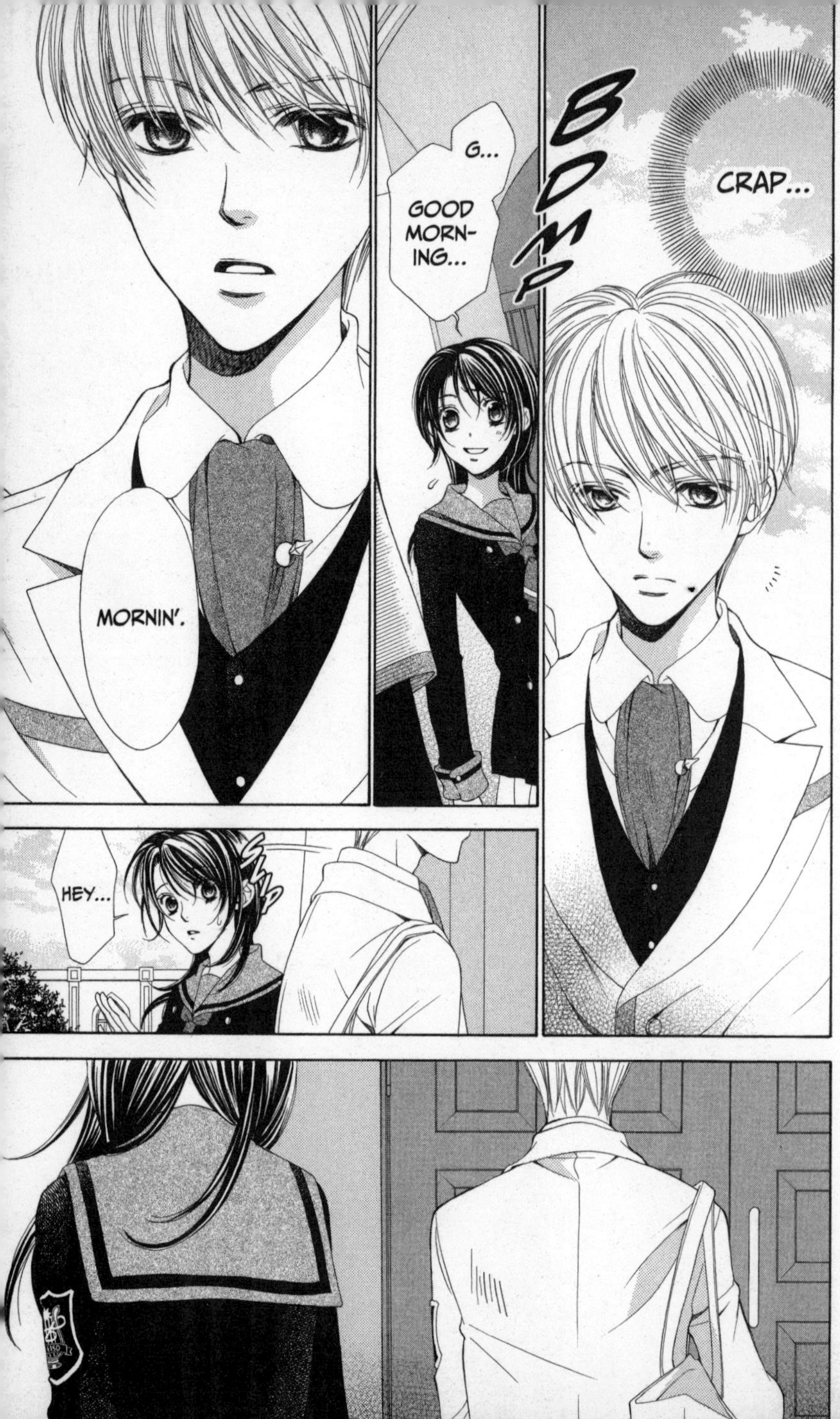
BDMP
CRAP...
G...
GOOD MORN-ING...
MORNIN'.
HEY...

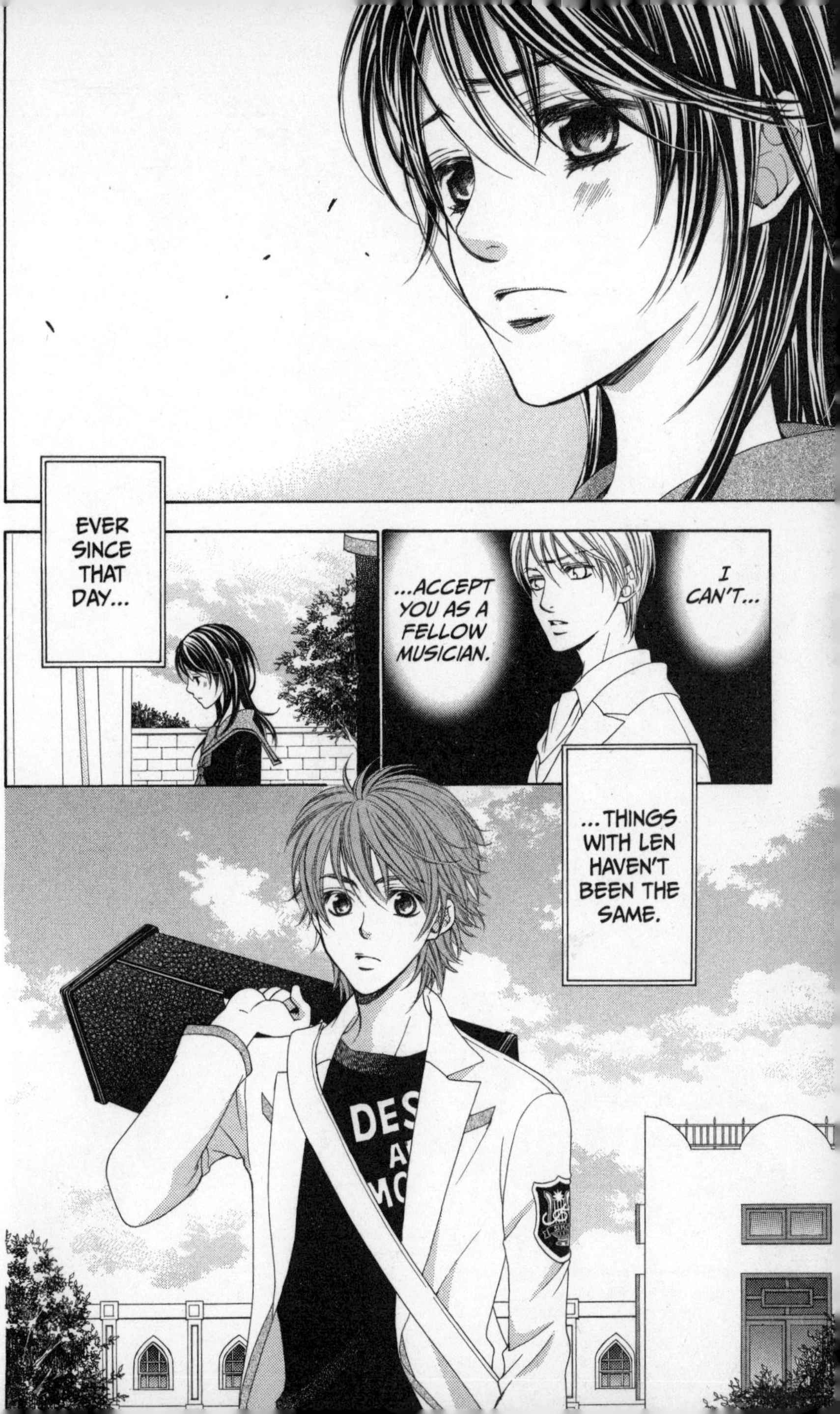
I CAN'T...
...ACCEPT YOU AS A FELLOW MUSICIAN.
EVER SINCE THAT DAY...
...THINGS WITH LEN HAVEN'T BEEN THE SAME.

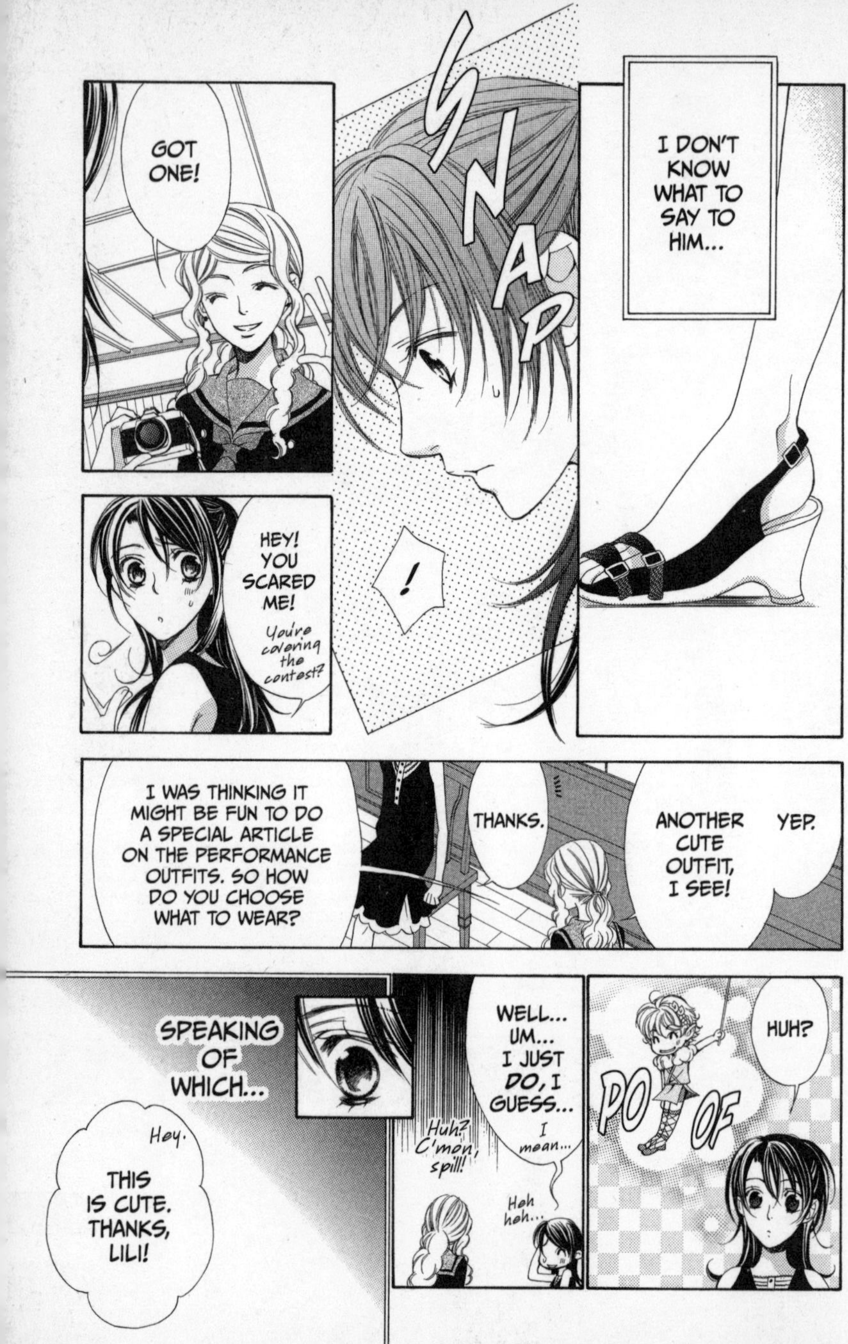
I DON'T KNOW WHAT TO SAY TO HIM...
SNAP
!
GOT ONE!
HEY! YOU SCARED ME!
You're covering the contest?
ANOTHER CUTE OUTFIT, I SEE!
YEP.
THANKS.
I WAS THINKING IT MIGHT BE FUN TO DO A SPECIAL ARTICLE ON THE PERFORMANCE OUTFITS. SO HOW DO YOU CHOOSE WHAT TO WEAR?
HUH?
POOF
WELL... UM... I JUST DO, I GUESS...
I mean...
Huh? C'mon, spill!
Heh heh...
SPEAKING OF WHICH...
Hey.
THIS IS CUTE. THANKS, LILI!

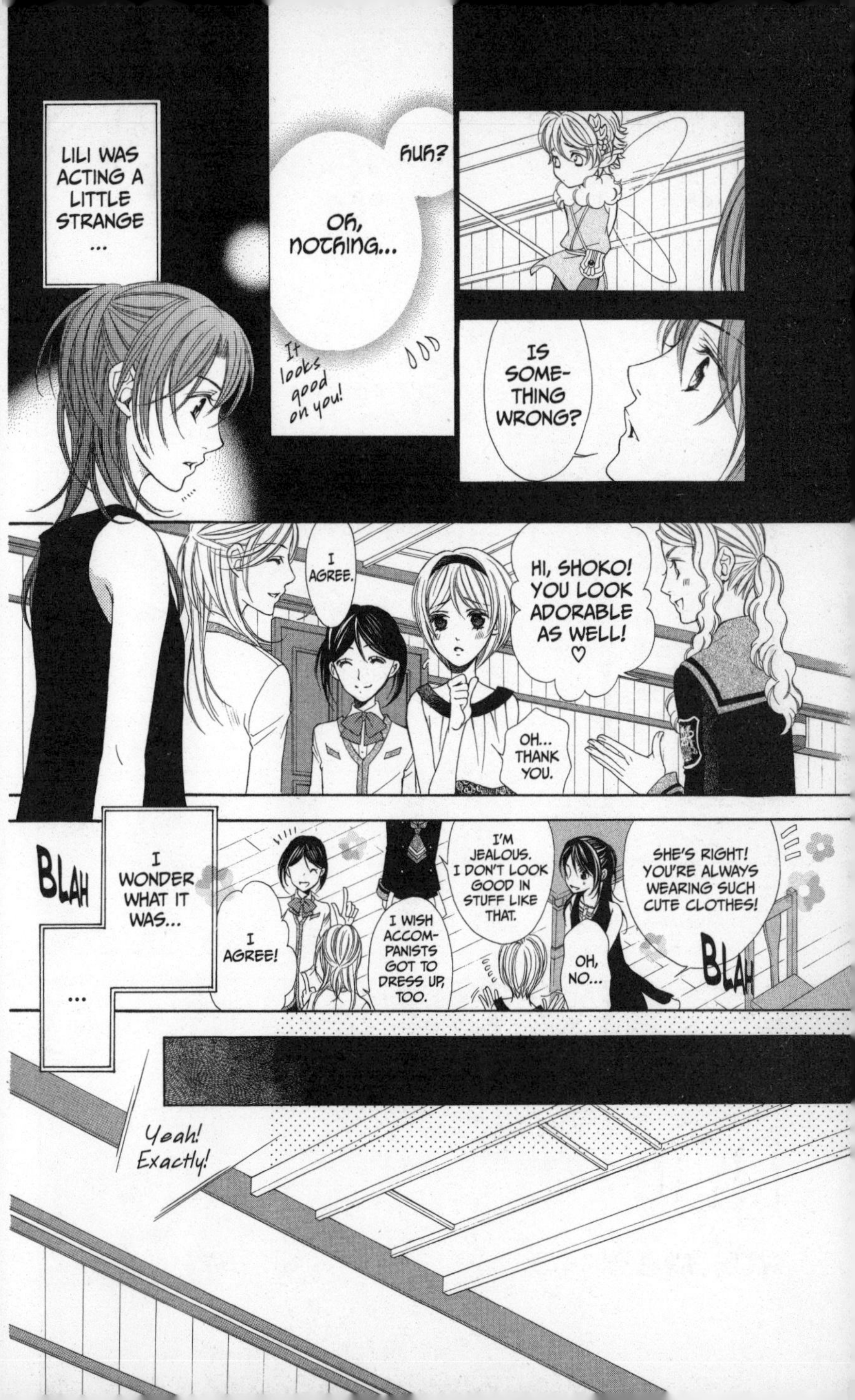
IS SOME-THING WRONG?
HUH?
OH, NOTHING...
It looks good on you!
LILI WAS ACTING A LITTLE STRANGE ...
HI, SHOKO! YOU LOOK ADORABLE AS WELL! ♡
OH... THANK YOU.
I AGREE.
SHE'S RIGHT! YOU'RE ALWAYS WEARING SUCH CUTE CLOTHES!
BLAH
I'M JEALOUS. I DON'T LOOK GOOD IN STUFF LIKE THAT.
OH, NO...
I WISH ACCOM-PANISTS GOT TO DRESS UP, TOO.
I AGREE!
BLAH
I WONDER WHAT IT WAS...
...
Yeah! Exactly!

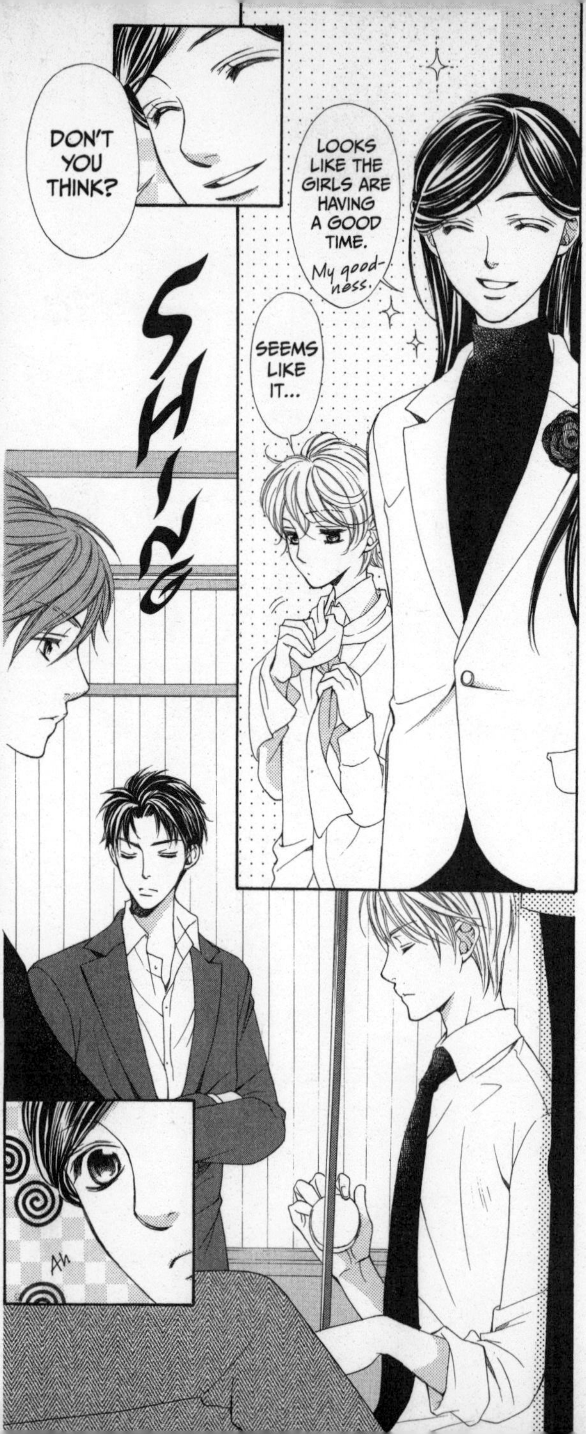
LOOKS LIKE THE GIRLS ARE HAVING A GOOD TIME.
My good-ness.
SEEMS LIKE IT...
DON'T YOU THINK?
SHING
Ah

THREE

I was able to go to a music recording for the anime soundtrack.

It was very professional. It's not like I get to sit in on live recordings every day, so it was a lot of fun.

The musicians were all current music students or recent graduates and were ALL extremely good-looking! There was only one day slotted for the recording, though, so it was a pretty tight schedule. I think the cellist doing Keiichi's part was there past midnight... I'm sure the producers and staff members were there until the wee hours of the morning.

Great work, everybody!

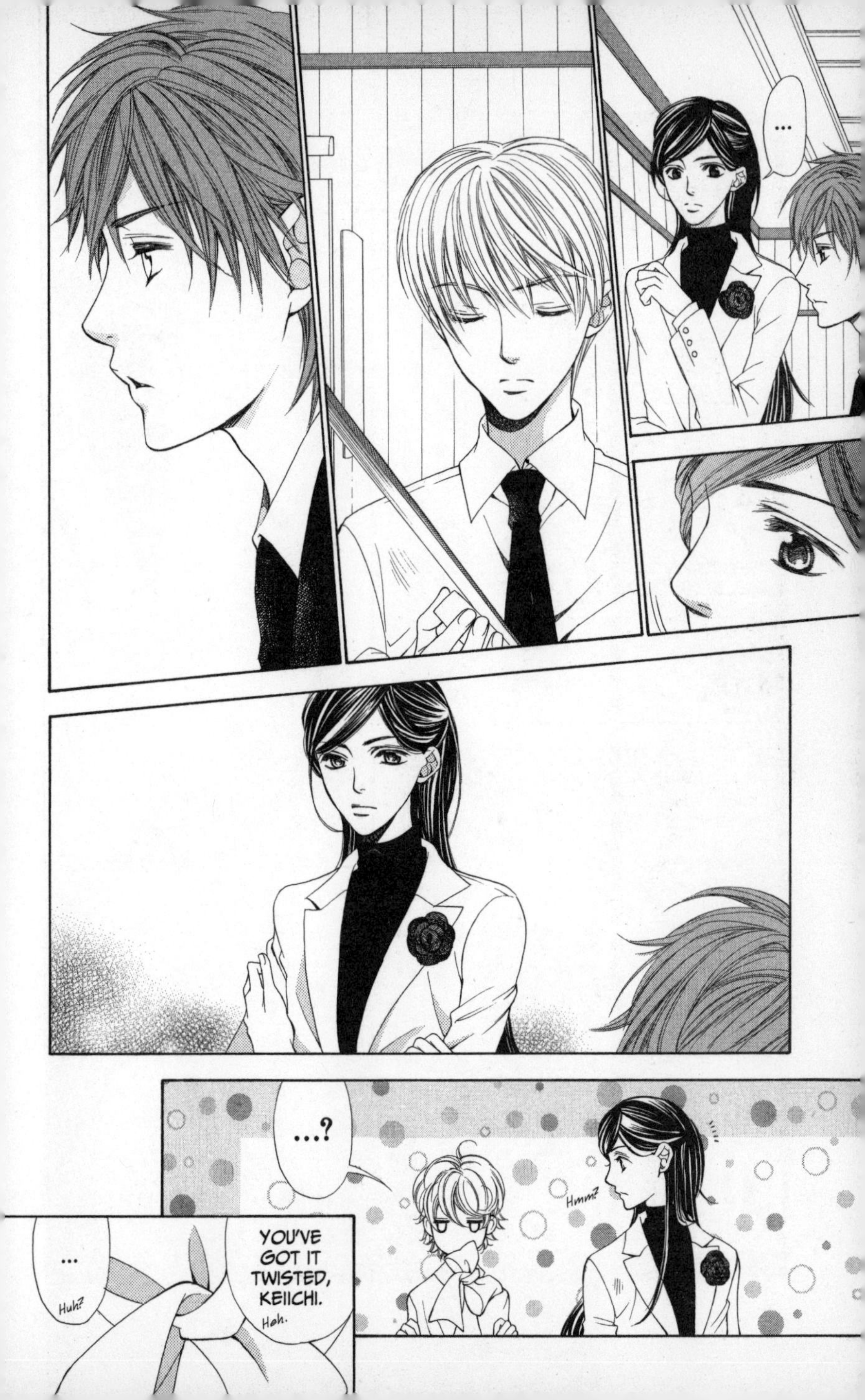
...
...?
Hmm?
YOU'VE GOT IT TWISTED, KEIICHI.
Heh.
...
Huh?

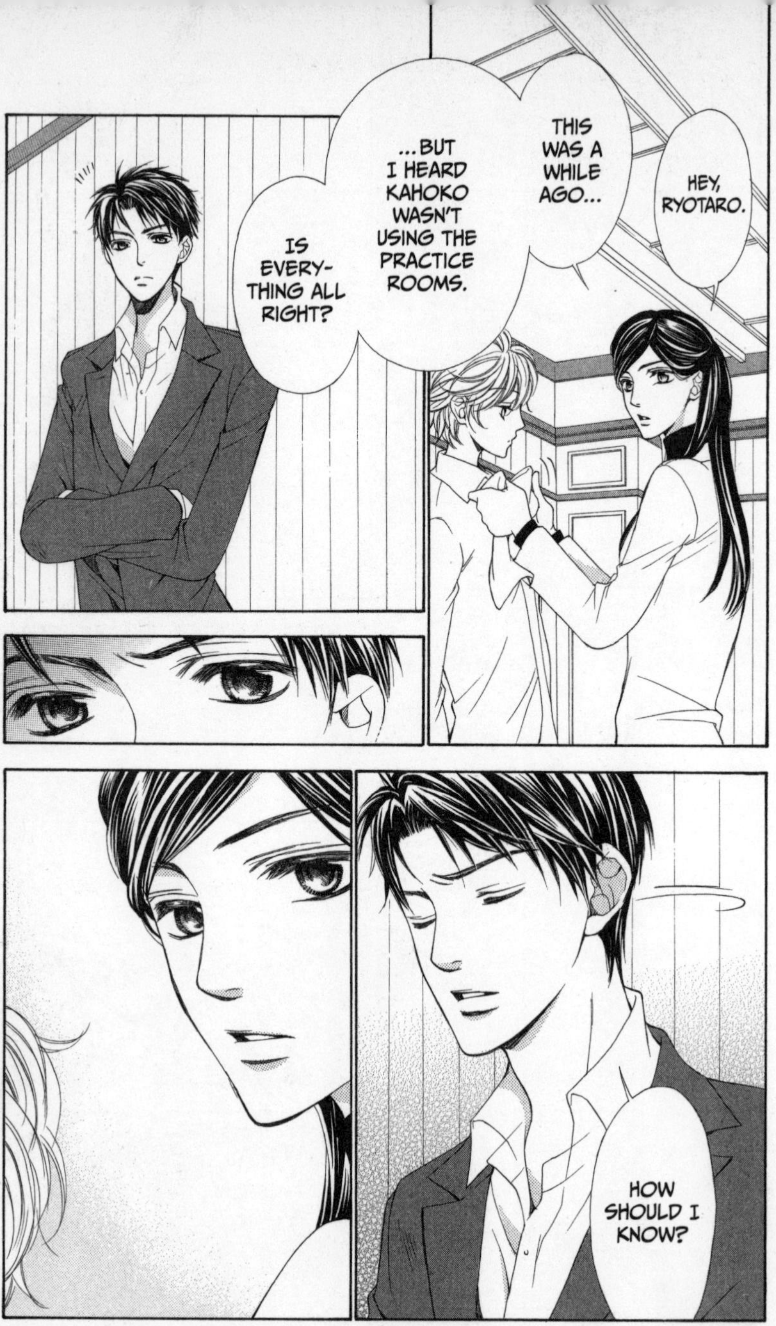
HEY, RYOTARO.
THIS WAS A WHILE AGO...
...BUT I HEARD KAHOKO WASN'T USING THE PRACTICE ROOMS.
IS EVERYTHING ALL RIGHT?
HOW SHOULD I KNOW?

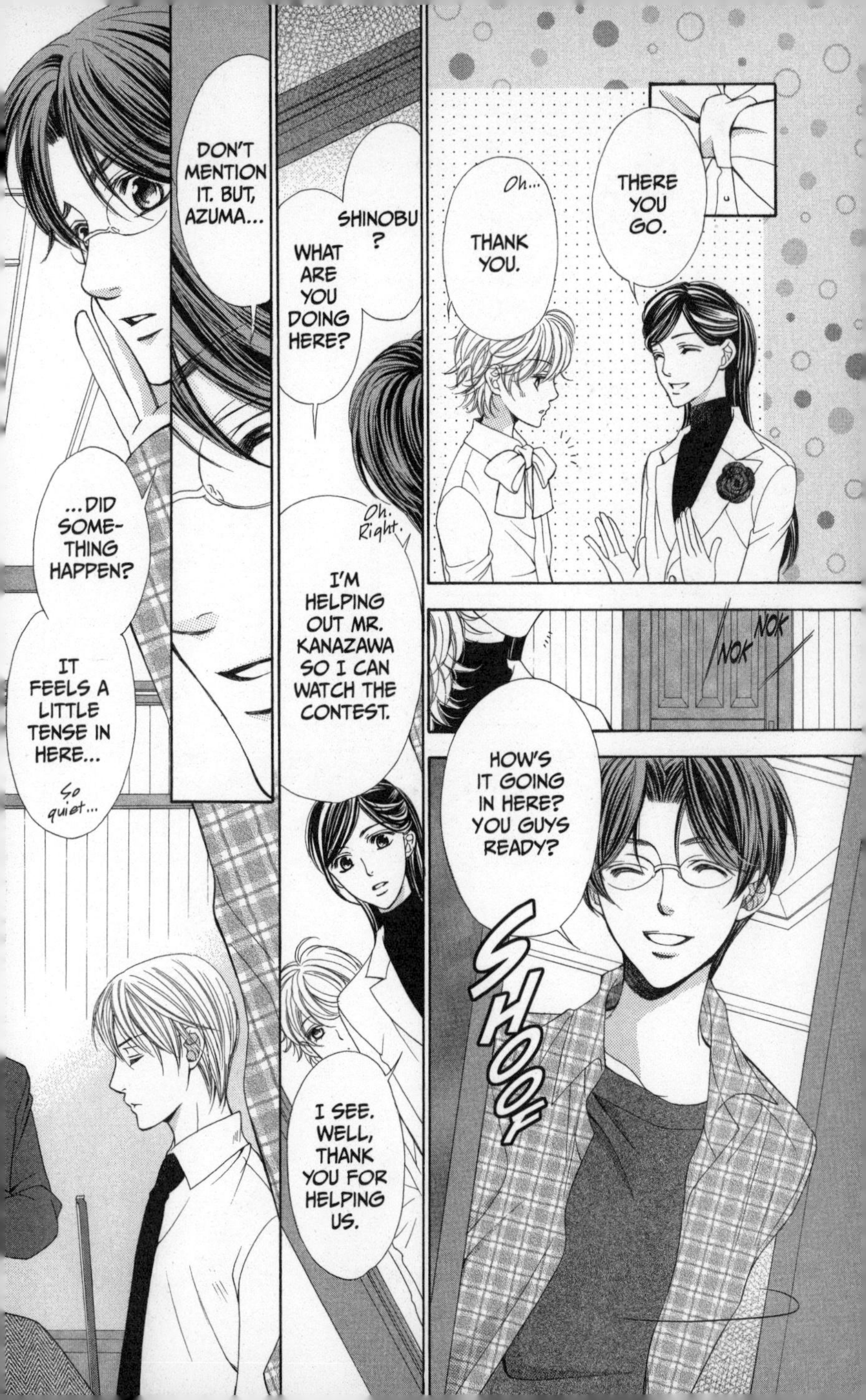
THERE YOU GO.
Oh...
THANK YOU.
NOK NOK
HOW'S IT GOING IN HERE? YOU GUYS READY?
SHOOP
SHINOBU?
WHAT ARE YOU DOING HERE?
Oh. Right.
I'M HELPING OUT MR. KANAZAWA SO I CAN WATCH THE CONTEST.
I SEE. WELL, THANK YOU FOR HELPING US.
DON'T MENTION IT. BUT, AZUMA...
...DID SOME-THING HAPPEN?
IT FEELS A LITTLE TENSE IN HERE...
So quiet...

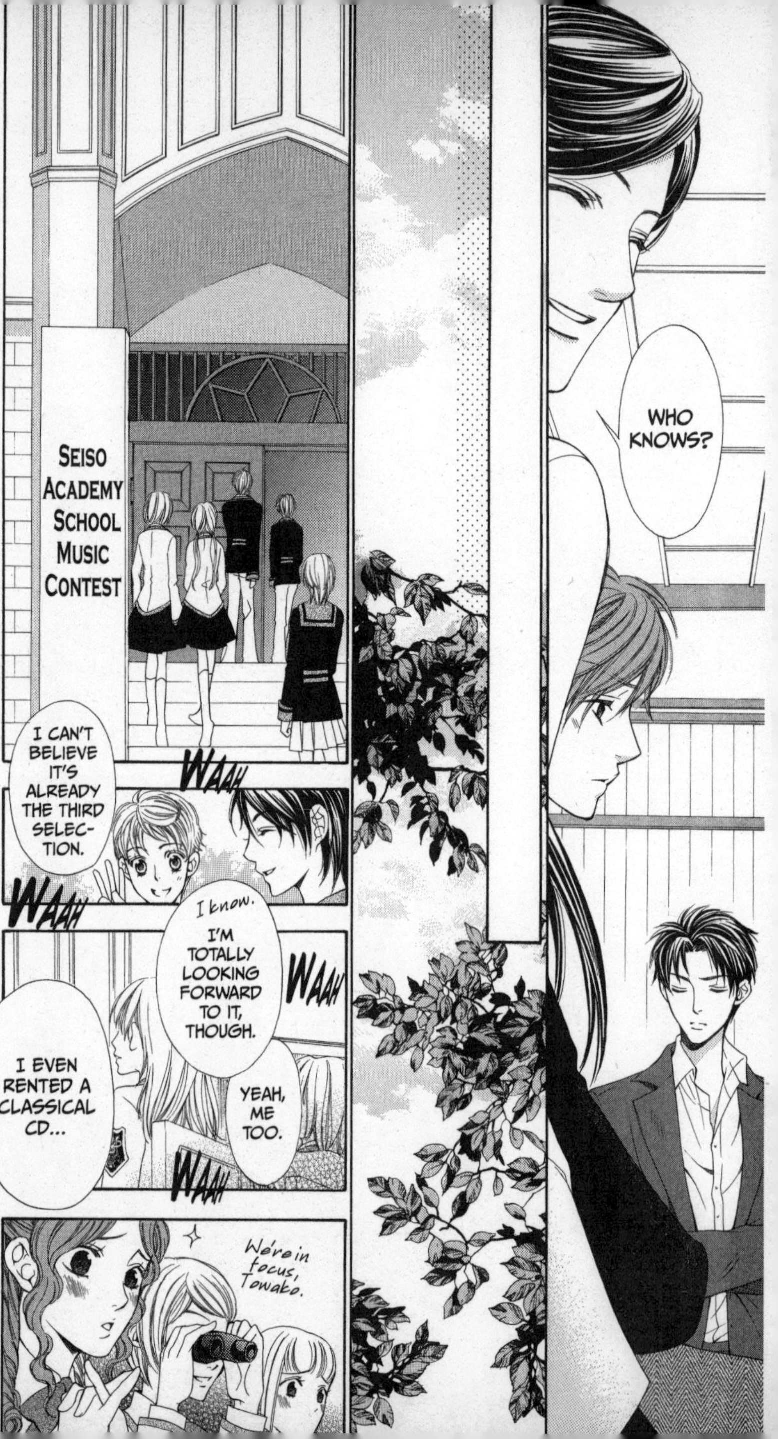
WHO KNOWS?
SEISO ACADEMY SCHOOL MUSIC CONTEST
WAAH
I CAN'T BELIEVE IT'S ALREADY THE THIRD SELECTION.
WAAH
I know.
I'M TOTALLY LOOKING FORWARD TO IT, THOUGH.
WAAH
YEAH, ME TOO.
I EVEN RENTED A CLASSICAL CD...
WAAH
We're in focus, Towako.

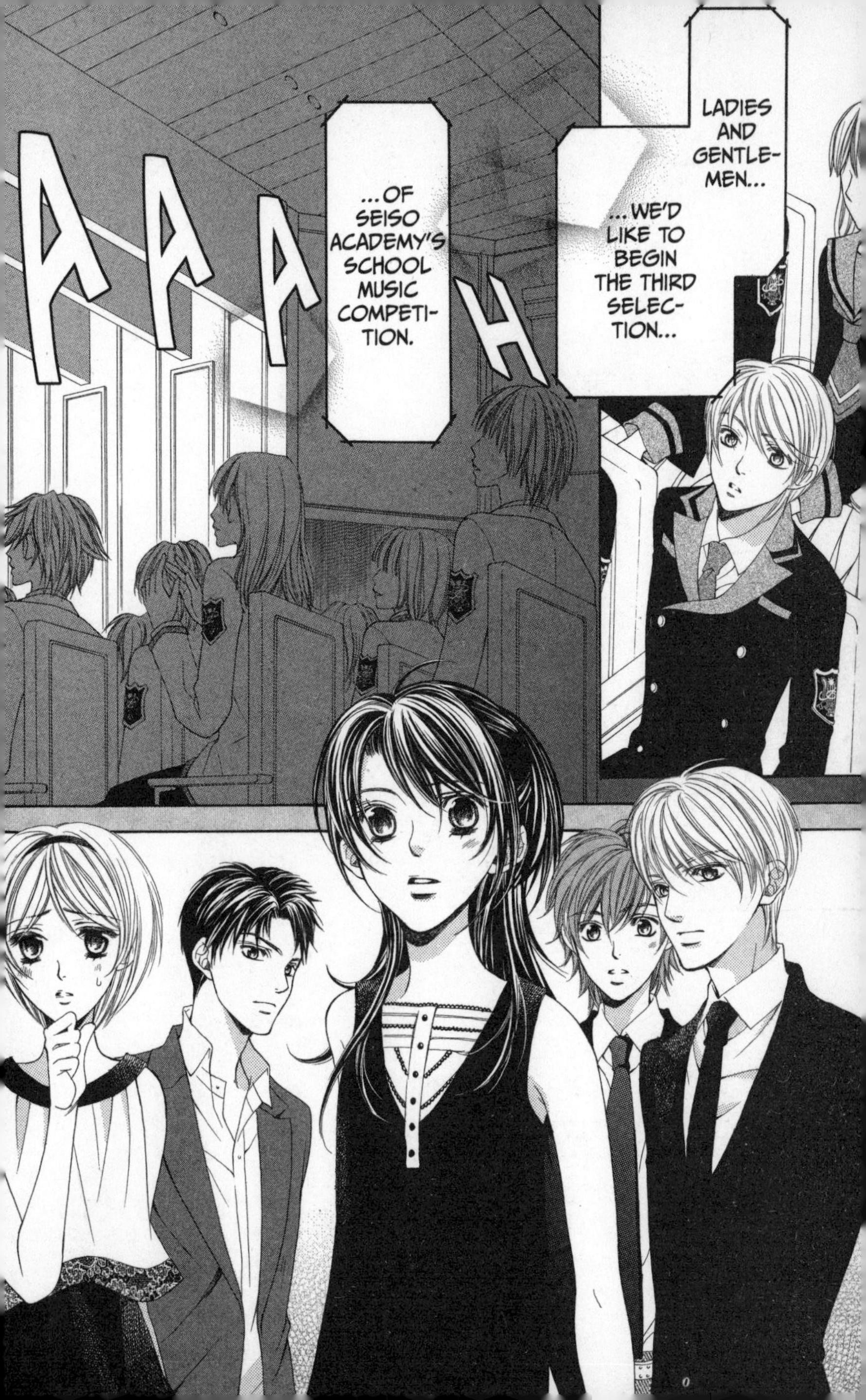
LADIES AND GENTLE-MEN...
...WE'D LIKE TO BEGIN THE THIRD SELEC-TION...
...OF SEISO ACADEMY'S SCHOOL MUSIC COMPETI-TION.
AAAAH

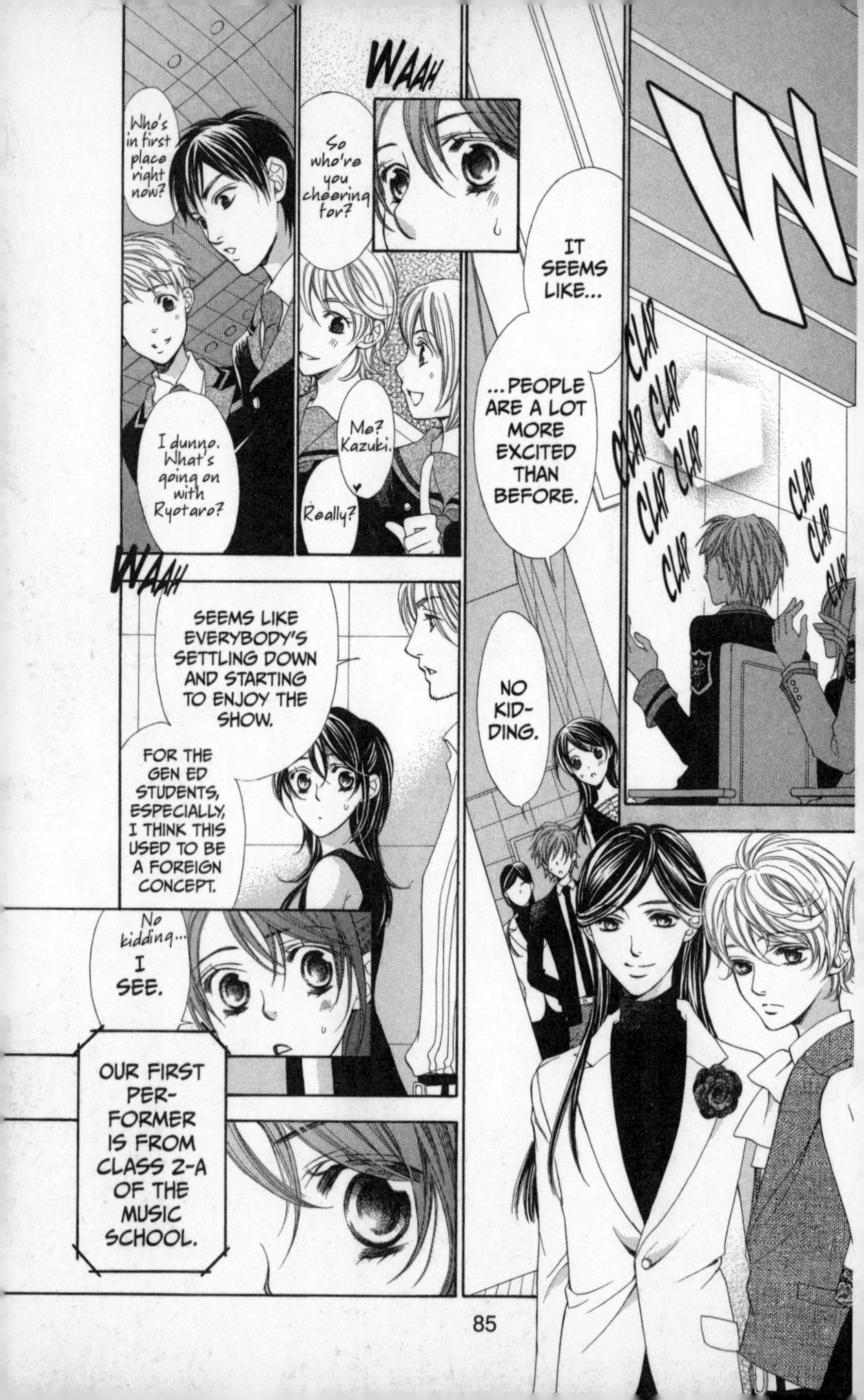
W
CLAP CLAP CLAP CLAP CLAP CLAP
CLAP CLAP CLAP
IT SEEMS LIKE...
...PEOPLE ARE A LOT MORE EXCITED THAN BEFORE.
NO KID-DING.
WAAH
So who're you cheering for?
Me? Kazuki.
Really?
Who's in first place right now?
I dunno. What's going on with Ryotaro?
WAAH
SEEMS LIKE EVERYBODY'S SETTLING DOWN AND STARTING TO ENJOY THE SHOW.
FOR THE GEN ED STUDENTS, ESPECIALLY, I THINK THIS USED TO BE A FOREIGN CONCEPT.
No kidding...
I SEE.
OUR FIRST PER-FORMER IS FROM CLASS 2-A OF THE MUSIC SCHOOL.

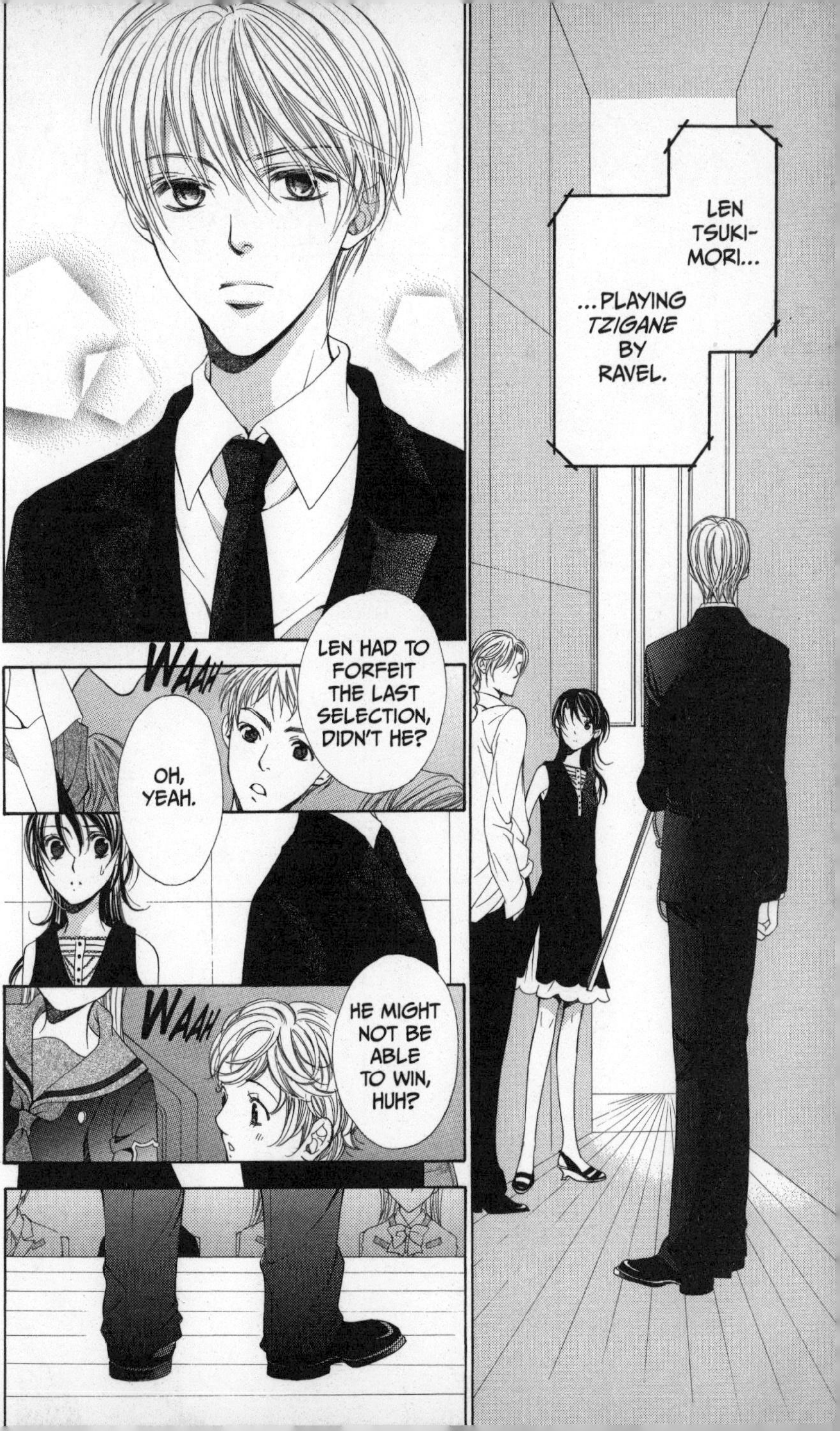
LEN TSUKI-MORI...
...PLAYING *TZIGANE* BY RAVEL.
LEN HAD TO FORFEIT THE LAST SELECTION, DIDN'T HE?
WAAH
OH, YEAH.
HE MIGHT NOT BE ABLE TO WIN, HUH?
WAAH

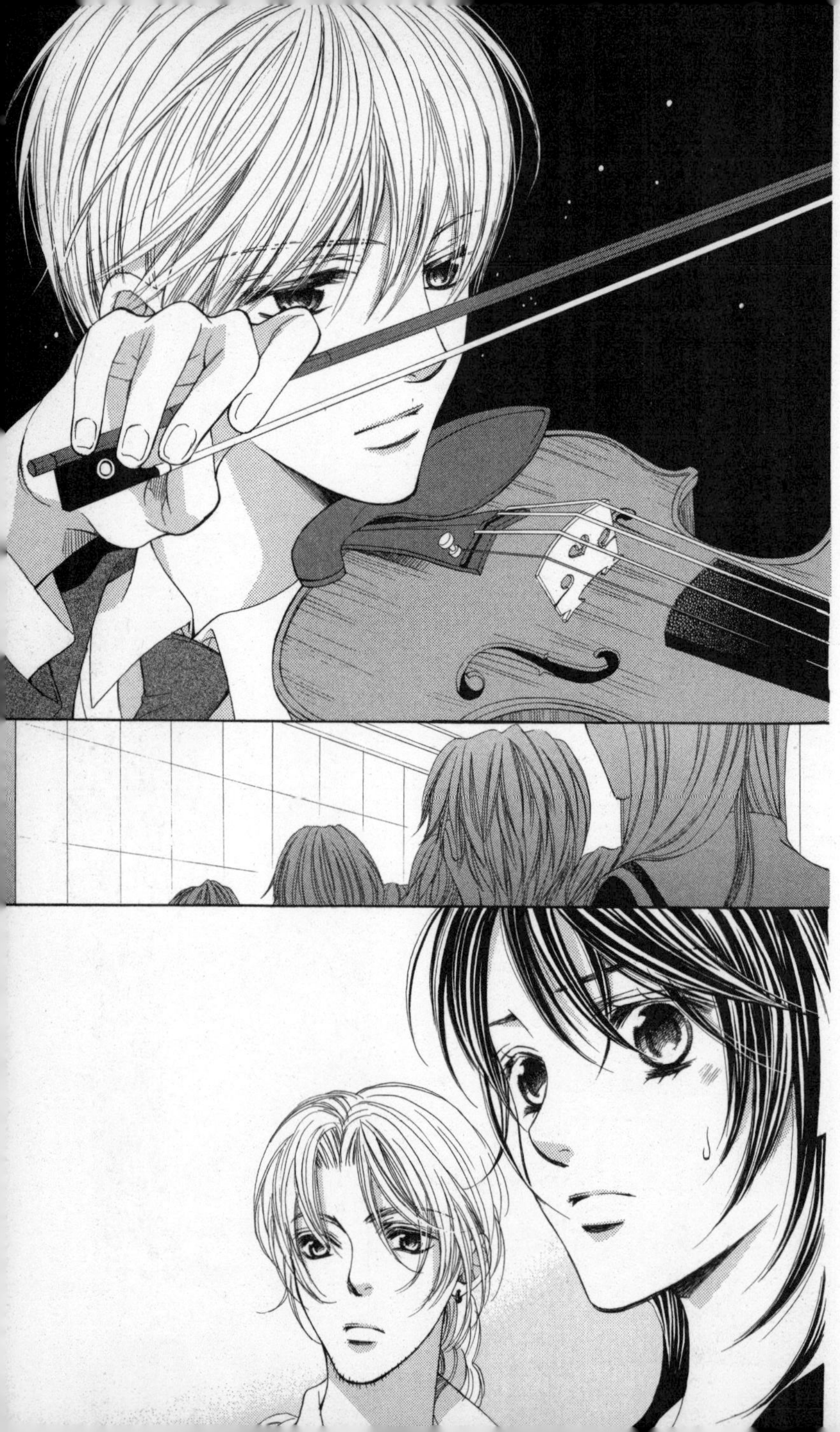

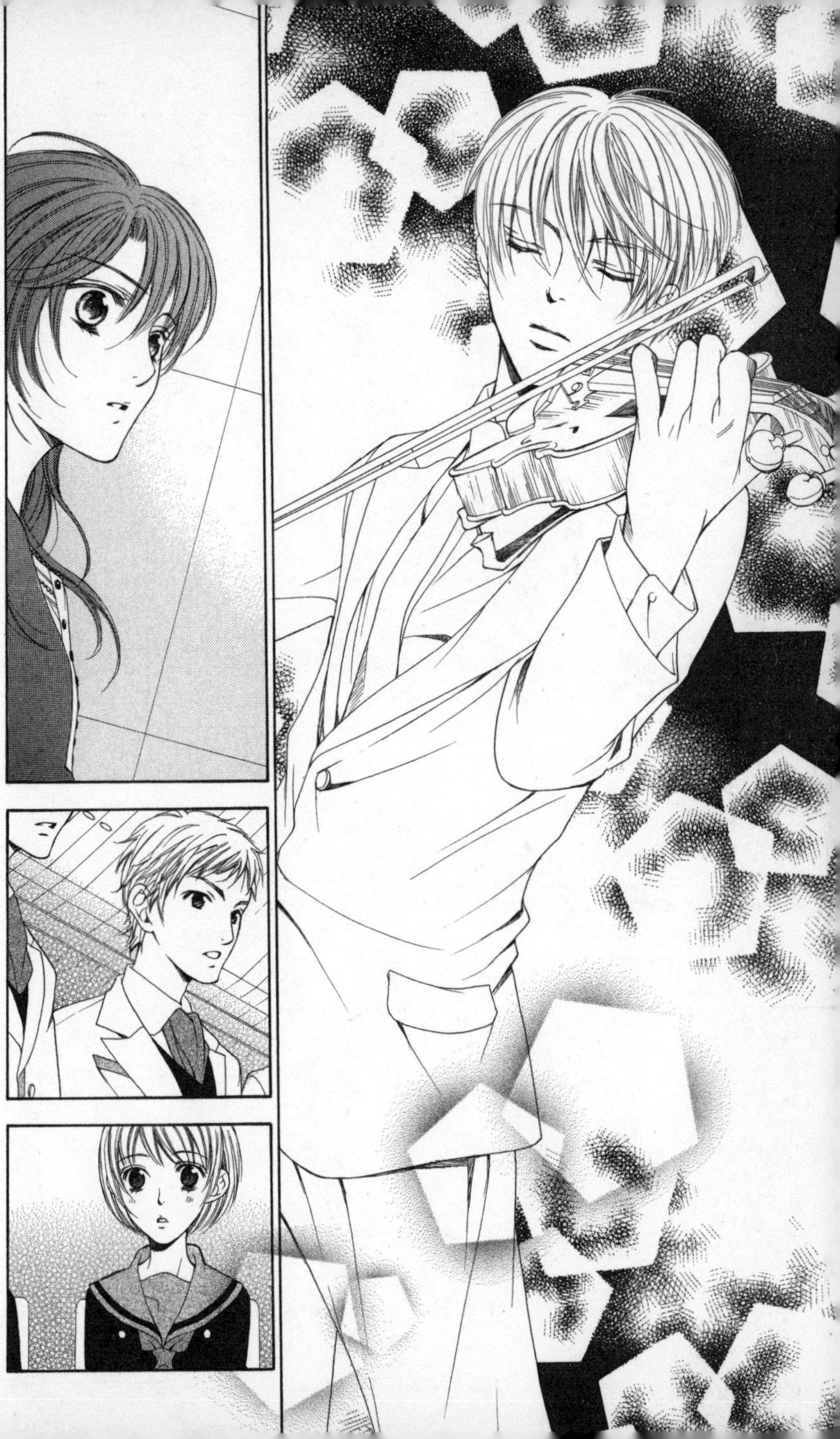

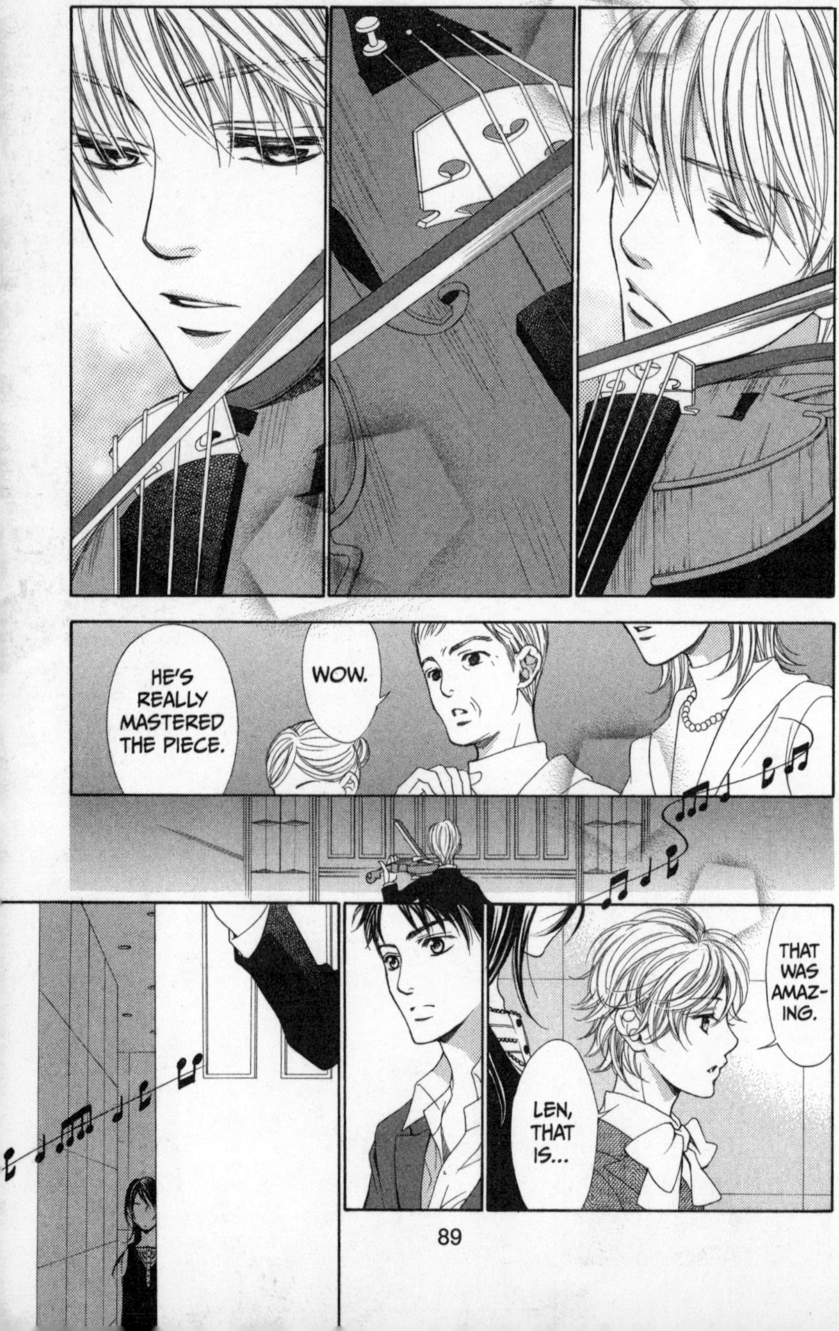
WOW.
HE'S REALLY MASTERED THE PIECE.
THAT WAS AMAZ-ING.
LEN, THAT IS...

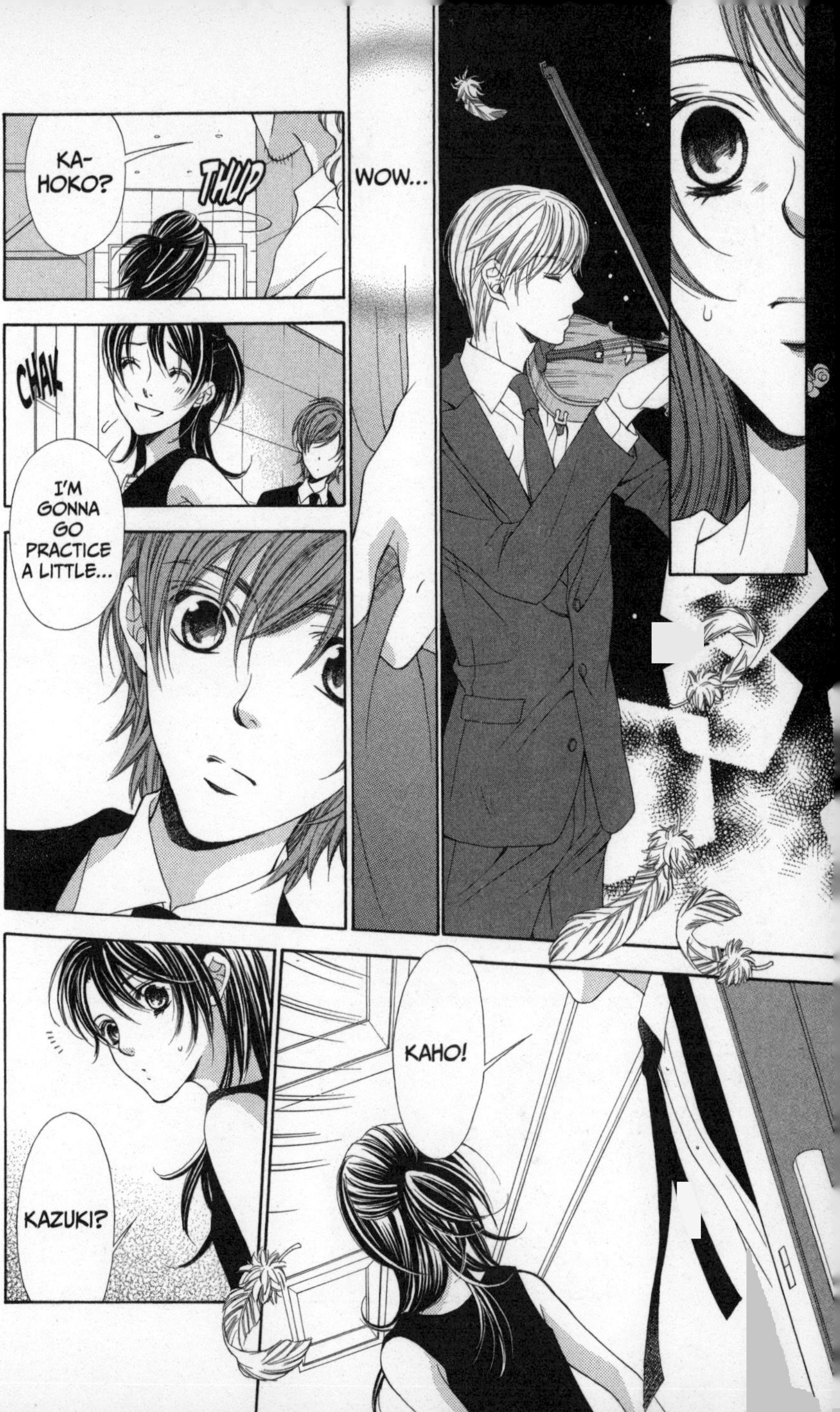
WOW...
KA-HOKO?
THUP
CHAK
I'M GONNA GO PRACTICE A LITTLE...
KAHO!
KAZUKI?

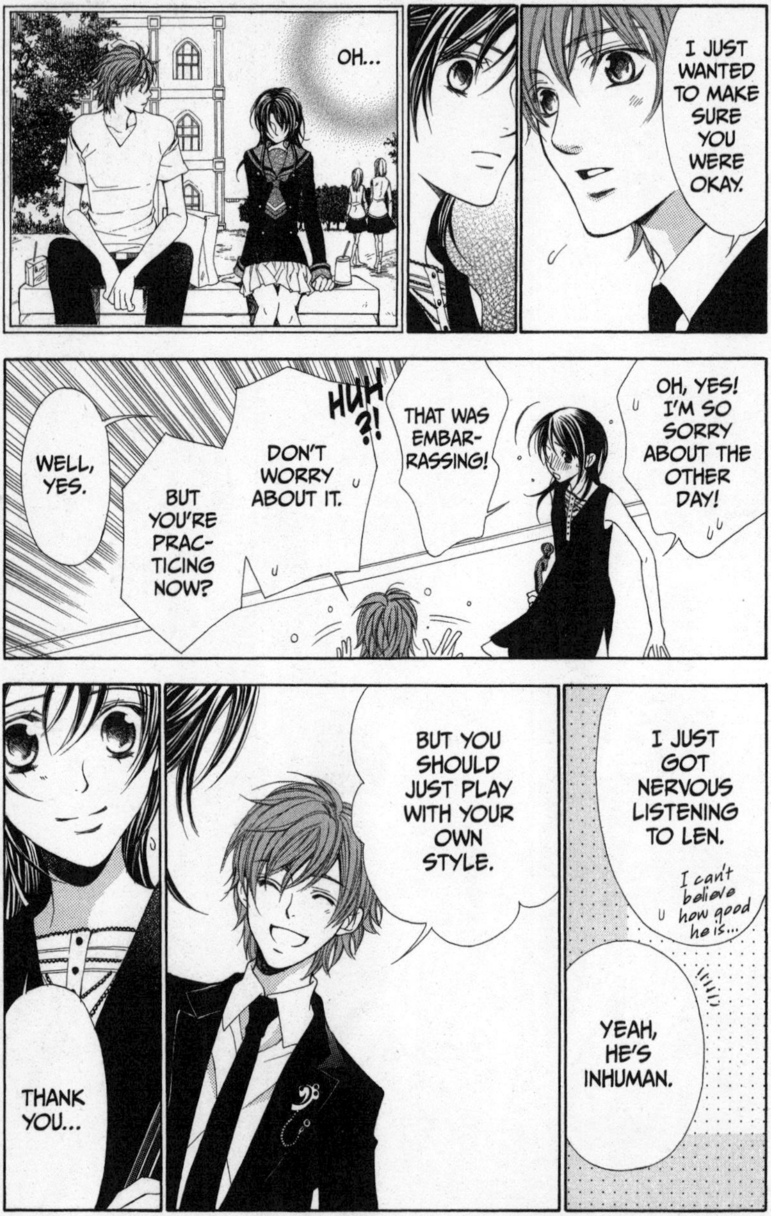
I JUST WANTED TO MAKE SURE YOU WERE OKAY.
OH...
OH, YES! I'M SO SORRY ABOUT THE OTHER DAY!
THAT WAS EMBARRASSING!
HUH?!
DON'T WORRY ABOUT IT.
BUT YOU'RE PRACTICING NOW?
WELL, YES.
I JUST GOT NERVOUS LISTENING TO LEN.
I can't believe how good he is...
YEAH, HE'S INHUMAN.
BUT YOU SHOULD JUST PLAY WITH YOUR OWN STYLE.
THANK YOU...

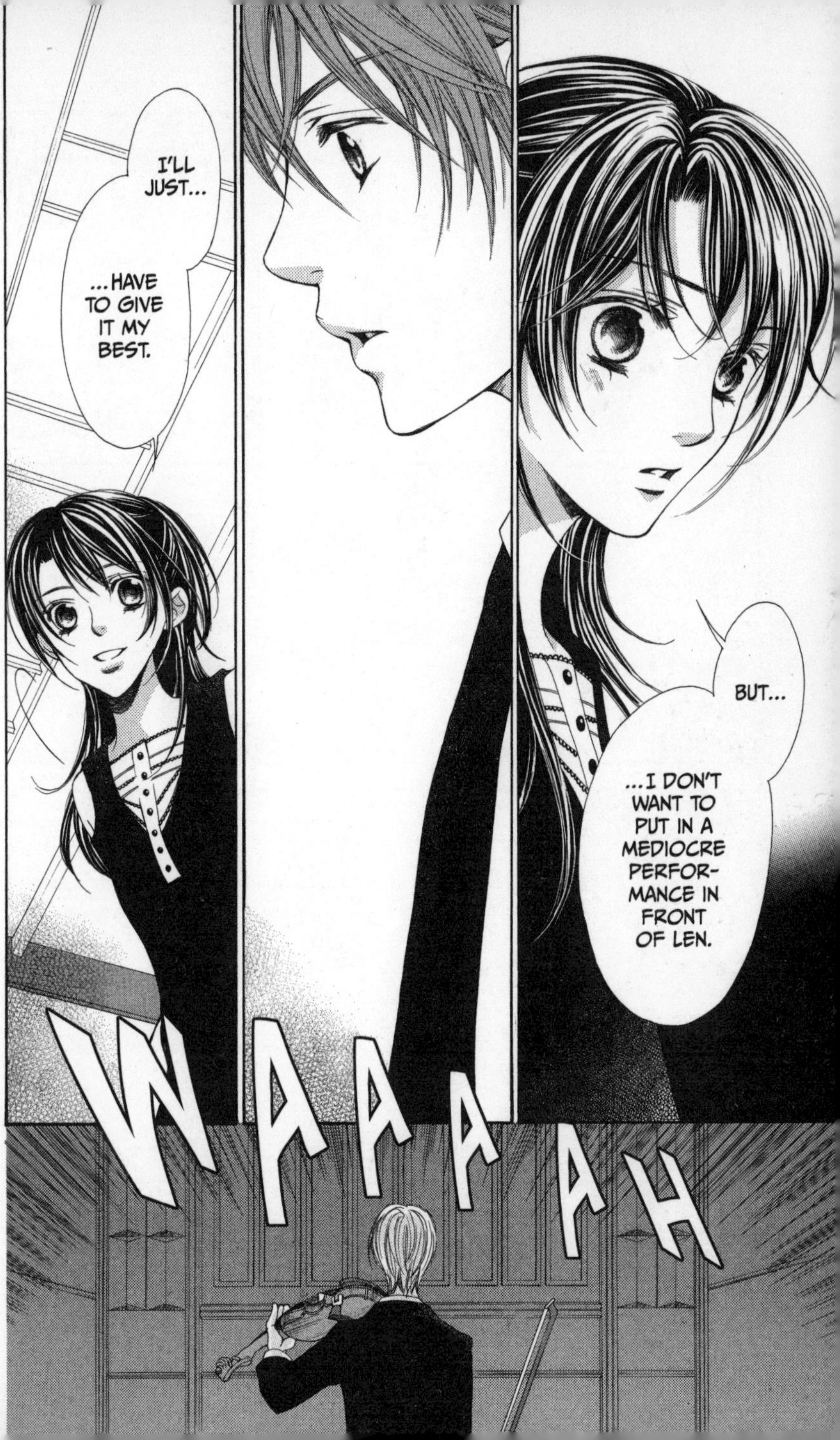
BUT...
...I DON'T WANT TO PUT IN A MEDIOCRE PERFORMANCE IN FRONT OF LEN.
I'LL JUST...
...HAVE TO GIVE IT MY BEST.
WAAAAH

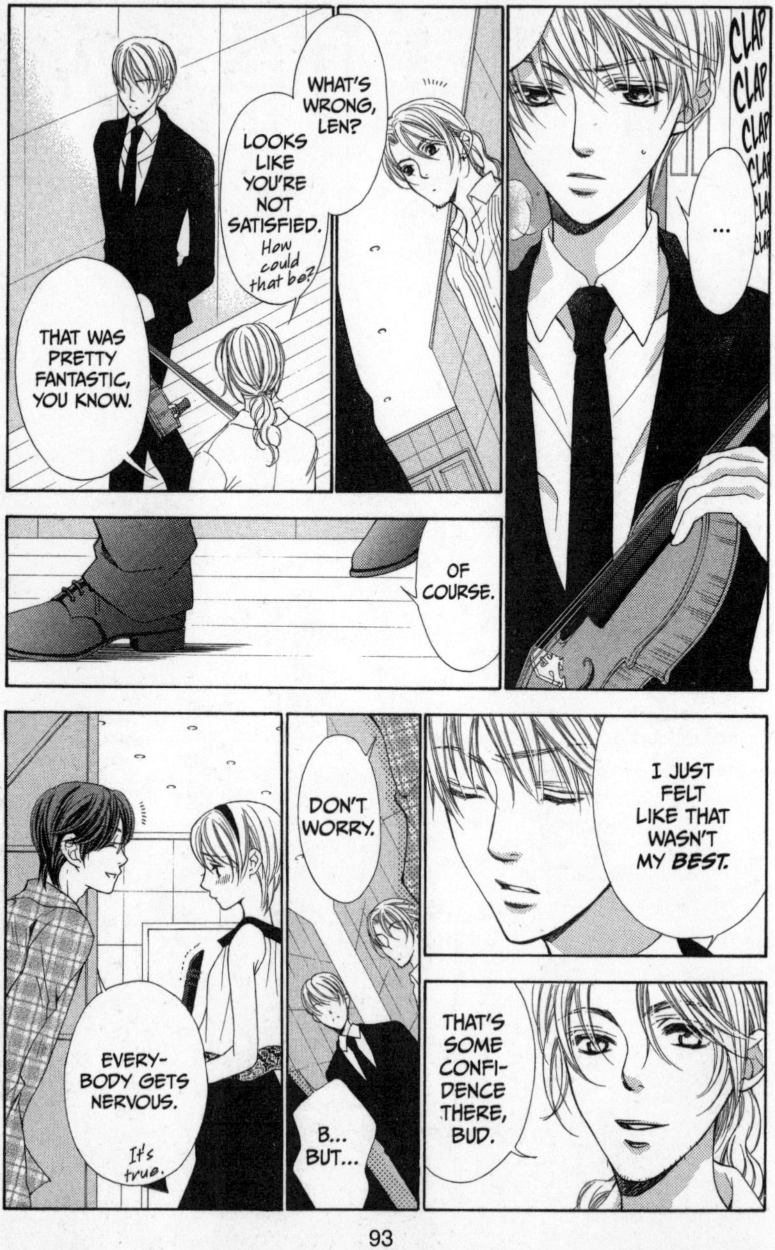
CLAP CLAP CLAP CLAP CLAP CLAP
...
WHAT'S WRONG, LEN? LOOKS LIKE YOU'RE NOT SATISFIED.
How could that be?
THAT WAS PRETTY FANTASTIC, YOU KNOW.
OF COURSE.
I JUST FELT LIKE THAT WASN'T MY *BEST.*
THAT'S SOME CONFI-DENCE THERE, BUD.
DON'T WORRY.
B... BUT...
EVERY-BODY GETS NERVOUS.
It's true.

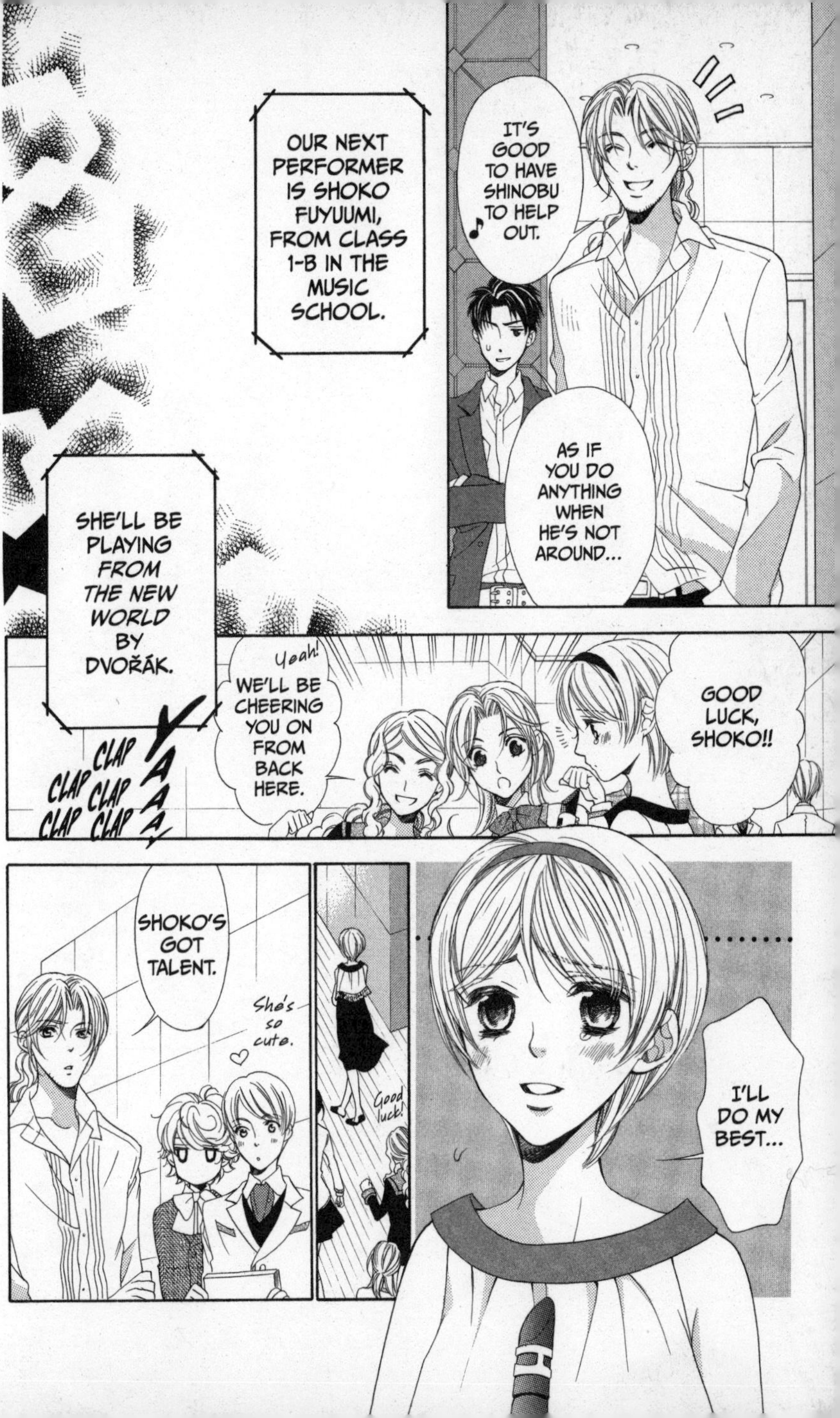
IT'S GOOD TO HAVE SHINOBU TO HELP OUT. ♪
AS IF YOU DO ANYTHING WHEN HE'S NOT AROUND...
OUR NEXT PERFORMER IS SHOKO FUYUUMI, FROM CLASS 1-B IN THE MUSIC SCHOOL.
SHE'LL BE PLAYING FROM THE NEW WORLD BY DVOŘÁK.
GOOD LUCK, SHOKO!!
Yeah!
WE'LL BE CHEERING YOU ON FROM BACK HERE.
YAAAA
CLAP CLAP CLAP CLAP CLAP CLAP
I'LL DO MY BEST...
Good luck!
SHOKO'S GOT TALENT.
She's so cute.

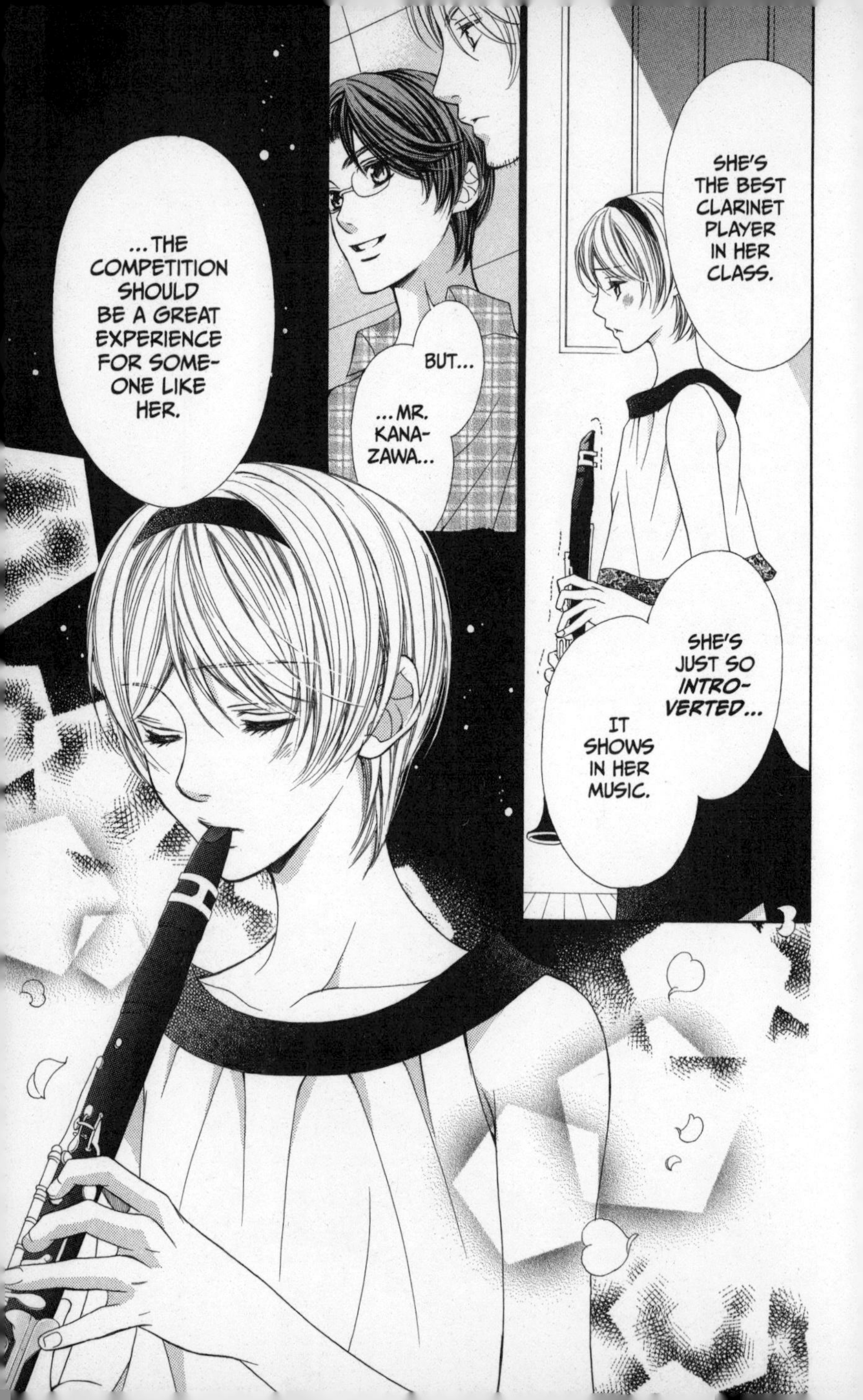
SHE'S THE BEST CLARINET PLAYER IN HER CLASS.
SHE'S JUST SO *INTRO-VERTED*...
IT SHOWS IN HER MUSIC.
BUT...
...MR. KANA-ZAWA...
...THE COMPETITION SHOULD BE A GREAT EXPERIENCE FOR SOME-ONE LIKE HER.

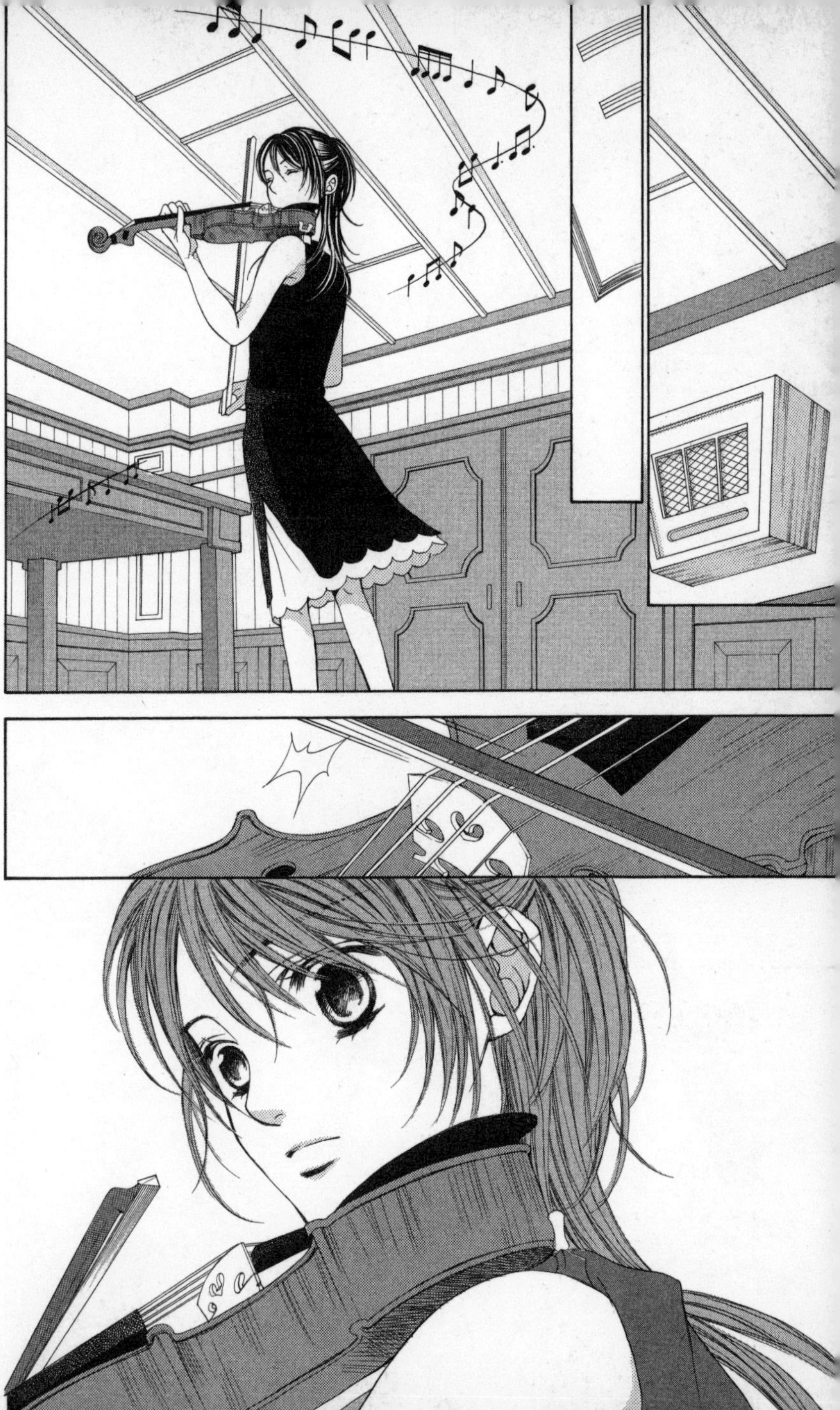

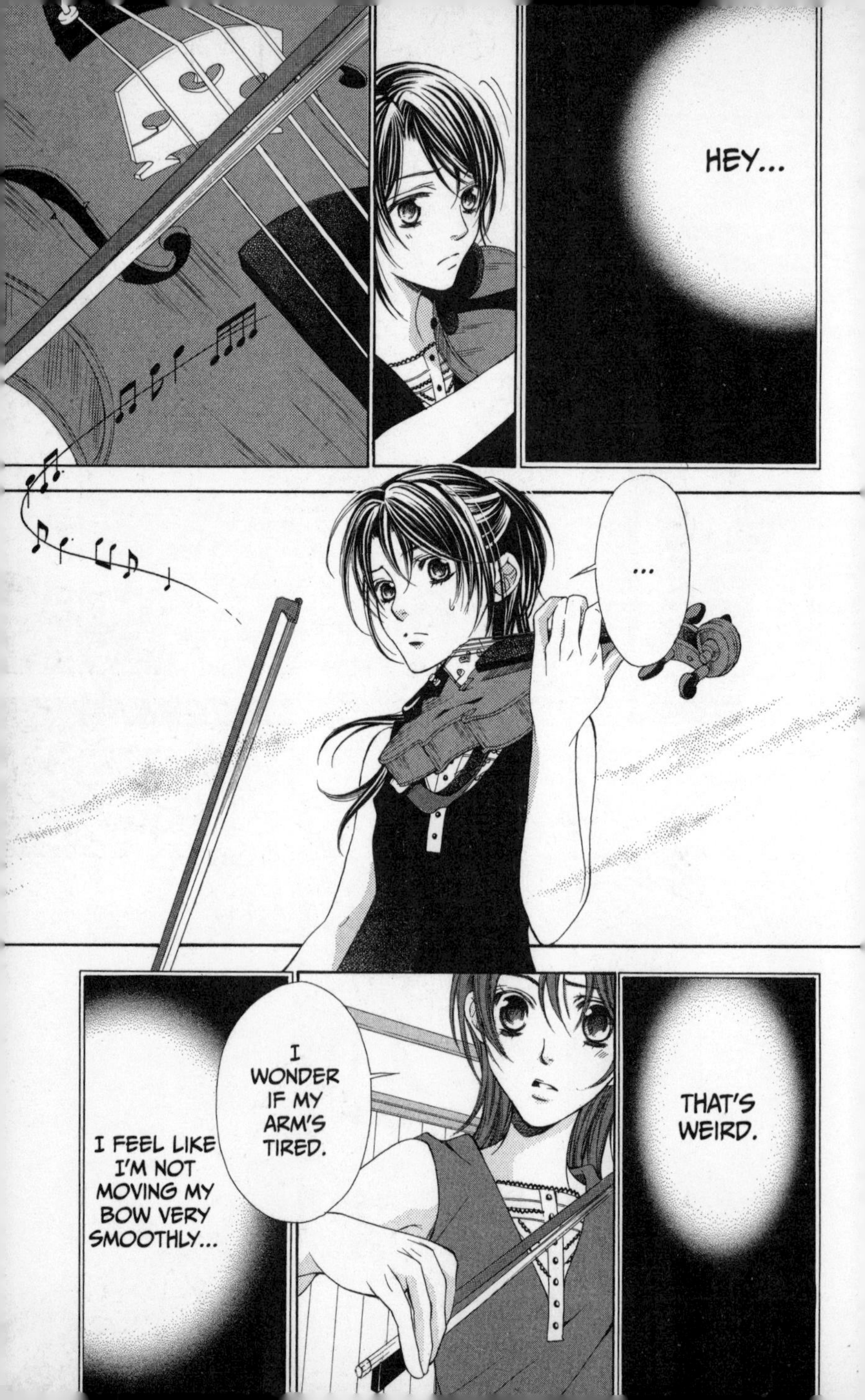
HEY...
...
THAT'S WEIRD.
I WONDER IF MY ARM'S TIRED.
I FEEL LIKE I'M NOT MOVING MY BOW VERY SMOOTHLY...

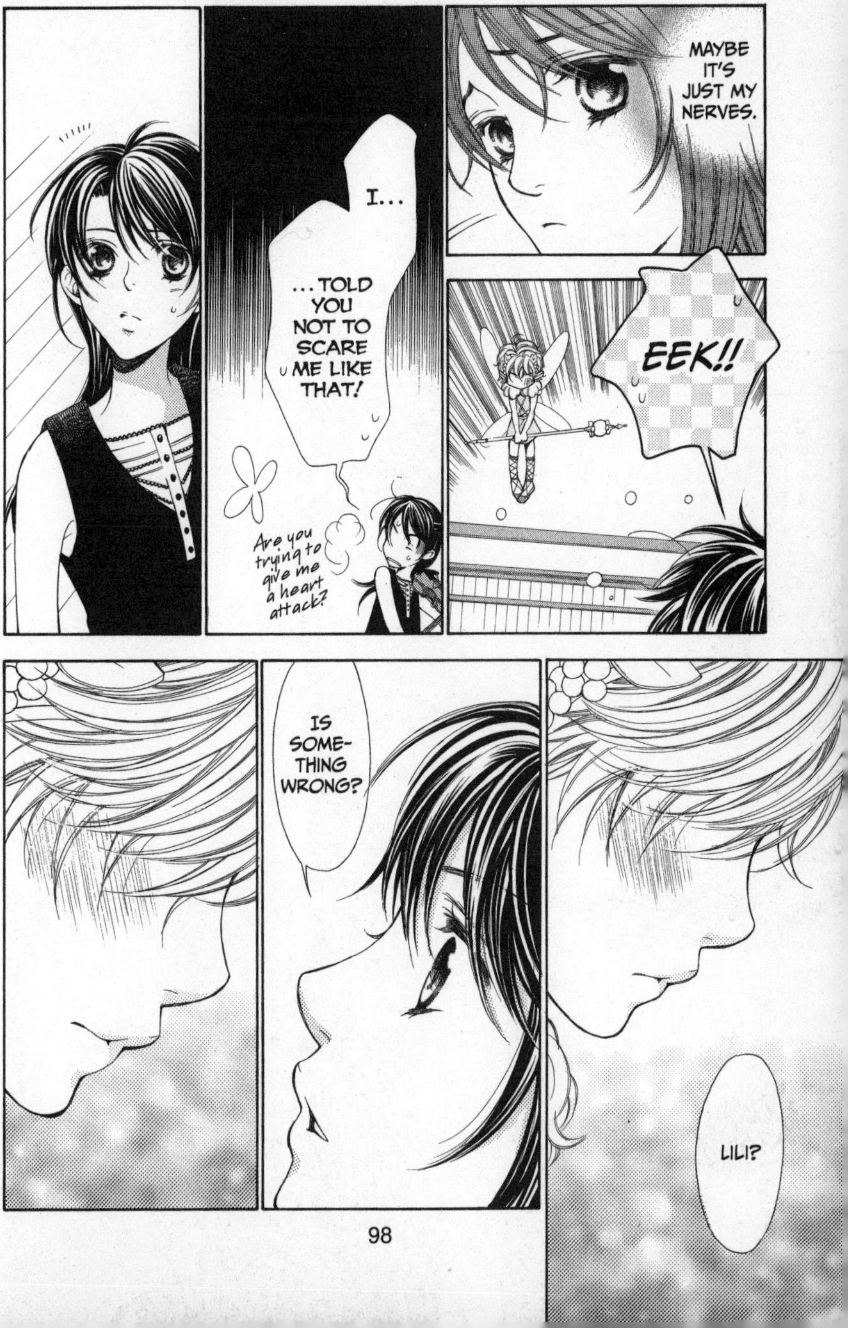
MAYBE IT'S JUST MY NERVES.
EEK!!
I...
...TOLD YOU NOT TO SCARE ME LIKE THAT!
Are you trying to give me a heart attack?
LILI?
IS SOME-THING WRONG?

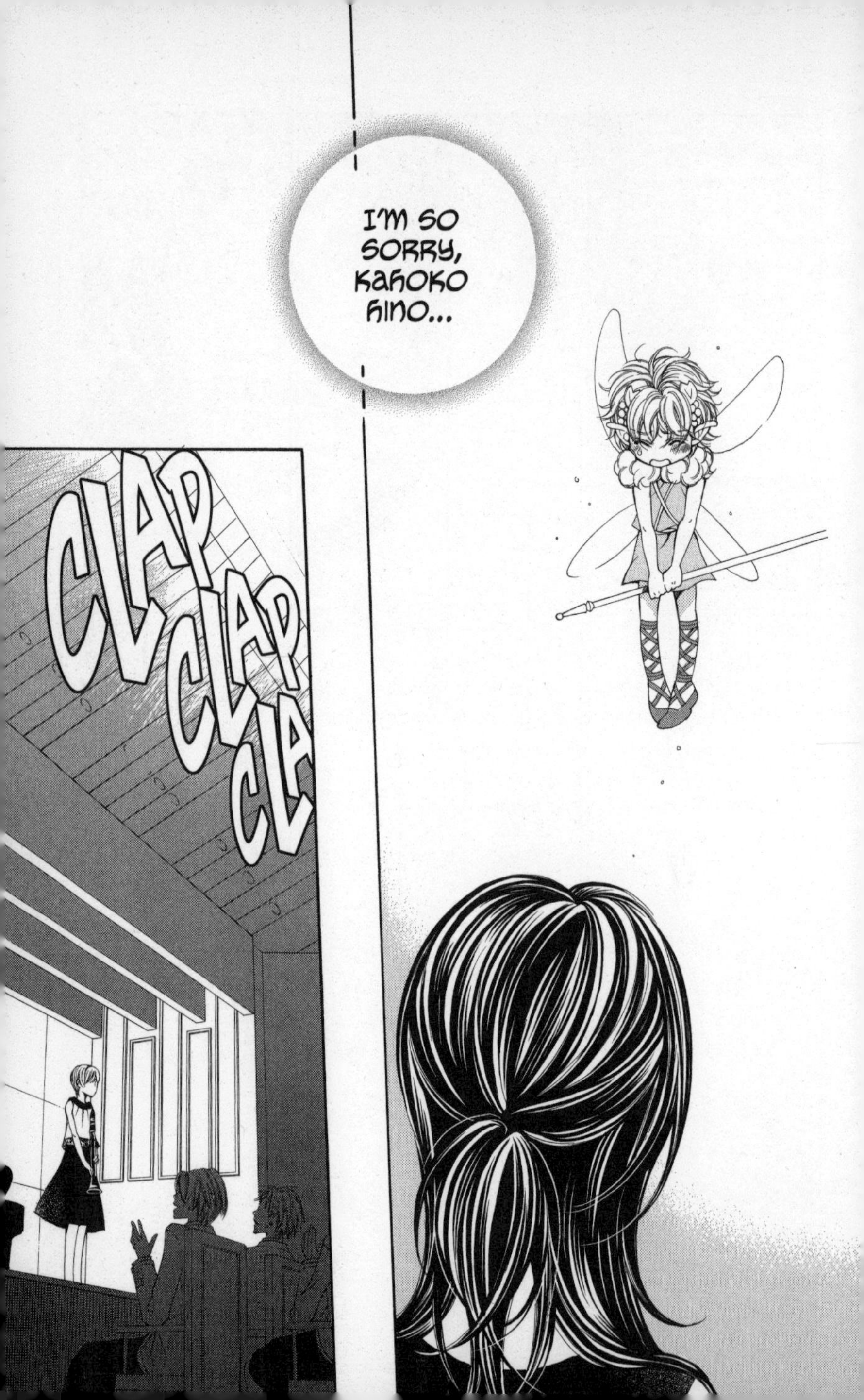
I'M SO SORRY, KAHOKO HINO...
CLAP
CLAP
CLA

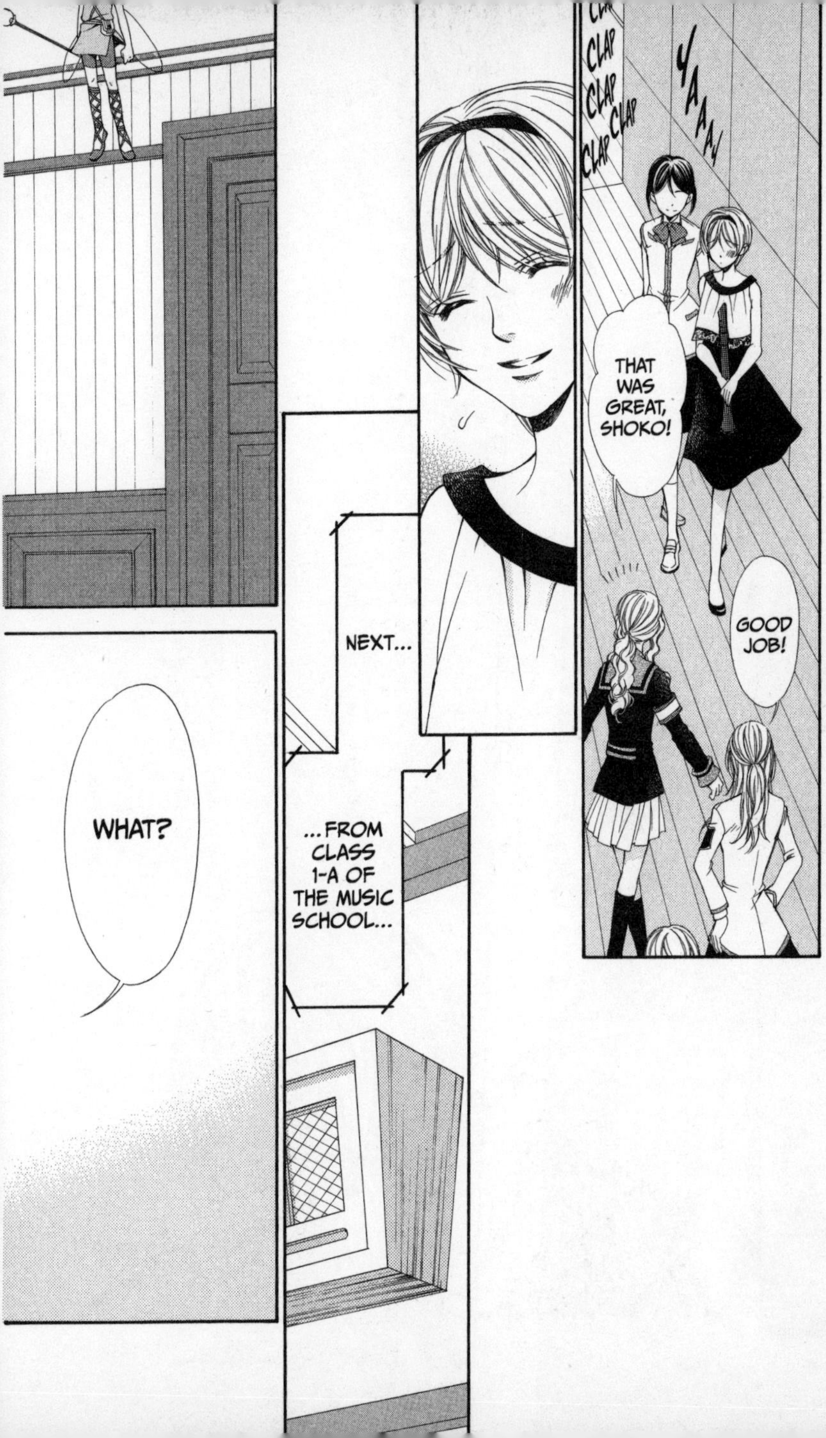
CLAP CLAP CLAP CLAP CLAP CLAP
YAAAAY
THAT WAS GREAT, SHOKO!
GOOD JOB!
NEXT...
...FROM CLASS 1-A OF THE MUSIC SCHOOL...
WHAT?

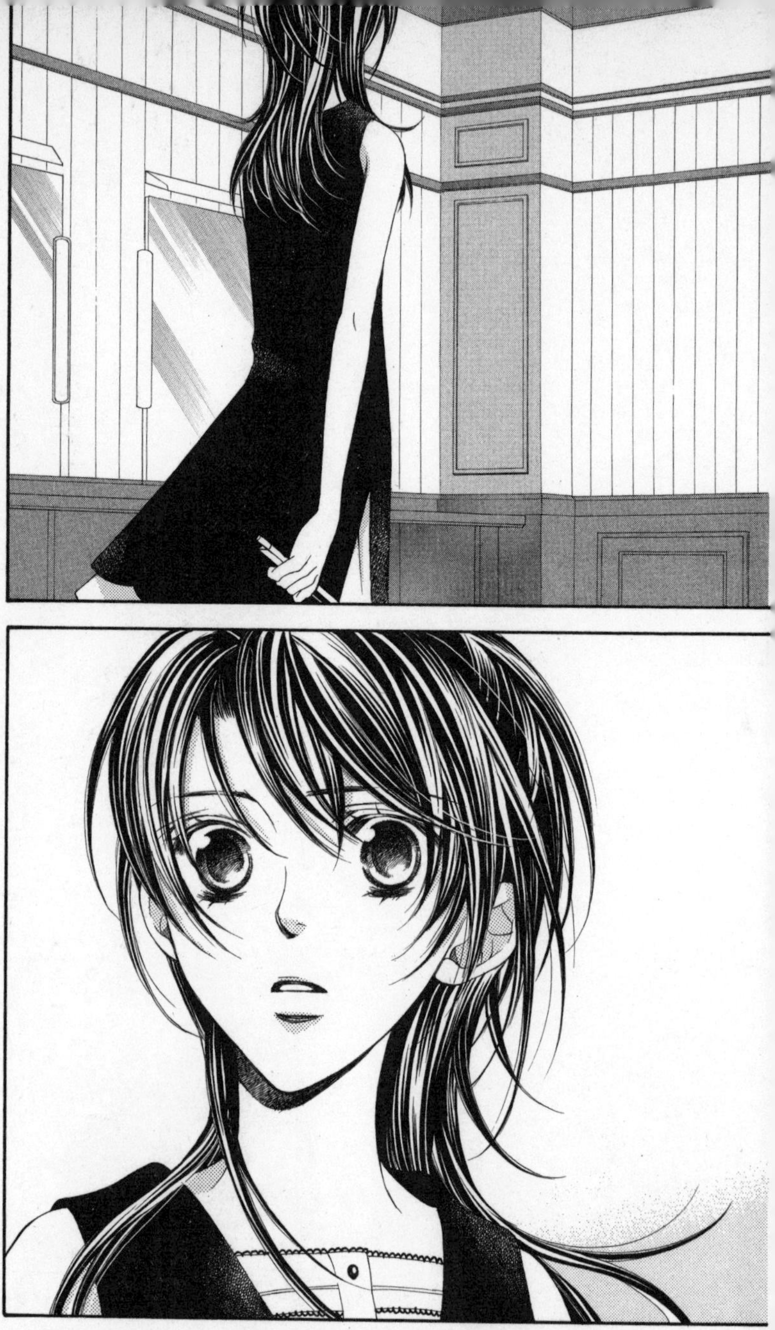

END OF MEASURE 30

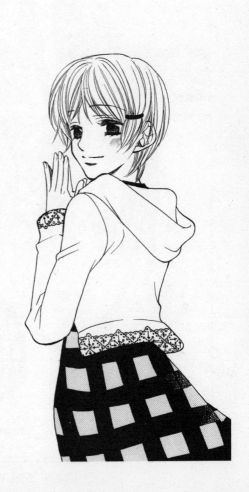

La Corda d'Oro

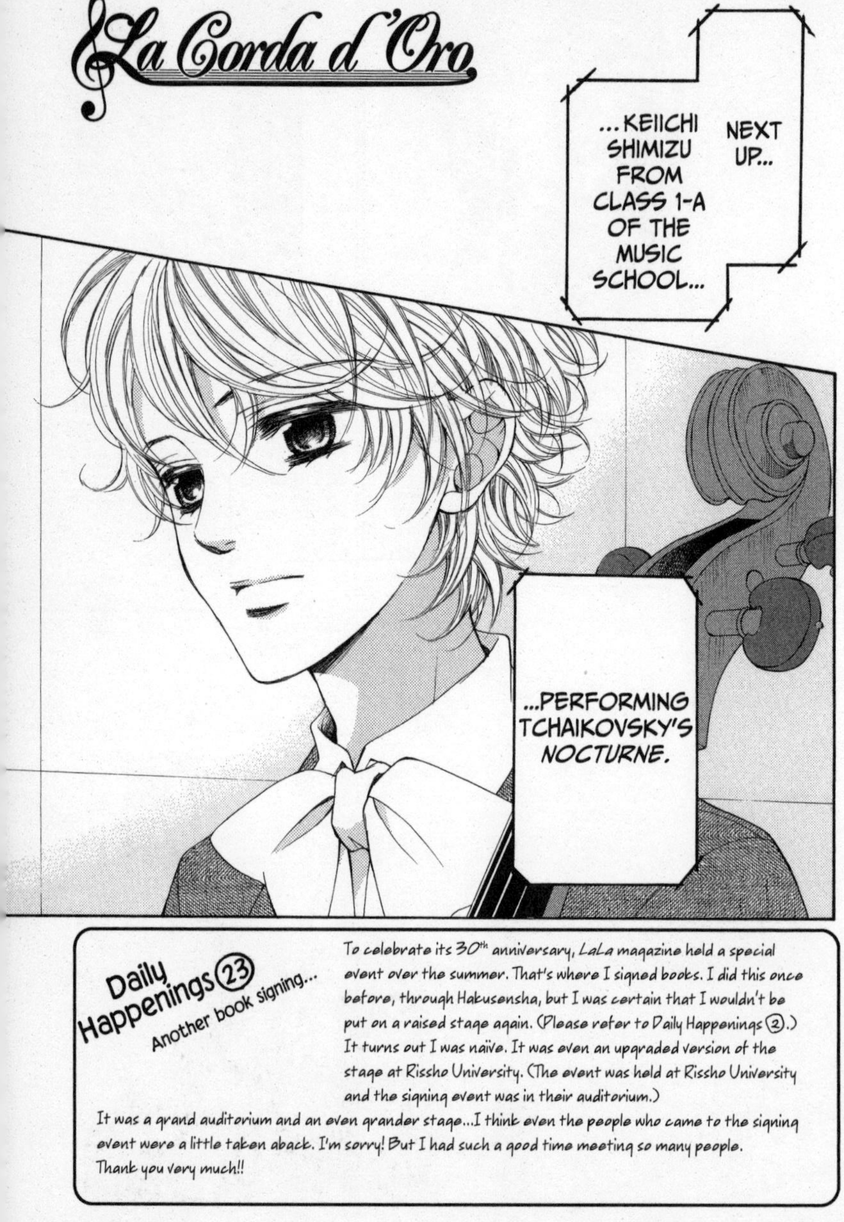
NEXT UP...
...KEIICHI SHIMIZU FROM CLASS 1-A OF THE MUSIC SCHOOL...
...PERFORMING TCHAIKOVSKY'S *NOCTURNE.*

Daily Happenings ㉓
Another book signing...

To celebrate its 30th anniversary, *LaLa* magazine held a special event over the summer. That's where I signed books. I did this once before, through Hakusensha, but I was certain that I wouldn't be put on a raised stage again. (Please refer to Daily Happenings ②.) It turns out I was naïve. It was even an upgraded version of the stage at Rissho University. (The event was held at Rissho University and the signing event was in their auditorium.) It was a grand auditorium and an even grander stage...I think even the people who came to the signing event were a little taken aback. I'm sorry! But I had such a good time meeting so many people. Thank you very much!!

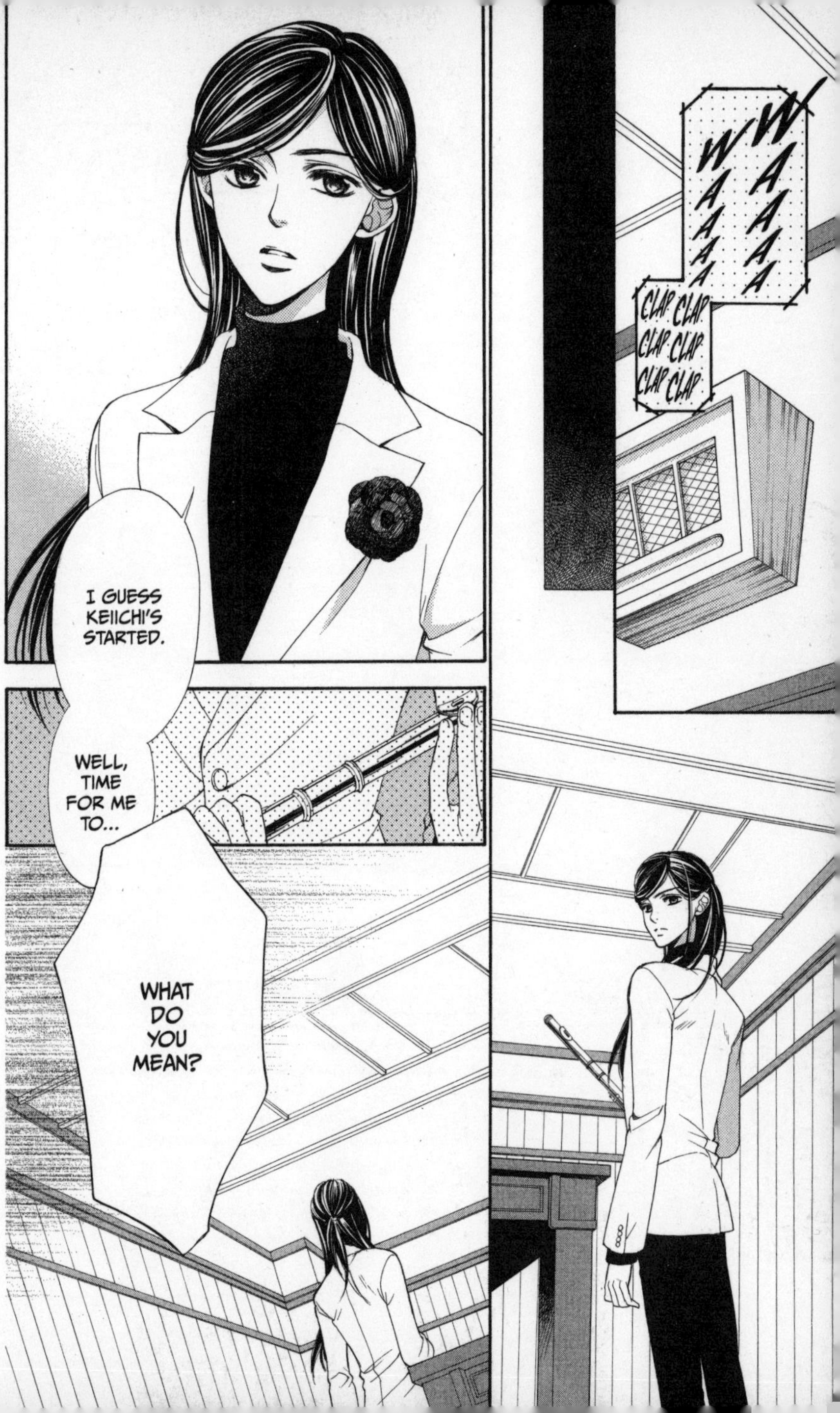
WAAAAA
WAAAAA
CLAP CLAP CLAP CLAP CLAP CLAP
I GUESS KEIICHI'S STARTED.
WELL, TIME FOR ME TO...
WHAT DO YOU MEAN?

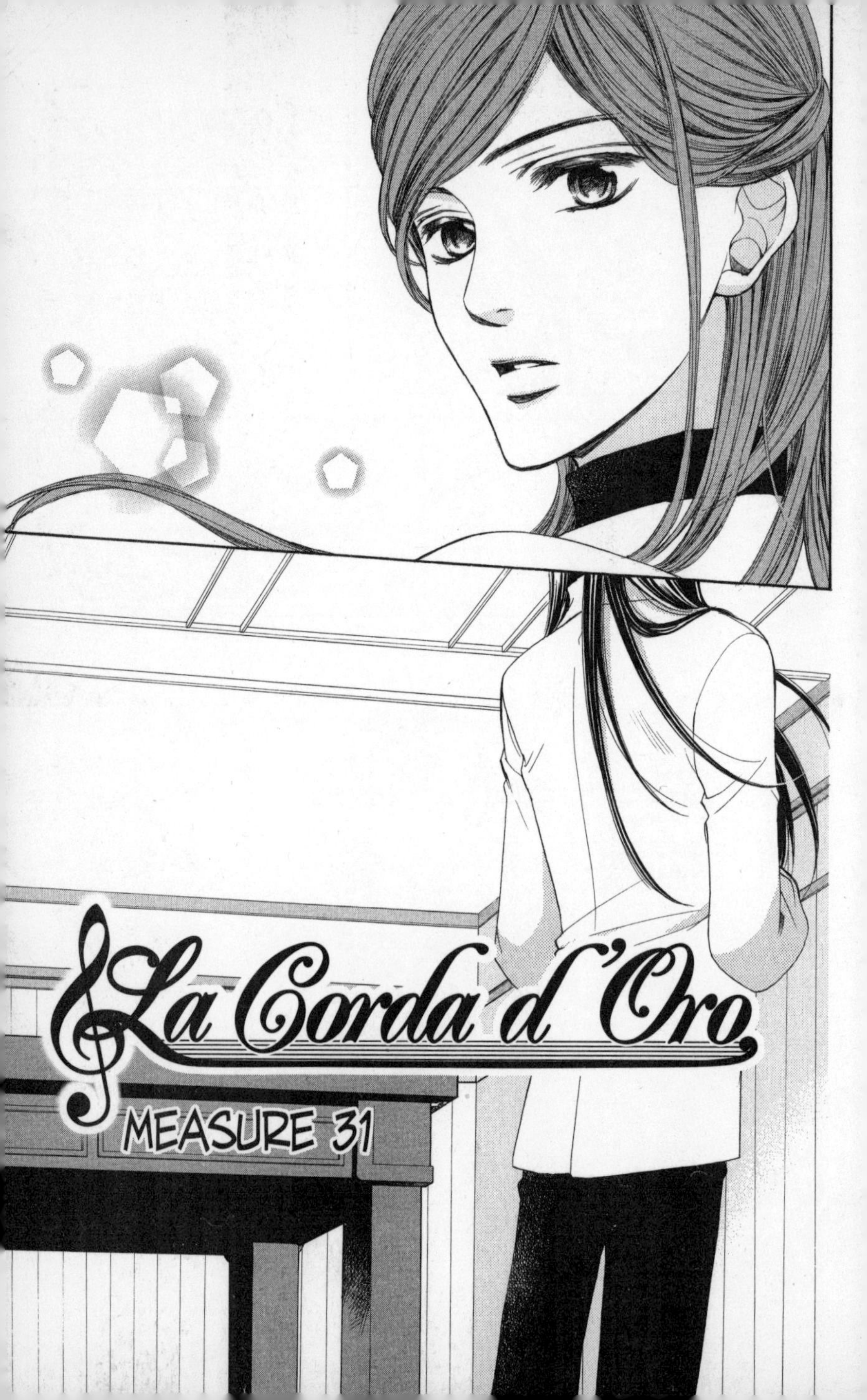
La Corda d'Oro
MEASURE 31

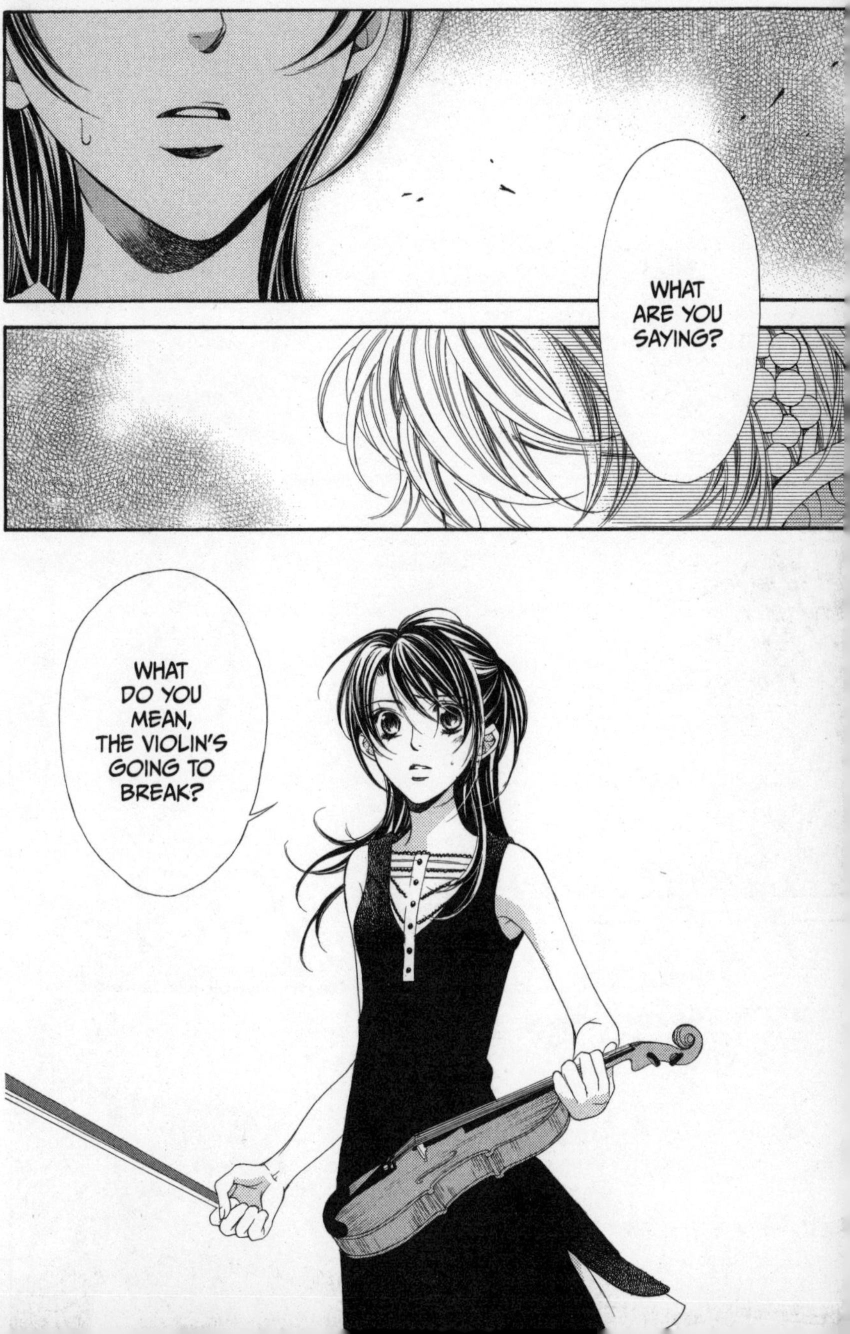
WHAT ARE YOU SAYING?
WHAT DO YOU MEAN, THE VIOLIN'S GOING TO BREAK?

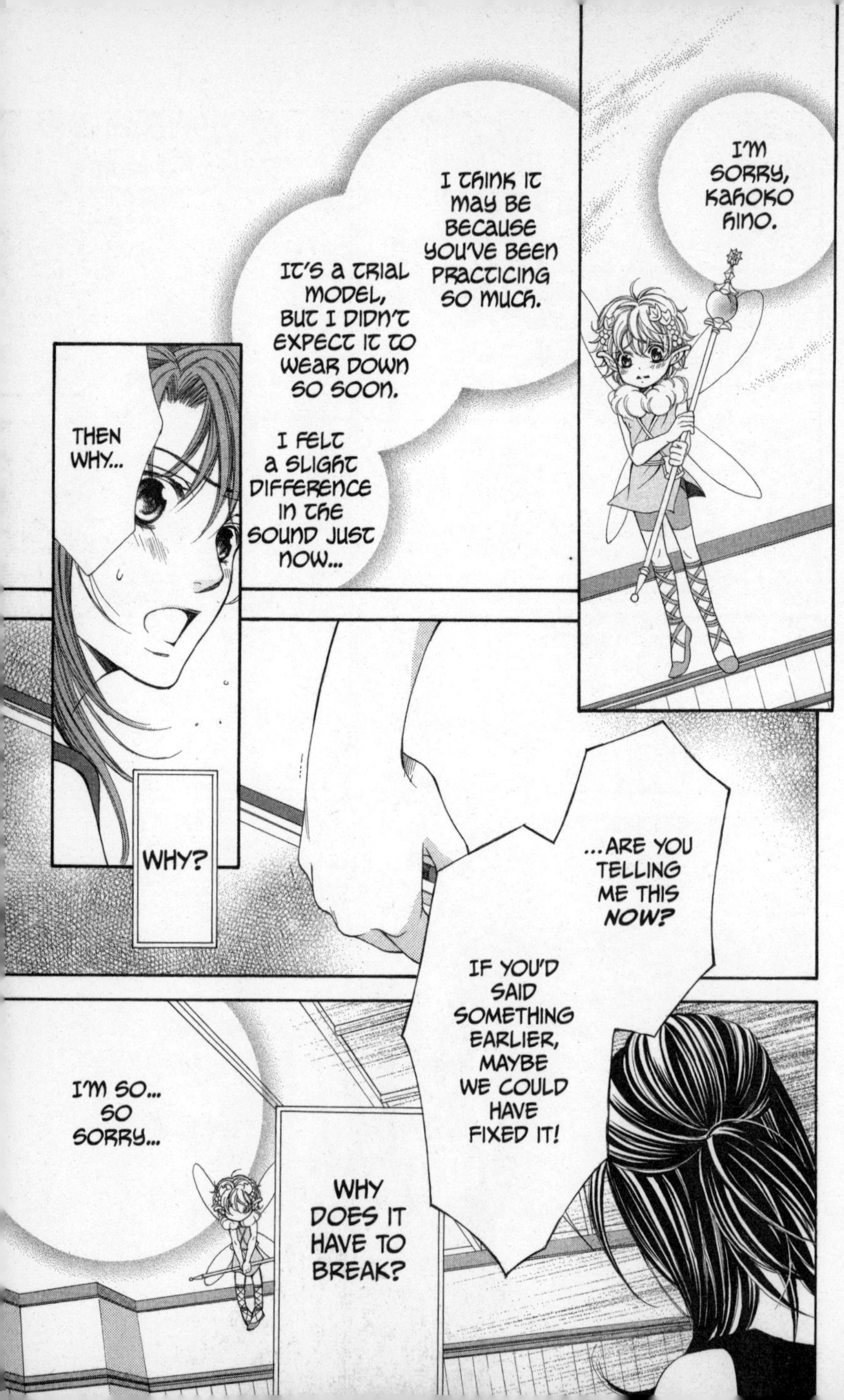
I'M SORRY, KAHOKO HINO.
I THINK IT MAY BE BECAUSE YOU'VE BEEN PRACTICING SO MUCH.
IT'S A TRIAL MODEL, BUT I DIDN'T EXPECT IT TO WEAR DOWN SO SOON.
I FELT A SLIGHT DIFFERENCE IN THE SOUND JUST NOW...
THEN WHY...
WHY?
...ARE YOU TELLING ME THIS *NOW?*
IF YOU'D SAID SOMETHING EARLIER, MAYBE WE COULD HAVE FIXED IT!
WHY DOES IT HAVE TO BREAK?
I'M SO... SO SORRY...

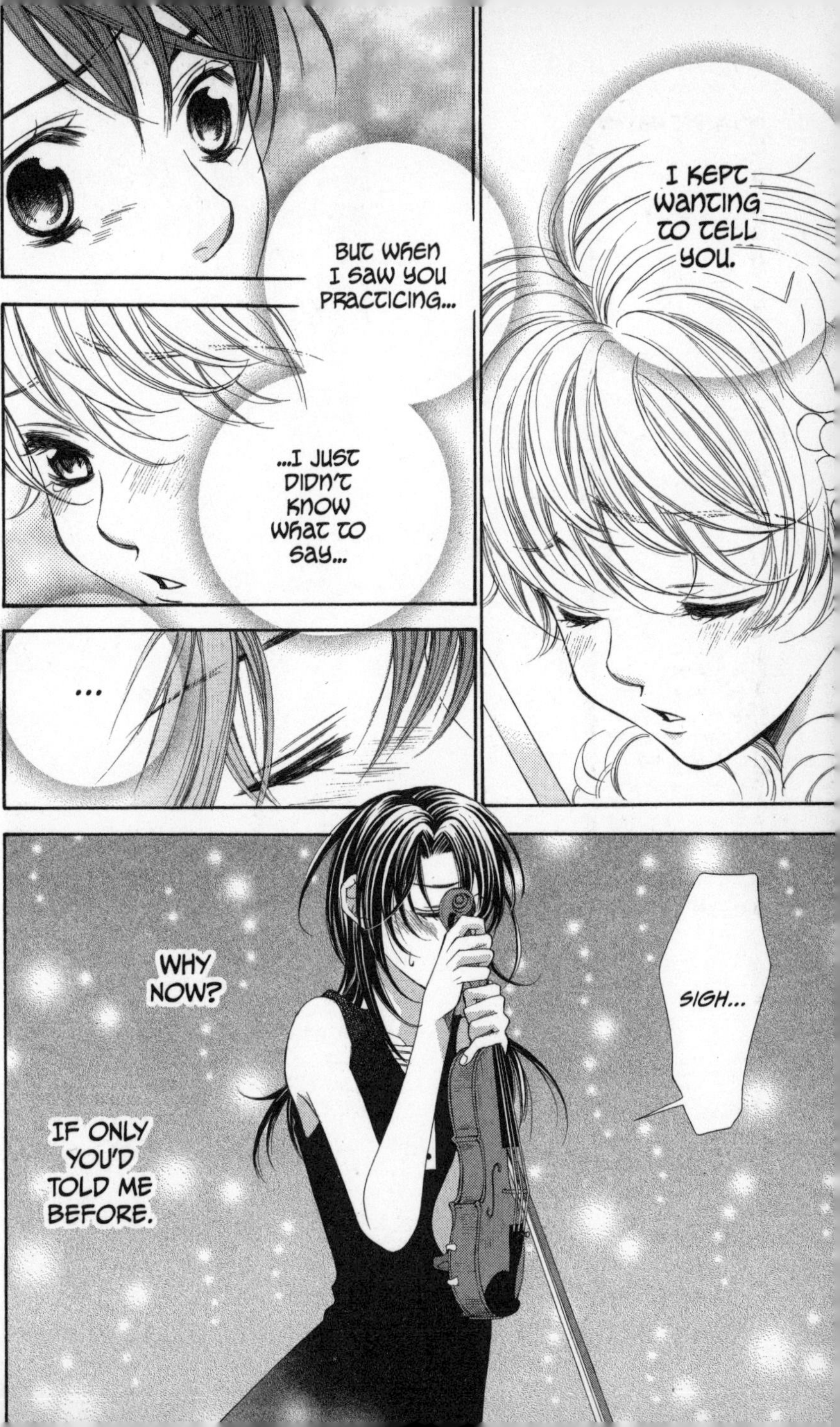
I KEPT WANTING TO TELL YOU.
BUT WHEN I SAW YOU PRACTICING...
...I JUST DIDN'T KNOW WHAT TO SAY...
...
SIGH...
WHY NOW?
IF ONLY YOU'D TOLD ME BEFORE.

FOUR

Thank you so much for reading! Come to think of it, I haven't used these columns to talk about the story in this volume at all. Well, let's ride this out to the end and avoid the topic altogether. This volume also includes a short story from a long time ago, like volume 6.

I hope to see you again in volume 8!

Until then, 'bye!

IF ONLY...

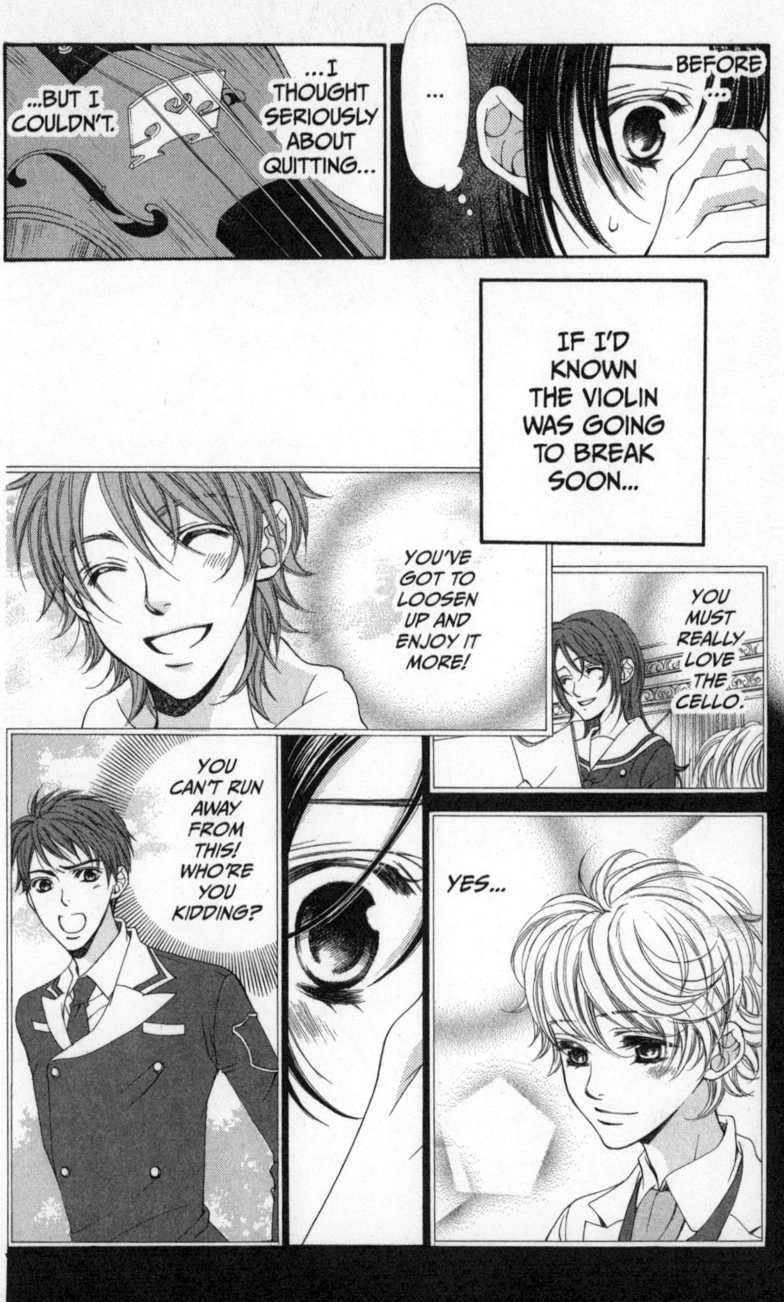
BEFORE...
...
...I THOUGHT SERIOUSLY ABOUT QUITTING...
...BUT I COULDN'T.
IF I'D KNOWN THE VIOLIN WAS GOING TO BREAK SOON...
YOU MUST REALLY LOVE THE CELLO.
YOU'VE GOT TO LOOSEN UP AND ENJOY IT MORE!
YES...
YOU CAN'T RUN AWAY FROM THIS! WHO'RE YOU KIDDING?

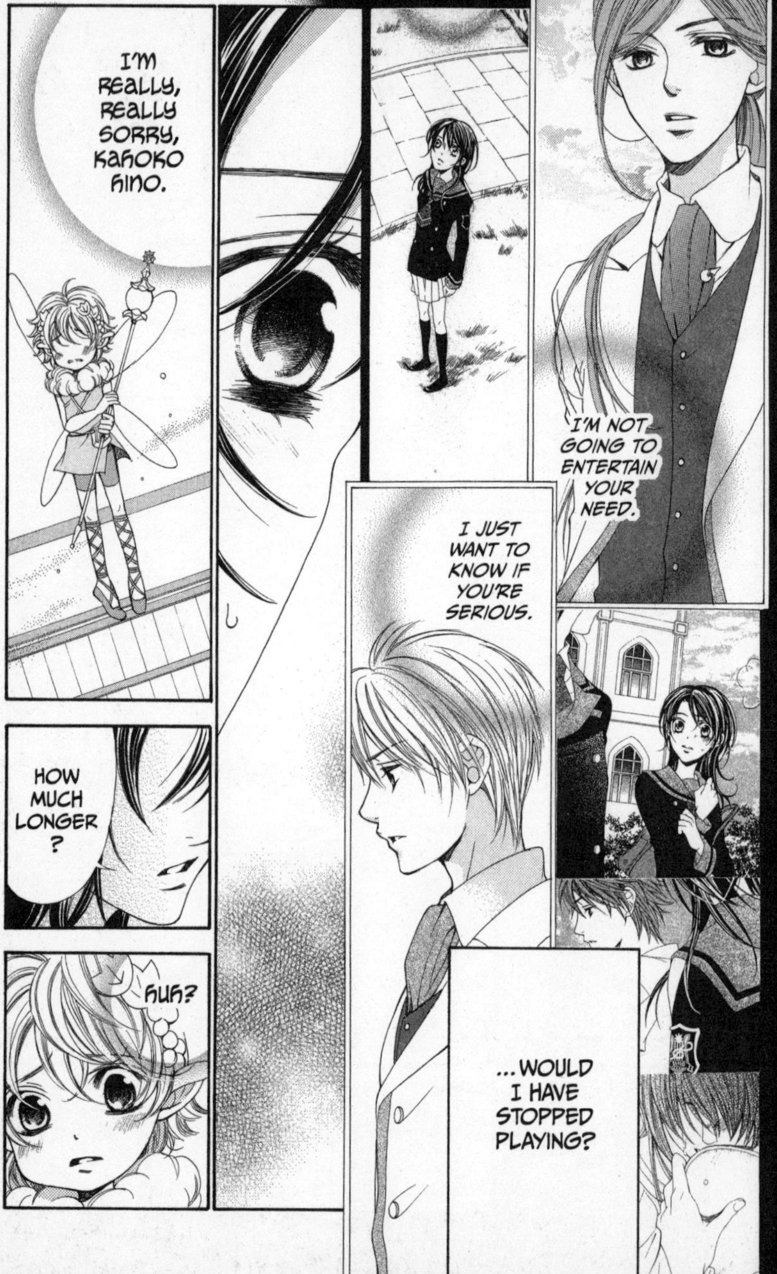
I'M NOT GOING TO ENTERTAIN YOUR NEED.
I JUST WANT TO KNOW IF YOU'RE SERIOUS.
...WOULD I HAVE STOPPED PLAYING?
I'M REALLY, REALLY SORRY, KAHOKO HINO.
HOW MUCH LONGER?
HUH?

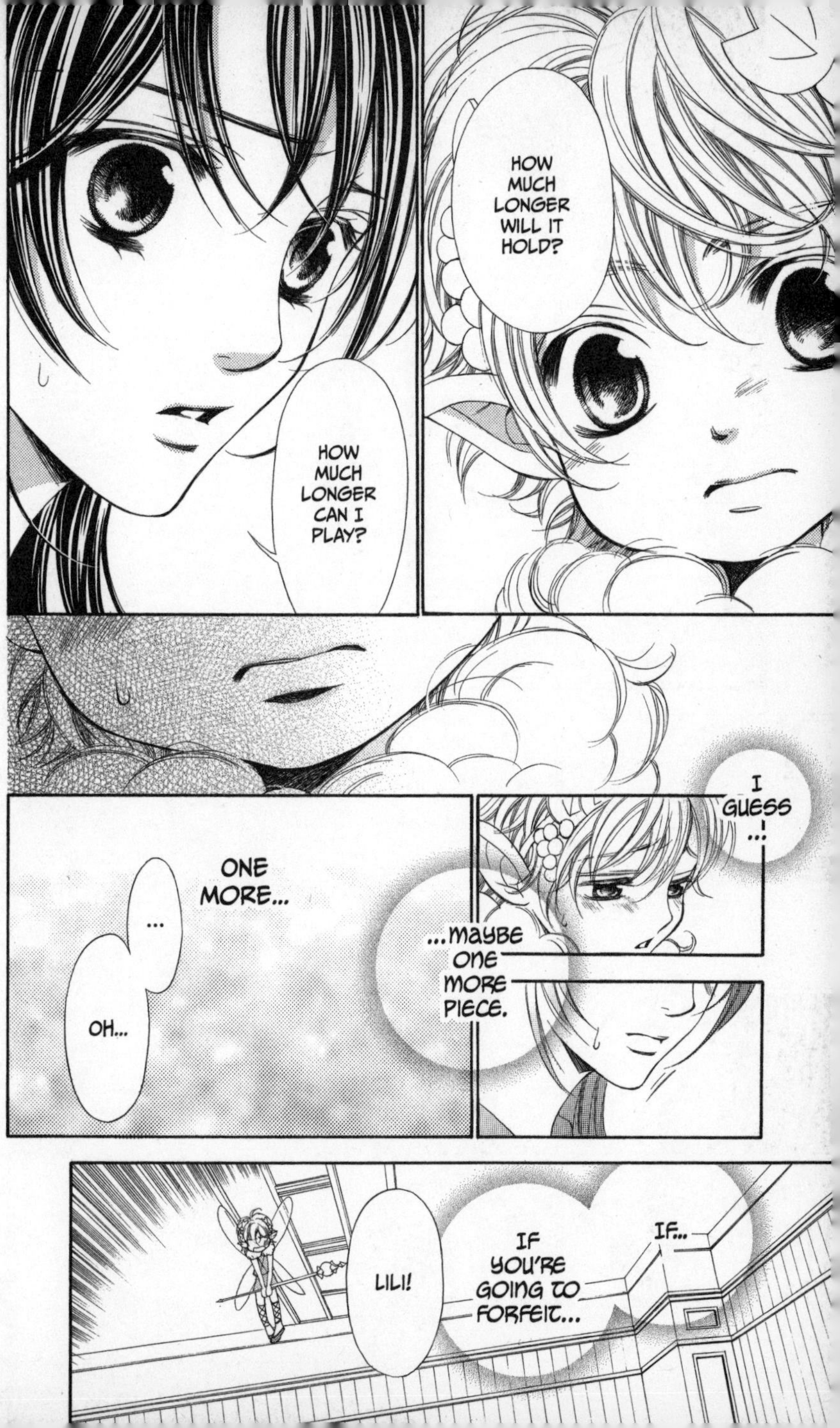
HOW MUCH LONGER WILL IT HOLD?
HOW MUCH LONGER CAN I PLAY?
I GUESS...
...MAYBE ONE MORE PIECE.
ONE MORE...
...
OH...
IF...
IF YOU'RE GOING TO FORFEIT...
LILI!

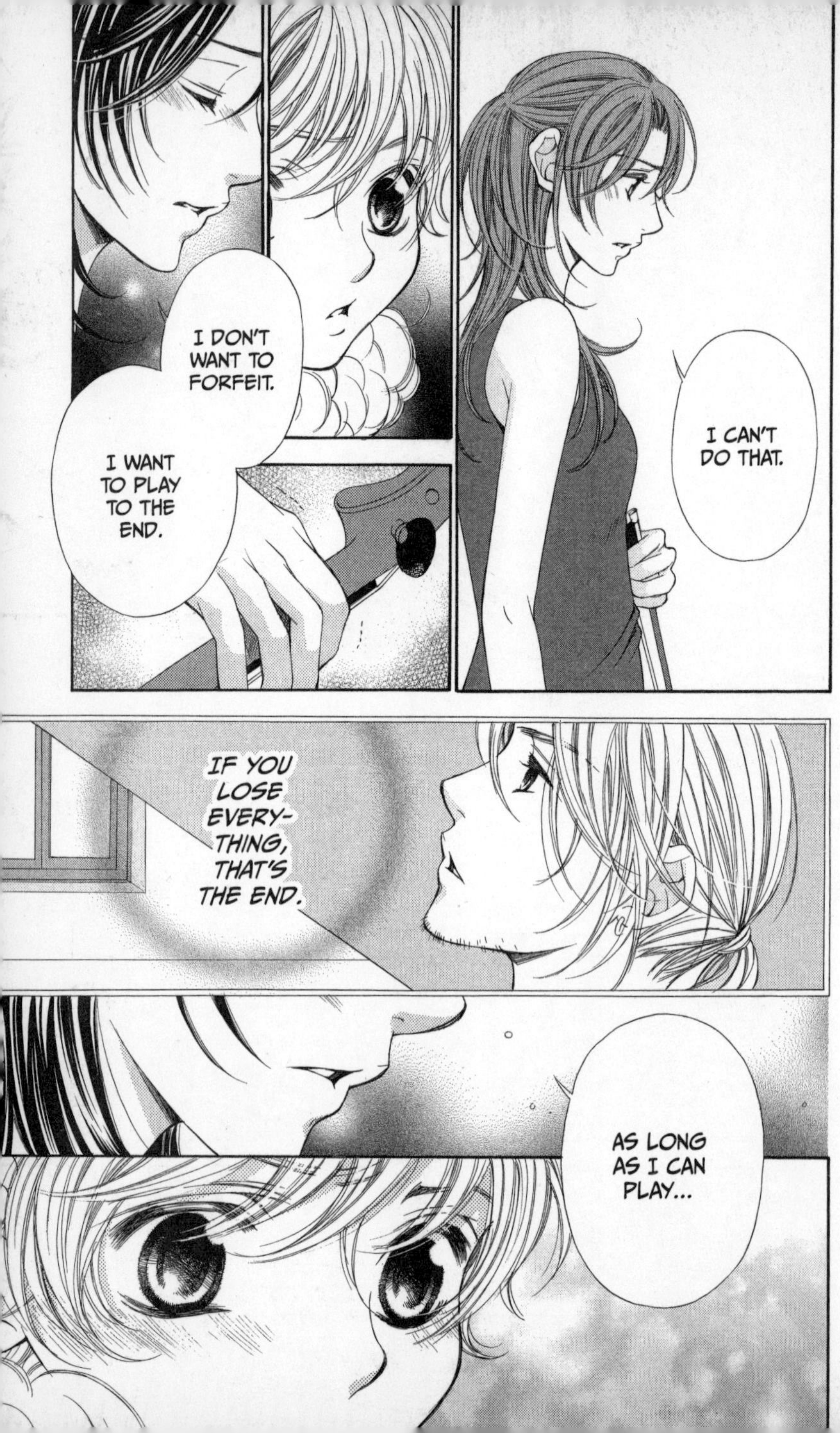
I CAN'T DO THAT.
I DON'T WANT TO FORFEIT.
I WANT TO PLAY TO THE END.
IF YOU LOSE EVERYTHING, THAT'S THE END.
AS LONG AS I CAN PLAY...

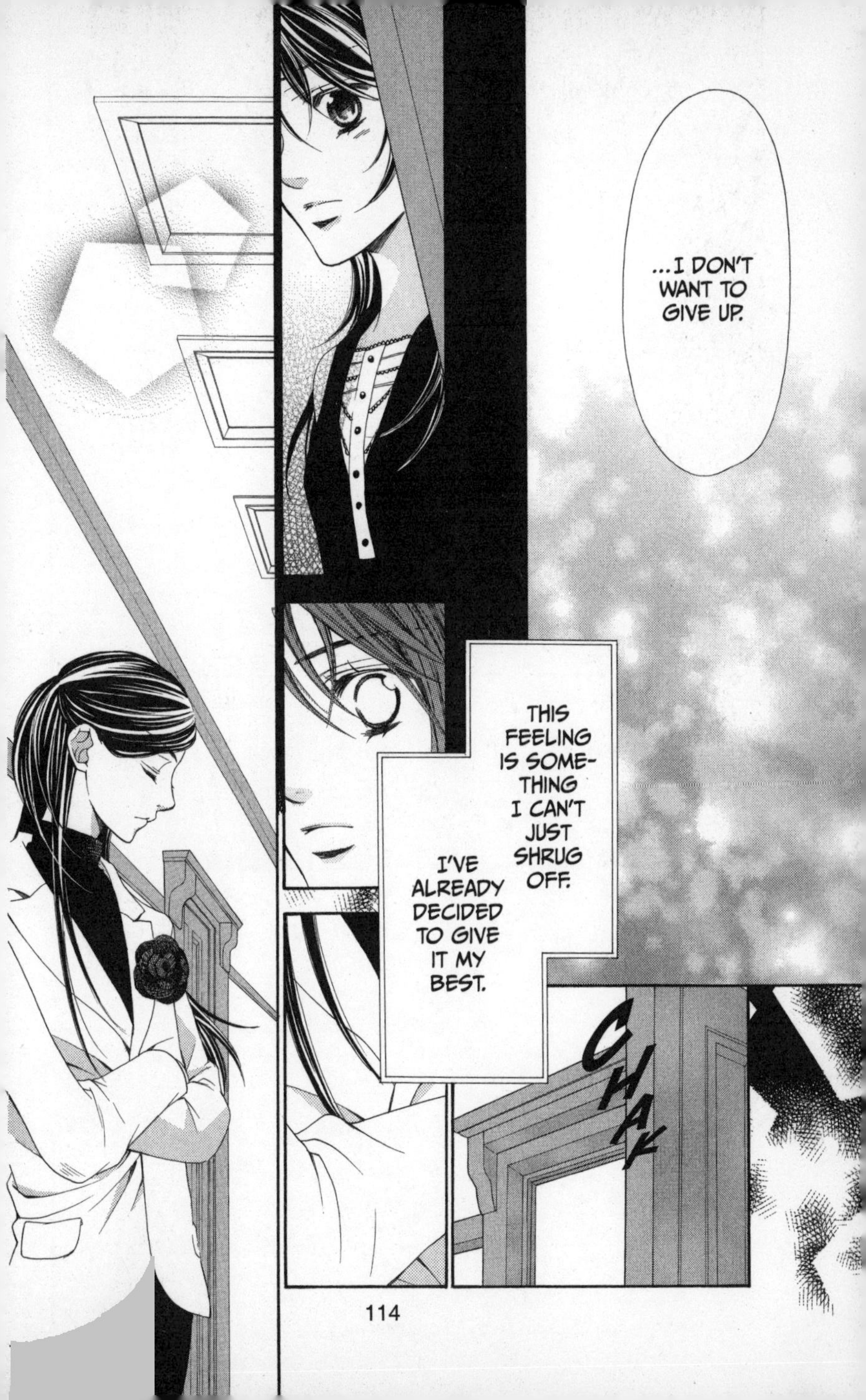
...I DON'T WANT TO GIVE UP.
THIS FEELING IS SOMETHING I CAN'T JUST SHRUG OFF.
I'VE ALREADY DECIDED TO GIVE IT MY BEST.
CHAK

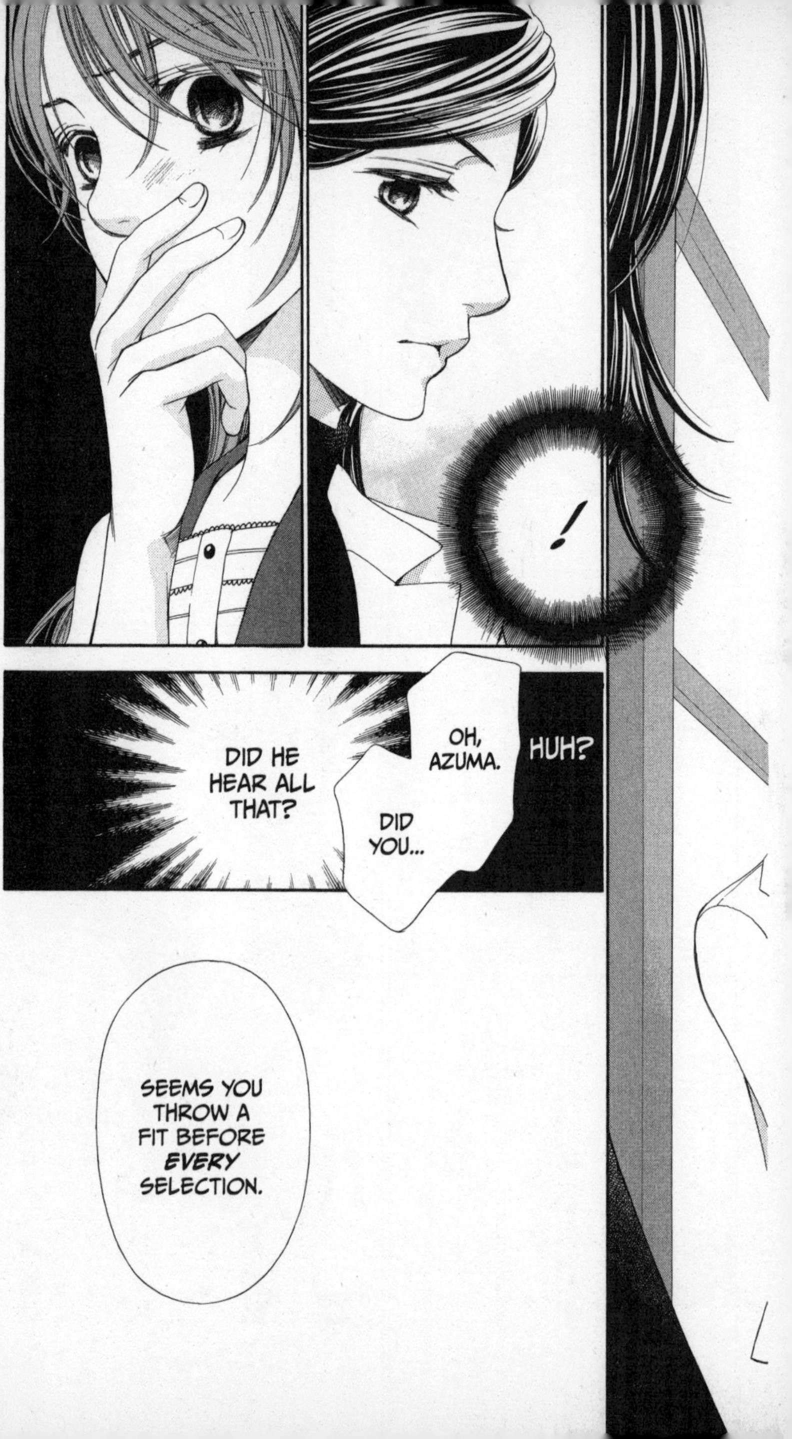
!
HUH?
OH, AZUMA.
DID YOU...
DID HE HEAR ALL THAT?
SEEMS YOU THROW A FIT BEFORE *EVERY* SELECTION.

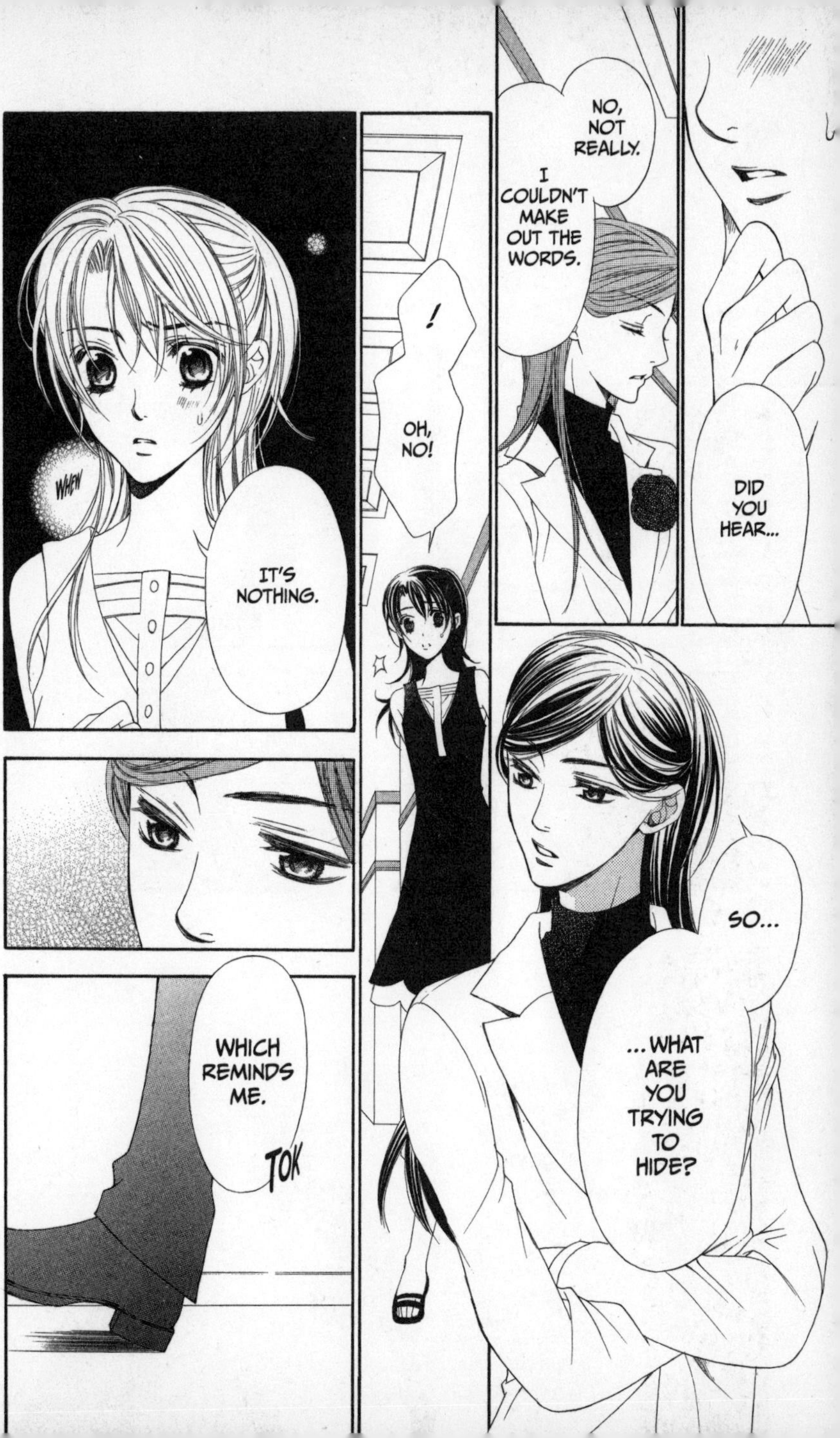
DID YOU HEAR...
NO, NOT REALLY.
I COULDN'T MAKE OUT THE WORDS.
SO...
...WHAT ARE YOU TRYING TO HIDE?
!
OH, NO!
WHEW
IT'S NOTHING.
WHICH REMINDS ME.
TOK

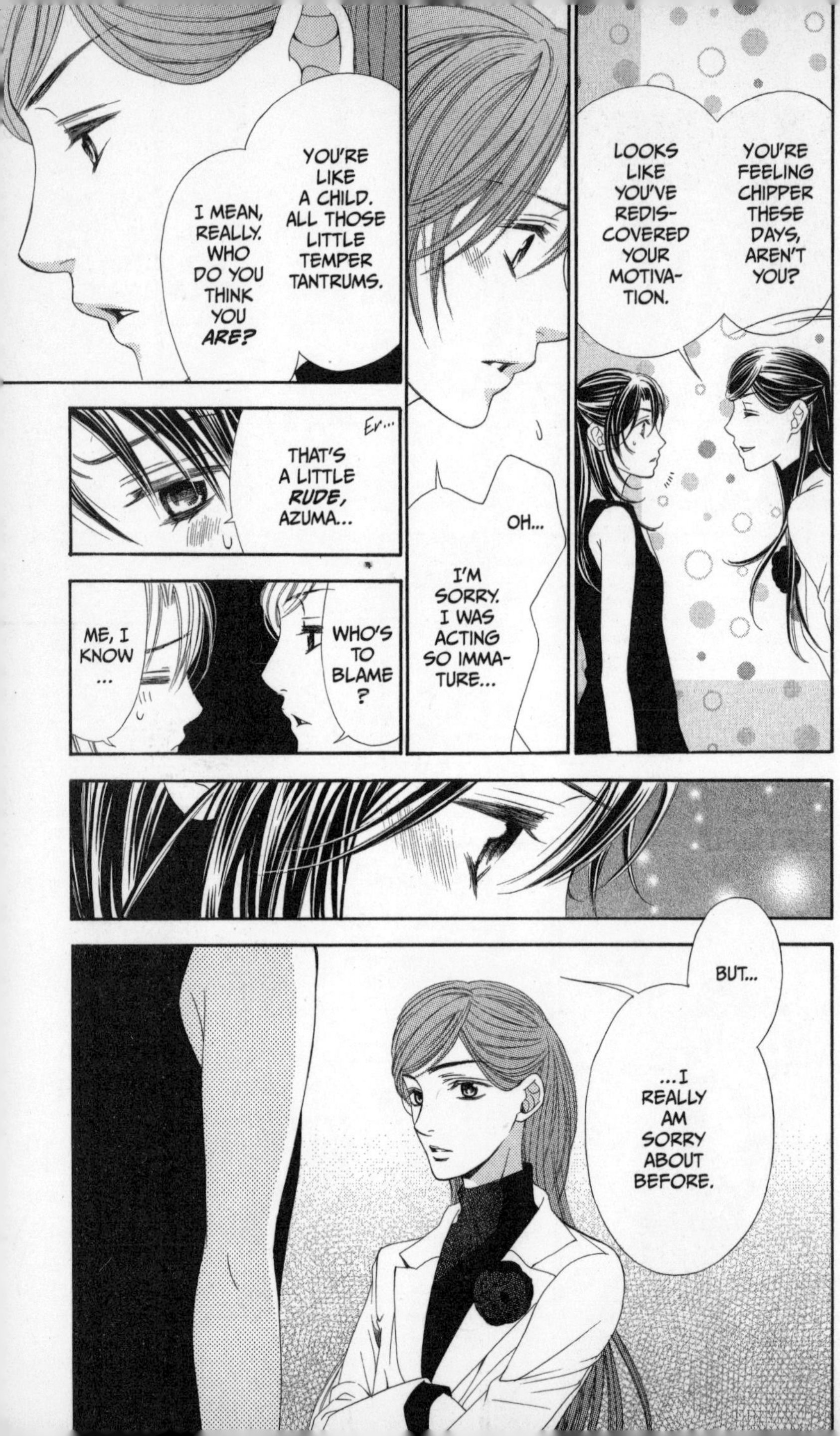
YOU'RE FEELING CHIPPER THESE DAYS, AREN'T YOU?
LOOKS LIKE YOU'VE REDISCOVERED YOUR MOTIVATION.
OH...
I'M SORRY. I WAS ACTING SO IMMATURE...
YOU'RE LIKE A CHILD. ALL THOSE LITTLE TEMPER TANTRUMS.
I MEAN, REALLY. WHO DO YOU THINK YOU *ARE?*
Er...
THAT'S A LITTLE *RUDE,* AZUMA...
WHO'S TO BLAME?
ME, I KNOW...
BUT...
...I REALLY AM SORRY ABOUT BEFORE.

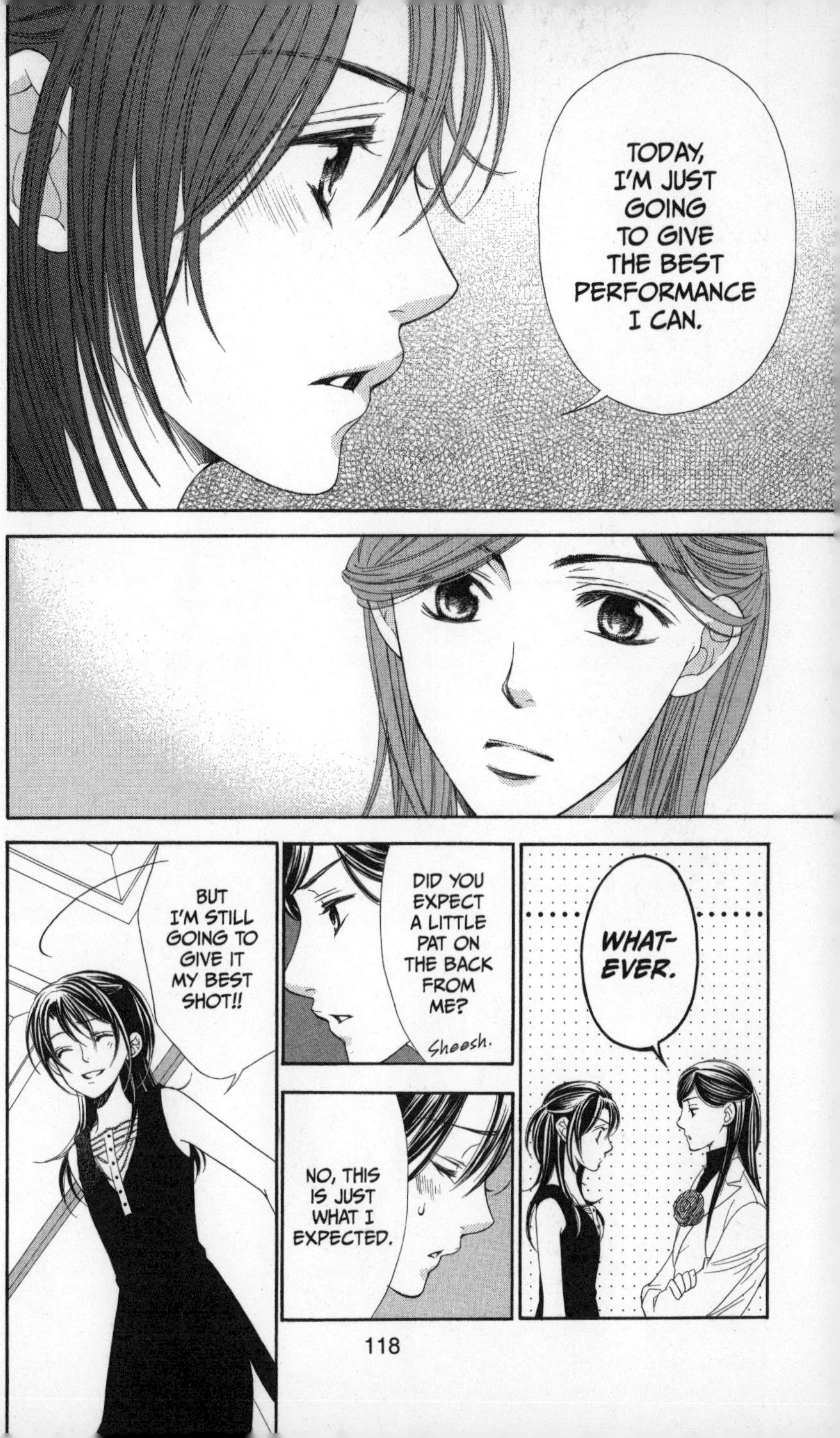
TODAY, I'M JUST GOING TO GIVE THE BEST PERFORMANCE I CAN.
......
WHAT-EVER.
......
DID YOU EXPECT A LITTLE PAT ON THE BACK FROM ME?
Sheesh.
NO, THIS IS JUST WHAT I EXPECTED.
BUT I'M STILL GOING TO GIVE IT MY BEST SHOT!!

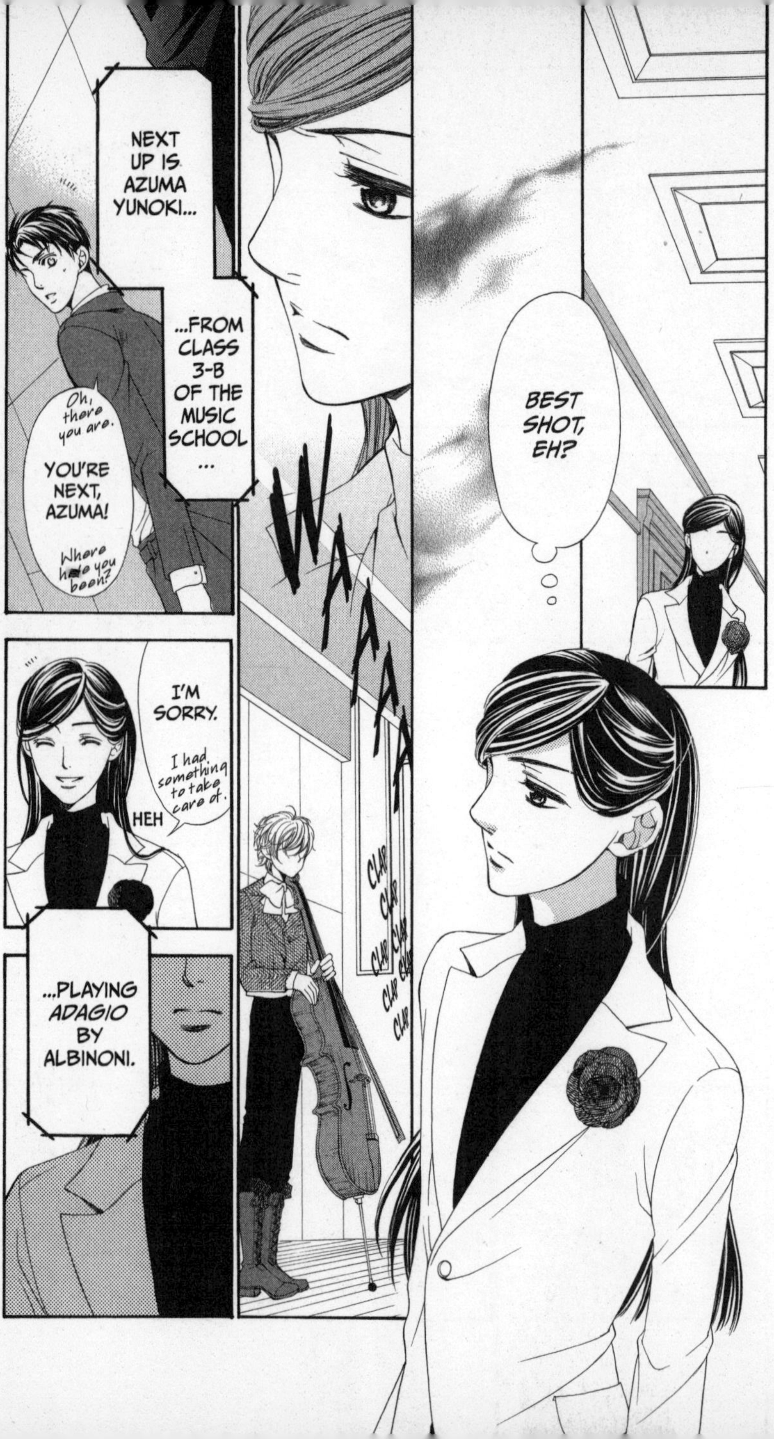
BEST SHOT, EH?
WAAAA
CLAP CLAP CLAP CLAP CLAP CLAP CLAP CLAP
NEXT UP IS AZUMA YUNOKI...
...FROM CLASS 3-B OF THE MUSIC SCHOOL ...
Oh, there you are. YOU'RE NEXT, AZUMA! Where have you been?
I'M SORRY. I had something to take care of.
HEH
...PLAYING ADAGIO BY ALBINONI.

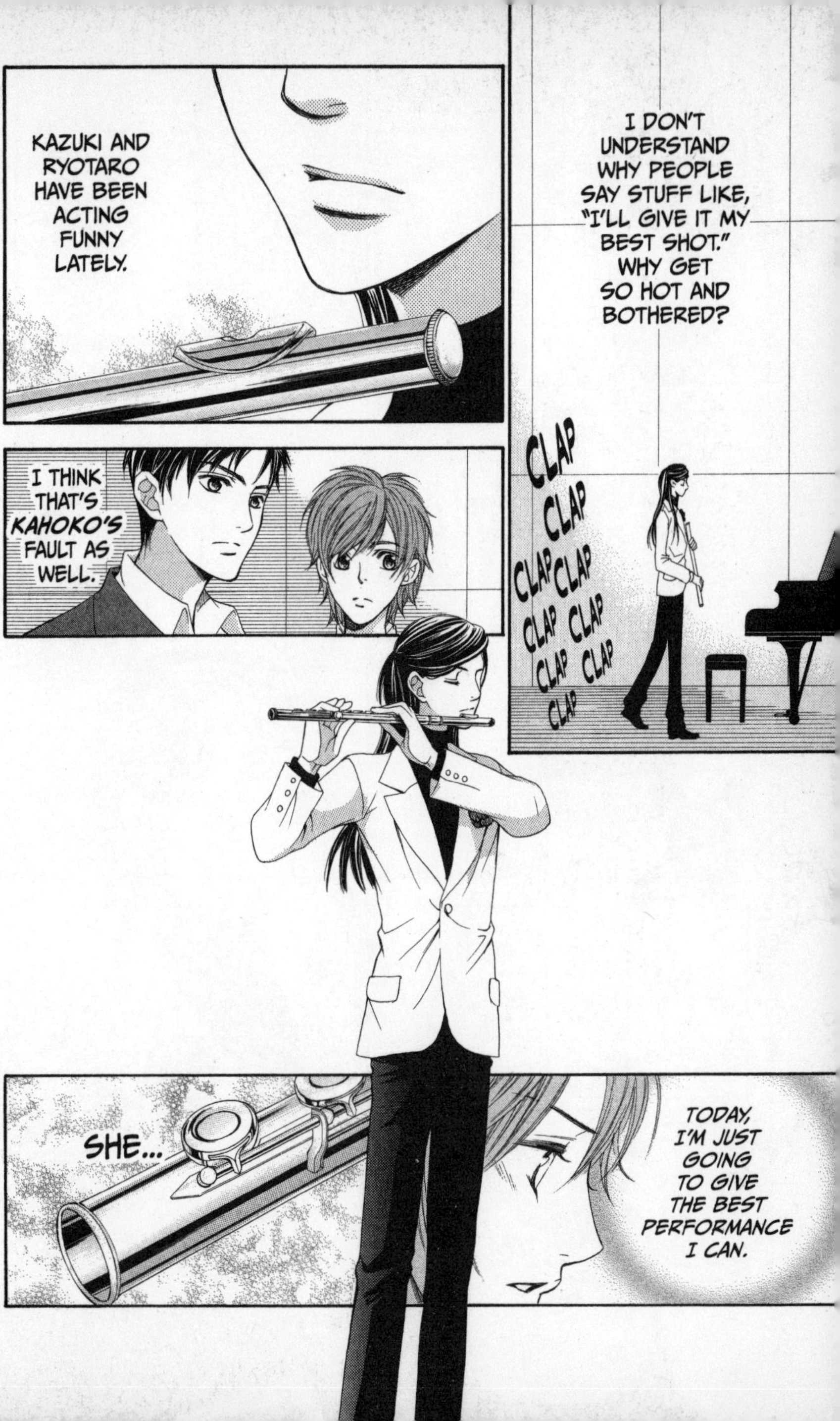
I DON'T UNDERSTAND WHY PEOPLE SAY STUFF LIKE, "I'LL GIVE IT MY BEST SHOT." WHY GET SO HOT AND BOTHERED?
CLAP CLAP CLAP CLAP CLAP CLAP CLAP CLAP CLAP
KAZUKI AND RYOTARO HAVE BEEN ACTING FUNNY LATELY.
I THINK THAT'S *KAHOKO'S* FAULT AS WELL.
TODAY, I'M JUST GOING TO GIVE THE BEST PERFORMANCE I CAN.
SHE...

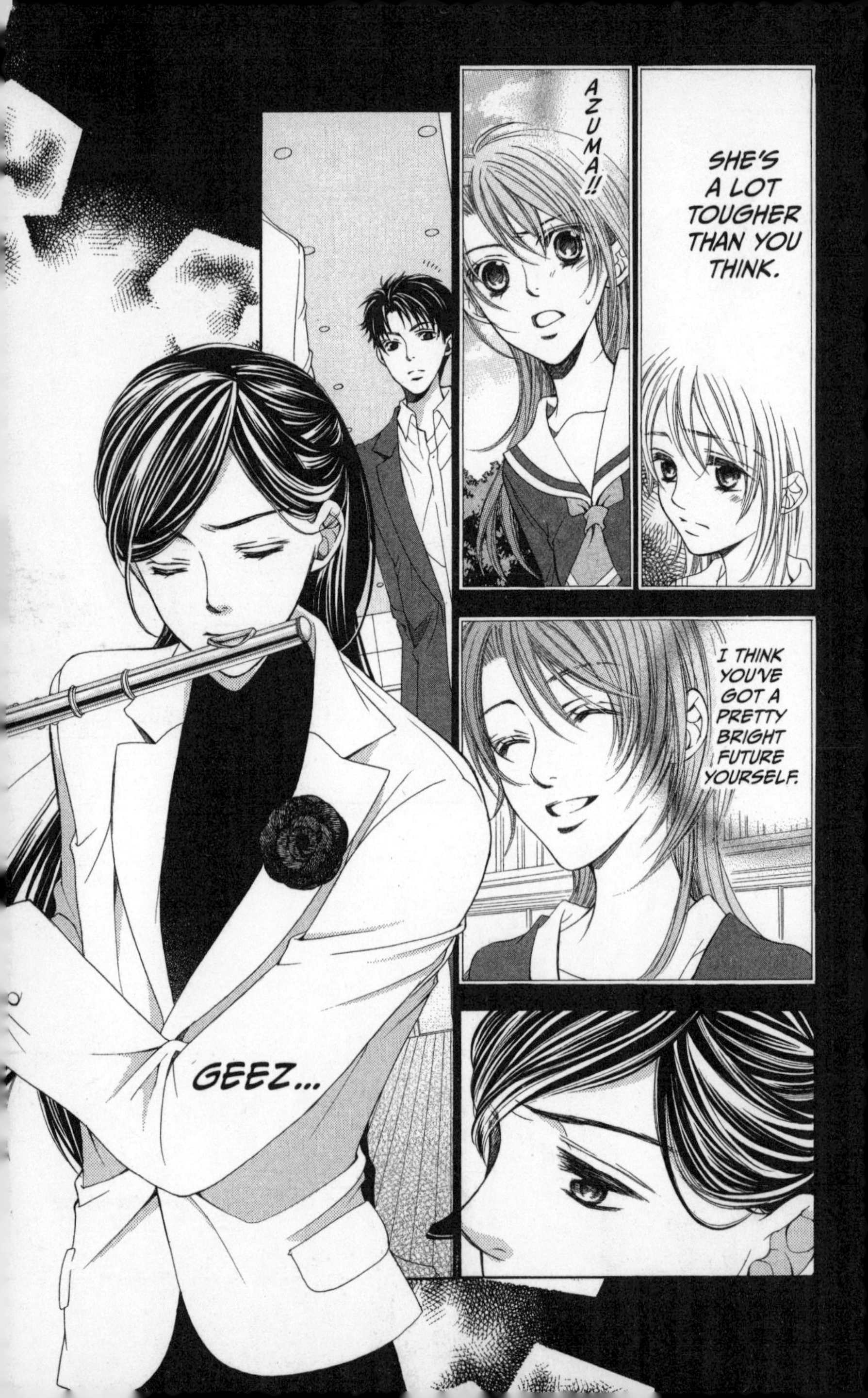
SHE'S A LOT TOUGHER THAN YOU THINK.
AZUMA!!
I THINK YOU'VE GOT A PRETTY BRIGHT FUTURE YOURSELF.
GEEZ...

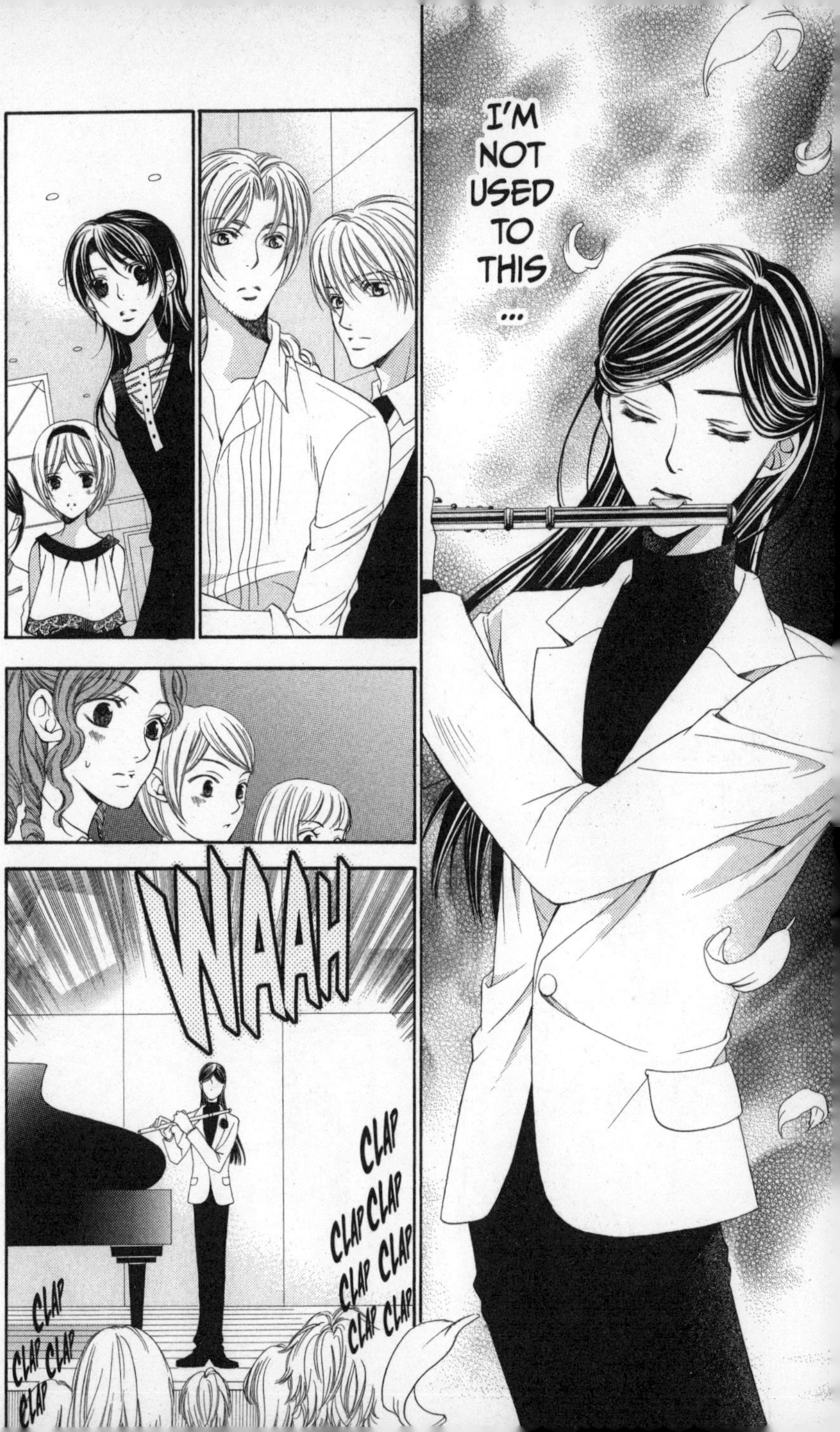
I'M NOT USED TO THIS ...
WAAH
CLAP
CLAP CLAP
CLAP CLAP
CLAP CLAP
CLAP CLAP
CLAP
CLAP CLAP
CLAP

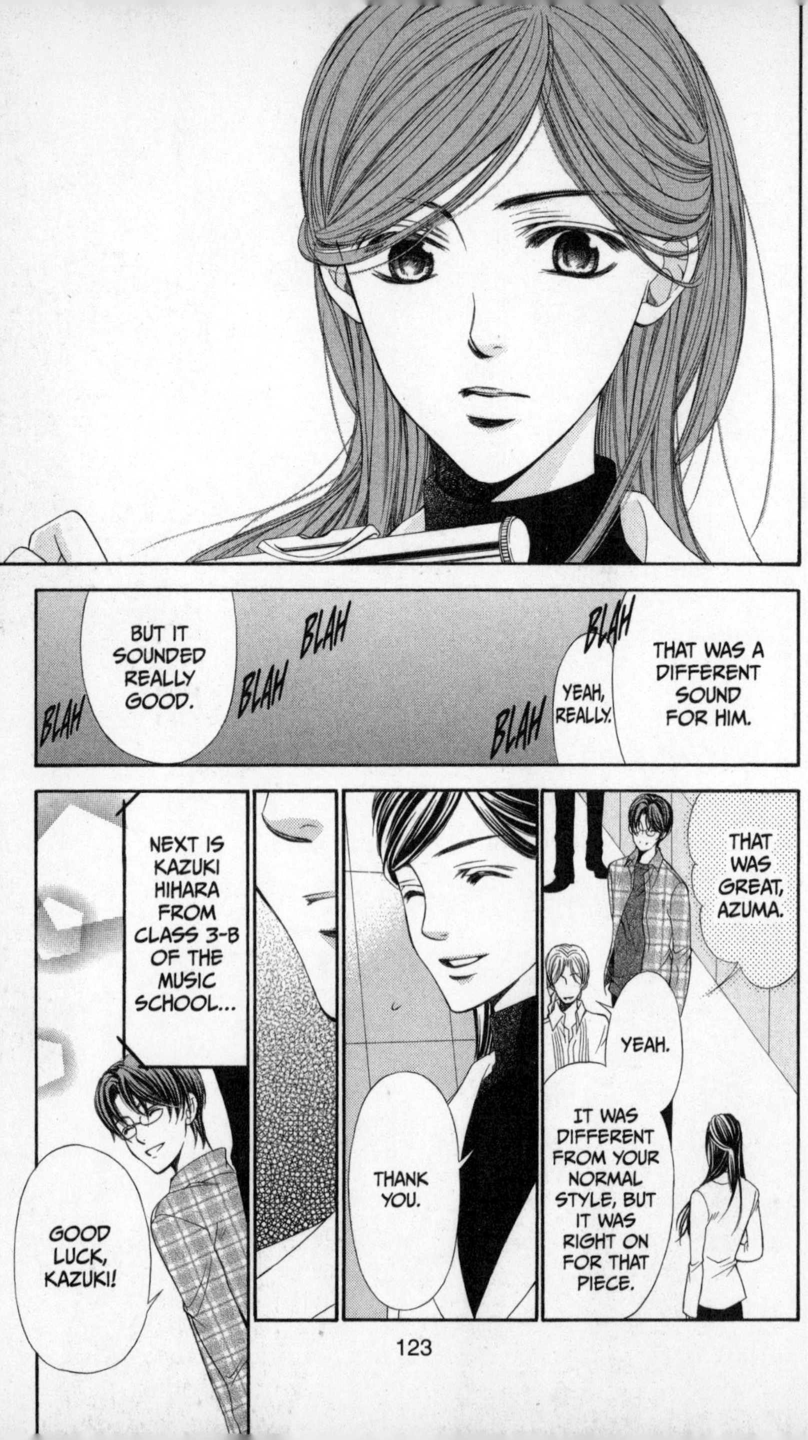

THAT WAS A DIFFERENT SOUND FOR HIM.
BLAH
YEAH, REALLY.
BLAH
BLAH
BLAH
BUT IT SOUNDED REALLY GOOD.
BLAH
THAT WAS GREAT, AZUMA.
YEAH.
IT WAS DIFFERENT FROM YOUR NORMAL STYLE, BUT IT WAS RIGHT ON FOR THAT PIECE.
THANK YOU.
NEXT IS KAZUKI HIHARA FROM CLASS 3-B OF THE MUSIC SCHOOL...
GOOD LUCK, KAZUKI!

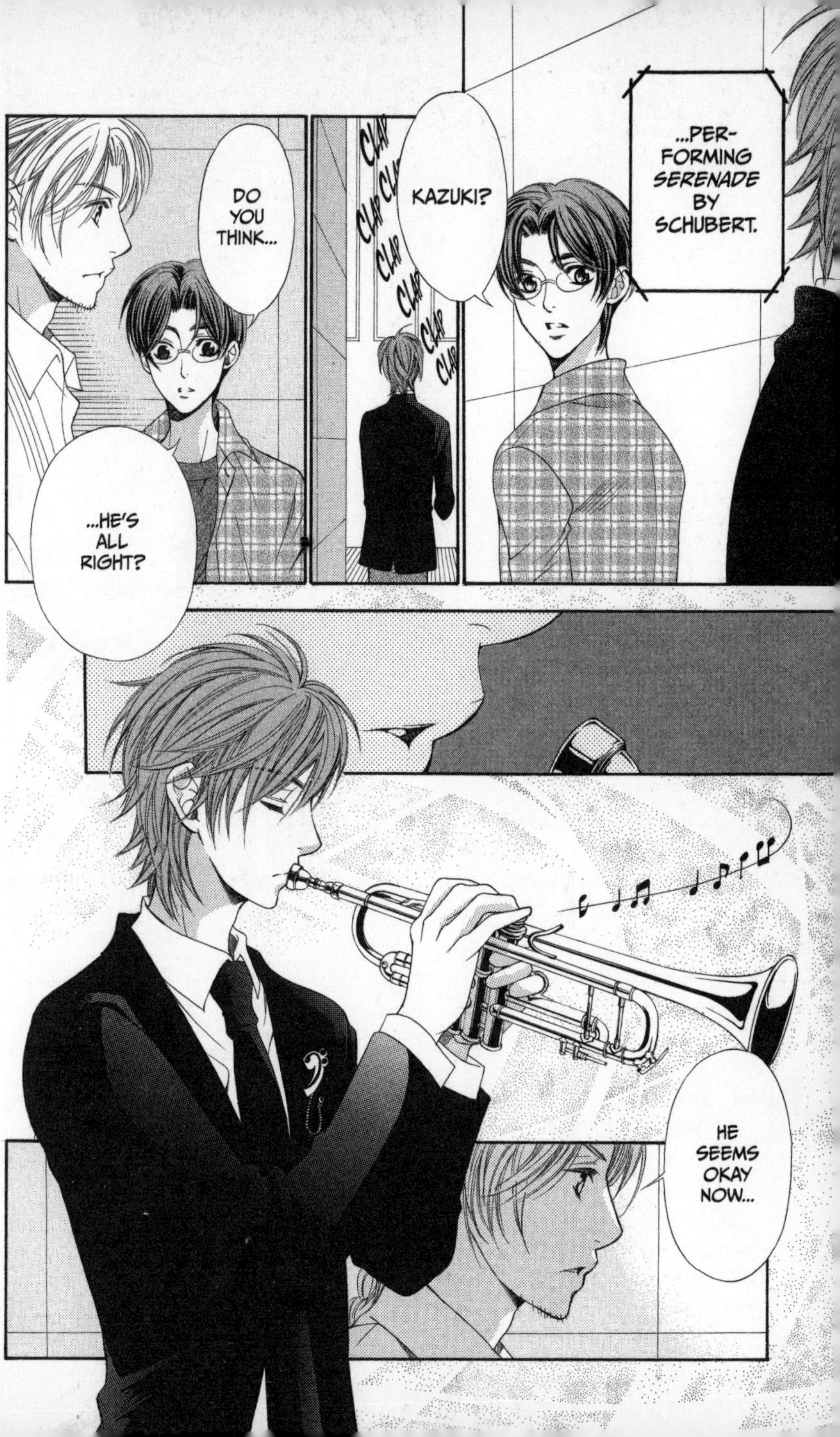
...PER-FORMING SERENADE BY SCHUBERT.
KAZUKI?
CLAP CLAP CLAP CLAP CLAP CLAP CLAP CLAP
DO YOU THINK...
...HE'S ALL RIGHT?
HE SEEMS OKAY NOW...

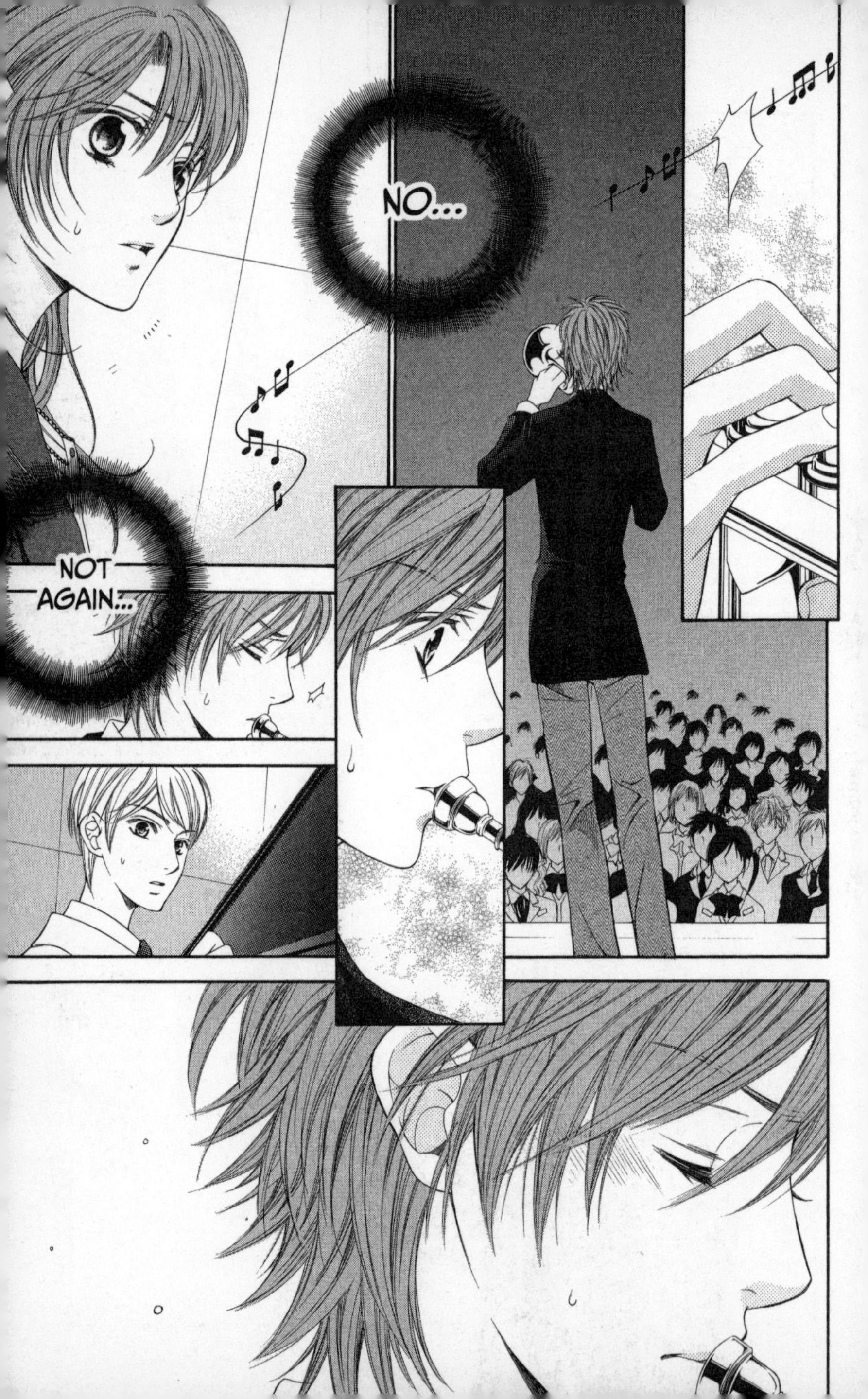
NO...
NOT AGAIN...

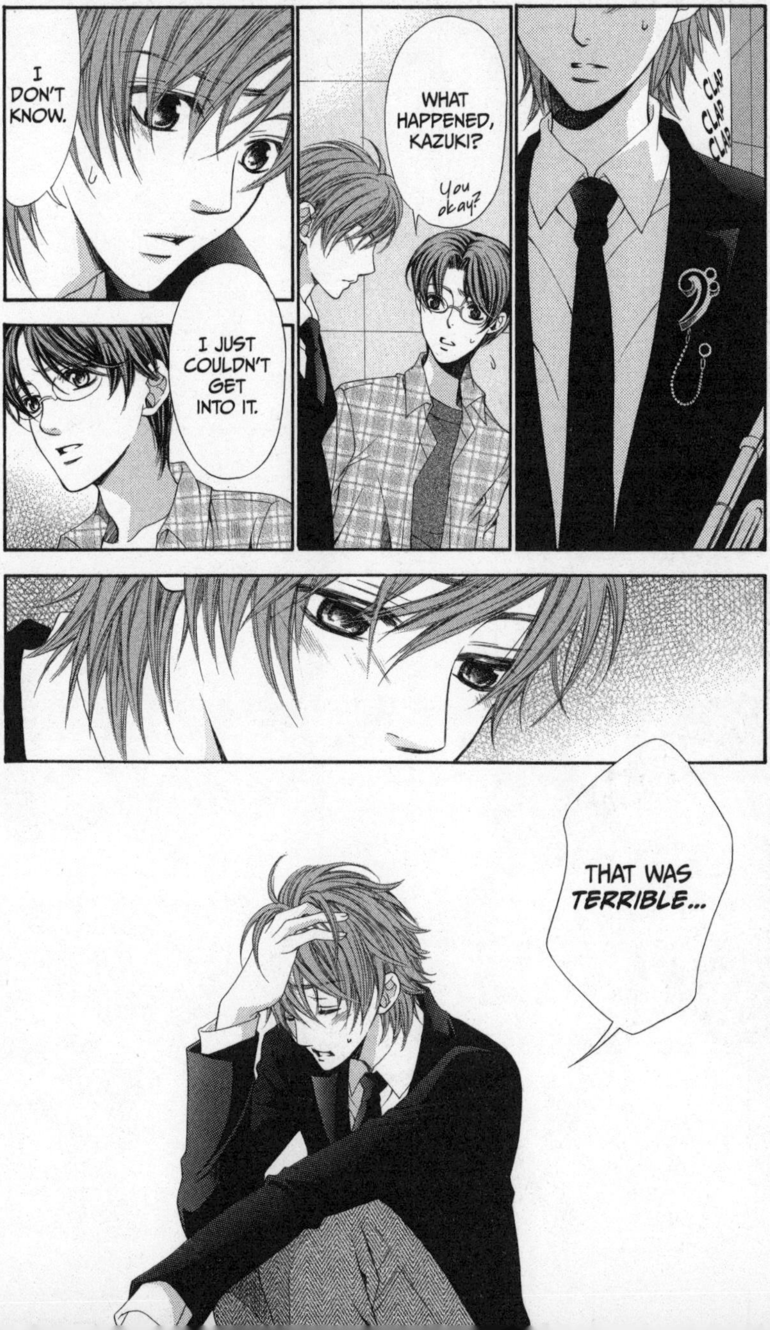
CLAP CLAP CLAP
WHAT HAPPENED, KAZUKI?
You okay?
I DON'T KNOW.
I JUST COULDN'T GET INTO IT.
THAT WAS TERRIBLE...

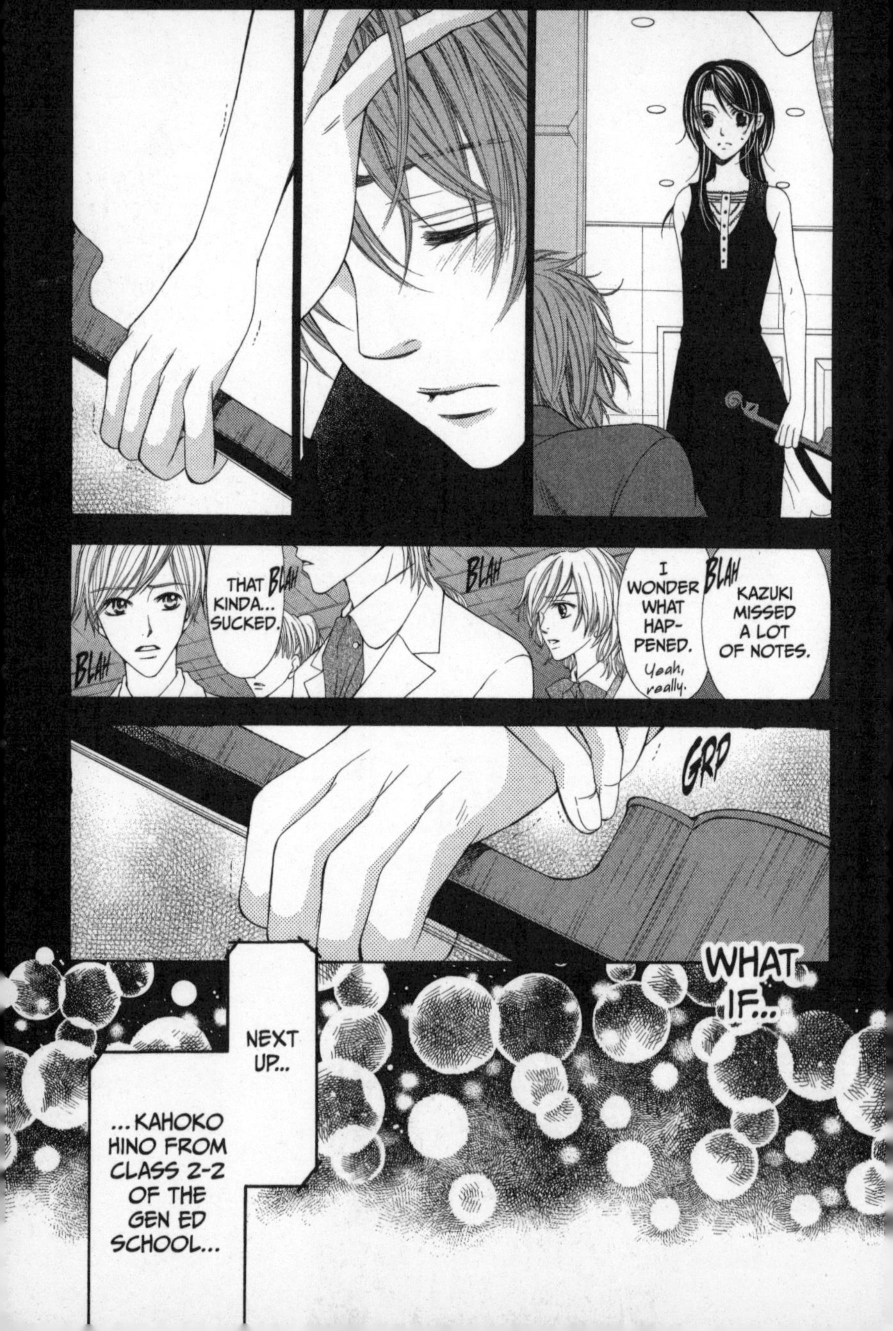
KAZUKI MISSED A LOT OF NOTES.
BLAH
I WONDER WHAT HAP-PENED.
Yeah, really.
BLAH
THAT KINDA... SUCKED.
BLAH
BLAH
GRP
WHAT IF...
NEXT UP...
...KAHOKO HINO FROM CLASS 2-2 OF THE GEN ED SCHOOL...

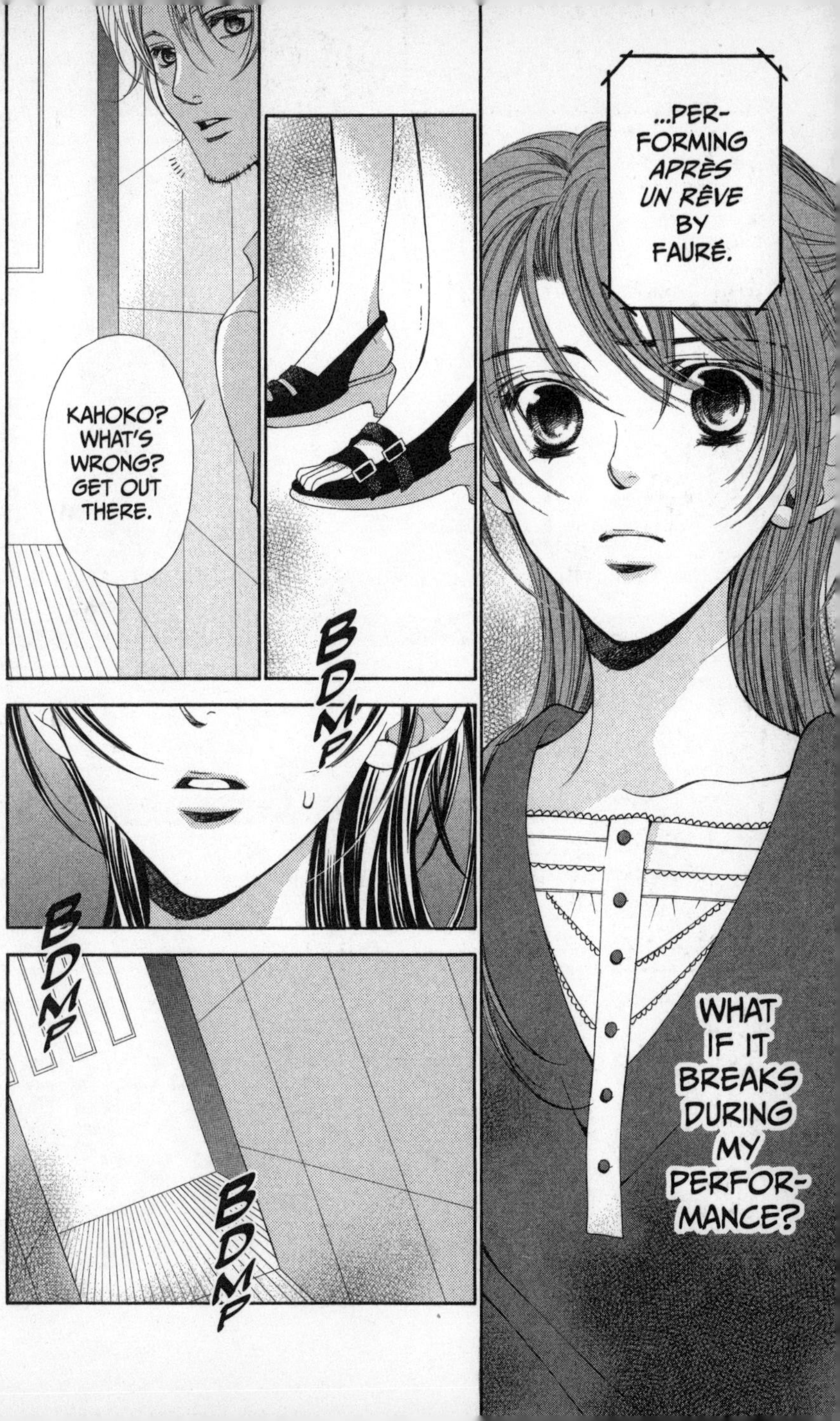
...PER-FORMING APRÈS UN RÊVE BY FAURÉ.
WHAT IF IT BREAKS DURING MY PERFOR-MANCE?
BDMP
KAHOKO? WHAT'S WRONG? GET OUT THERE.
BDMP
BDMP

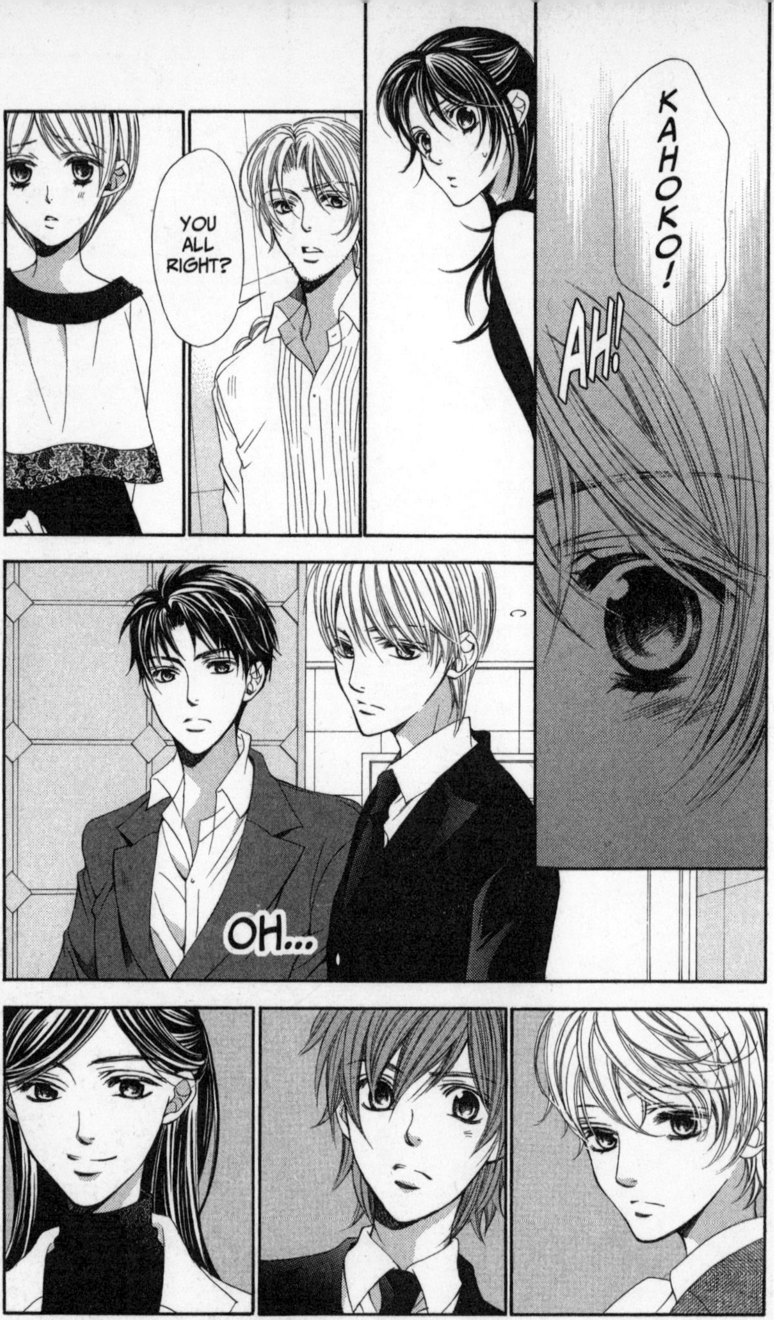
KAHOKO!
AH!
YOU ALL RIGHT?
OH...

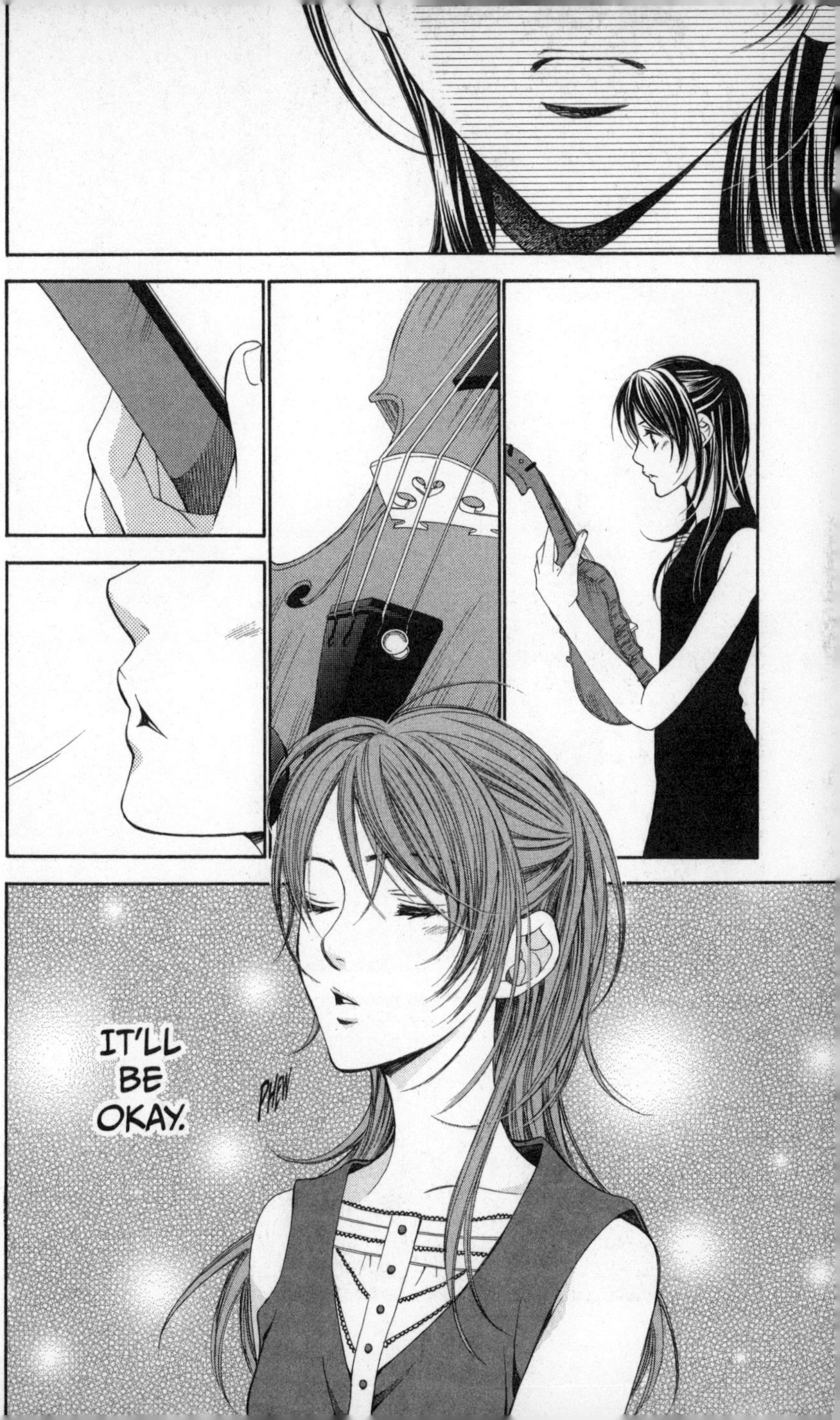
IT'LL BE OKAY.
PHEW

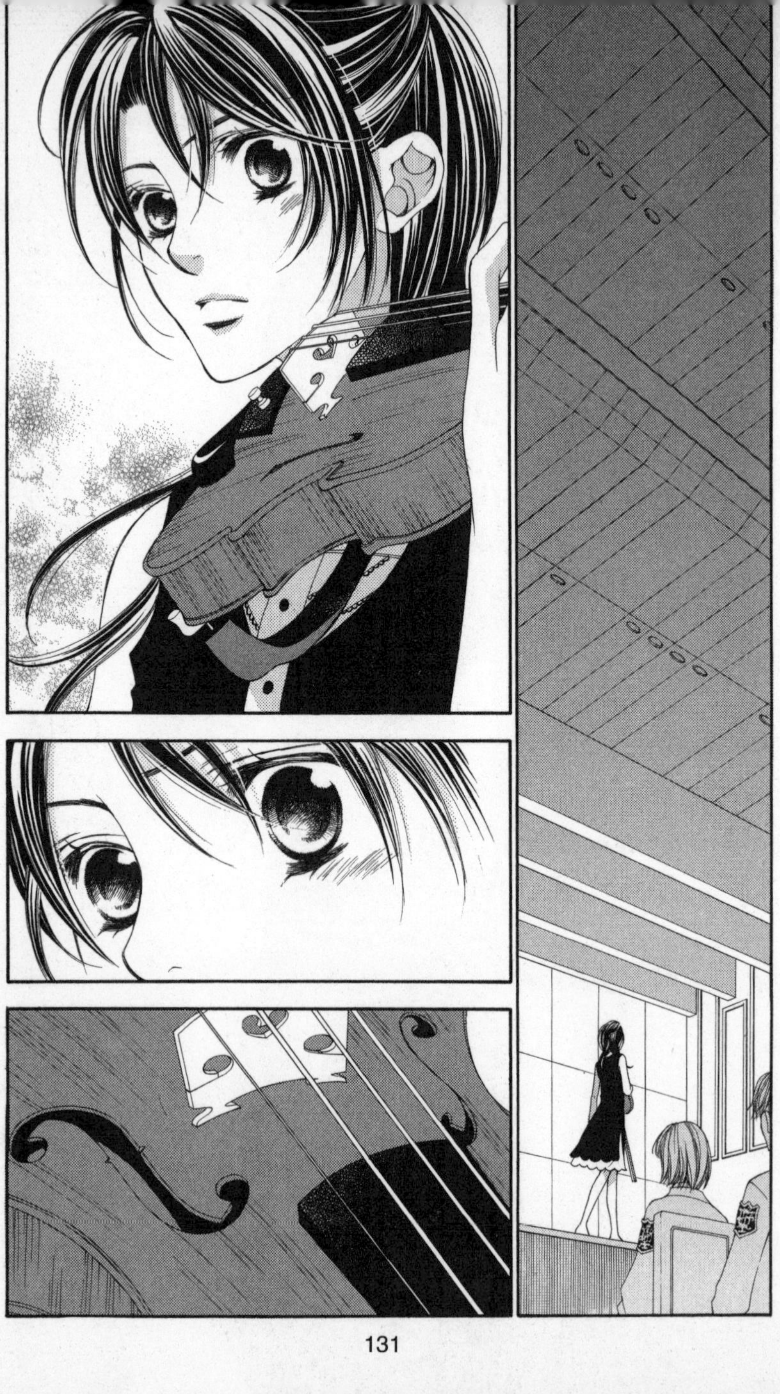

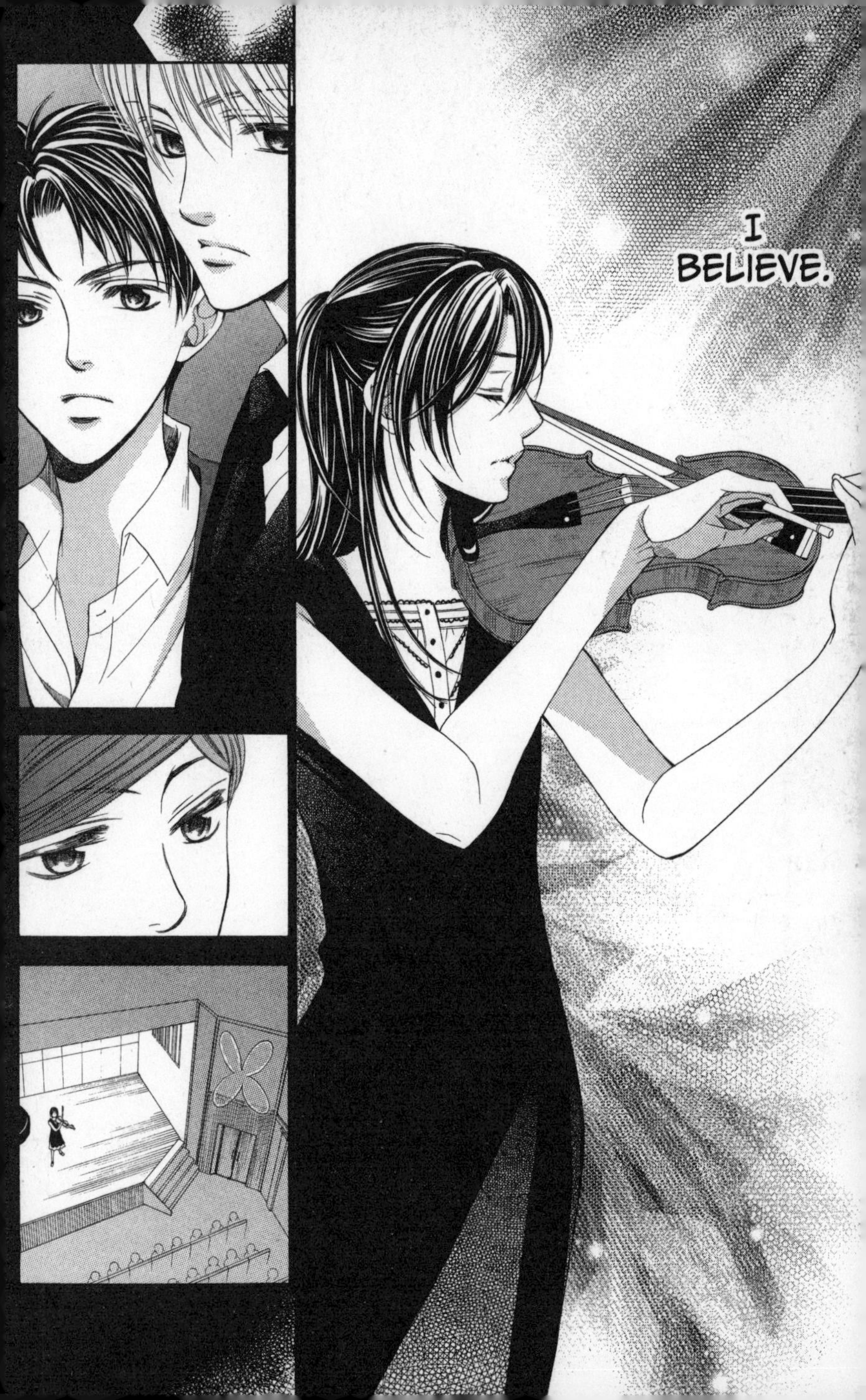
I BELIEVE.

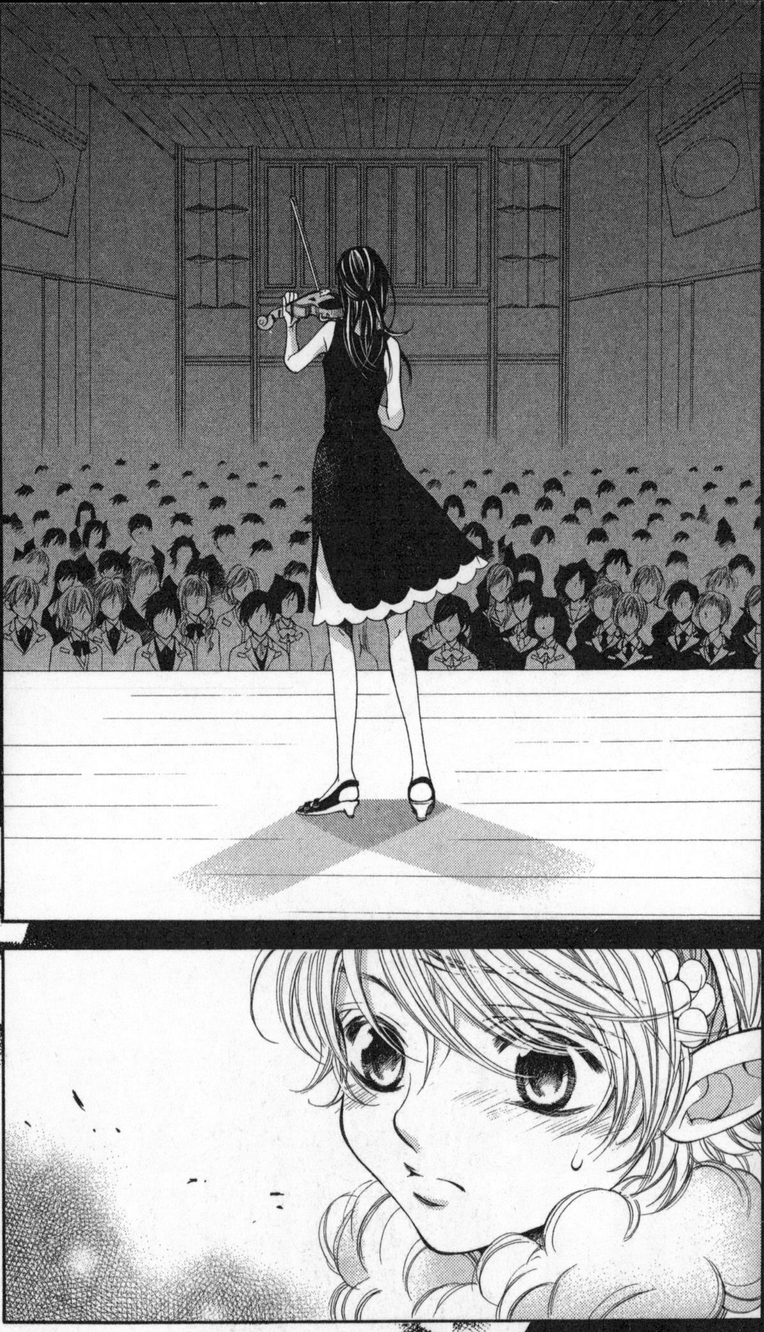

END OF MEASURE 31

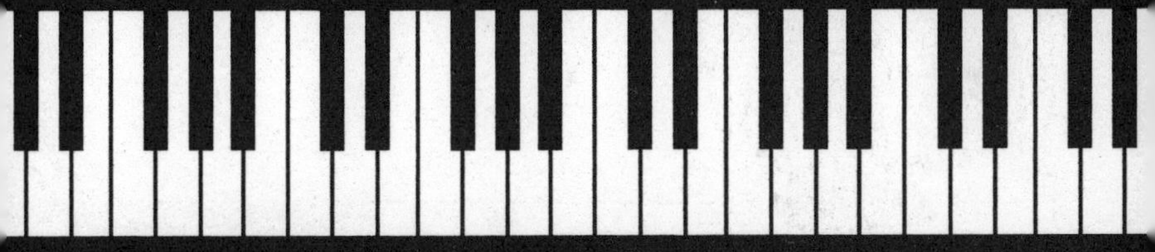

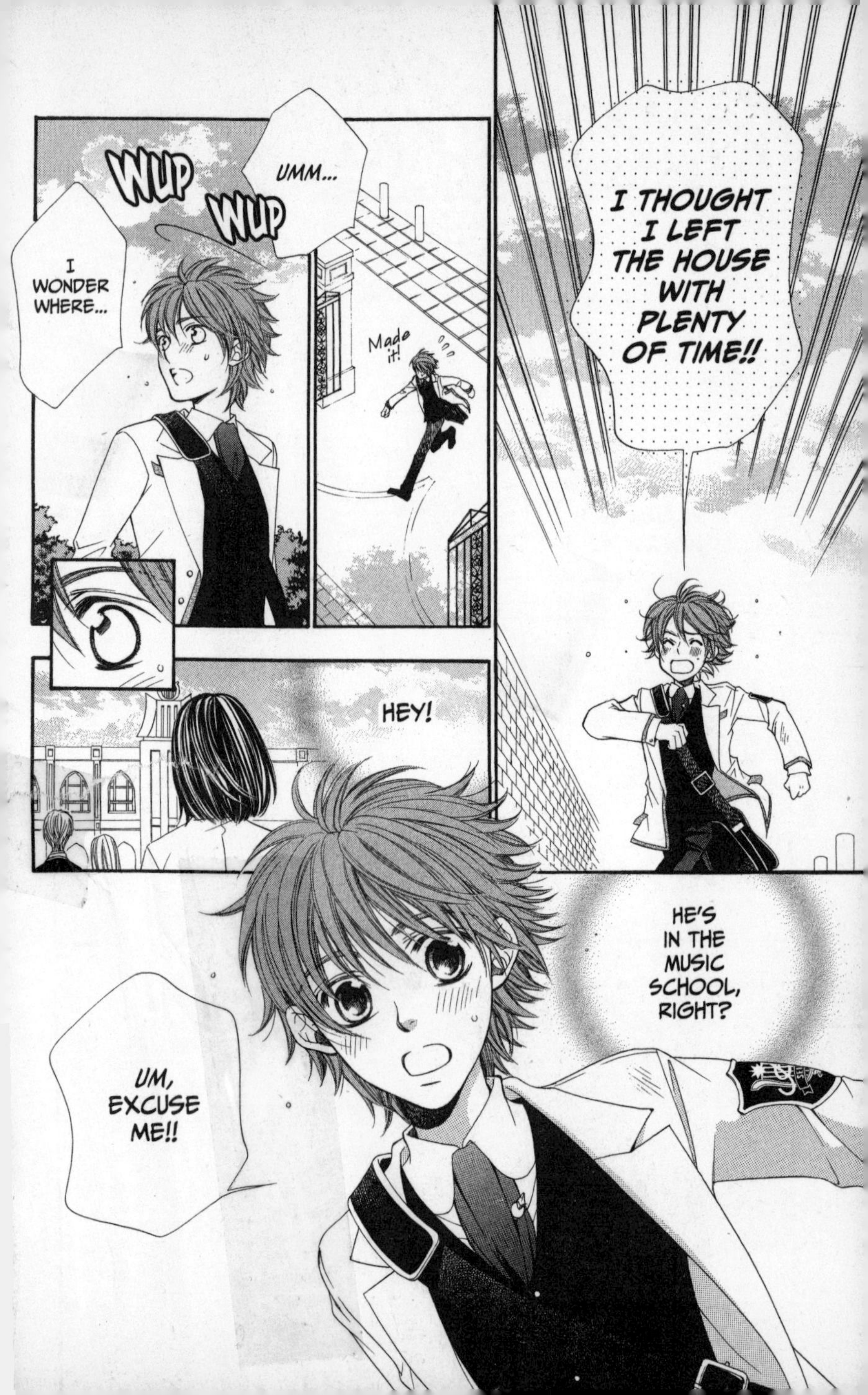
I THOUGHT I LEFT THE HOUSE WITH PLENTY OF TIME!!
Made it!
UMM...
WUP
WUP
I WONDER WHERE...
HEY!
HE'S IN THE MUSIC SCHOOL, RIGHT?
UM, EXCUSE ME!!

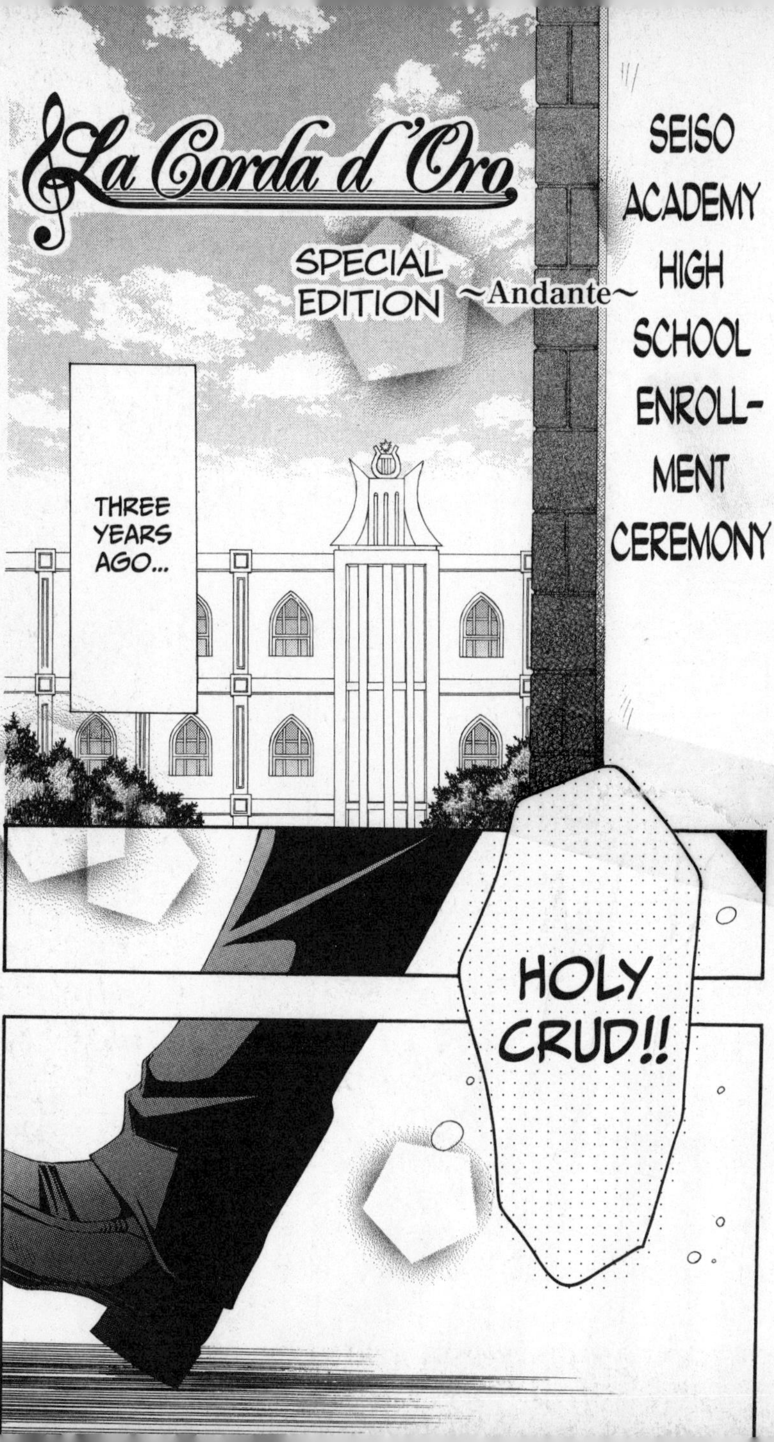
La Corda d'Oro
SPECIAL EDITION ~Andante~
SEISO ACADEMY HIGH SCHOOL ENROLLMENT CEREMONY
THREE YEARS AGO...
HOLY CRUD!!

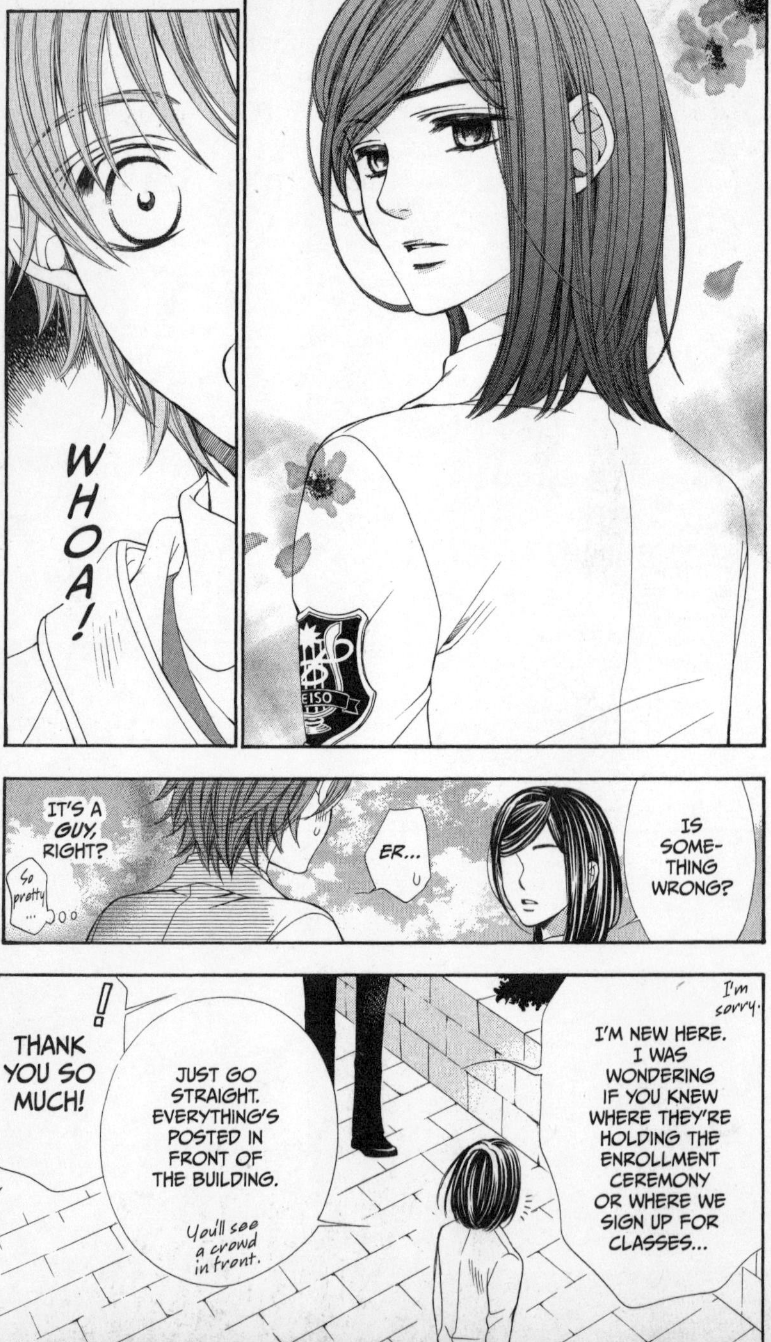
WHOA!
IS SOMETHING WRONG?
ER...
IT'S A GUY, RIGHT?
So pretty...
I'm sorry.
I'M NEW HERE. I WAS WONDERING IF YOU KNEW WHERE THEY'RE HOLDING THE ENROLLMENT CEREMONY OR WHERE WE SIGN UP FOR CLASSES...
JUST GO STRAIGHT. EVERYTHING'S POSTED IN FRONT OF THE BUILDING.
You'll see a crowd in front.
!
THANK YOU SO MUCH!

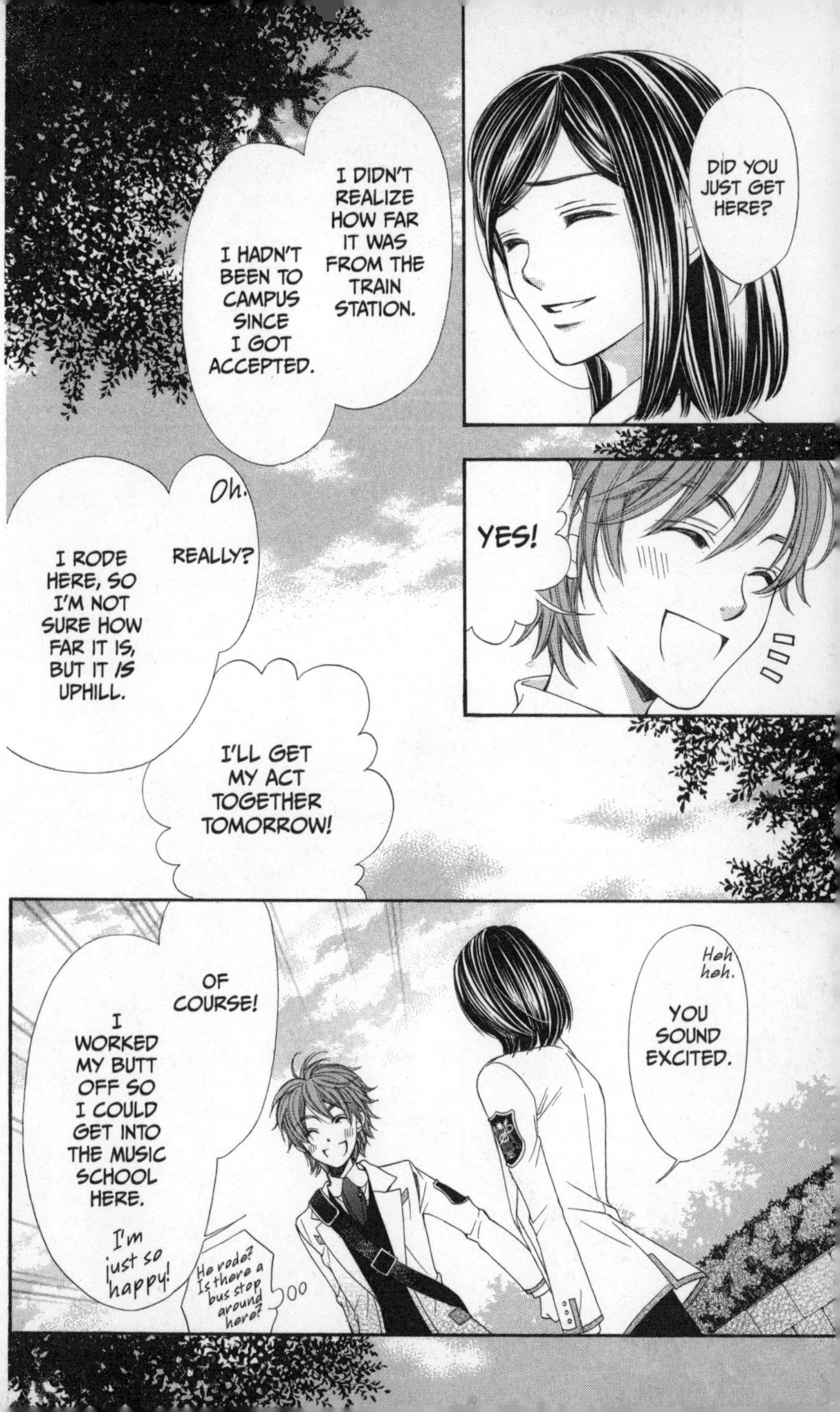
DID YOU JUST GET HERE?
YES!
I DIDN'T REALIZE HOW FAR IT WAS FROM THE TRAIN STATION.
I HADN'T BEEN TO CAMPUS SINCE I GOT ACCEPTED.
Oh.
REALLY?
I RODE HERE, SO I'M NOT SURE HOW FAR IT IS, BUT IT *IS* UPHILL.
I'LL GET MY ACT TOGETHER TOMORROW!
Heh heh.
YOU SOUND EXCITED.
OF COURSE!
I WORKED MY BUTT OFF SO I COULD GET INTO THE MUSIC SCHOOL HERE.
I'm just so happy!
He rode? Is there a bus stop around here?

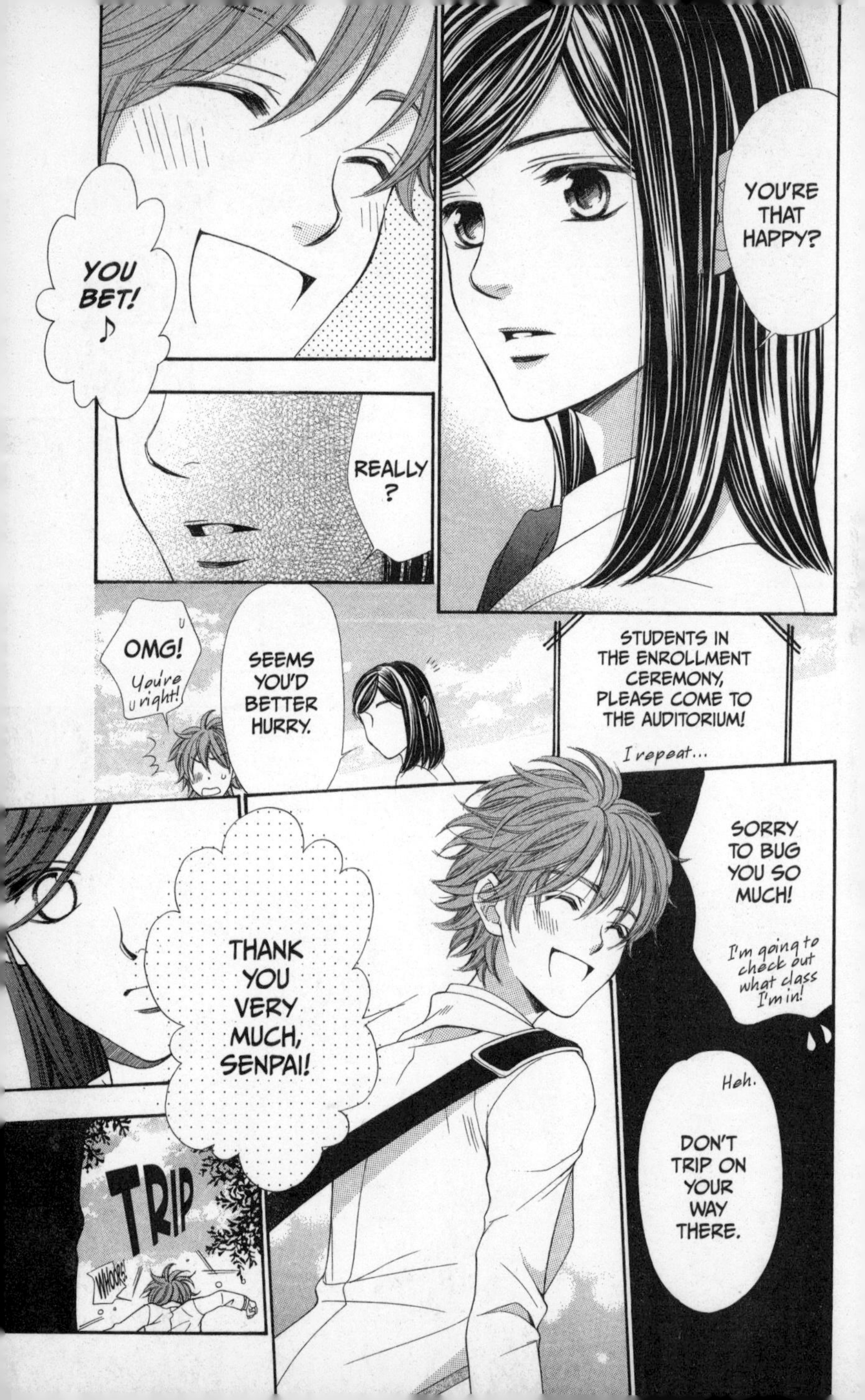
YOU'RE THAT HAPPY?
YOU BET! ♪
REALLY ?
STUDENTS IN THE ENROLLMENT CEREMONY, PLEASE COME TO THE AUDITORIUM!
I repeat...
SEEMS YOU'D BETTER HURRY.
OMG!
You're right!
SORRY TO BUG YOU SO MUCH!
I'm going to check out what class I'm in!
THANK YOU VERY MUCH, SENPAI!
Heh.
DON'T TRIP ON YOUR WAY THERE.
TRIP
WHOOPS!

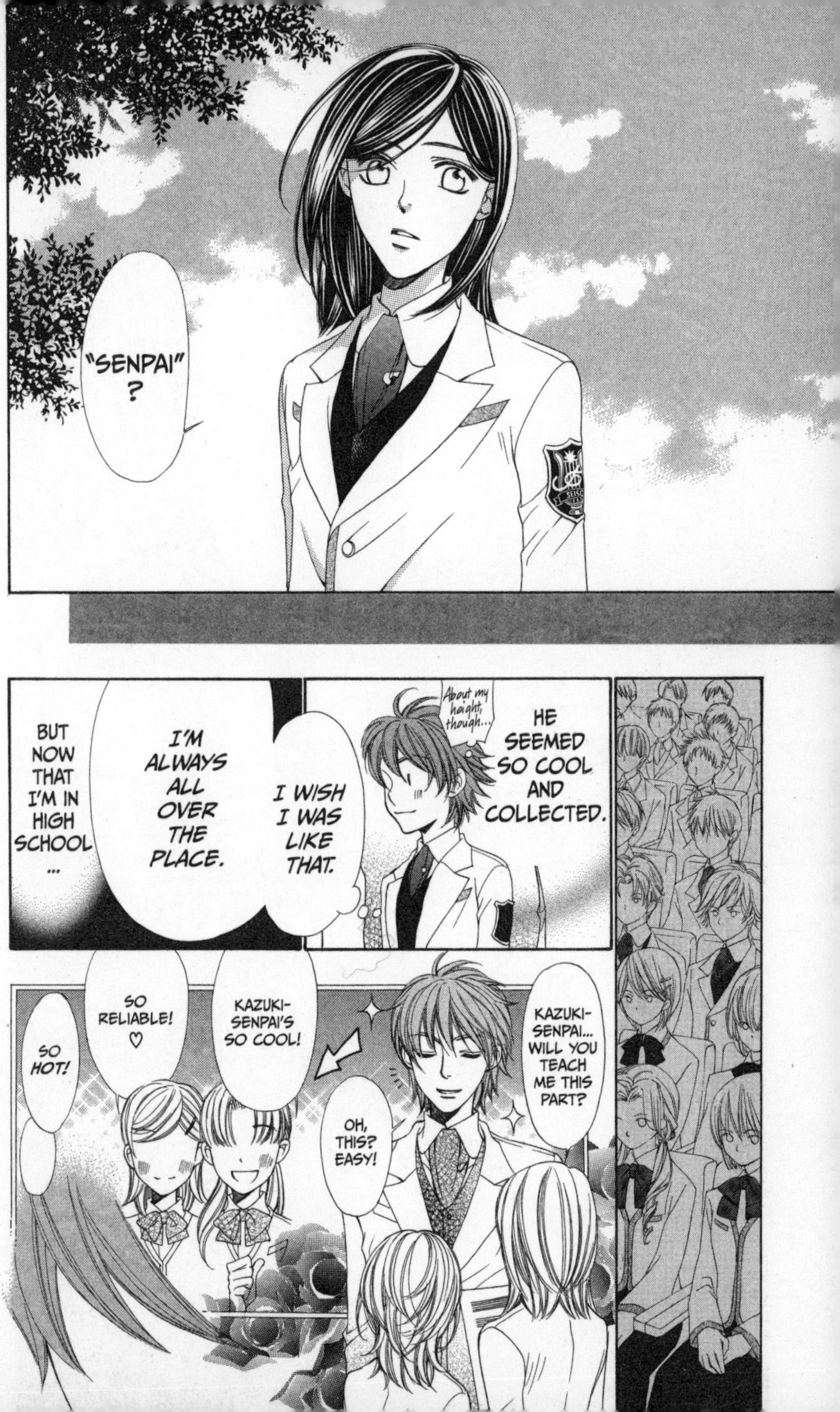
"SENPAI"?
HE SEEMED SO COOL AND COLLECTED.
About my height, though...
I WISH I WAS LIKE THAT.
I'M ALWAYS ALL OVER THE PLACE.
BUT NOW THAT I'M IN HIGH SCHOOL...
KAZUKI-SENPAI... WILL YOU TEACH ME THIS PART?
OH, THIS? EASY!
KAZUKI-SENPAI'S SO COOL!
SO RELIABLE! ♡
SO HOT!

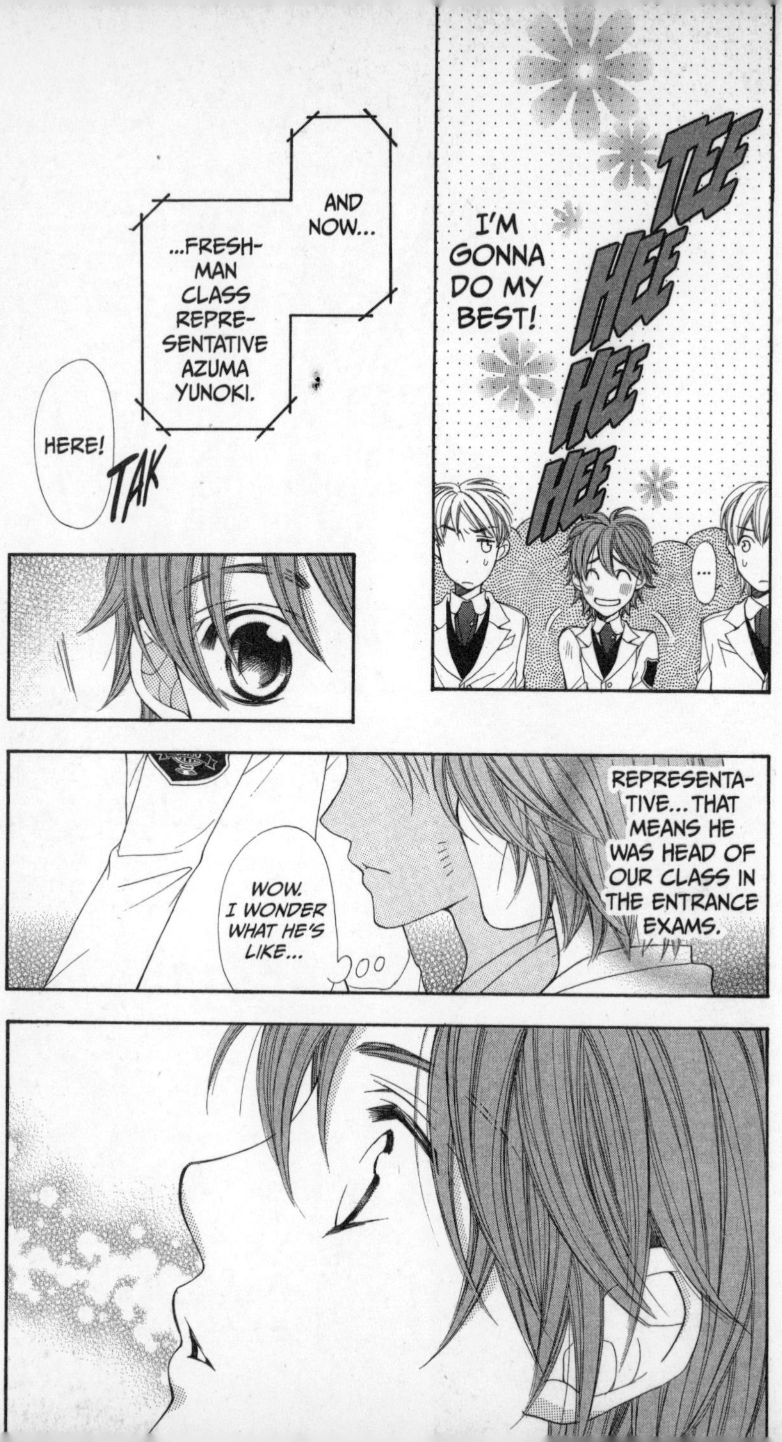
TEE HEE HEE HEE
I'M GONNA DO MY BEST!
...
AND NOW...
...FRESHMAN CLASS REPRESENTATIVE AZUMA YUNOKI.
HERE!
TAK
REPRESENTATIVE... THAT MEANS HE WAS HEAD OF OUR CLASS IN THE ENTRANCE EXAMS.
WOW. I WONDER WHAT HE'S LIKE...

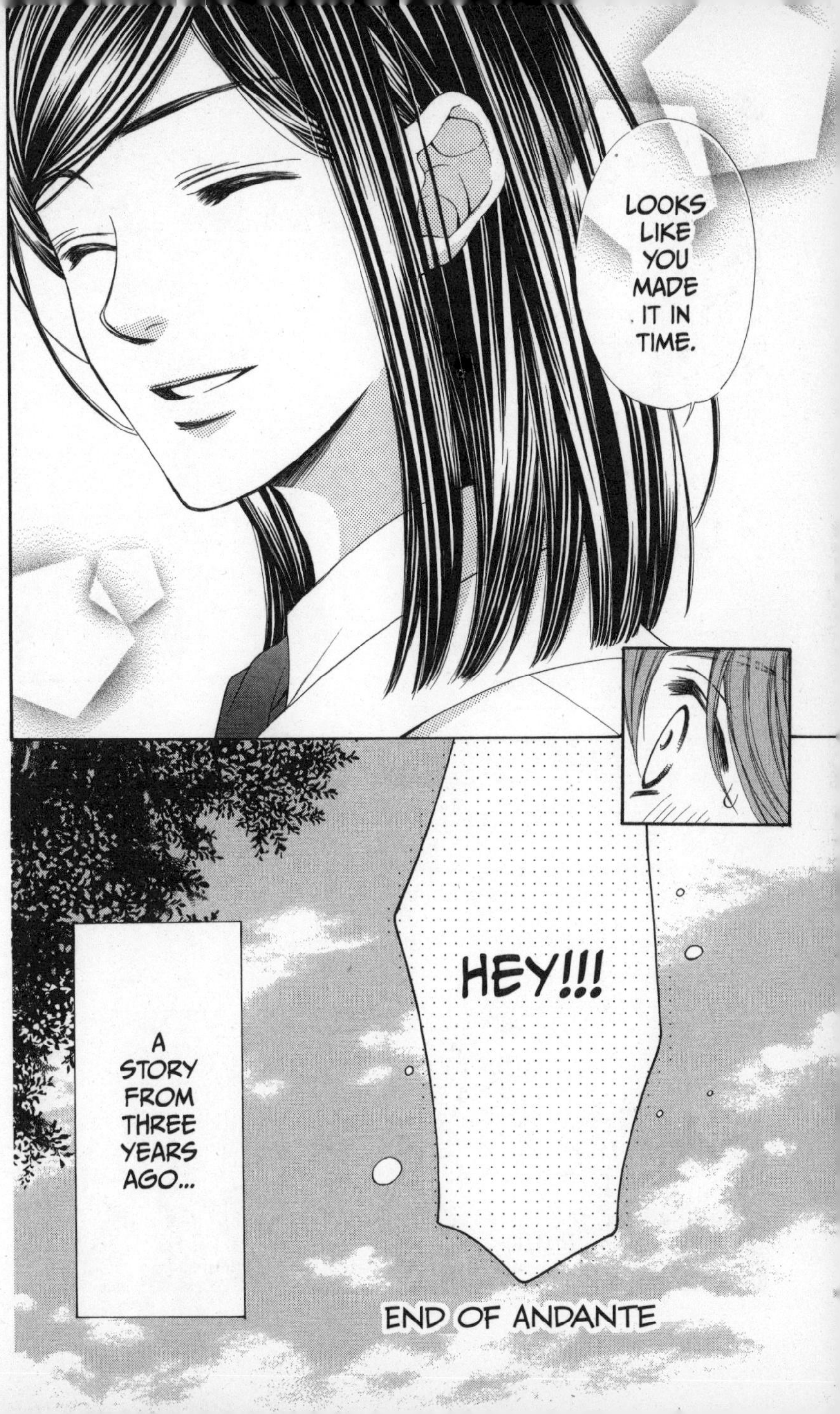
LOOKS LIKE YOU MADE IT IN TIME.
HEY!!!
A STORY FROM THREE YEARS AGO...
END OF ANDANTE

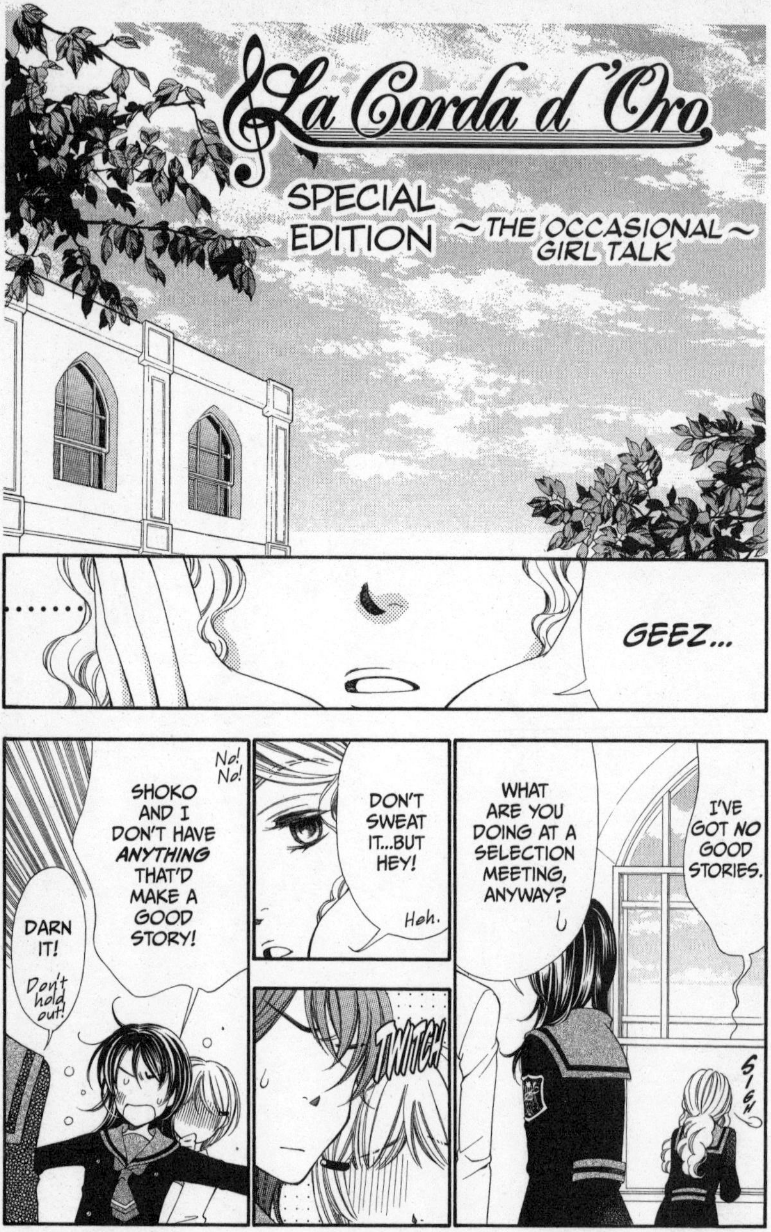
La Corda d'Oro
SPECIAL EDITION
~THE OCCASIONAL~ GIRL TALK
GEEZ...
......
I'VE GOT NO GOOD STORIES.
SIGH
WHAT ARE YOU DOING AT A SELECTION MEETING, ANYWAY?
DON'T SWEAT IT...BUT HEY!
Heh.
TWITCH
No! No!
SHOKO AND I DON'T HAVE ANYTHING THAT'D MAKE A GOOD STORY!
DARN IT!
Don't hold out!

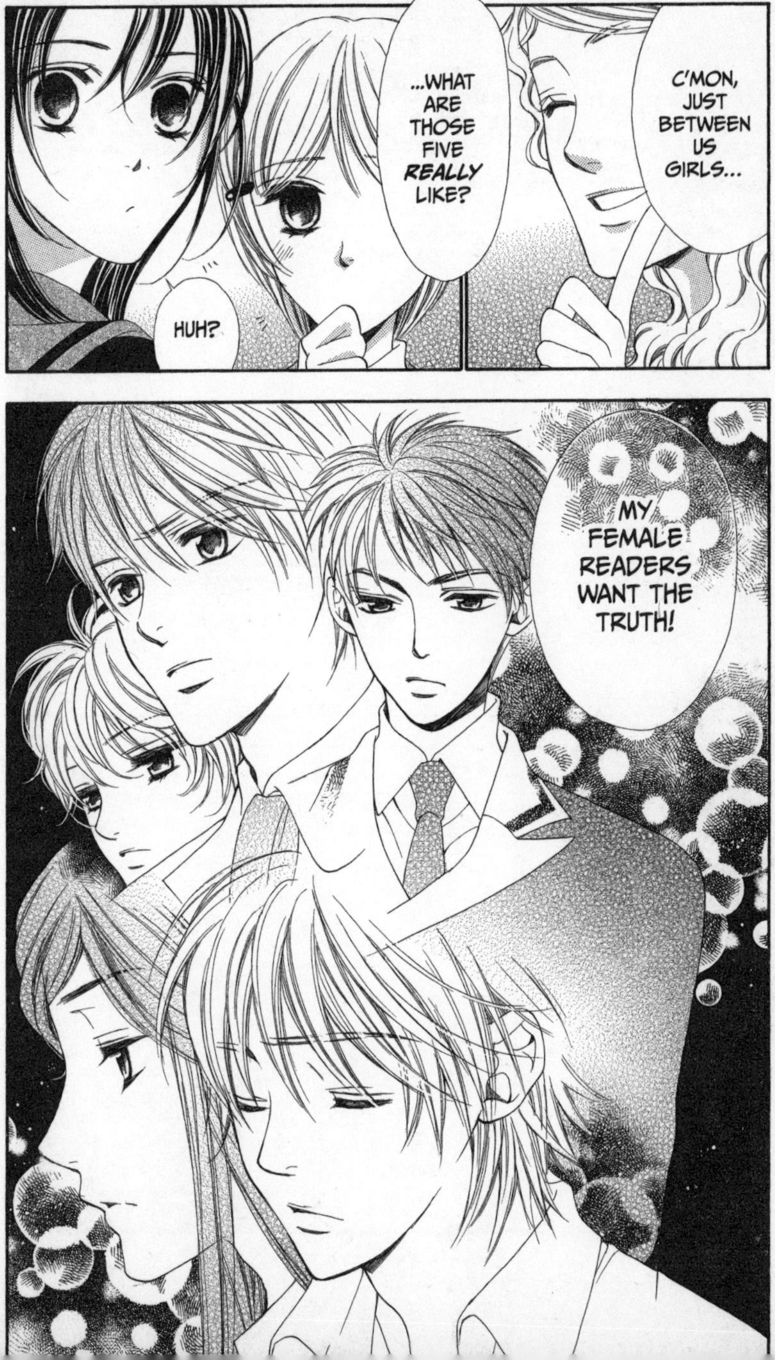
C'MON, JUST BETWEEN US GIRLS...
...WHAT ARE THOSE FIVE *REALLY* LIKE?
HUH?
MY FEMALE READERS WANT THE TRUTH!

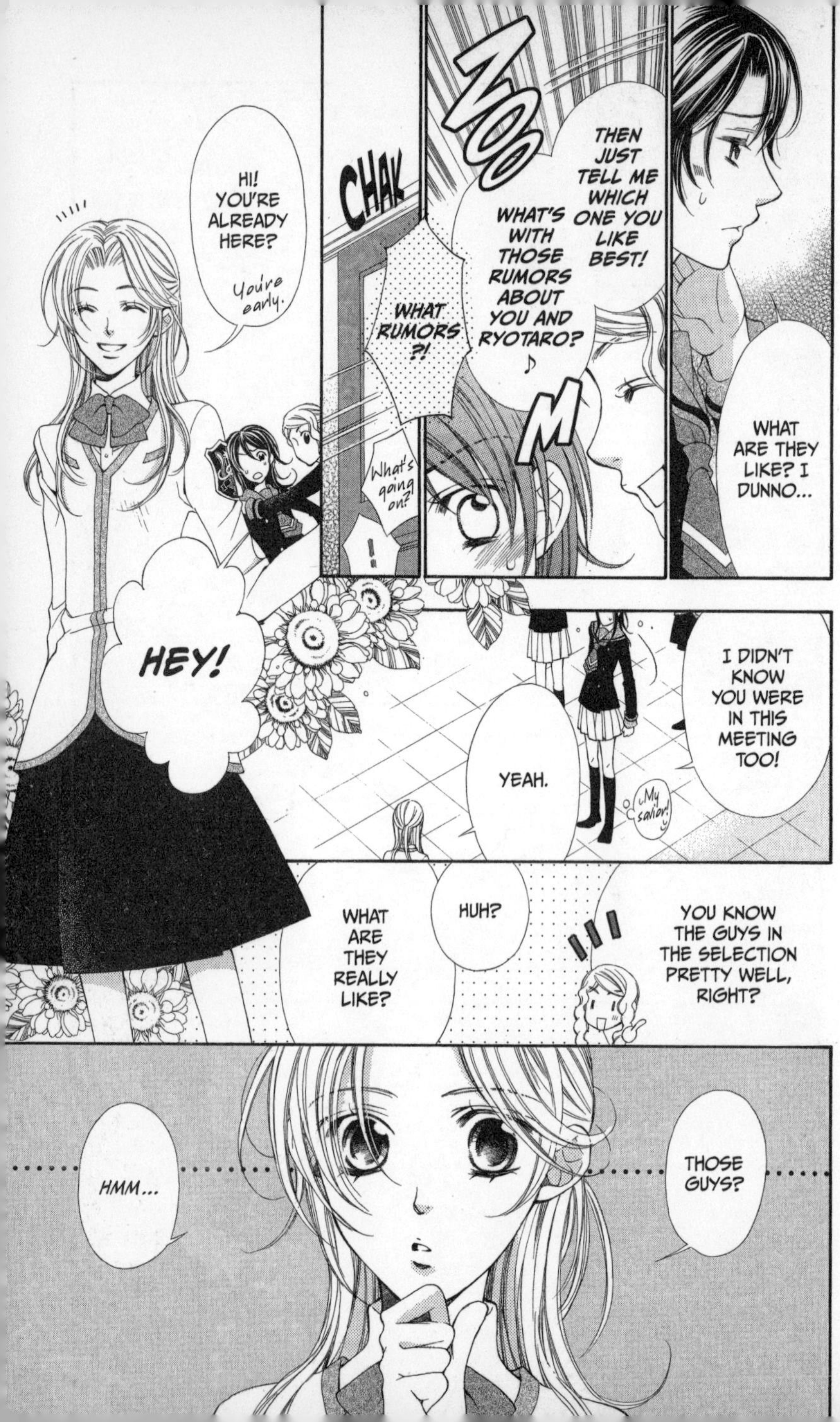
THEN JUST TELL ME WHICH ONE YOU LIKE BEST!
WHAT ARE THEY LIKE? I DUNNO...
NOO
WHAT'S WITH THOSE RUMORS ABOUT YOU AND RYOTARO? ♪
M
CHAK
WHAT RUMORS ?!
What's going on?!
!
I DIDN'T KNOW YOU WERE IN THIS MEETING TOO!
YEAH.
My savior!
YOU KNOW THE GUYS IN THE SELECTION PRETTY WELL, RIGHT?
HUH?
WHAT ARE THEY REALLY LIKE?
HI! YOU'RE ALREADY HERE?
You're early.
HEY!
THOSE GUYS?
HMM...

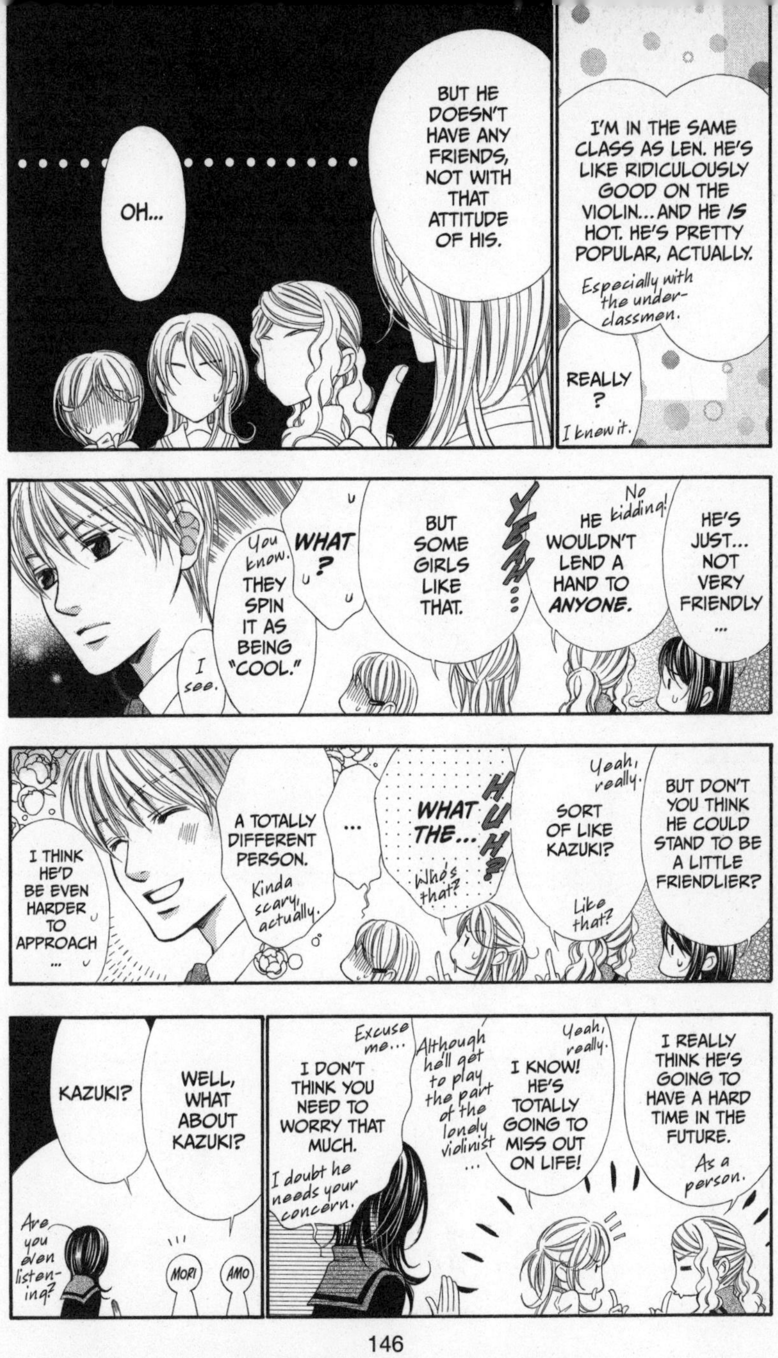
I'M IN THE SAME CLASS AS LEN. HE'S LIKE RIDICULOUSLY GOOD ON THE VIOLIN... AND HE *IS* HOT. HE'S PRETTY POPULAR, ACTUALLY.
Especially with the underclassmen.
REALLY?
I knew it.
BUT HE DOESN'T HAVE ANY FRIENDS, NOT WITH THAT ATTITUDE OF HIS.
OH...
....
HE'S JUST... NOT VERY FRIENDLY...
HE WOULDN'T LEND A HAND TO *ANYONE.*
No kidding!
YEAH...
BUT SOME GIRLS LIKE THAT.
WHAT?
THEY SPIN IT AS BEING "COOL."
You know.
I see.
BUT DON'T YOU THINK HE COULD STAND TO BE A LITTLE FRIENDLIER?
Yeah, really.
SORT OF LIKE KAZUKI?
Like that?
HUH?
WHAT THE...
Who's that?
...
A TOTALLY DIFFERENT PERSON.
Kinda scary, actually.
I THINK HE'D BE EVEN HARDER TO APPROACH...
I REALLY THINK HE'S GOING TO HAVE A HARD TIME IN THE FUTURE.
As a person.
I KNOW! HE'S TOTALLY GOING TO MISS OUT ON LIFE!
Yeah, really.
Although he'll get to play the part of the lonely violinist...
I DON'T THINK YOU NEED TO WORRY THAT MUCH.
Excuse me...
I doubt he needs your concern.
WELL, WHAT ABOUT KAZUKI?
KAZUKI?
MORI
AMO
Are you even listening?

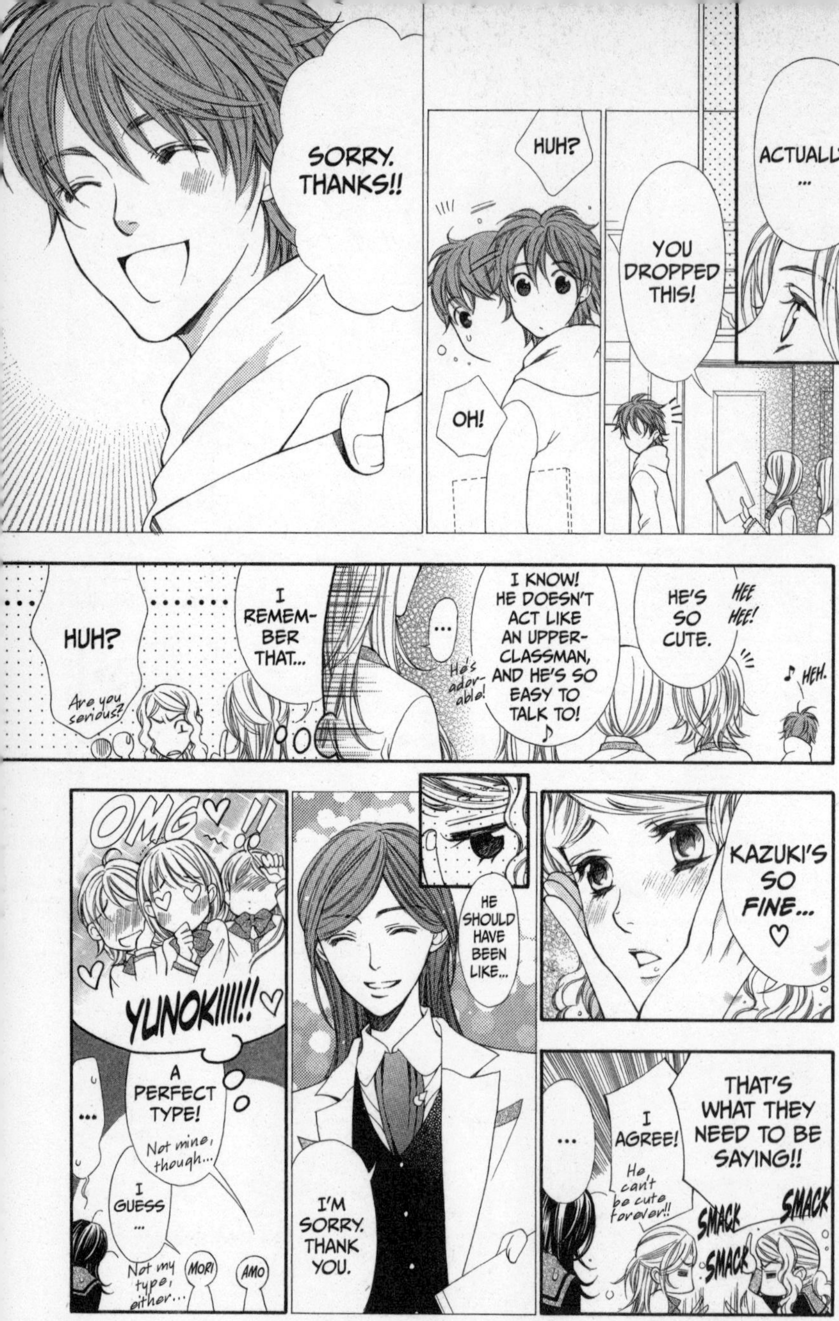
ACTUALLY ...
YOU DROPPED THIS!
HUH?
OH!
SORRY. THANKS!!
HEE HEE!
♪ HEH.
HE'S SO CUTE.
I KNOW! HE DOESN'T ACT LIKE AN UPPER-CLASSMAN, AND HE'S SO EASY TO TALK TO! ♪
He's adorable!
...
I REMEMBER THAT...
HUH?
Are you serious?
KAZUKI'S SO FINE... ♡
THAT'S WHAT THEY NEED TO BE SAYING!!
I AGREE!
He can't be cute forever!!
...
SMACK
SMACK
SMACK
HE SHOULD HAVE BEEN LIKE...
I'M SORRY. THANK YOU.
OMG♡!!
YUNOKIIIII!!
A PERFECT TYPE!
Not mine, though...
I GUESS ...
Not my type, either...
MORI
AMO
...

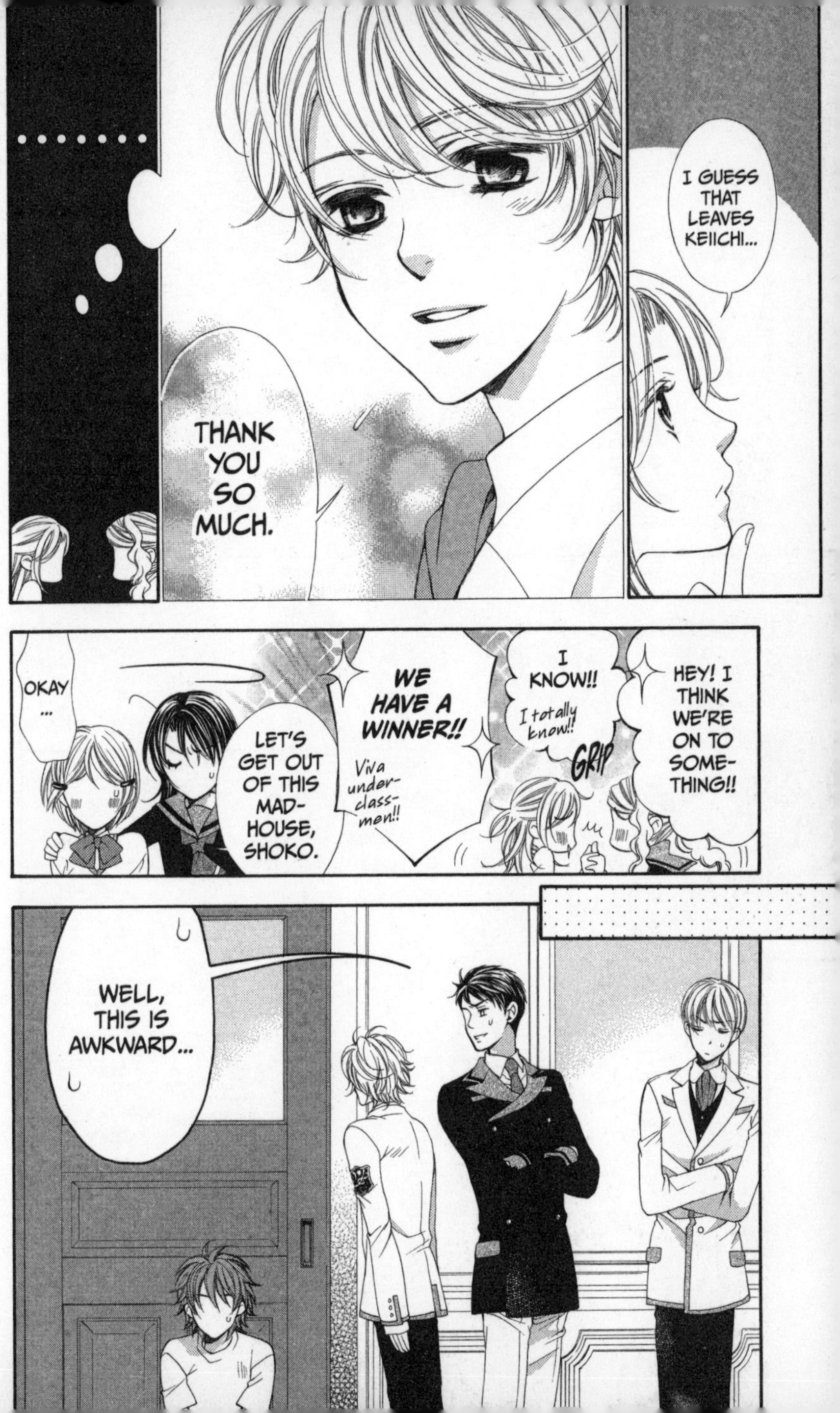
I GUESS THAT LEAVES KEIICHI...
THANK YOU SO MUCH.
....
HEY! I THINK WE'RE ON TO SOME-THING!!
I KNOW!!
I totally know!!
GRIP
WE HAVE A WINNER!!
Viva under-class-men!!
LET'S GET OUT OF THIS MAD-HOUSE, SHOKO.
OKAY...
WELL, THIS IS AWKWARD...

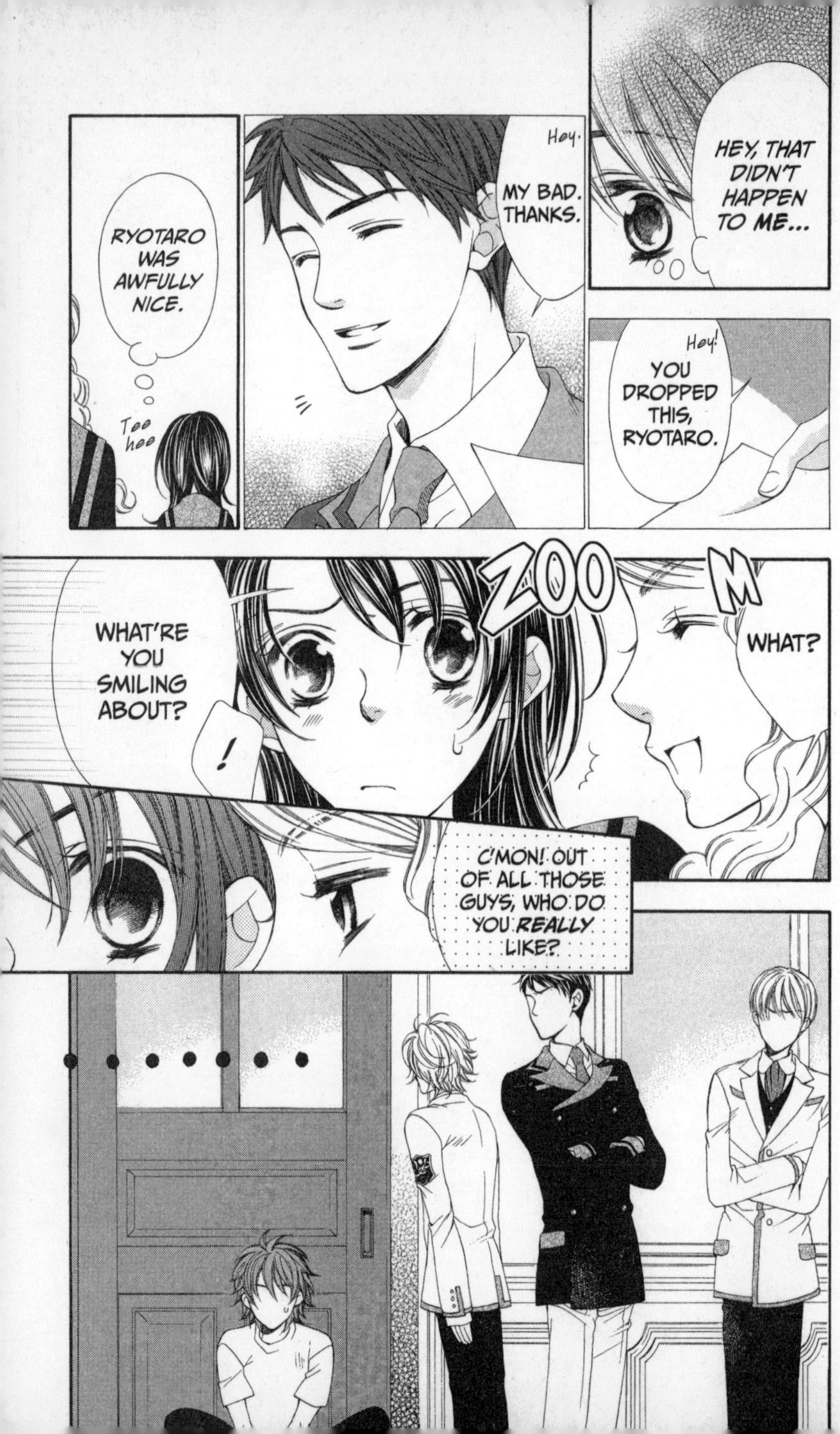
HEY, THAT DIDN'T HAPPEN TO ME...
Hey!
YOU DROPPED THIS, RYOTARO.
Hey.
MY BAD. THANKS.
RYOTARO WAS AWFULLY NICE.
Tee hee
ZOOM
WHAT?
WHAT'RE YOU SMILING ABOUT?
!
C'MON! OUT OF ALL THOSE GUYS, WHO DO YOU REALLY LIKE?
....

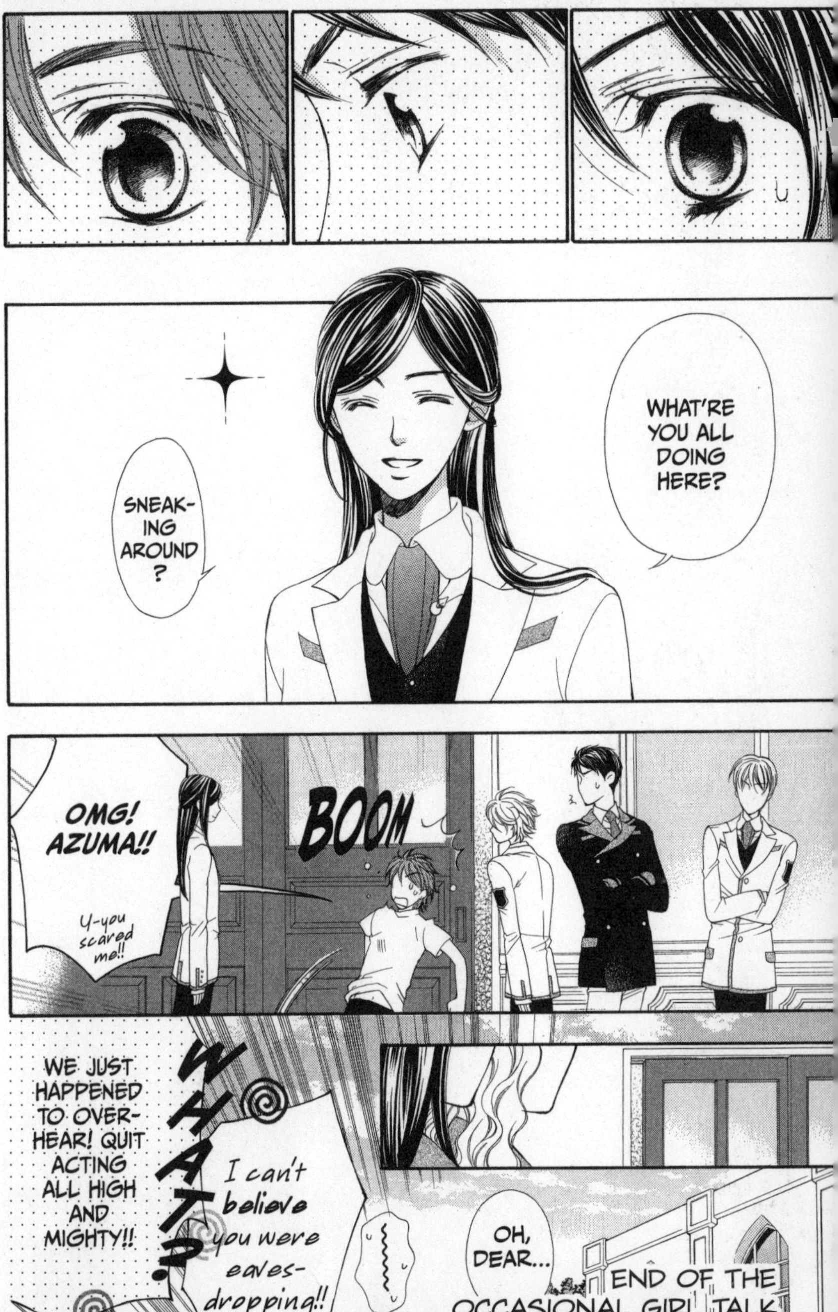
WHAT'RE YOU ALL DOING HERE?
SNEAKING AROUND?
BOOM
OMG! AZUMA!!
Y-you scared me!!
OH, DEAR...
END OF THE OCCASIONAL GIRL TALK
WHAT?
WE JUST HAPPENED TO OVERHEAR! QUIT ACTING ALL HIGH AND MIGHTY!!
I can't believe you were eavesdropping!!

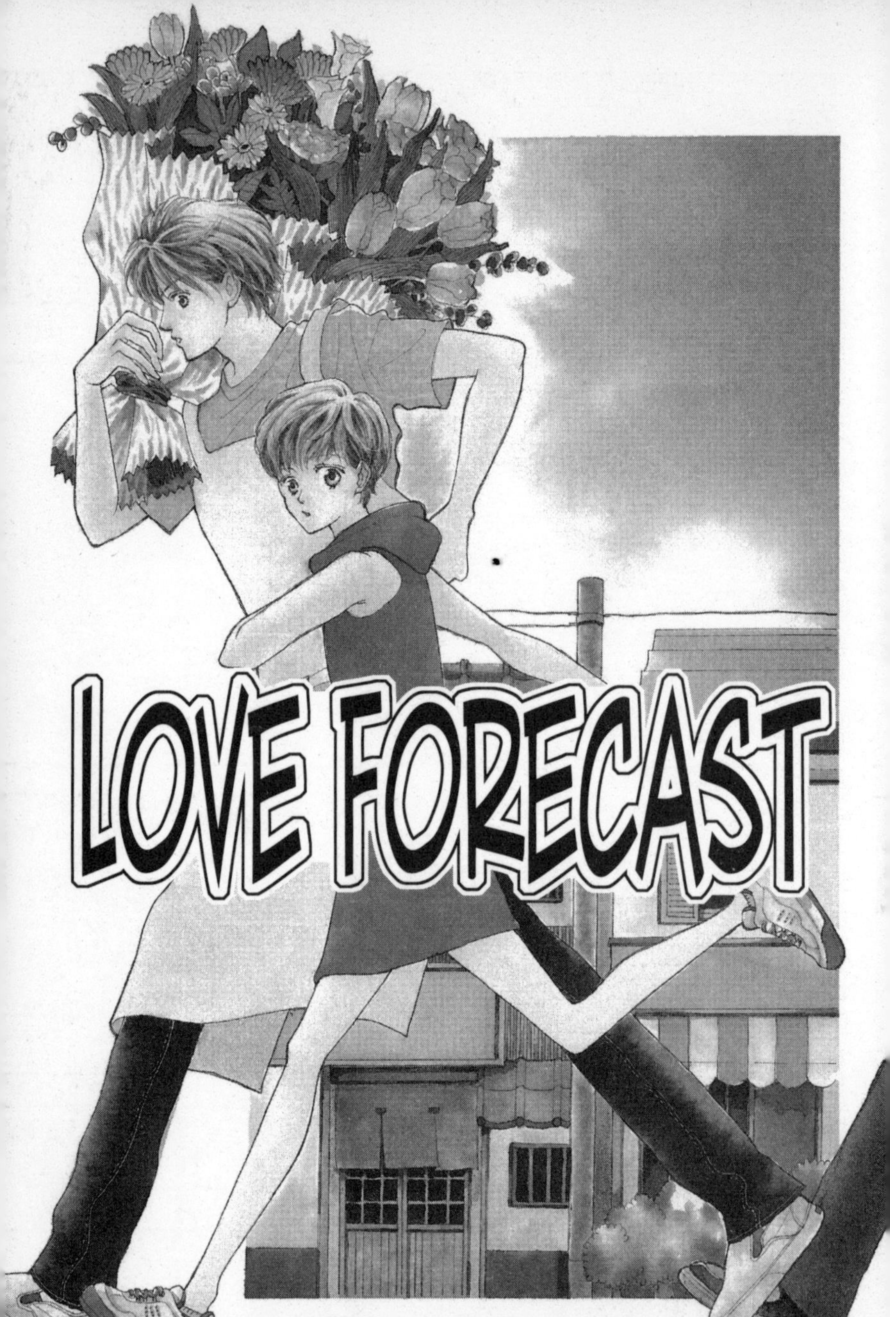
LOVE FORECAST

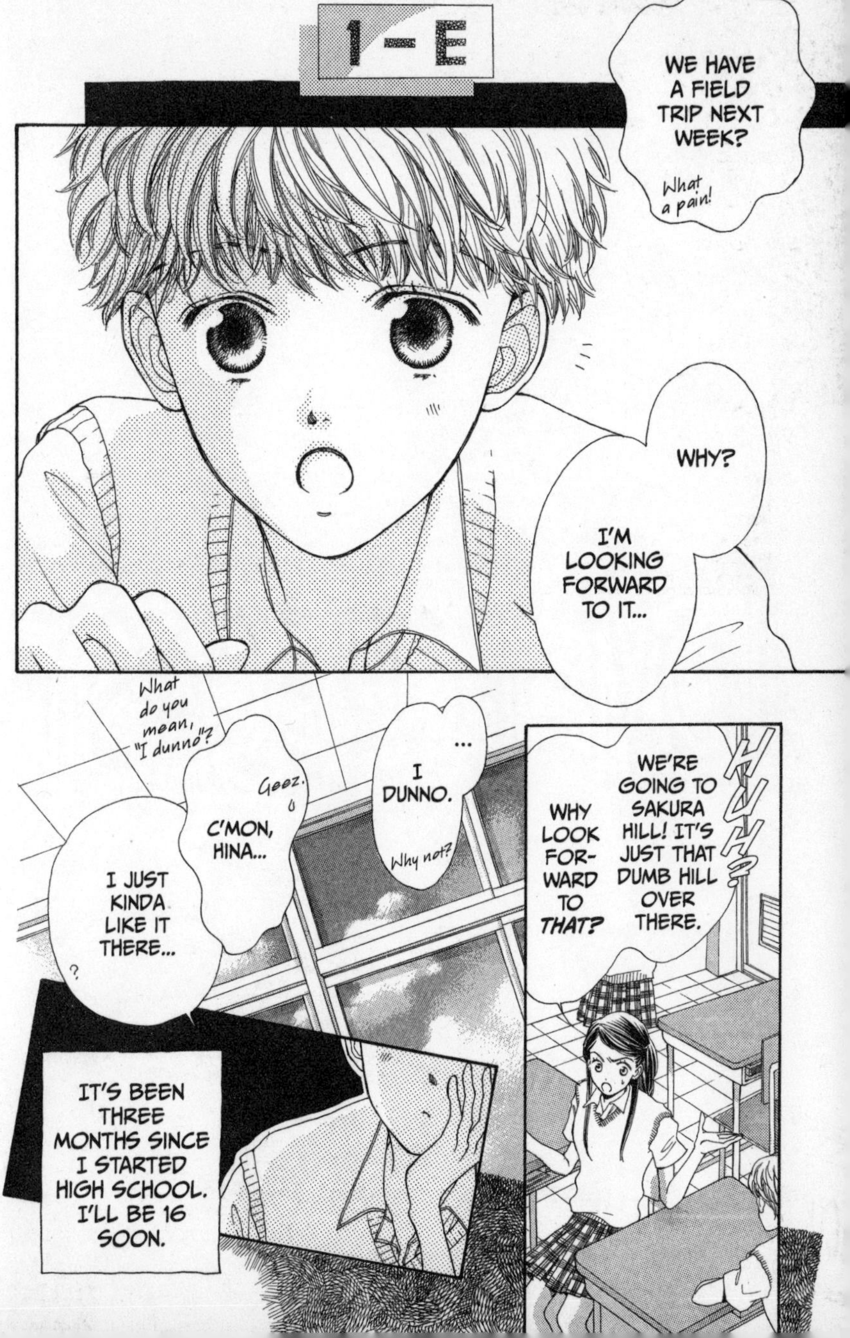
1-E
WE HAVE A FIELD TRIP NEXT WEEK?
What a pain!
WHY?
I'M LOOKING FORWARD TO IT...
HUH?
WE'RE GOING TO SAKURA HILL! IT'S JUST THAT DUMB HILL OVER THERE.
WHY LOOK FORWARD TO *THAT?*
... I DUNNO.
Why not?
C'MON, HINA...
Geez.
What do you mean, "I dunno"?
I JUST KINDA LIKE IT THERE...
?
IT'S BEEN THREE MONTHS SINCE I STARTED HIGH SCHOOL. I'LL BE 16 SOON.

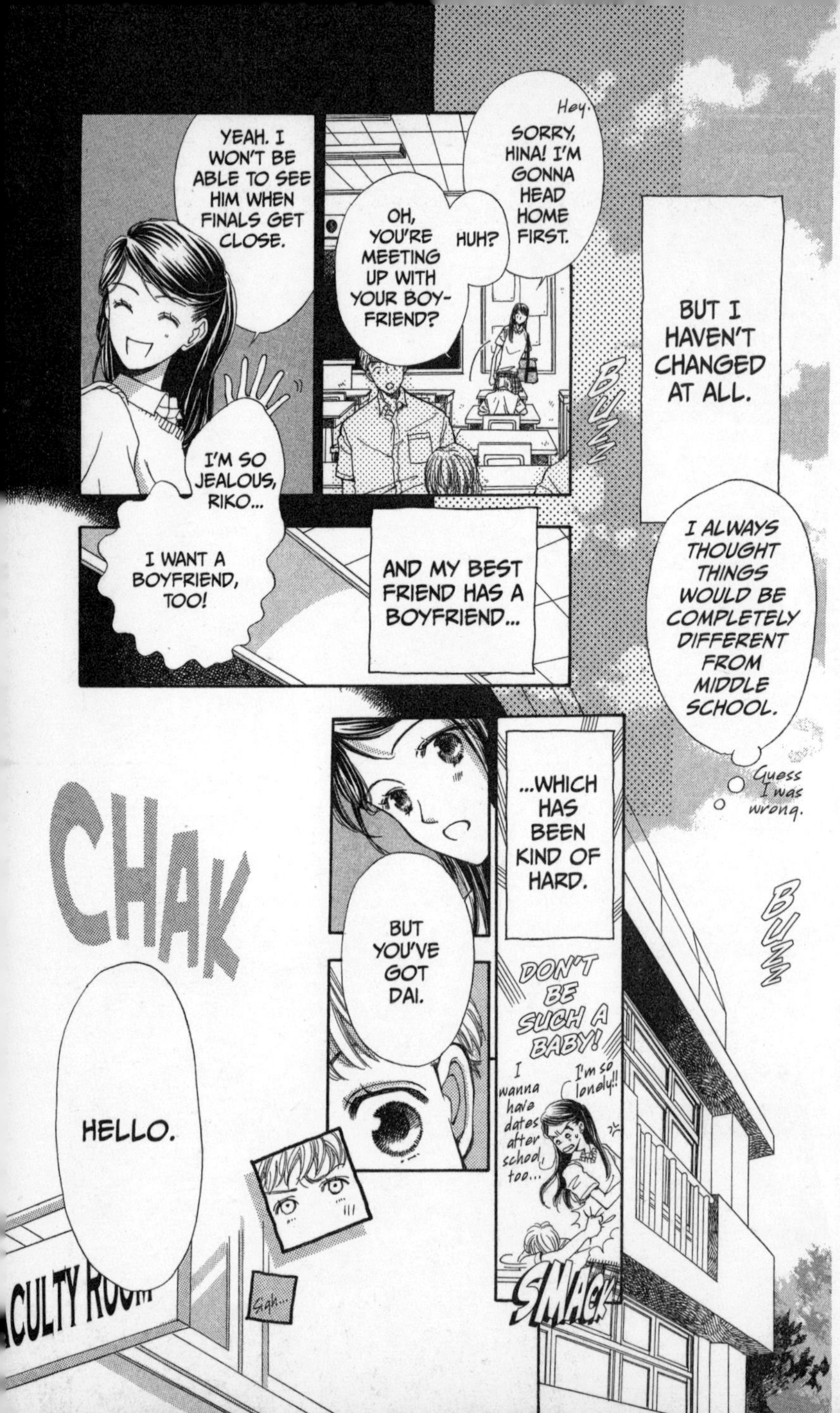

Hey.
SORRY, HINA! I'M GONNA HEAD HOME FIRST.
HUH?
OH, YOU'RE MEETING UP WITH YOUR BOY-FRIEND?
YEAH. I WON'T BE ABLE TO SEE HIM WHEN FINALS GET CLOSE.
I'M SO JEALOUS, RIKO...
I WANT A BOYFRIEND, TOO!
AND MY BEST FRIEND HAS A BOYFRIEND...
BUT I HAVEN'T CHANGED AT ALL.
BUZZ
I ALWAYS THOUGHT THINGS WOULD BE COMPLETELY DIFFERENT FROM MIDDLE SCHOOL.
Guess I was wrong.
...WHICH HAS BEEN KIND OF HARD.
BUZZ
DON'T BE SUCH A BABY!
I'm so lonely!!
I wanna have dates after school, too...
SMACK
BUT YOU'VE GOT DAI.
CHAK
HELLO.
Sigh...

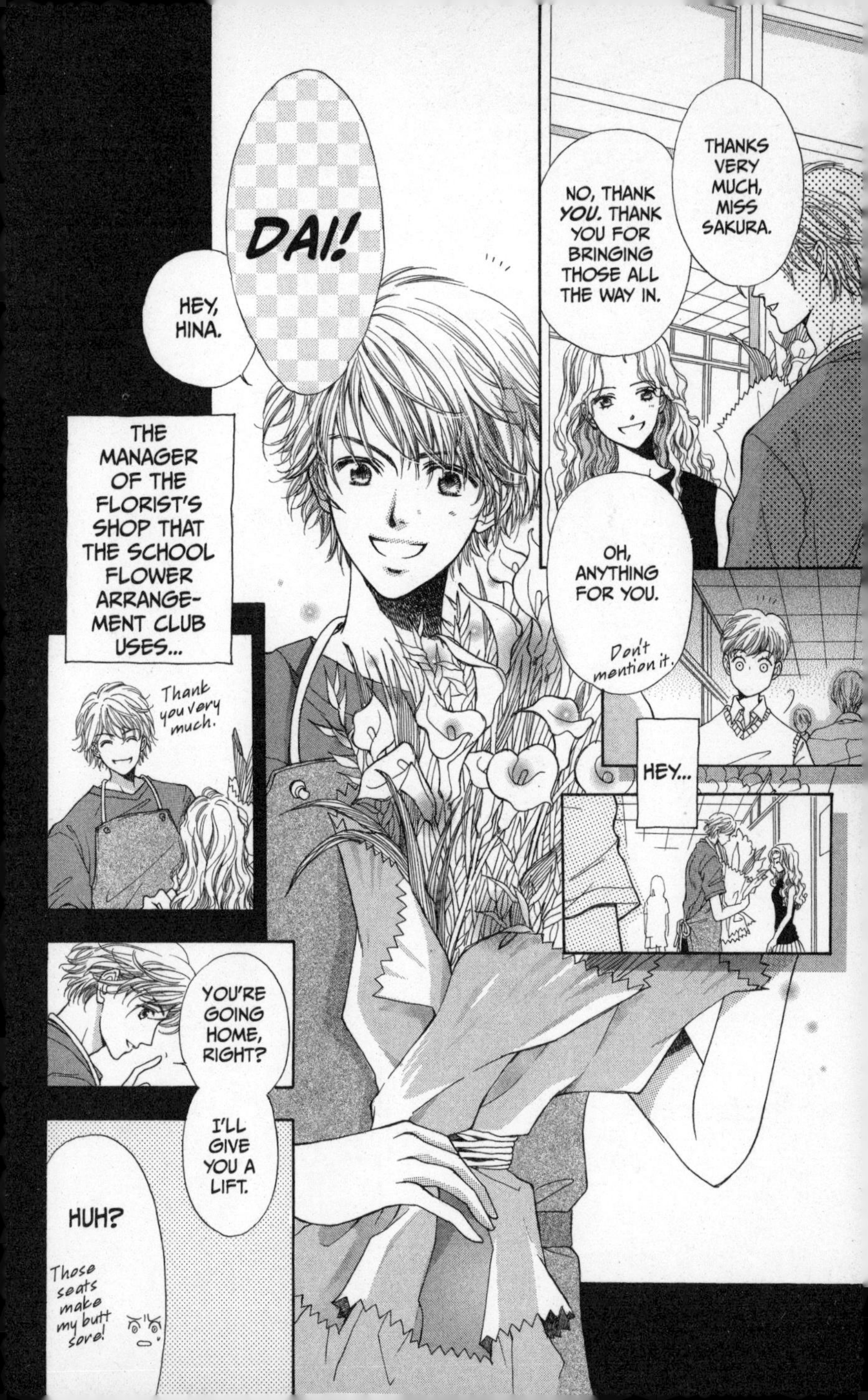
THANKS VERY MUCH, MISS SAKURA.
NO, THANK *YOU*. THANK YOU FOR BRINGING THOSE ALL THE WAY IN.
OH, ANYTHING FOR YOU.
Don't mention it.
HEY...
DAI!
HEY, HINA.
THE MANAGER OF THE FLORIST'S SHOP THAT THE SCHOOL FLOWER ARRANGE-MENT CLUB USES...
Thank you very much.
YOU'RE GOING HOME, RIGHT?
I'LL GIVE YOU A LIFT.
HUH?
Those seats make my butt sore!

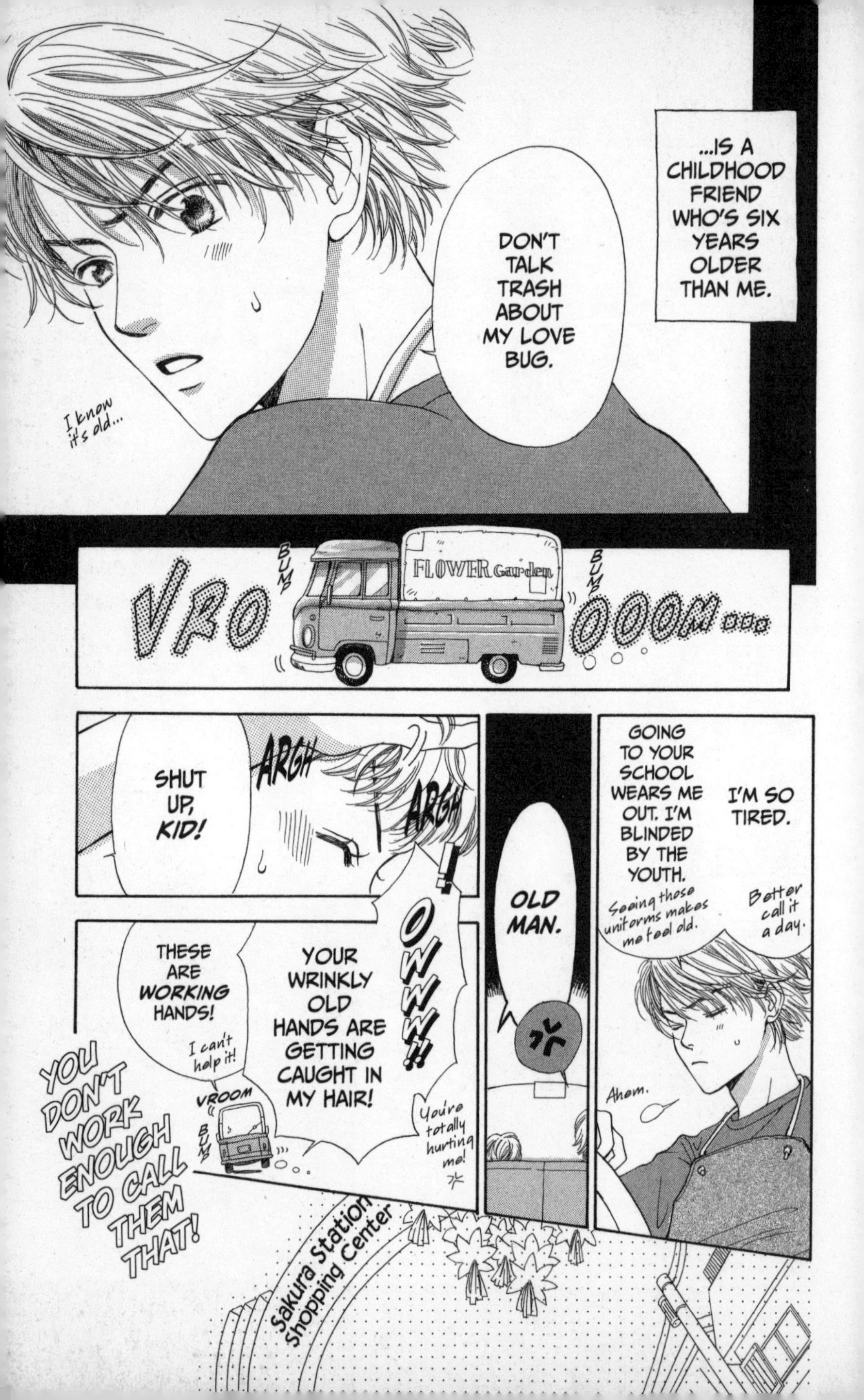
...IS A CHILDHOOD FRIEND WHO'S SIX YEARS OLDER THAN ME.
DON'T TALK TRASH ABOUT MY LOVE BUG.
I know it's old...
FLOWER Garden
BUMP
BUMP
VROOOOOM...
I'M SO TIRED.
GOING TO YOUR SCHOOL WEARS ME OUT. I'M BLINDED BY THE YOUTH.
Better call it a day.
Seeing those uniforms makes me feel old.
Ahem.
OLD MAN.
ARGH
ARGH
SHUT UP, KID!
!
OWWW!!
YOUR WRINKLY OLD HANDS ARE GETTING CAUGHT IN MY HAIR!
You're totally hurting me!
THESE ARE WORKING HANDS!
I can't help it!
VROOM
BUMP
YOU DON'T WORK ENOUGH TO CALL THEM THAT!
Sakura Station Shopping Center

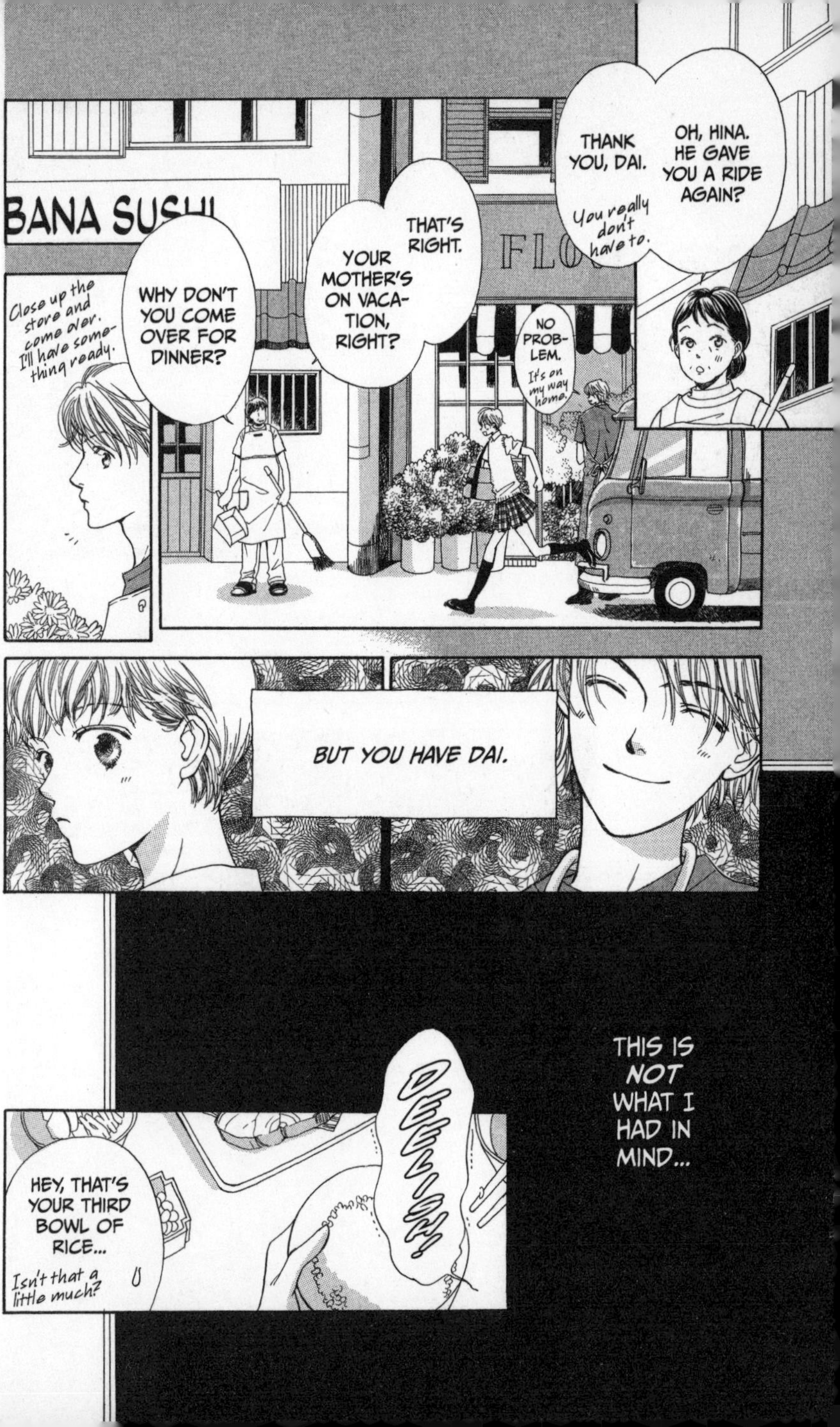
OH, HINA. HE GAVE YOU A RIDE AGAIN?
THANK YOU, DAI.
You really don't have to.
NO PROBLEM.
It's on my way home.
THAT'S RIGHT.
YOUR MOTHER'S ON VACATION, RIGHT?
WHY DON'T YOU COME OVER FOR DINNER?
Close up the store and come over. I'll have something ready.
BUT YOU HAVE DAI.
THIS IS NOT WHAT I HAD IN MIND...
HEY, THAT'S YOUR THIRD BOWL OF RICE...
Isn't that a little much?

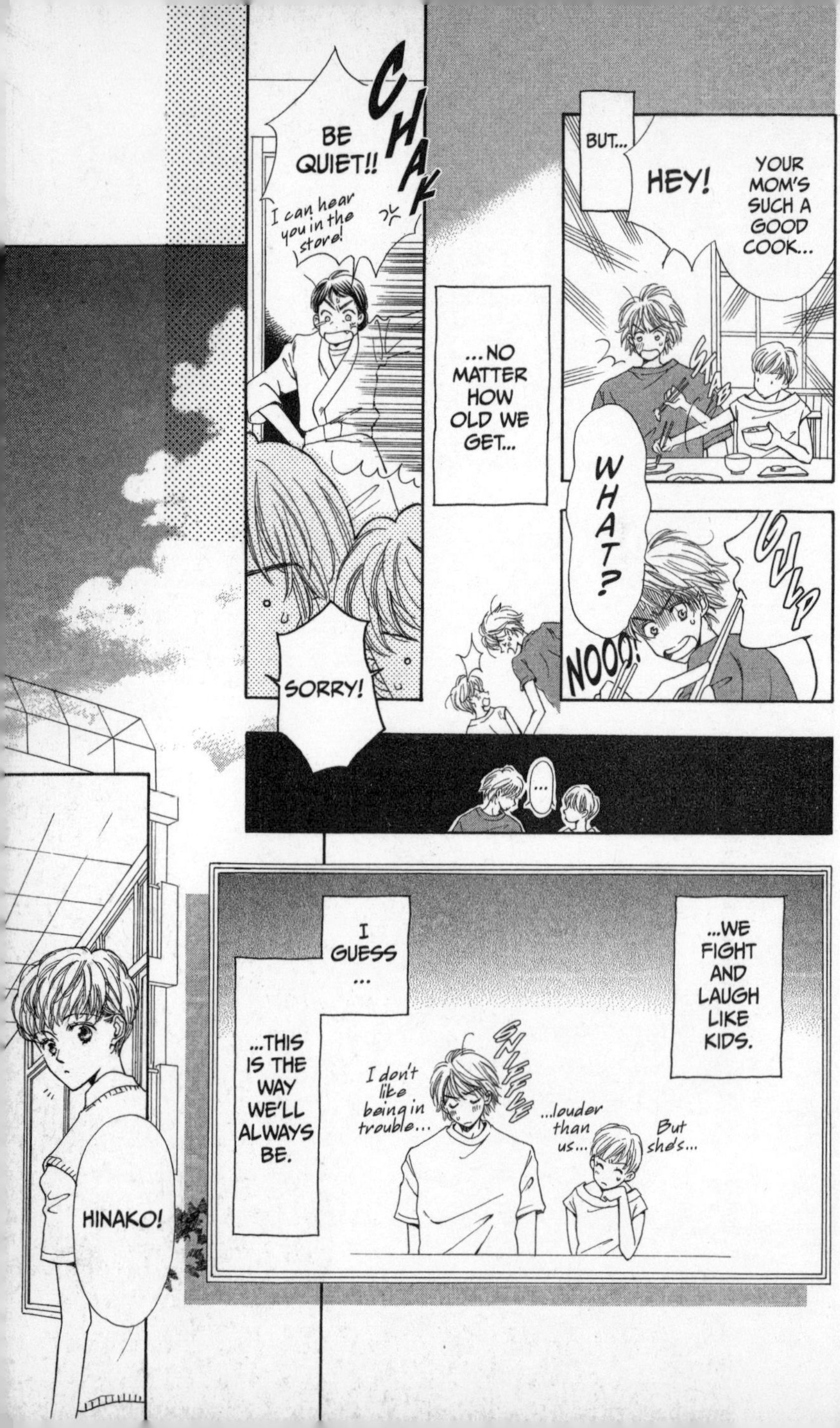
YOUR MOM'S SUCH A GOOD COOK...
BUT...
HEY!
WHAT?
NOOO!
...NO MATTER HOW OLD WE GET...
CHAK
BE QUIET!!
I can hear you in the store!
SORRY!
...
...WE FIGHT AND LAUGH LIKE KIDS.
I GUESS...
But she's...
...louder than us...
I don't like being in trouble...
...THIS IS THE WAY WE'LL ALWAYS BE.
HINAKO!

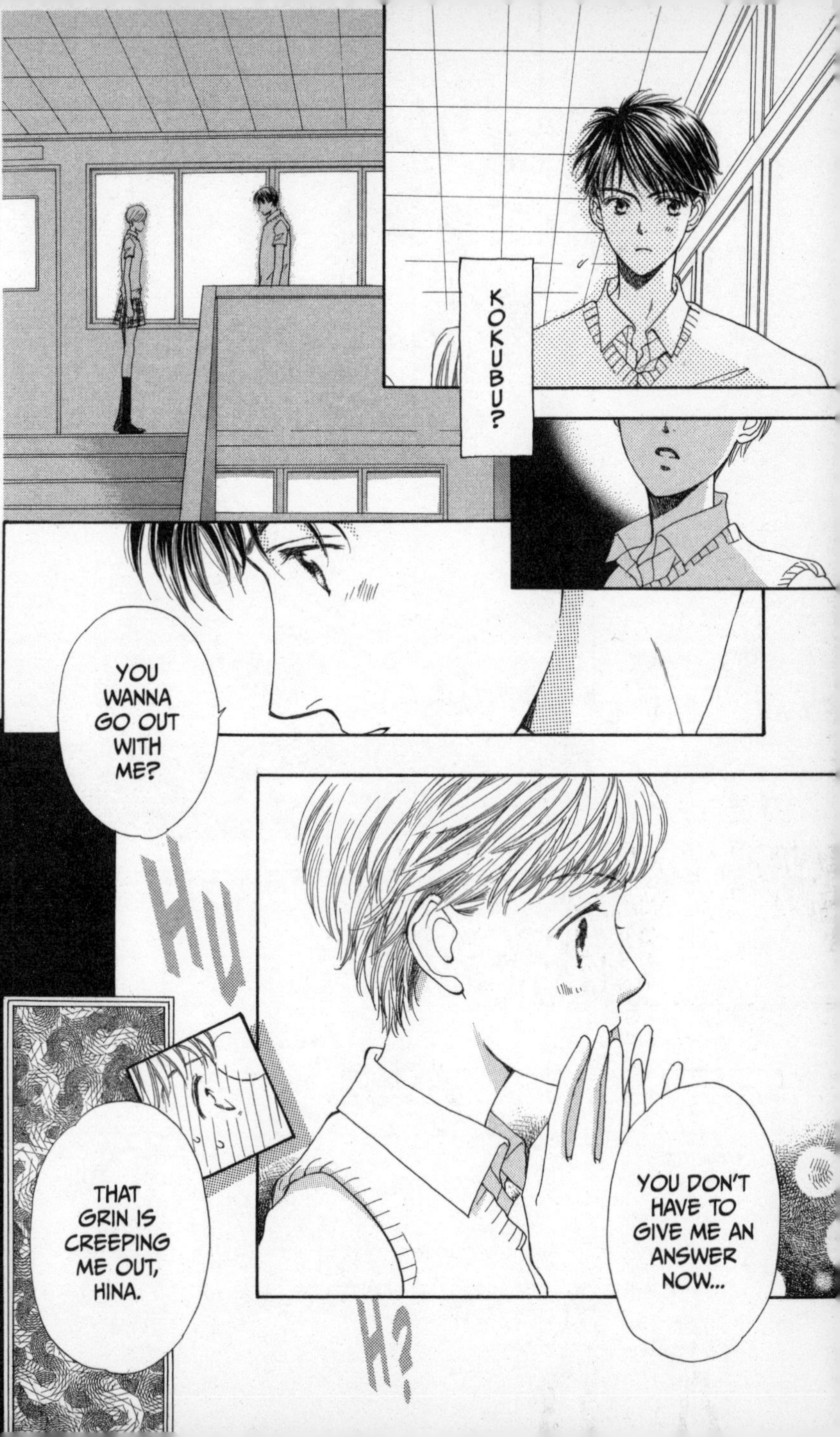
KOKUBU?
YOU WANNA GO OUT WITH ME?
HU
YOU DON'T HAVE TO GIVE ME AN ANSWER NOW...
THAT GRIN IS CREEPING ME OUT, HINA.
H?

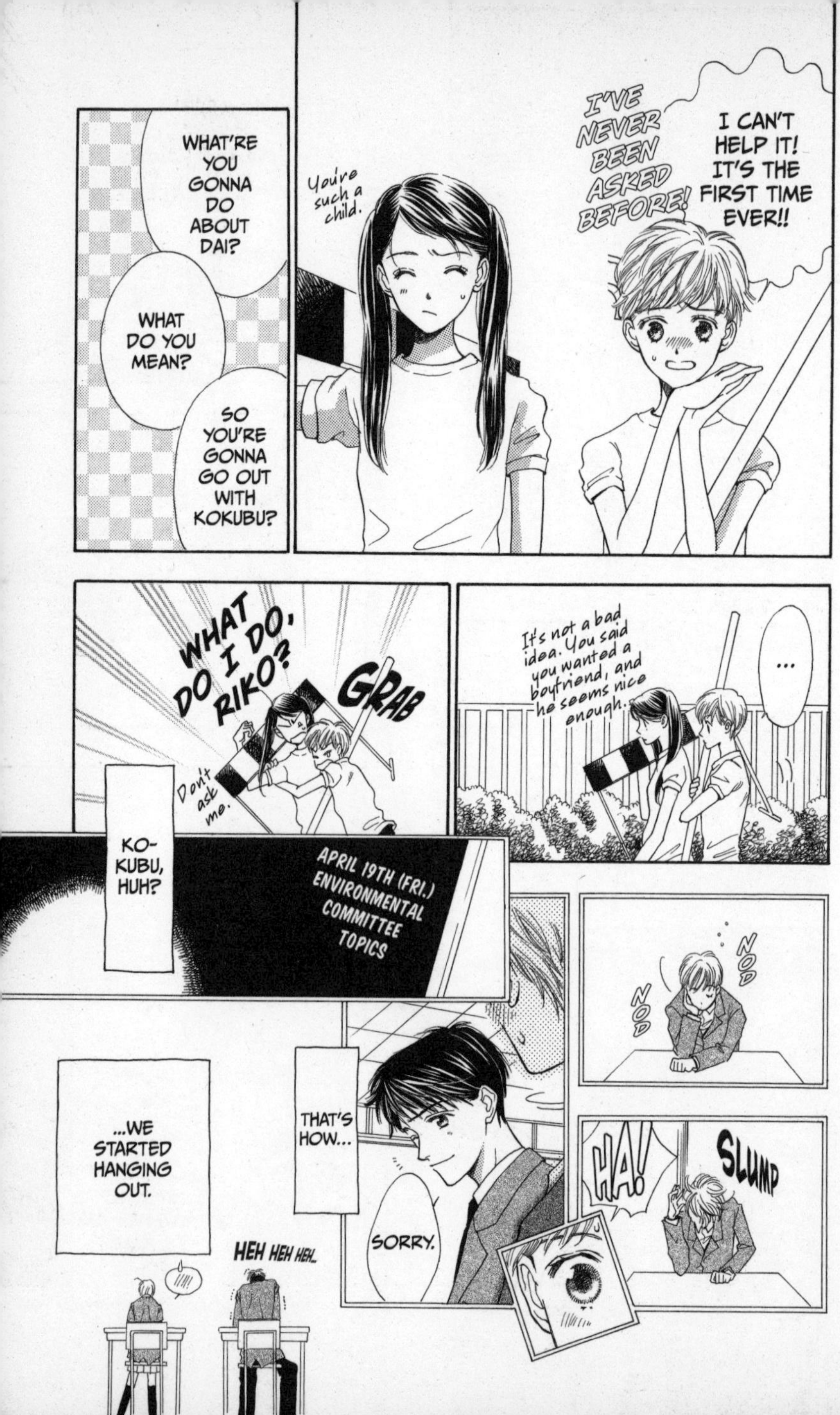
I'VE NEVER BEEN ASKED BEFORE!
I CAN'T HELP IT! IT'S THE FIRST TIME EVER!!
You're such a child.
WHAT'RE YOU GONNA DO ABOUT DAI?
WHAT DO YOU MEAN?
SO YOU'RE GONNA GO OUT WITH KOKUBU?
...
It's not a bad idea. You said you wanted a boyfriend, and he seems nice enough...
WHAT DO I DO, RIKO?
GRAB
Don't ask me.
KO-KUBU, HUH?
APRIL 19TH (FRI.) ENVIRONMENTAL COMMITTEE TOPICS
NOD NOD
HA!
SLUMP
THAT'S HOW...
SORRY.
...WE STARTED HANGING OUT.
HEH HEH HEH...

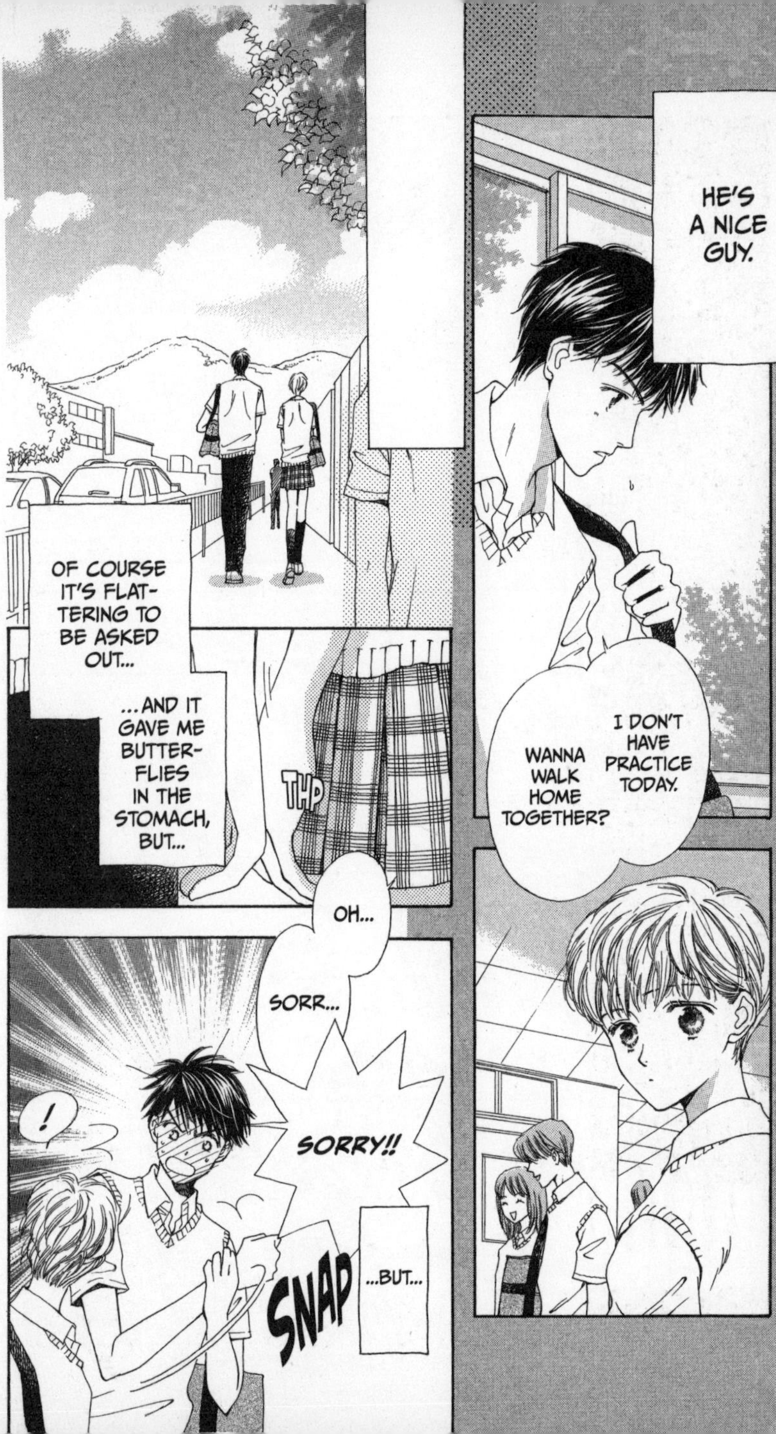
HE'S A NICE GUY.
I DON'T HAVE PRACTICE TODAY.
WANNA WALK HOME TOGETHER?
OF COURSE IT'S FLATTERING TO BE ASKED OUT...
...AND IT GAVE ME BUTTERFLIES IN THE STOMACH, BUT...
THP
OH...
SORR...
SORRY!!
!
SNAP
...BUT...

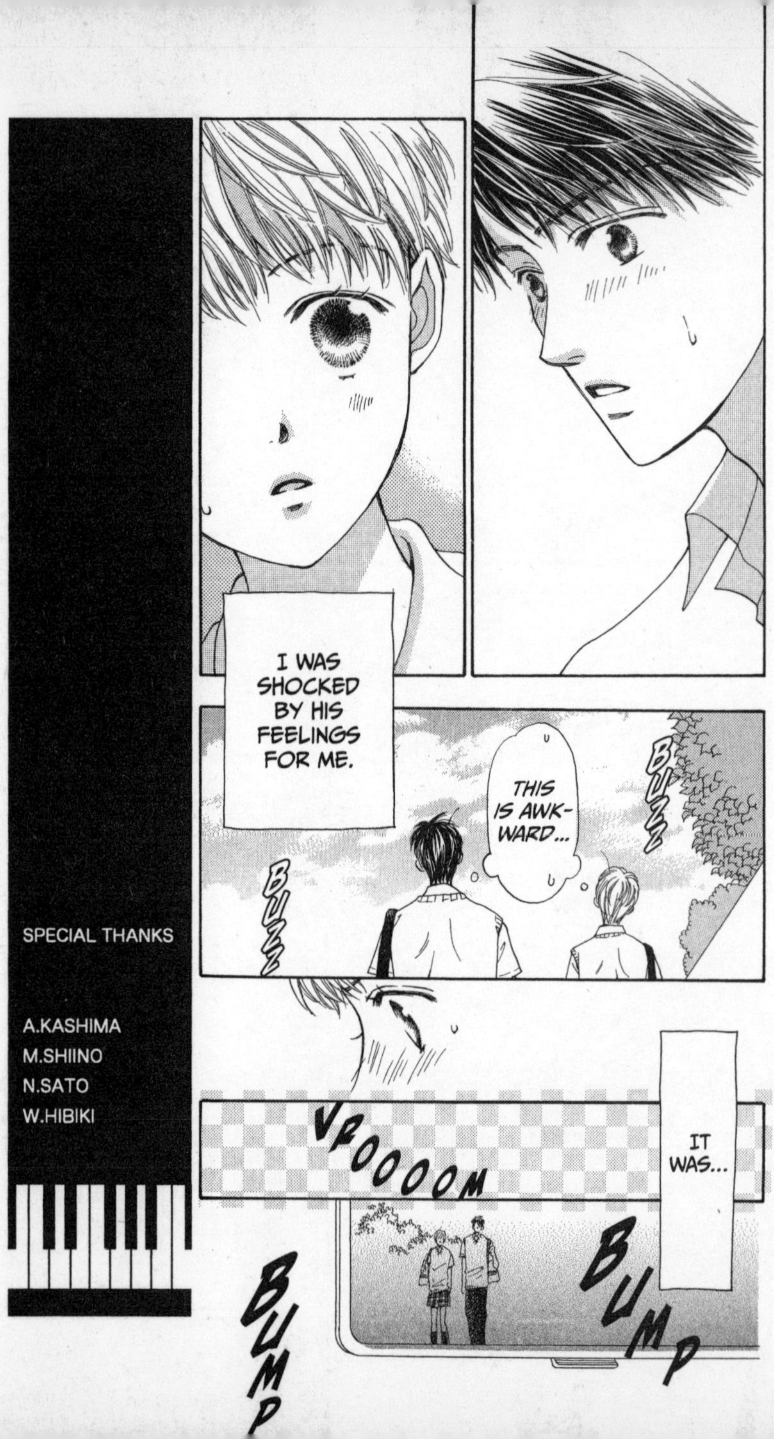
I WAS SHOCKED BY HIS FEELINGS FOR ME.
BUZZ
THIS IS AWK-WARD...
BUZZ
IT WAS...
VROOOOM
BUMP
BUMP

SPECIAL THANKS

A.KASHIMA
M.SHIINO
N.SATO
W.HIBIKI

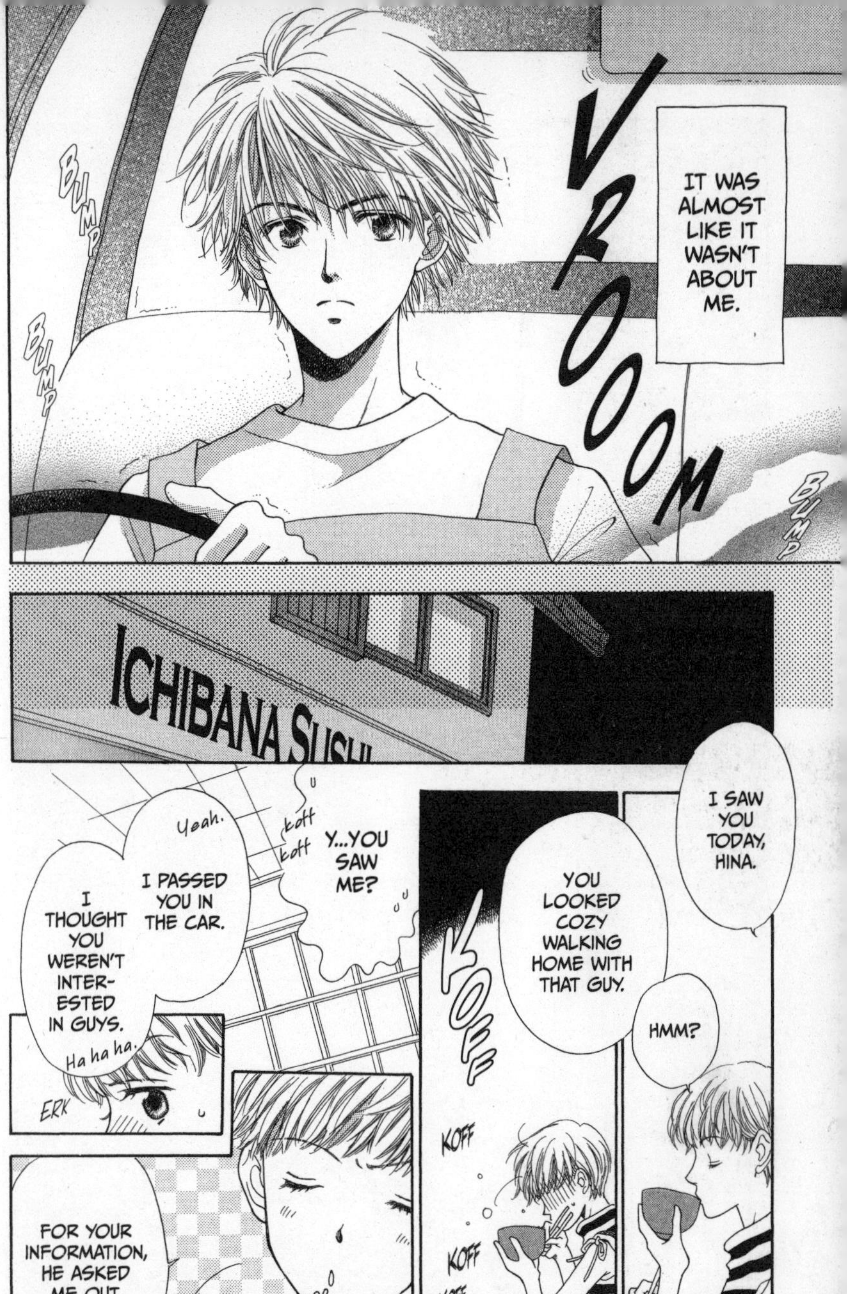
IT WAS ALMOST LIKE IT WASN'T ABOUT ME.
VROOOOM
BUMP
BUMP
BUMP
ICHIBANA SUSHI
I SAW YOU TODAY, HINA.
HMM?
YOU LOOKED COZY WALKING HOME WITH THAT GUY.
KOFF
KOFF
KOFF
KOFF
koff koff
Y...YOU SAW ME?
Yeah.
I PASSED YOU IN THE CAR.
I THOUGHT YOU WEREN'T INTER-ESTED IN GUYS.
Ha ha ha.
ERK
FOR YOUR INFORMATION, HE ASKED ME OUT.

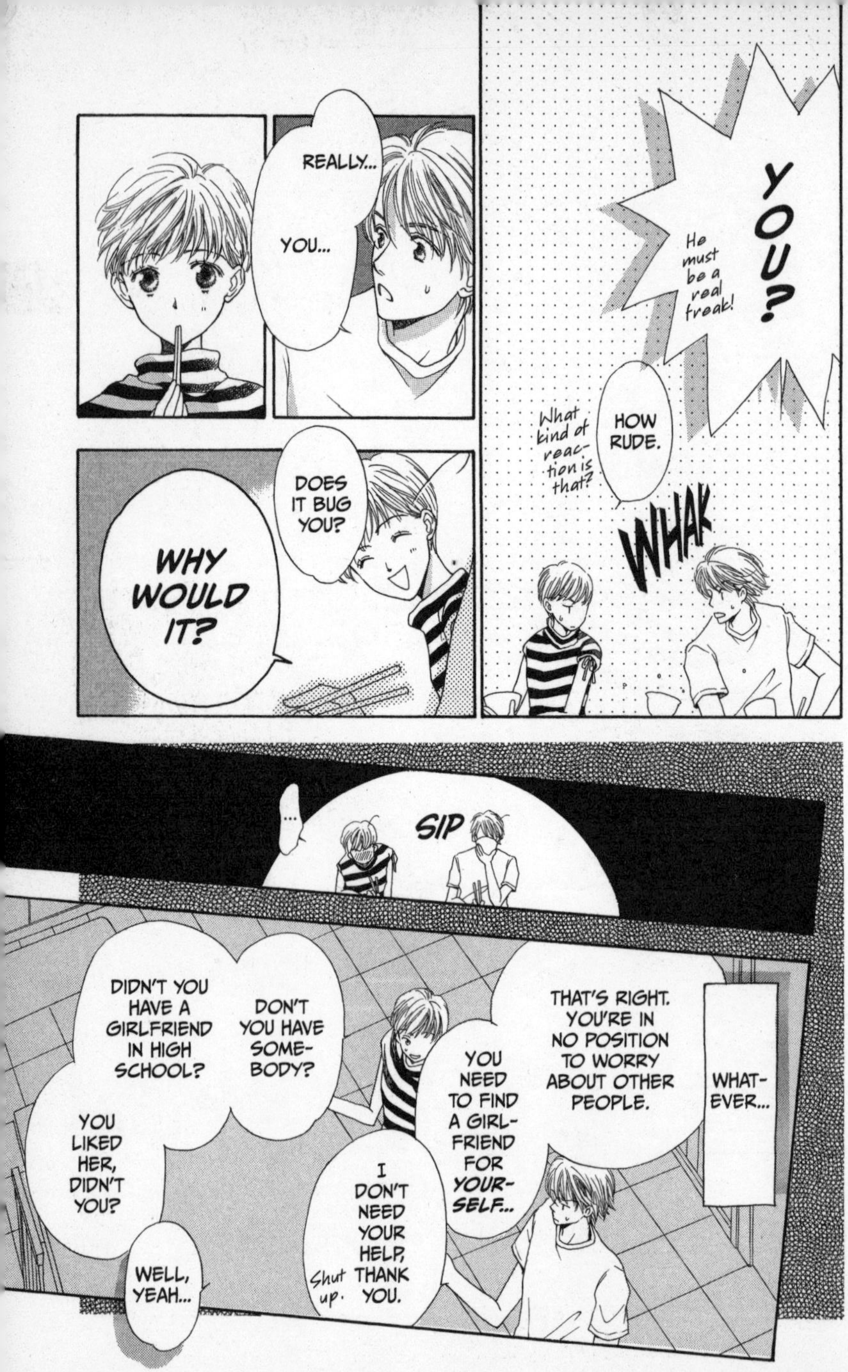
YOU?
He must be a real freak!
HOW RUDE.
What kind of reaction is that?
WHAK
REALLY...
YOU...
DOES IT BUG YOU?
WHY WOULD IT?
SIP
...
WHAT-EVER...
THAT'S RIGHT. YOU'RE IN NO POSITION TO WORRY ABOUT OTHER PEOPLE.
YOU NEED TO FIND A GIRL-FRIEND FOR *YOUR-SELF*...
DON'T YOU HAVE SOME-BODY?
DIDN'T YOU HAVE A GIRLFRIEND IN HIGH SCHOOL?
I DON'T NEED YOUR HELP, THANK YOU.
Shut up.
YOU LIKED HER, DIDN'T YOU?
WELL, YEAH...

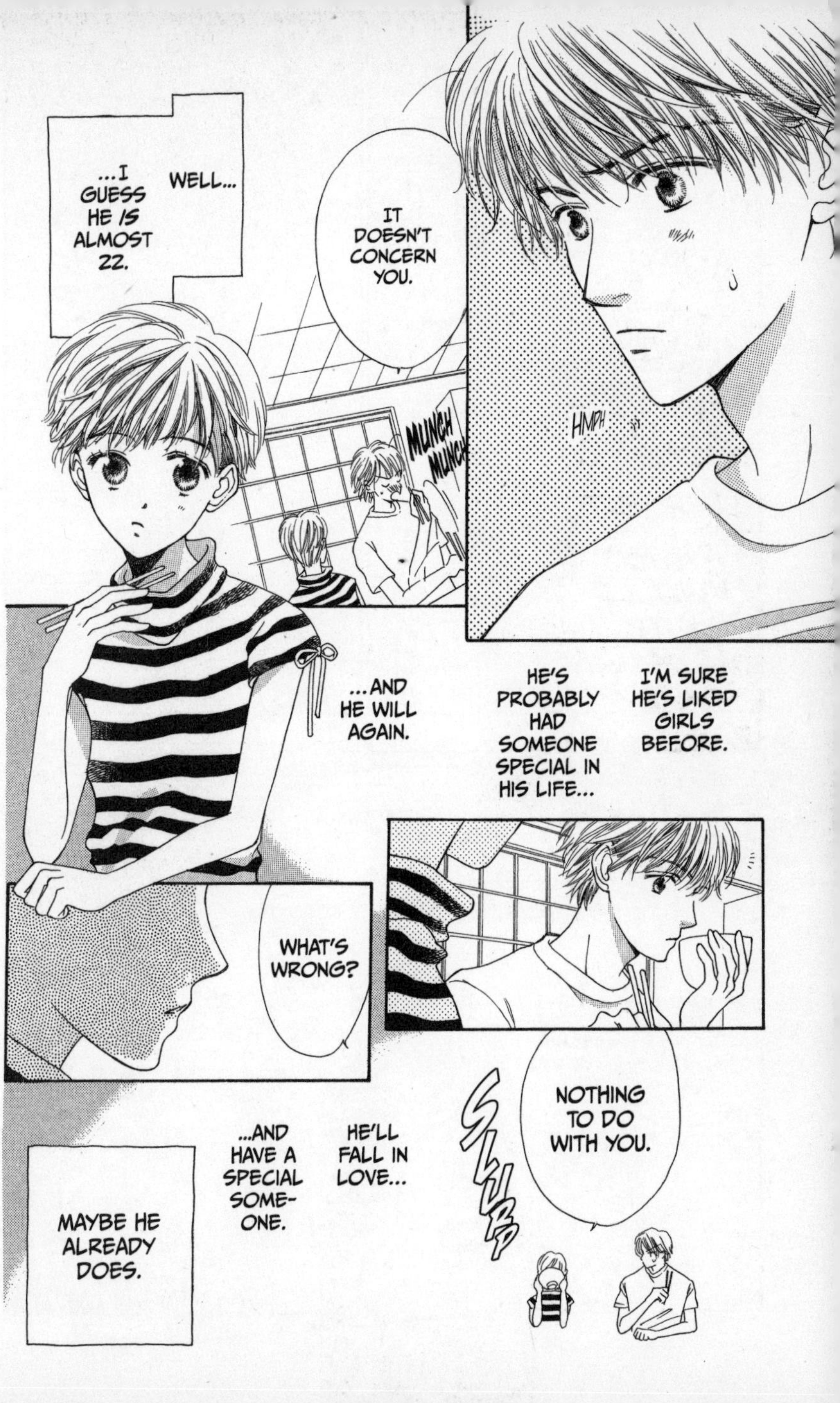

HMPH
IT DOESN'T CONCERN YOU.
MUNCH MUNCH
WELL...
...I GUESS HE IS ALMOST 22.
I'M SURE HE'S LIKED GIRLS BEFORE.
HE'S PROBABLY HAD SOMEONE SPECIAL IN HIS LIFE...
...AND HE WILL AGAIN.
WHAT'S WRONG?
NOTHING TO DO WITH YOU.
SLURP
HE'LL FALL IN LOVE...
...AND HAVE A SPECIAL SOME-ONE.
MAYBE HE ALREADY DOES.

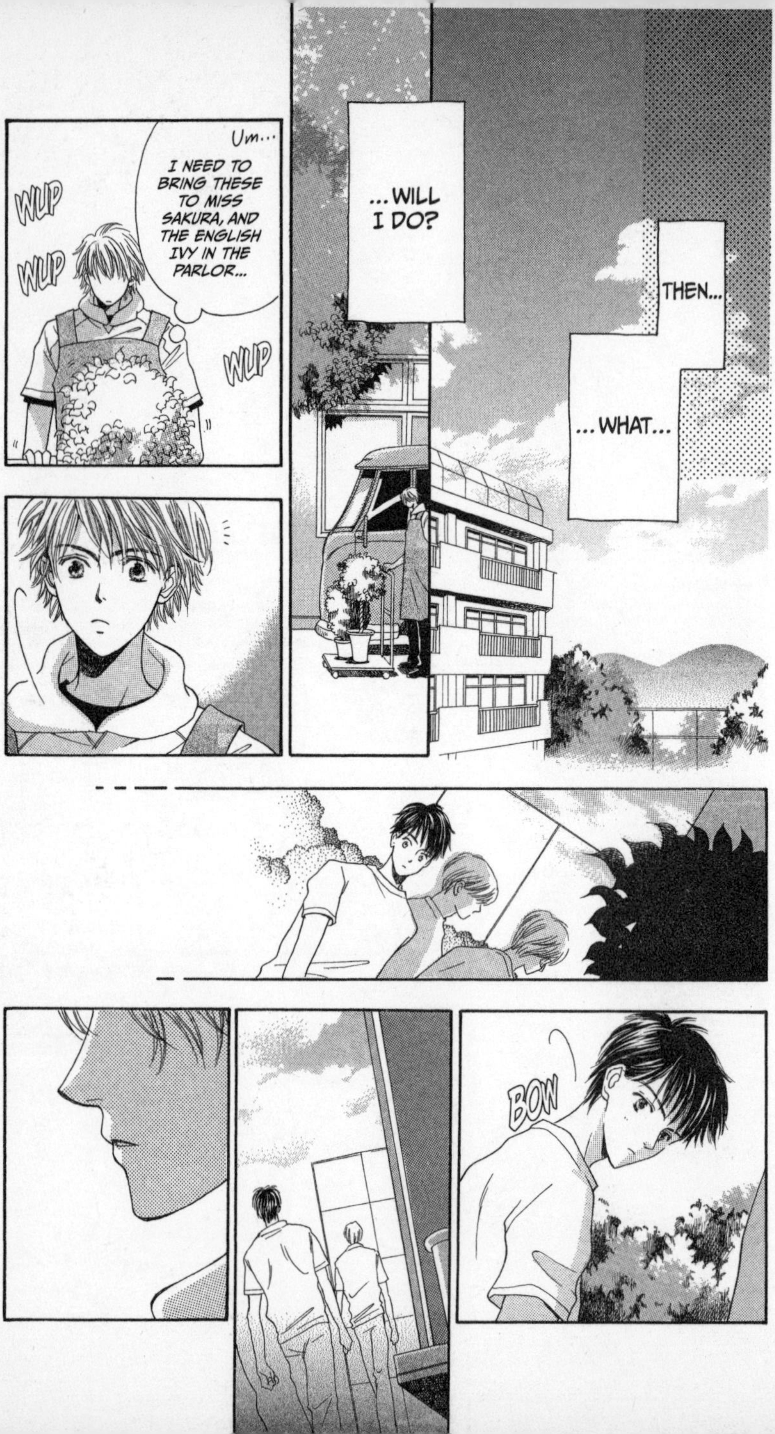
THEN...
...WHAT...
...WILL I DO?
Um...
I NEED TO BRING THESE TO MISS SAKURA, AND THE ENGLISH IVY IN THE PARLOR...
WULP
WULP
WULP
BOW

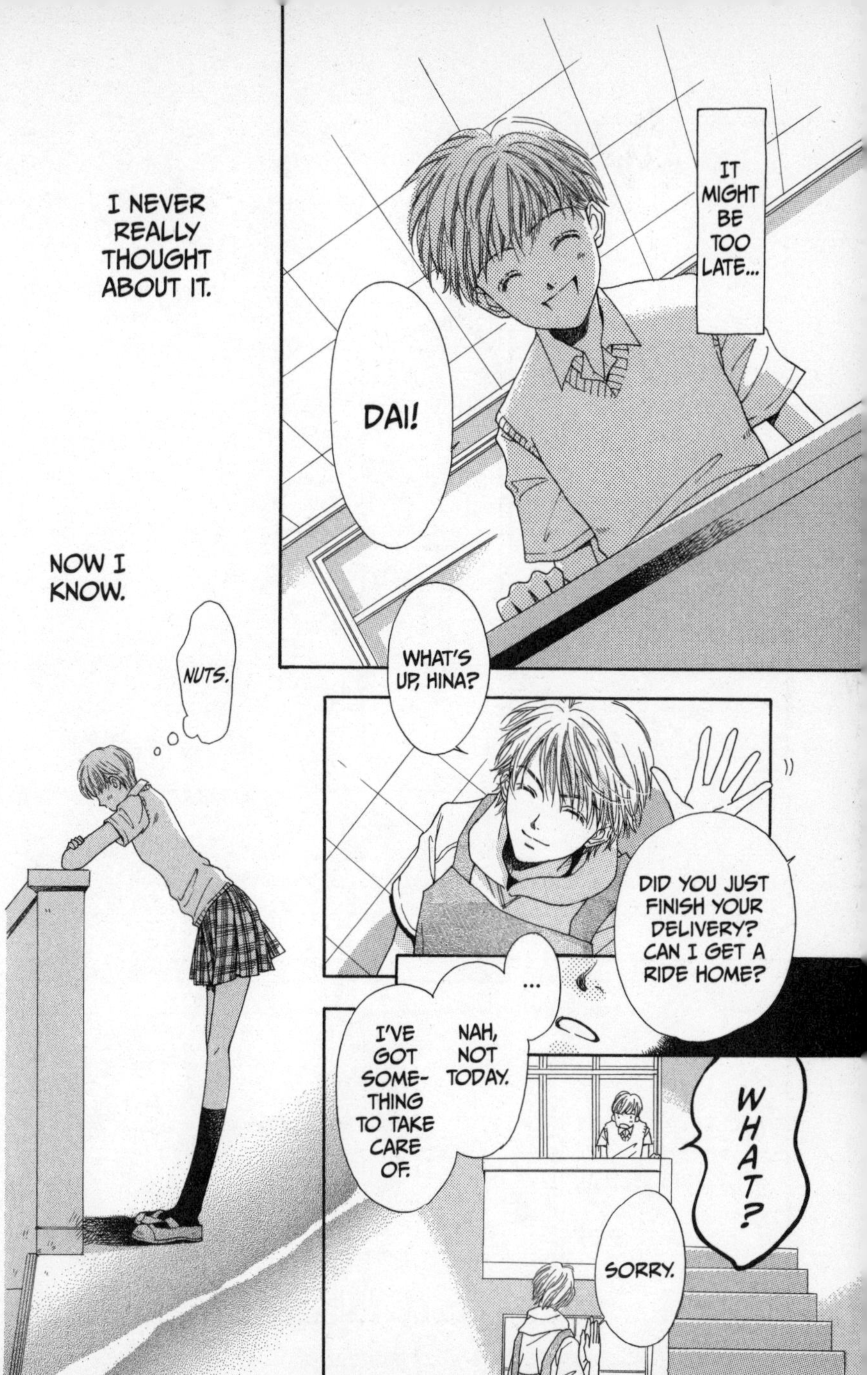
IT MIGHT BE TOO LATE...
DAI!
WHAT'S UP, HINA?
DID YOU JUST FINISH YOUR DELIVERY? CAN I GET A RIDE HOME?
...
NAH, NOT TODAY.
I'VE GOT SOME-THING TO TAKE CARE OF.
WHAT?
SORRY.
I NEVER REALLY THOUGHT ABOUT IT.
NOW I KNOW.
NUTS.

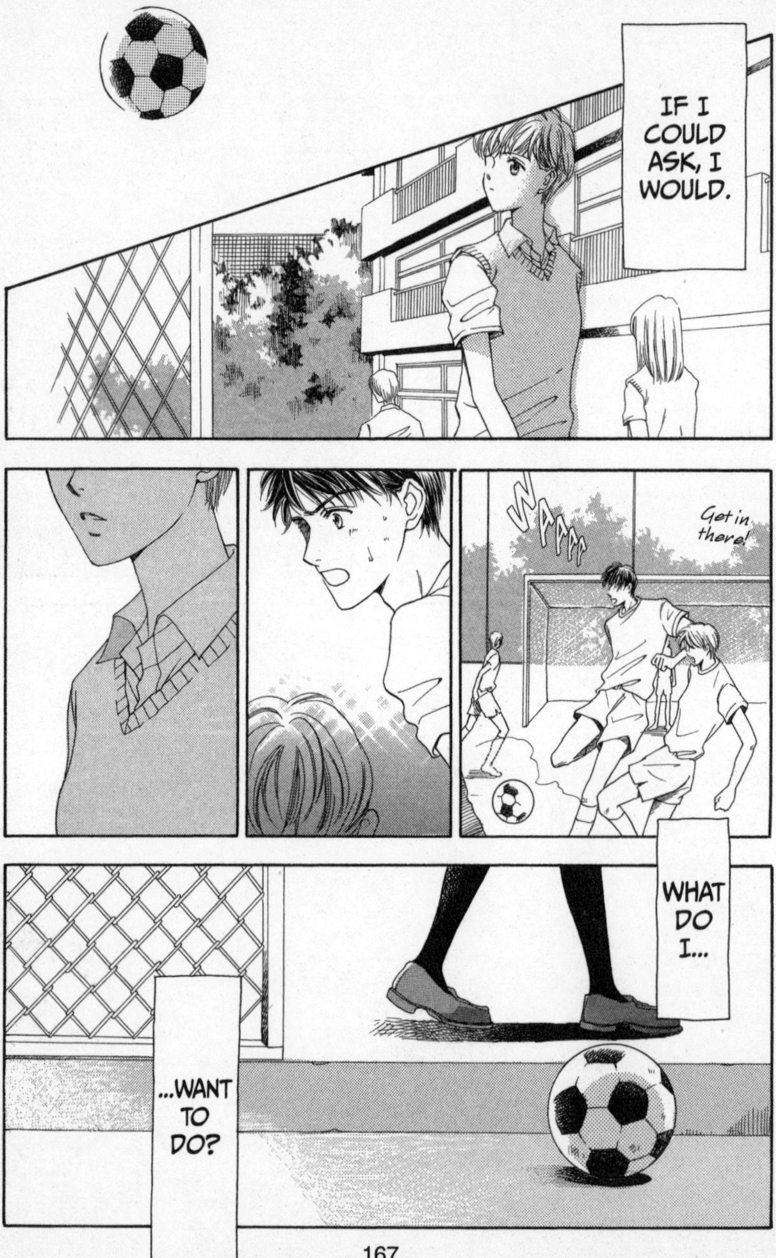
IF I COULD ASK, I WOULD.
Get in there!
WHAT DO I...
...WANT TO DO?

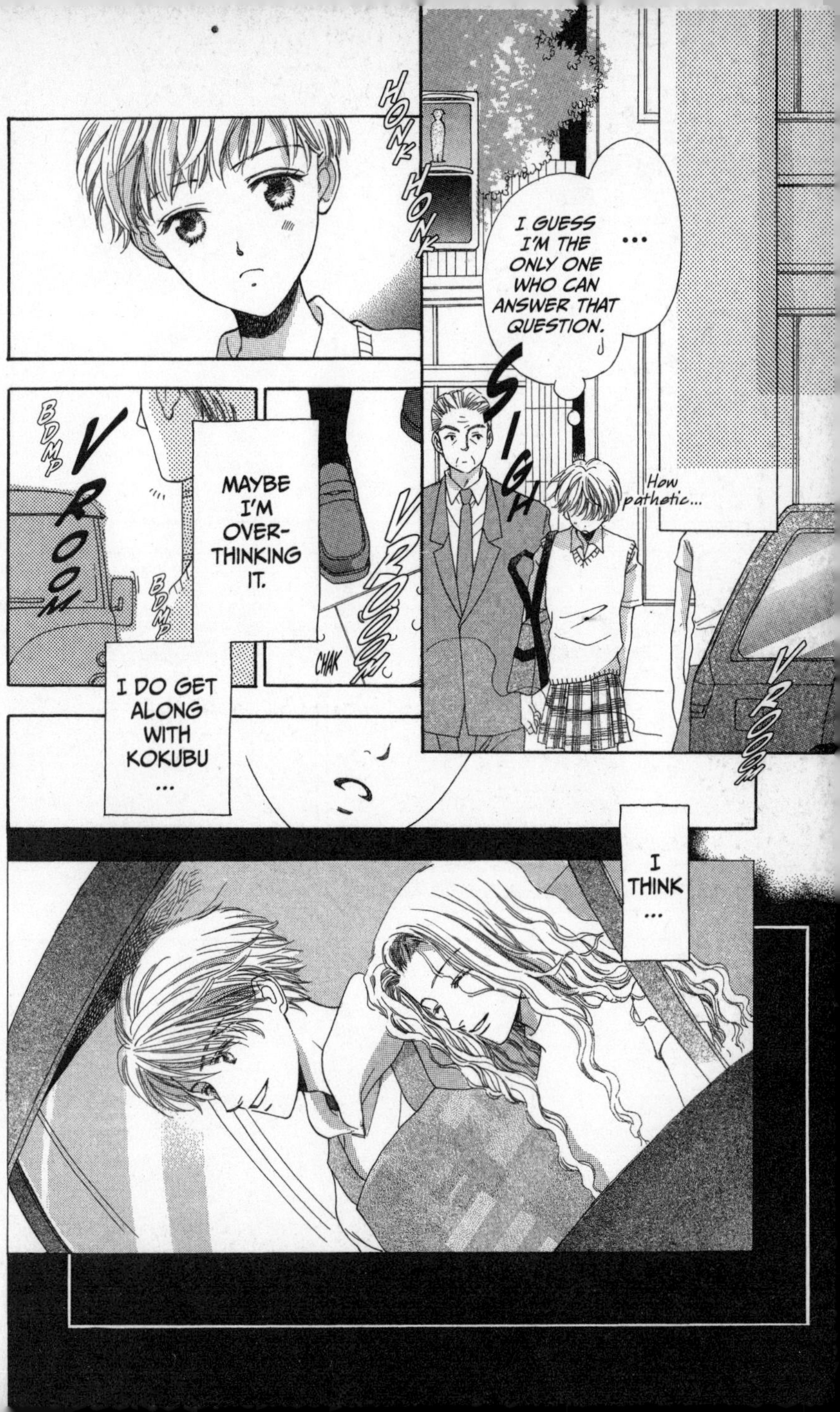
I GUESS I'M THE ONLY ONE WHO CAN ANSWER THAT QUESTION.
...
SIGH
How pathetic...
VROOOM
HONK HONK HONK
CHAK
VROOOOOOM
MAYBE I'M OVER-THINKING IT.
VROOOM
BDMP
BDMP
I DO GET ALONG WITH KOKUBU ...
I THINK ...

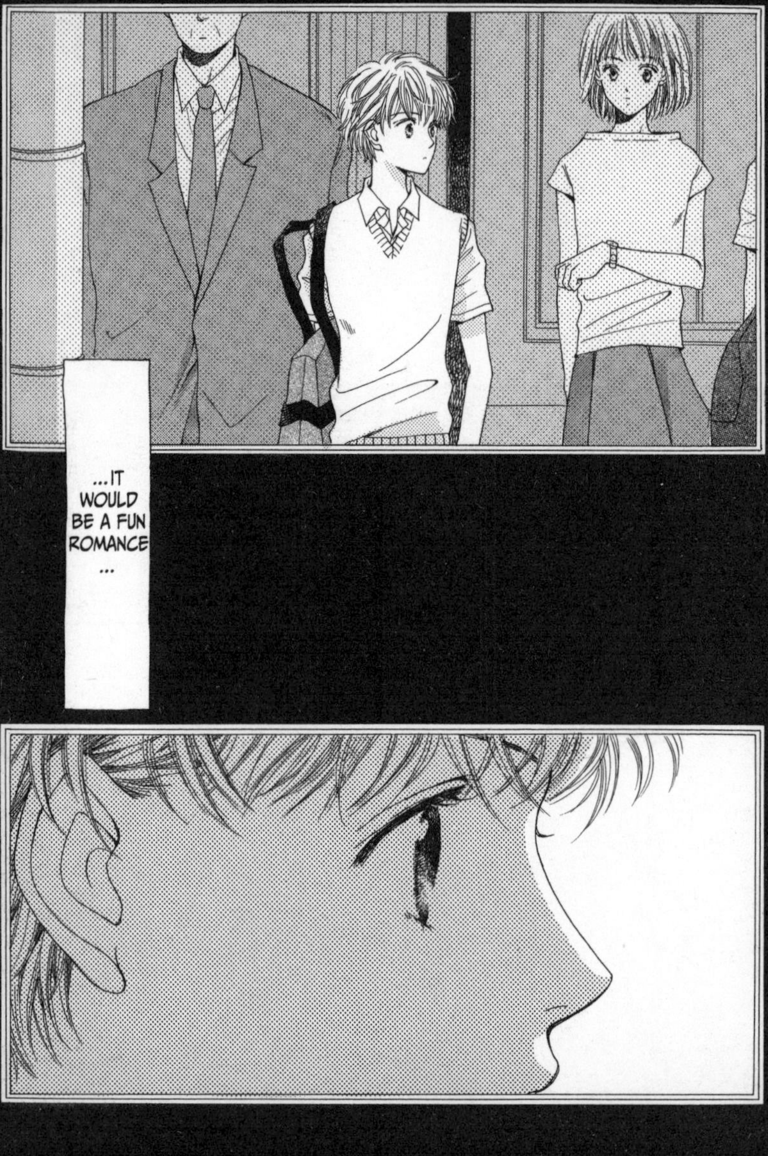
...IT WOULD BE A FUN ROMANCE ...

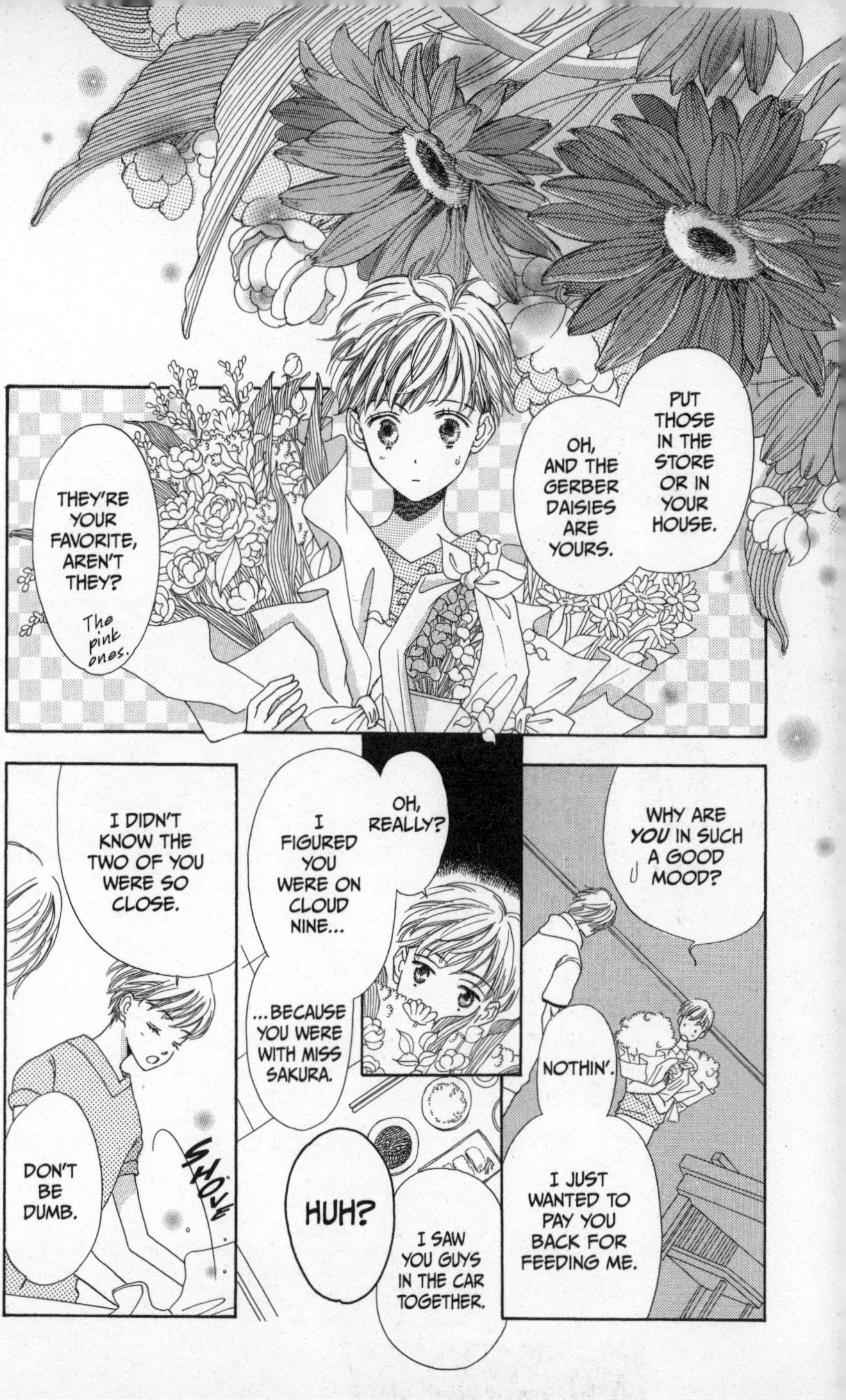
PUT THOSE IN THE STORE OR IN YOUR HOUSE.
OH, AND THE GERBER DAISIES ARE YOURS.
THEY'RE YOUR FAVORITE, AREN'T THEY?
The pink ones.
WHY ARE *YOU* IN SUCH A GOOD MOOD?
NOTHIN'.
I JUST WANTED TO PAY YOU BACK FOR FEEDING ME.
HUH?
I SAW YOU GUYS IN THE CAR TOGETHER.
OH, REALLY?
I FIGURED YOU WERE ON CLOUD NINE...
...BECAUSE YOU WERE WITH MISS SAKURA.
I DIDN'T KNOW THE TWO OF YOU WERE SO CLOSE.
DON'T BE DUMB.
SHOVE

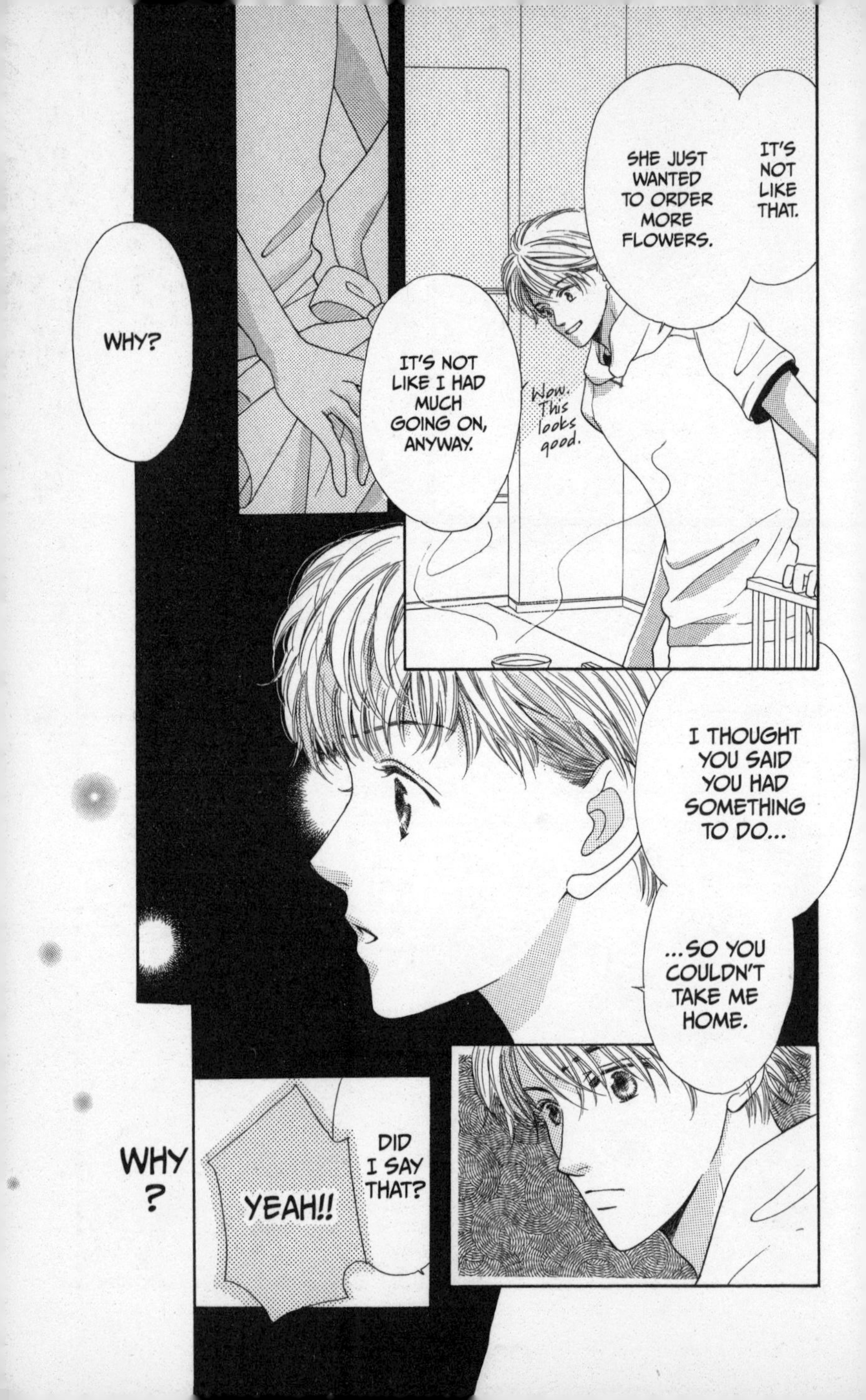
IT'S NOT LIKE THAT.
SHE JUST WANTED TO ORDER MORE FLOWERS.
Wow. This looks good.
IT'S NOT LIKE I HAD MUCH GOING ON, ANYWAY.
WHY?
I THOUGHT YOU SAID YOU HAD SOMETHING TO DO...
...SO YOU COULDN'T TAKE ME HOME.
DID I SAY THAT?
YEAH!!
WHY?

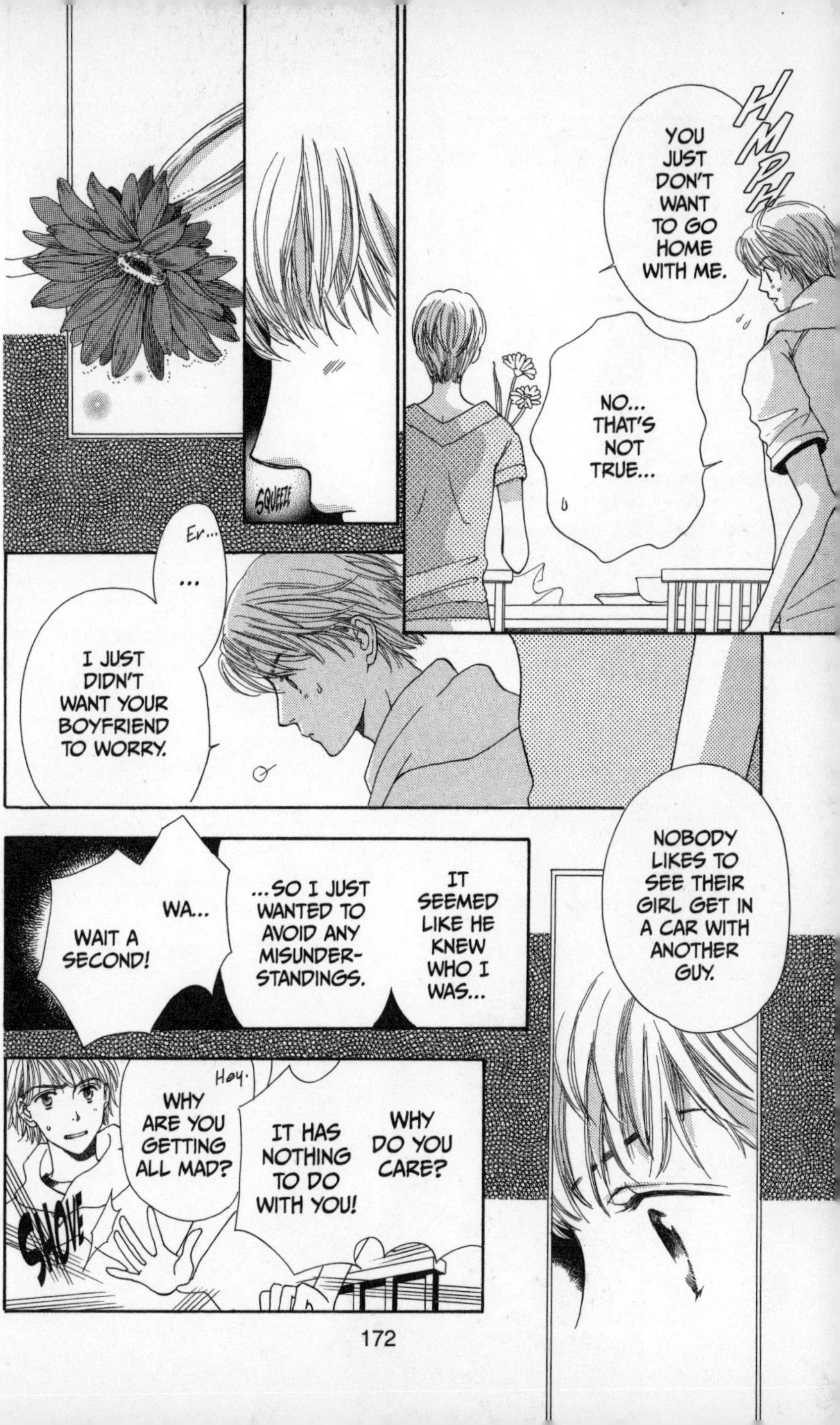
HMPH
YOU JUST DON'T WANT TO GO HOME WITH ME.
NO... THAT'S NOT TRUE...
SQUEEZE
Er...
...
I JUST DIDN'T WANT YOUR BOYFRIEND TO WORRY.
NOBODY LIKES TO SEE THEIR GIRL GET IN A CAR WITH ANOTHER GUY.
IT SEEMED LIKE HE KNEW WHO I WAS...
...SO I JUST WANTED TO AVOID ANY MISUNDER-STANDINGS.
WA...
WAIT A SECOND!
Hey.
WHY DO YOU CARE?
IT HAS NOTHING TO DO WITH YOU!
WHY ARE YOU GETTING ALL MAD?
SHOVE

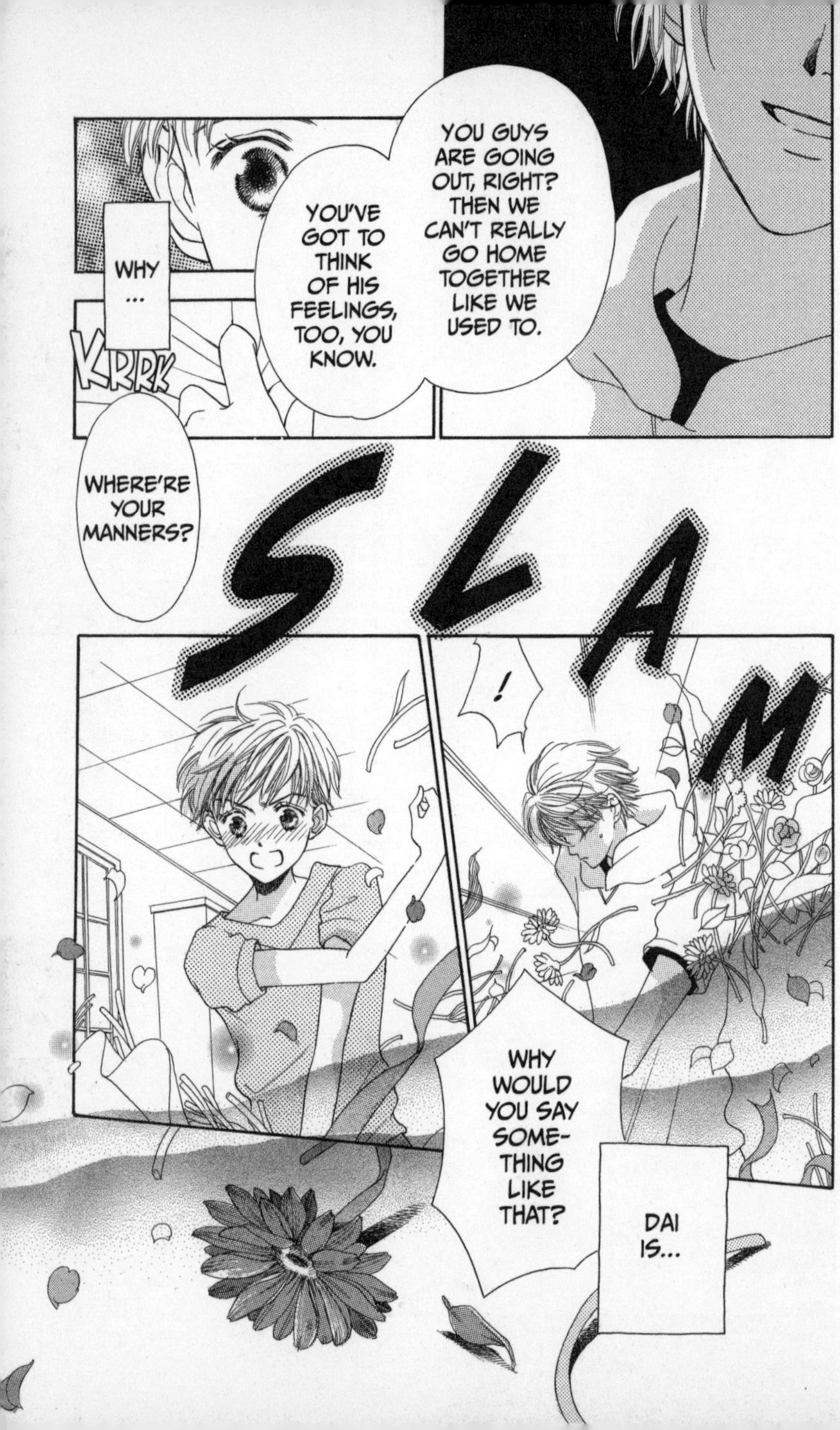
YOU GUYS ARE GOING OUT, RIGHT? THEN WE CAN'T REALLY GO HOME TOGETHER LIKE WE USED TO.
YOU'VE GOT TO THINK OF HIS FEELINGS, TOO, YOU KNOW.
WHY ...
KRRK
WHERE'RE YOUR MANNERS?
SLAM
!
WHY WOULD YOU SAY SOME-THING LIKE THAT?
DAI IS...

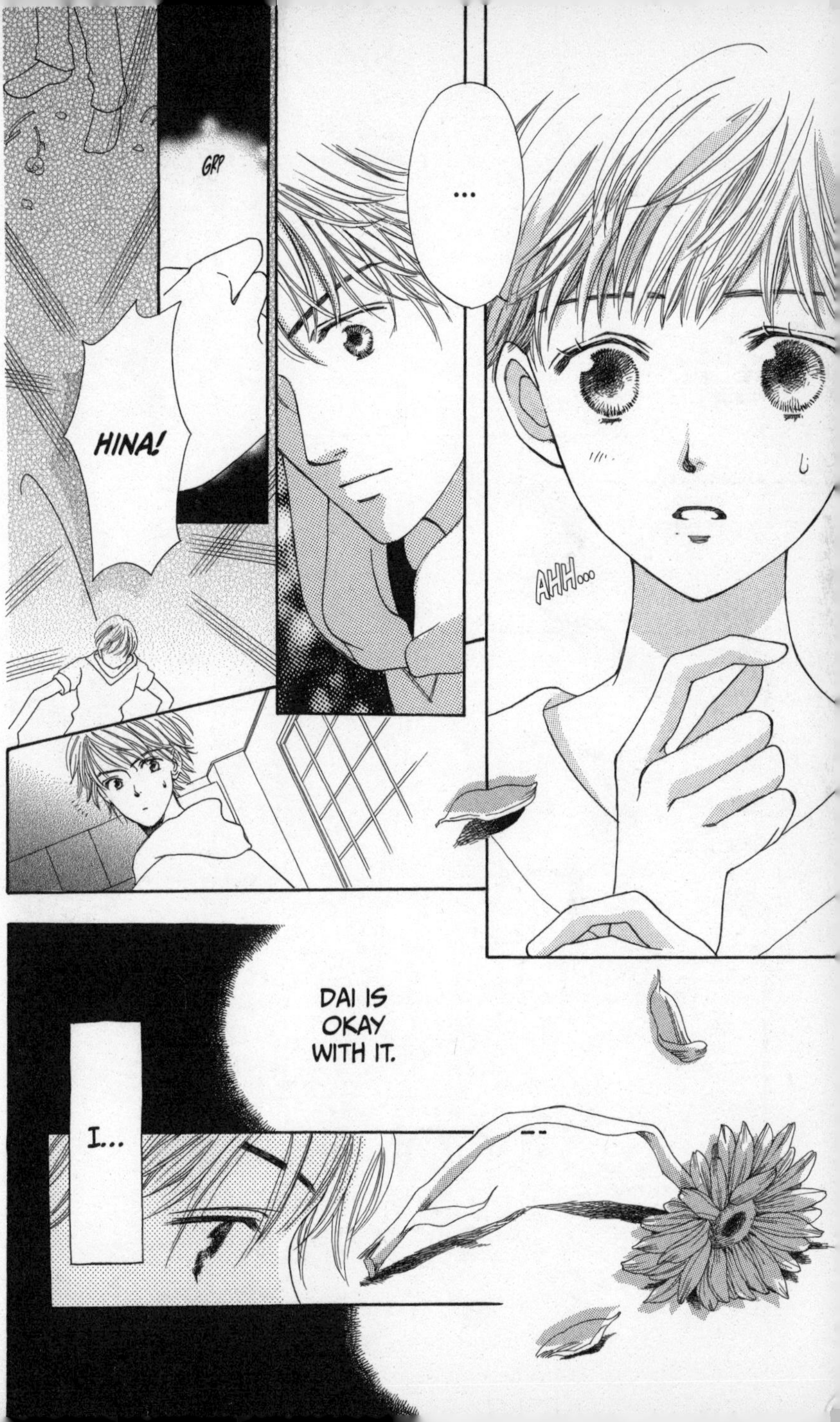
AHH...
...
GRP
HINA!
DAI IS OKAY WITH IT.
I...

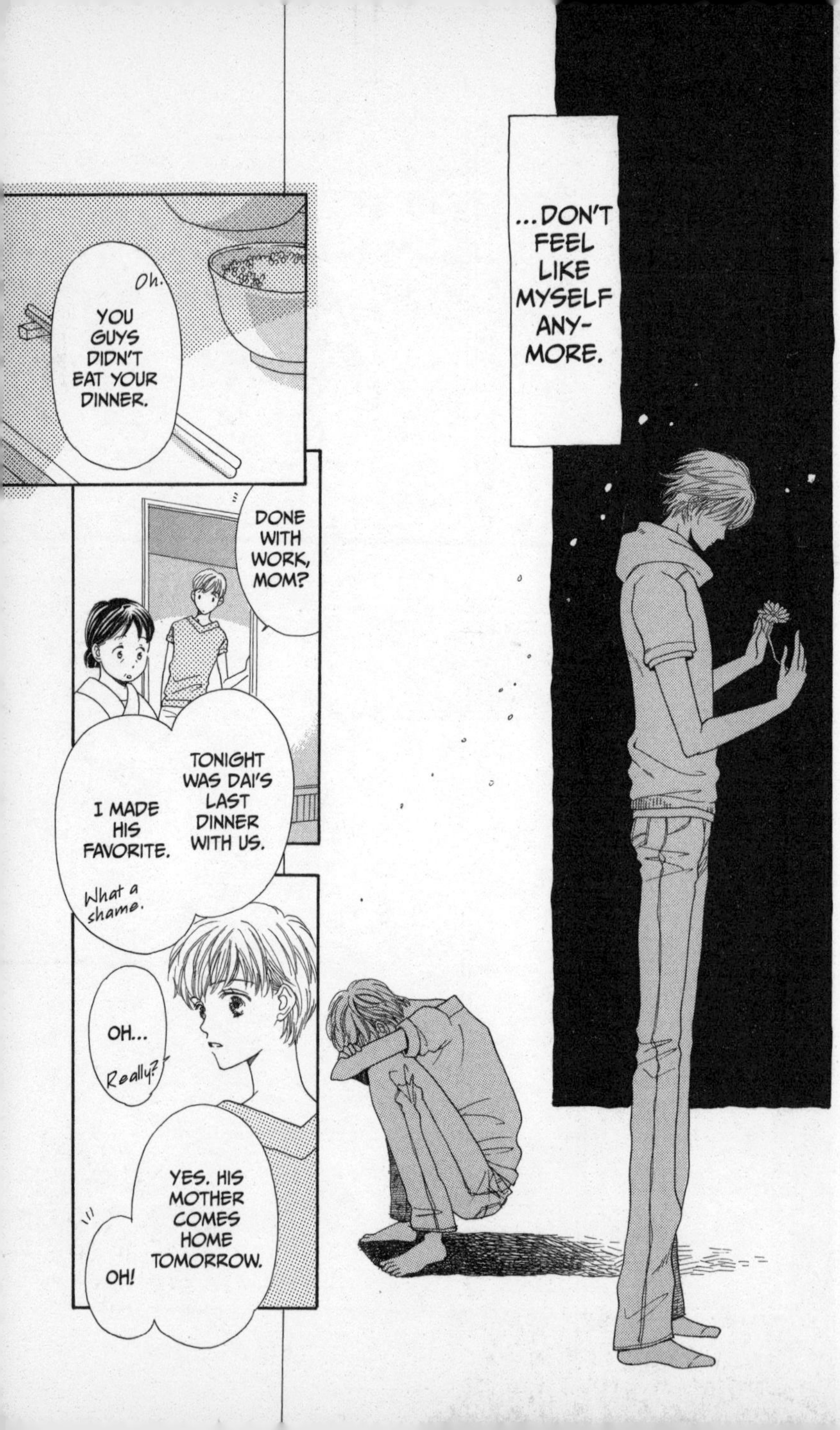
...DON'T FEEL LIKE MYSELF ANYMORE.
Oh.
YOU GUYS DIDN'T EAT YOUR DINNER.
DONE WITH WORK, MOM?
TONIGHT WAS DAI'S LAST DINNER WITH US.
I MADE HIS FAVORITE.
What a shame.
OH...
Really?
YES. HIS MOTHER COMES HOME TOMORROW.
OH!

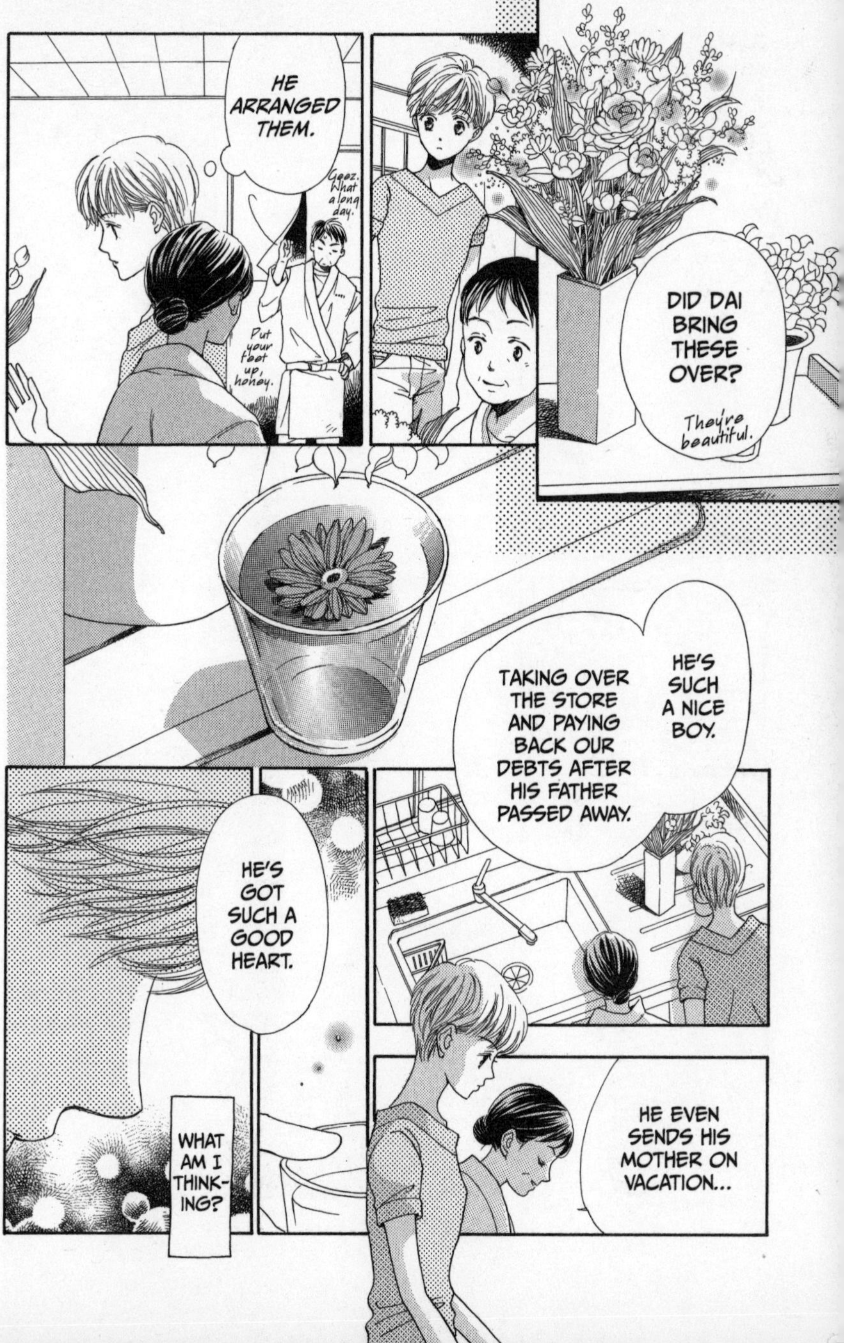
DID DAI BRING THESE OVER?
They're beautiful.
HE ARRANGED THEM.
Geez. What a long day.
Put your feet up, honey.
HE'S SUCH A NICE BOY.
TAKING OVER THE STORE AND PAYING BACK OUR DEBTS AFTER HIS FATHER PASSED AWAY.
HE EVEN SENDS HIS MOTHER ON VACATION...
HE'S GOT SUCH A GOOD HEART.
WHAT AM I THINK-ING?

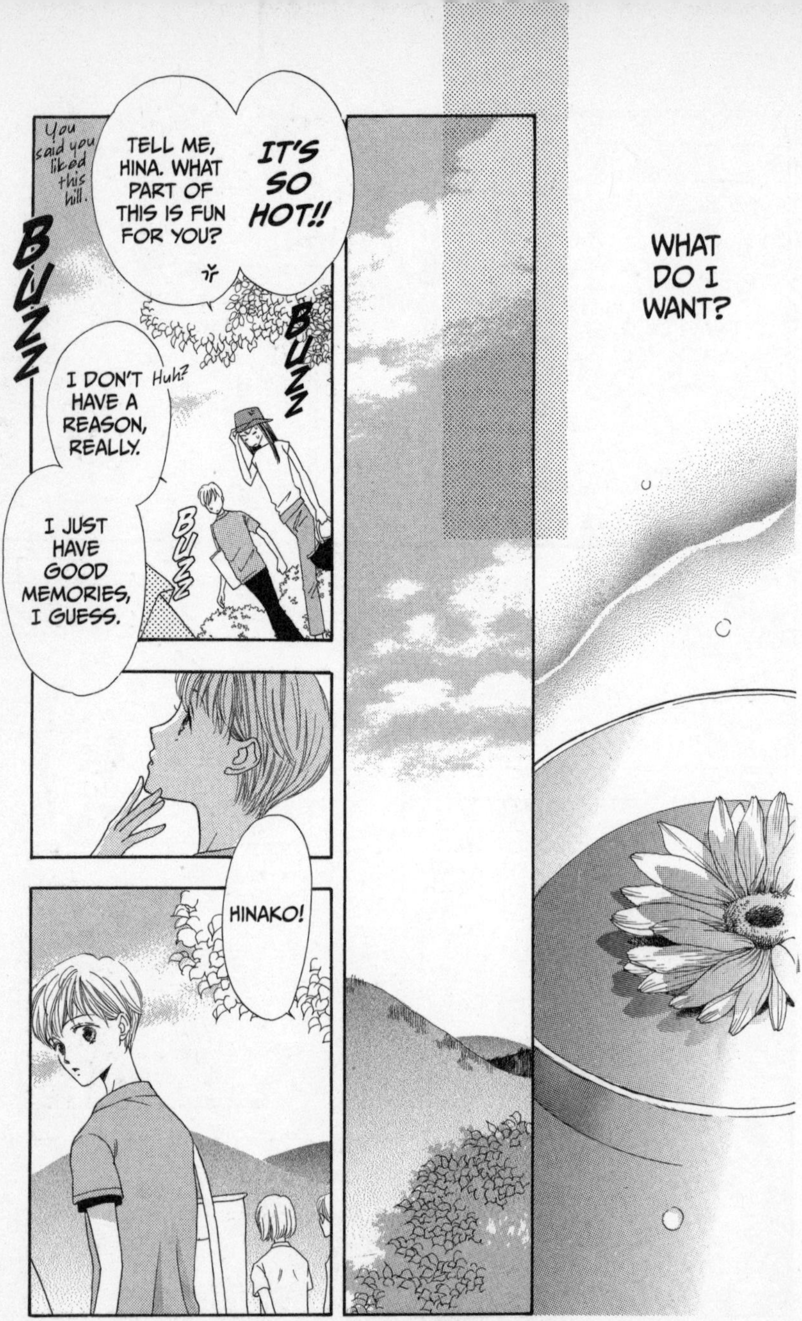
WHAT DO I WANT?
IT'S SO HOT!!
TELL ME, HINA. WHAT PART OF THIS IS FUN FOR YOU?
You said you liked this hill.
BUZZ
BUZZ
BUZZ
Huh?
I DON'T HAVE A REASON, REALLY.
I JUST HAVE GOOD MEMORIES, I GUESS.
HINAKO!

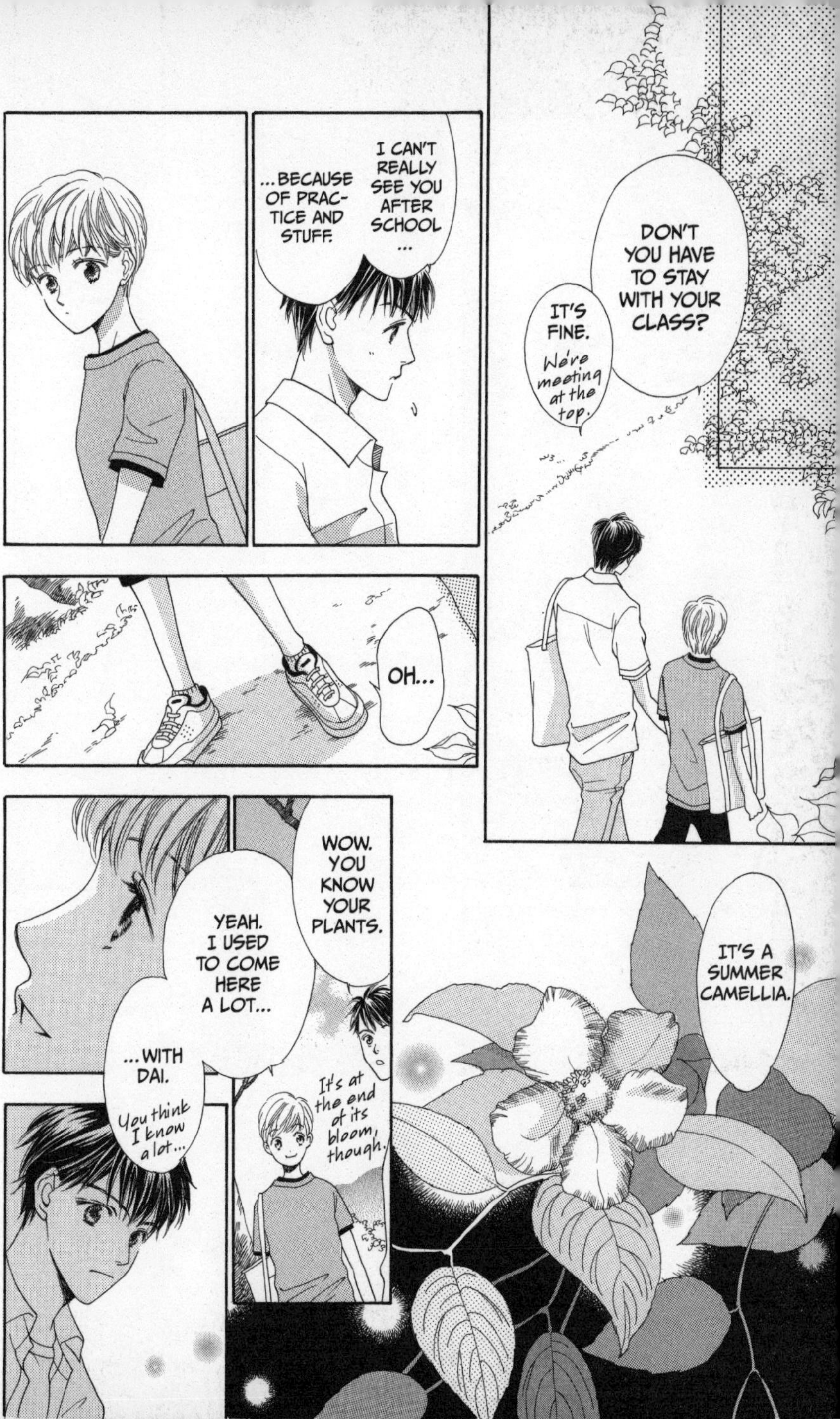
DON'T YOU HAVE TO STAY WITH YOUR CLASS?
IT'S FINE. We're meeting at the top.
I CAN'T REALLY SEE YOU AFTER SCHOOL...
...BECAUSE OF PRACTICE AND STUFF.
OH...
IT'S A SUMMER CAMELLIA.
WOW. YOU KNOW YOUR PLANTS.
It's at the end of its bloom, though.
YEAH. I USED TO COME HERE A LOT...
...WITH DAI.
You think I know a lot...

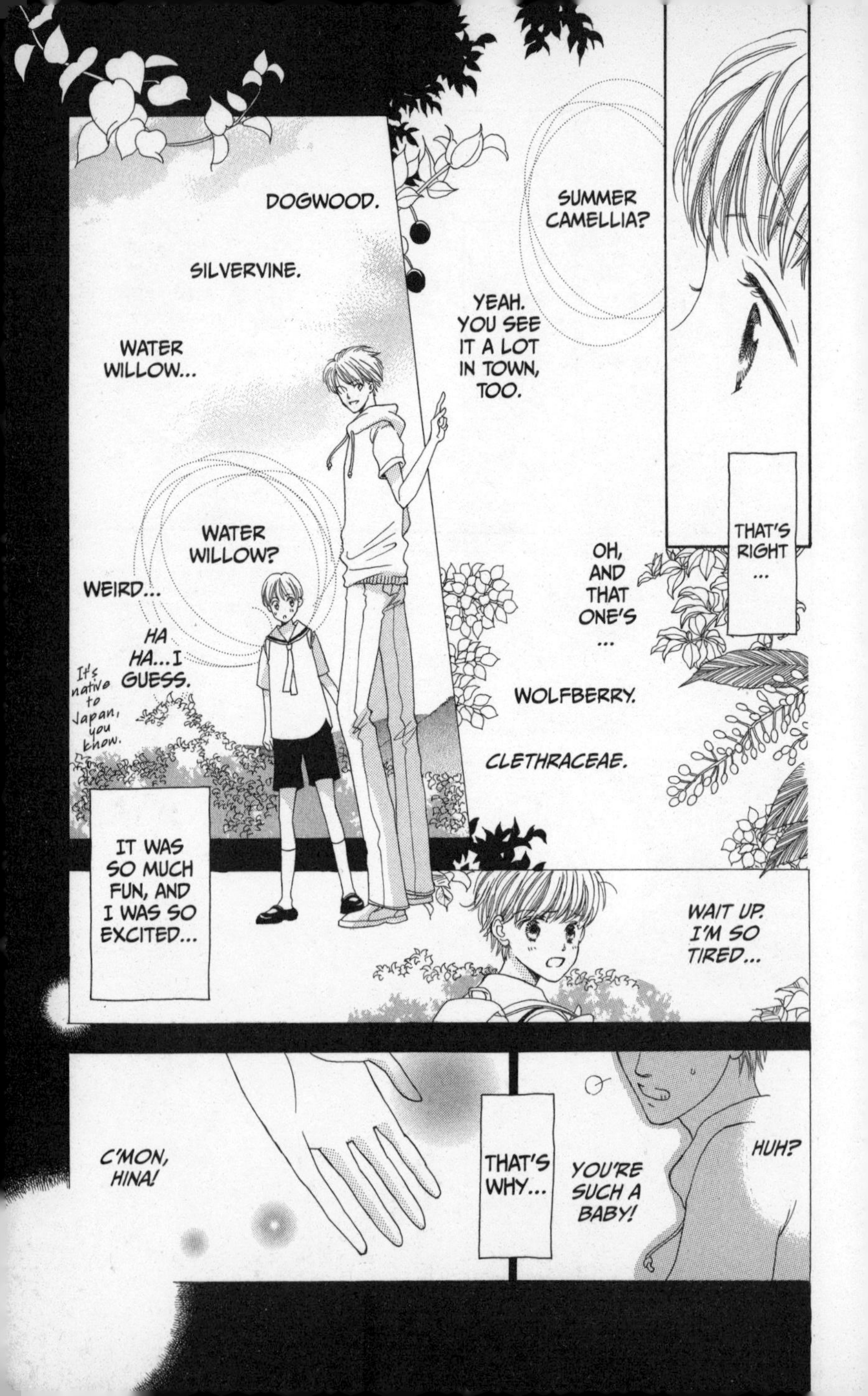
SUMMER CAMELLIA?
THAT'S RIGHT...
YEAH. YOU SEE IT A LOT IN TOWN, TOO.
DOGWOOD.
SILVERVINE.
WATER WILLOW...
OH, AND THAT ONE'S...
WOLFBERRY.
CLETHRACEAE.
WATER WILLOW?
WEIRD...
HA HA...I GUESS.
It's native to Japan, you know.
WAIT UP. I'M SO TIRED...
IT WAS SO MUCH FUN, AND I WAS SO EXCITED...
HUH?
YOU'RE SUCH A BABY!
THAT'S WHY...
C'MON, HINA!

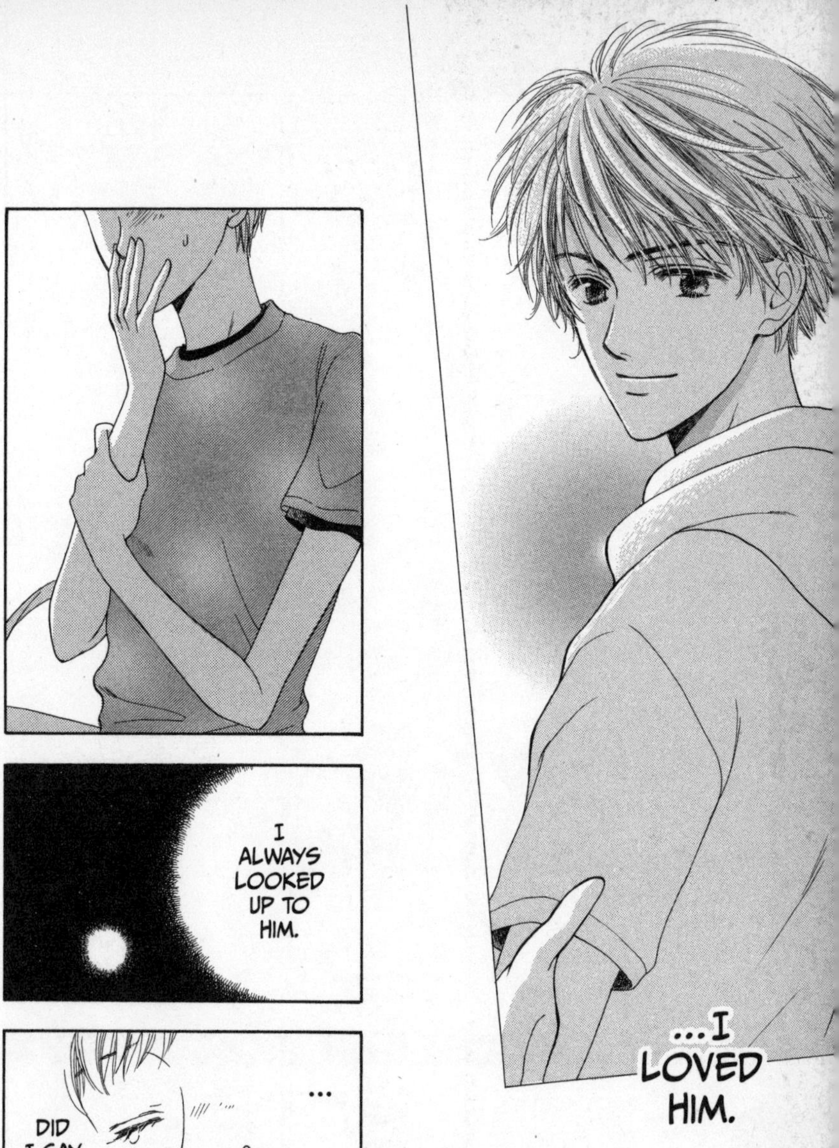
...I LOVED HIM.
I ALWAYS LOOKED UP TO HIM.
...
DID I SAY "LOVE"?

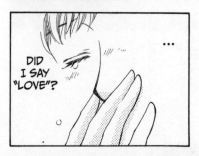

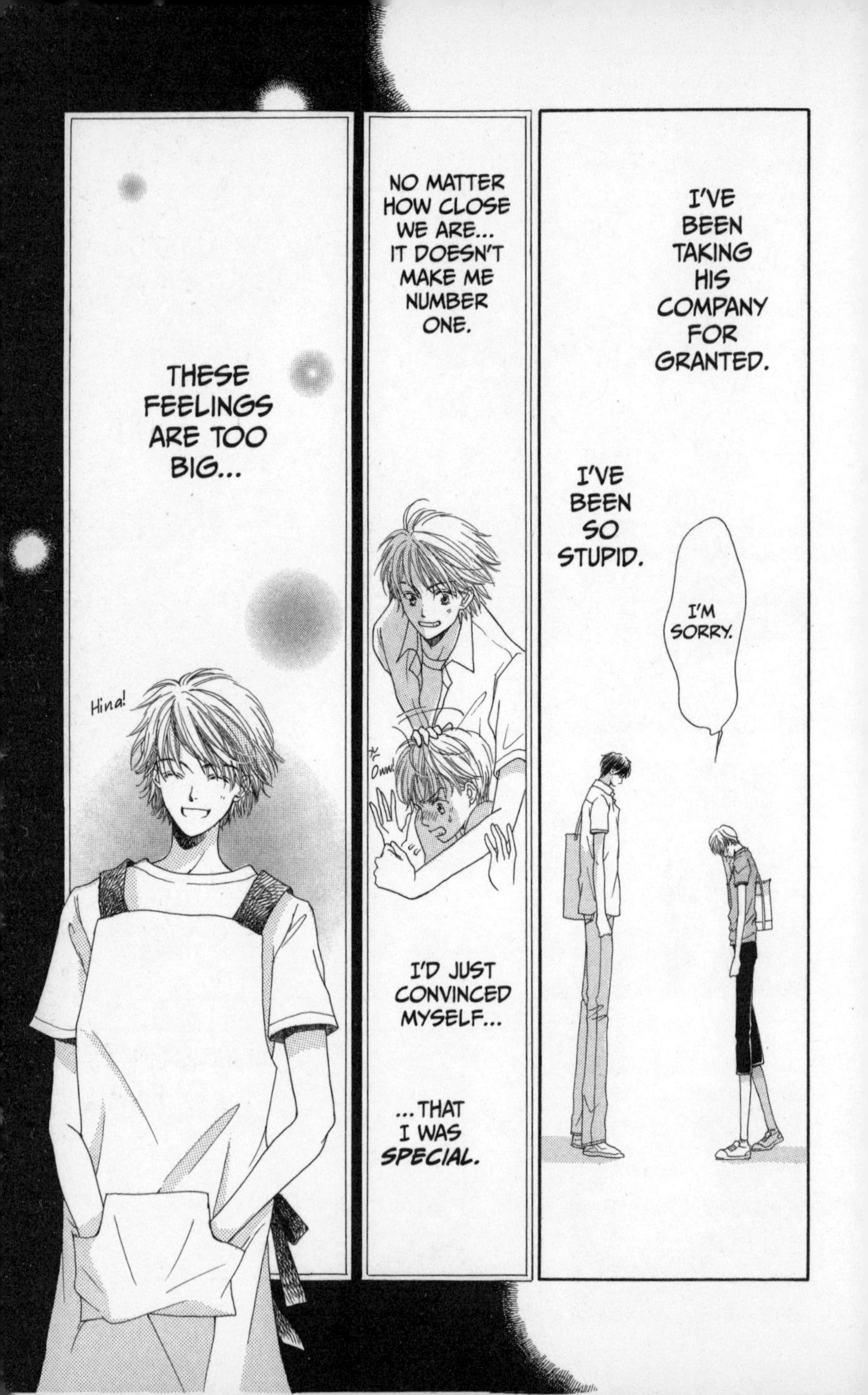
I'VE BEEN TAKING HIS COMPANY FOR GRANTED.
I'VE BEEN SO STUPID.
I'M SORRY.
NO MATTER HOW CLOSE WE ARE... IT DOESN'T MAKE ME NUMBER ONE.
Oww!
I'D JUST CONVINCED MYSELF...
...THAT I WAS SPECIAL.
THESE FEELINGS ARE TOO BIG...
Hina!

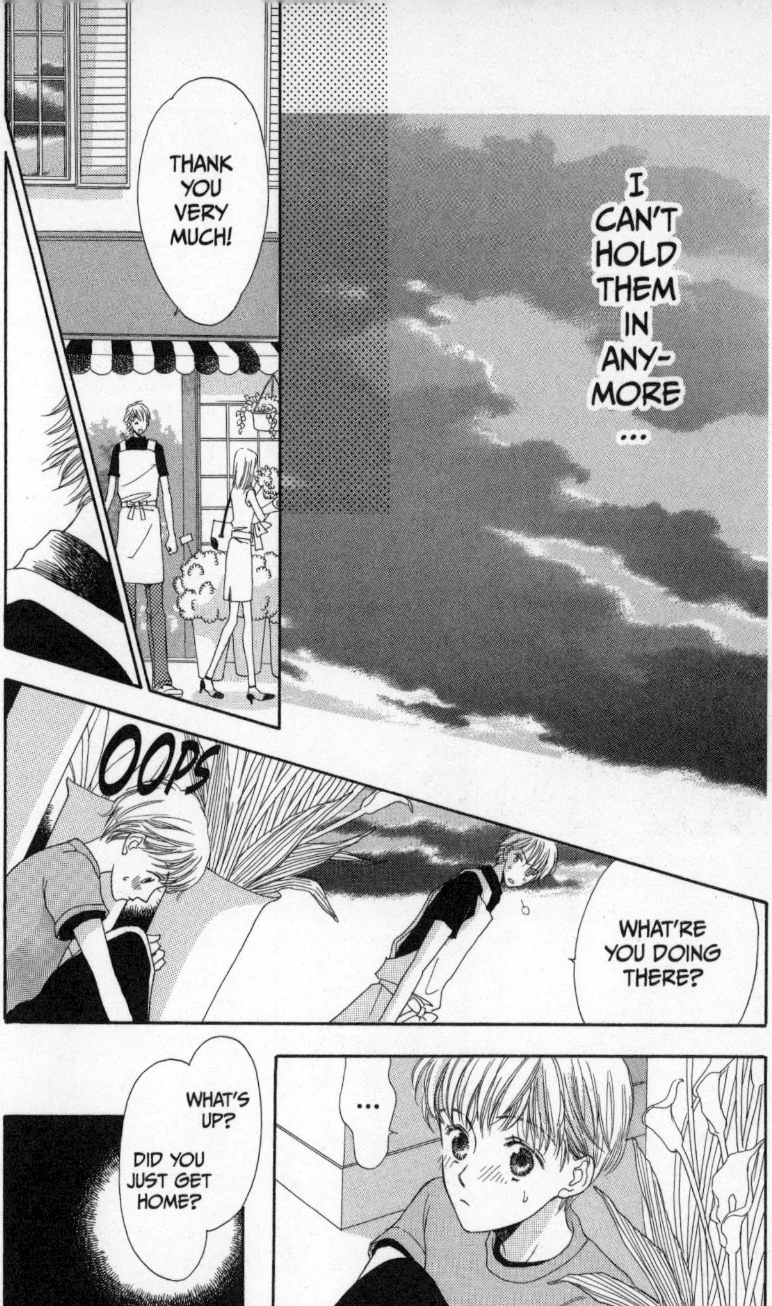
I CAN'T HOLD THEM IN ANY-MORE...
THANK YOU VERY MUCH!
OOPS
WHAT'RE YOU DOING THERE?
...
WHAT'S UP?
DID YOU JUST GET HOME?

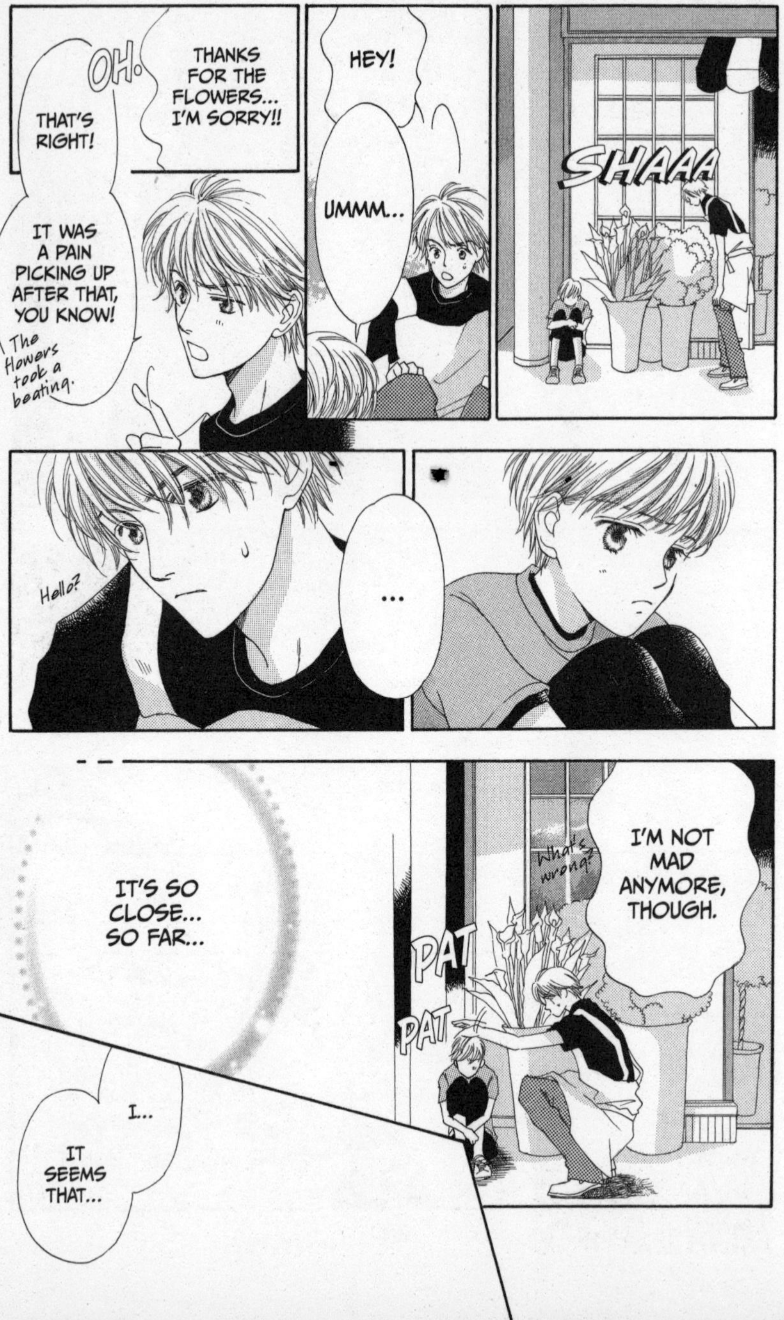
SHAAA
HEY!
UMMM...
THANKS FOR THE FLOWERS... I'M SORRY!!
OH!
THAT'S RIGHT!
IT WAS A PAIN PICKING UP AFTER THAT, YOU KNOW!
The flowers took a beating.
...
Hello?
I'M NOT MAD ANYMORE, THOUGH.
What's wrong?
PAT
PAT
IT'S SO CLOSE... SO FAR...
I...
IT SEEMS THAT...

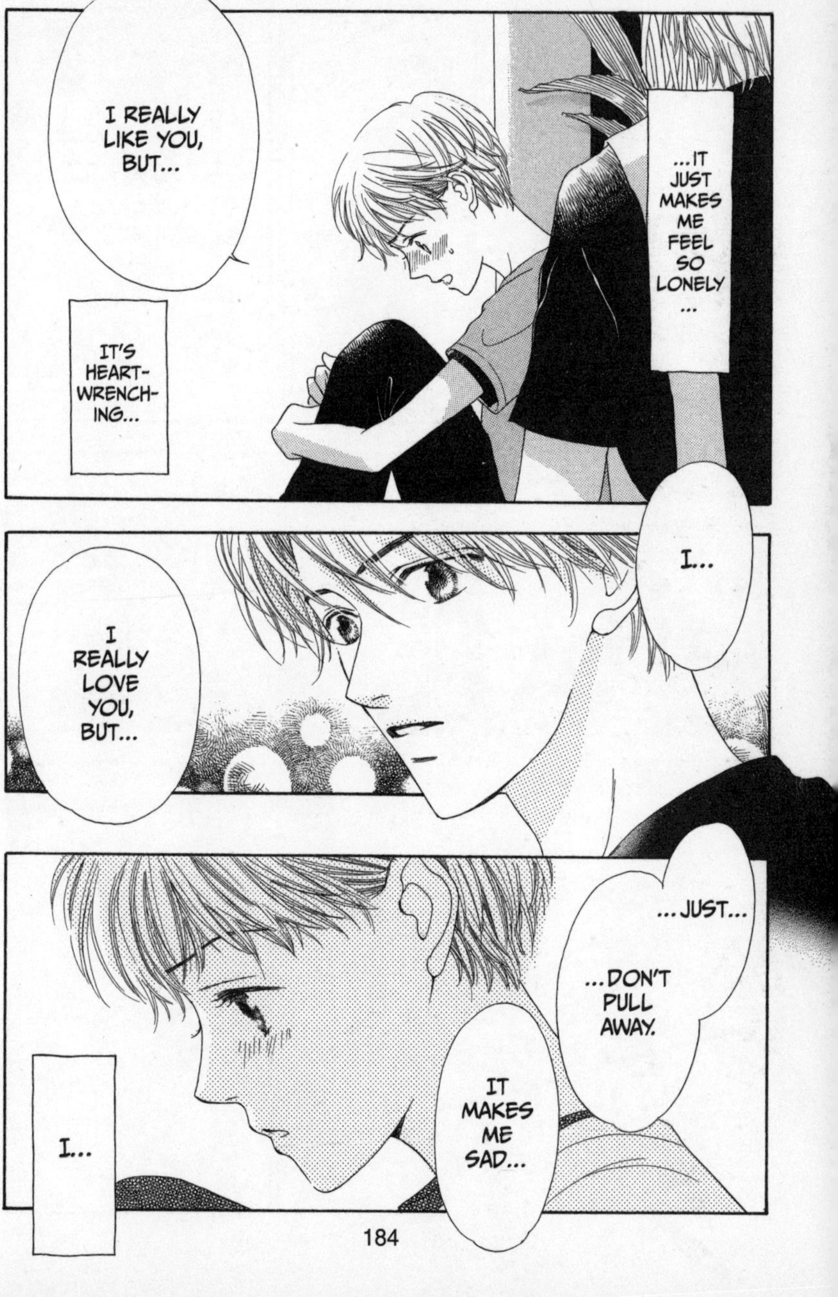
I REALLY LIKE YOU, BUT...
...IT JUST MAKES ME FEEL SO LONELY...
IT'S HEART-WRENCHING...
I...
I REALLY LOVE YOU, BUT...
...JUST...
...DON'T PULL AWAY.
IT MAKES ME SAD...
I...

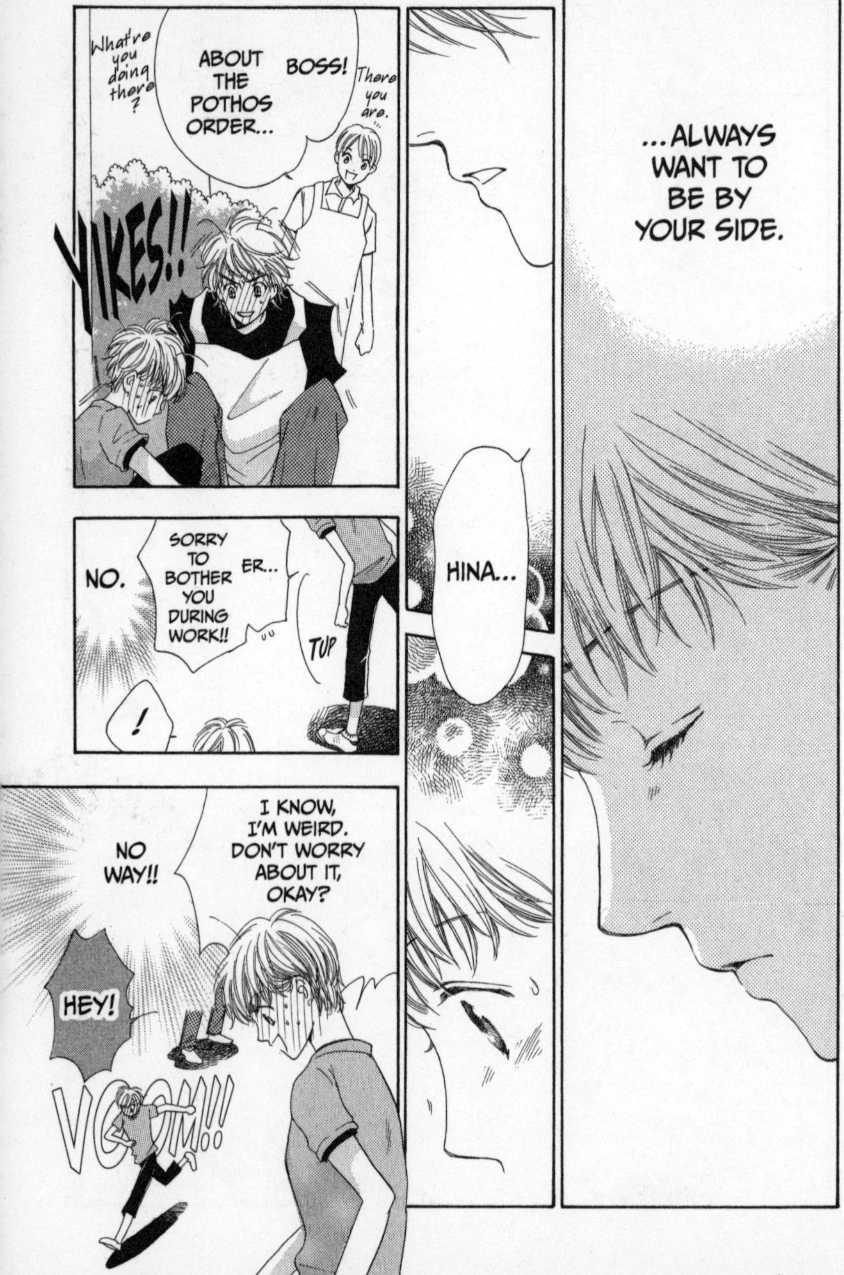
...ALWAYS WANT TO BE BY YOUR SIDE.
HINA...
BOSS!
There you are.
ABOUT THE POTHOS ORDER...
What're you doing there?
YIKES!!
ER...
SORRY TO BOTHER YOU DURING WORK!!
NO.
TUP
!
I KNOW, I'M WEIRD. DON'T WORRY ABOUT IT, OKAY?
NO WAY!!
HEY!
VOOM!!

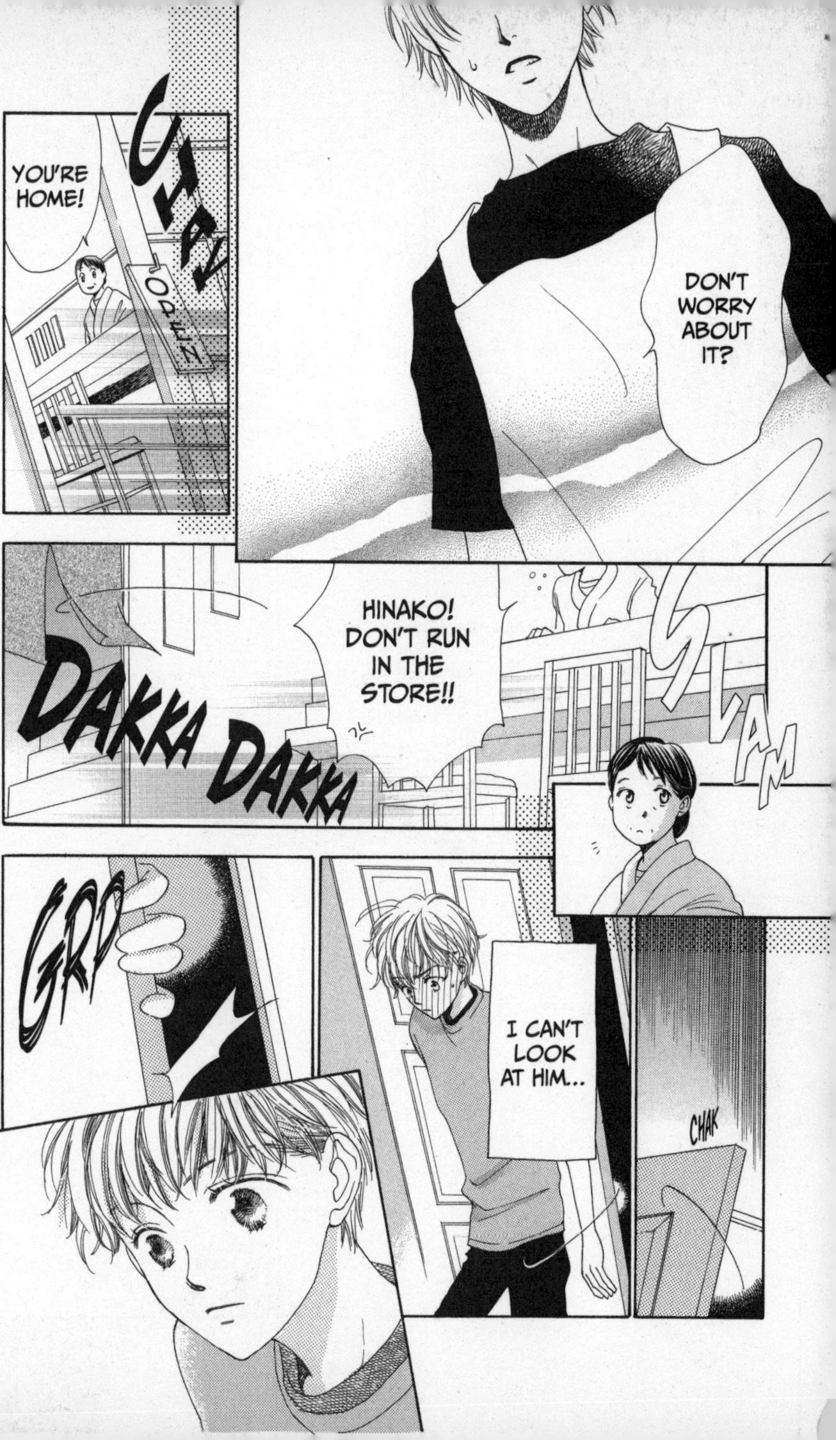
DON'T WORRY ABOUT IT?
YOU'RE HOME!
OPEN
SLAM
HINAKO! DON'T RUN IN THE STORE!!
DAKKA DAKKA
CHAK
I CAN'T LOOK AT HIM...
GRD

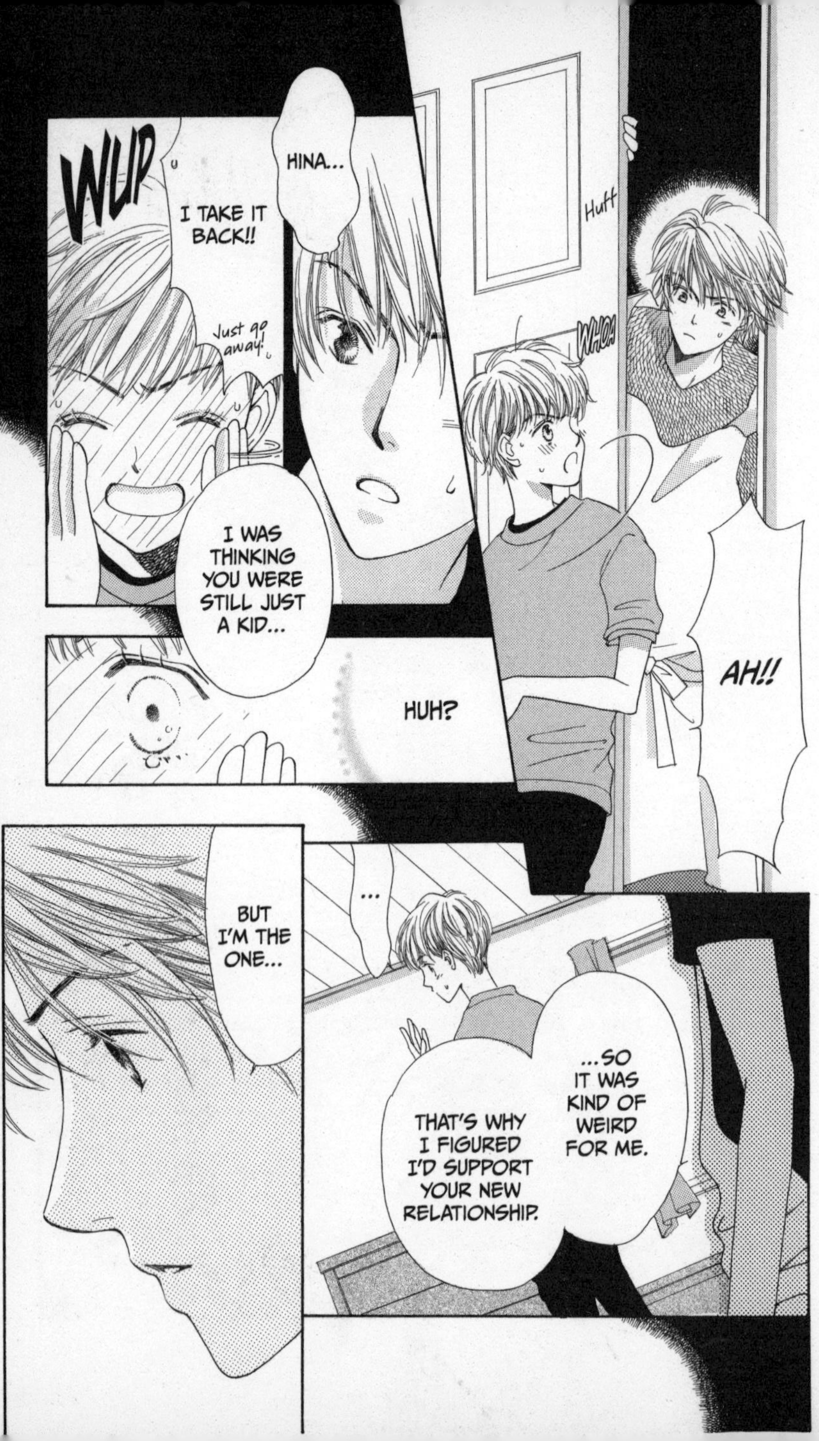
HINA...
WUP
I TAKE IT BACK!!
Just go away!
I WAS THINKING YOU WERE STILL JUST A KID...
HUH?
Huff
WHOA
AH!!
...
BUT I'M THE ONE...
...SO IT WAS KIND OF WEIRD FOR ME.
THAT'S WHY I FIGURED I'D SUPPORT YOUR NEW RELATIONSHIP.

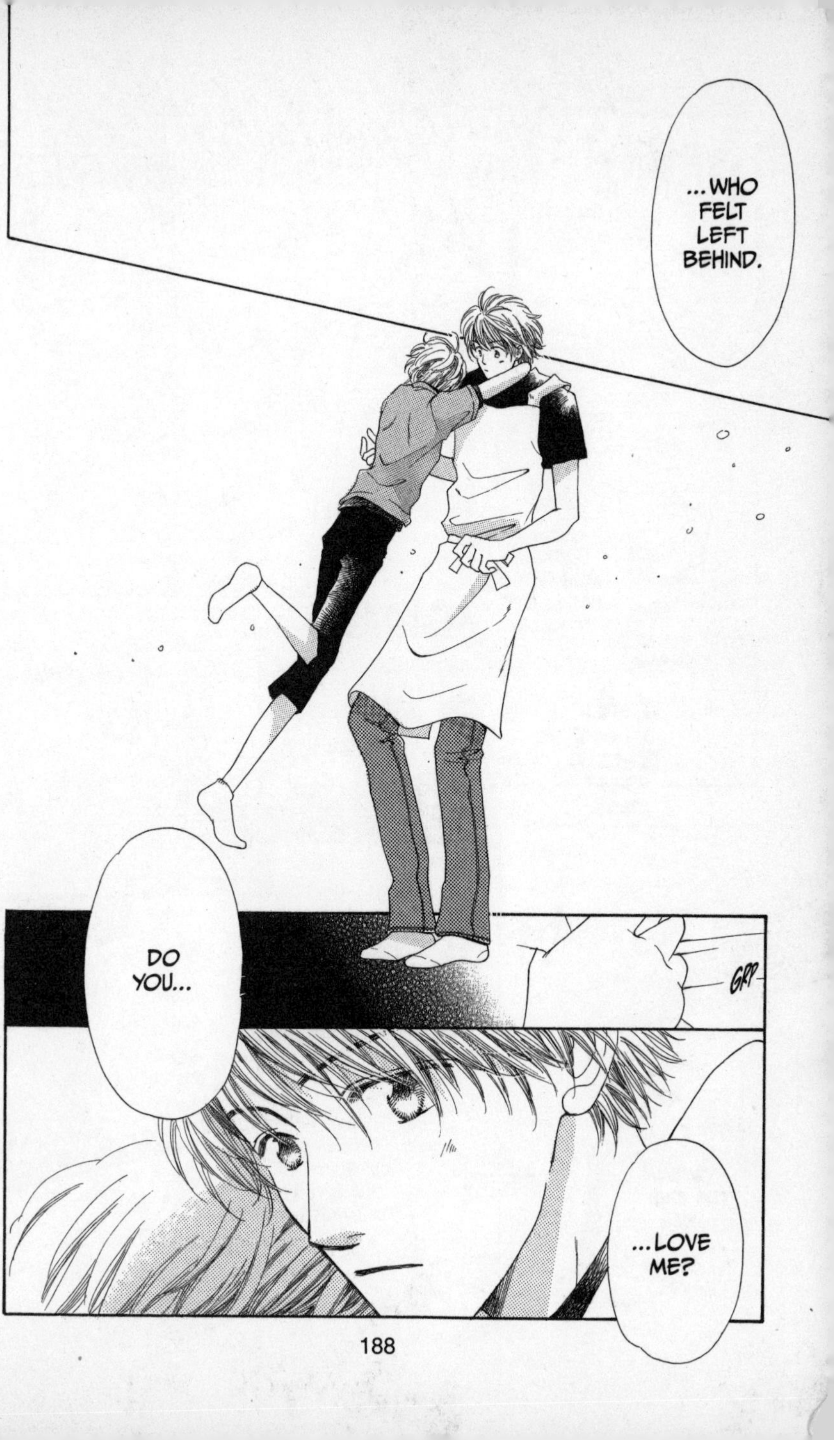
...WHO FELT LEFT BEHIND.
GRP
DO YOU...
...LOVE ME?

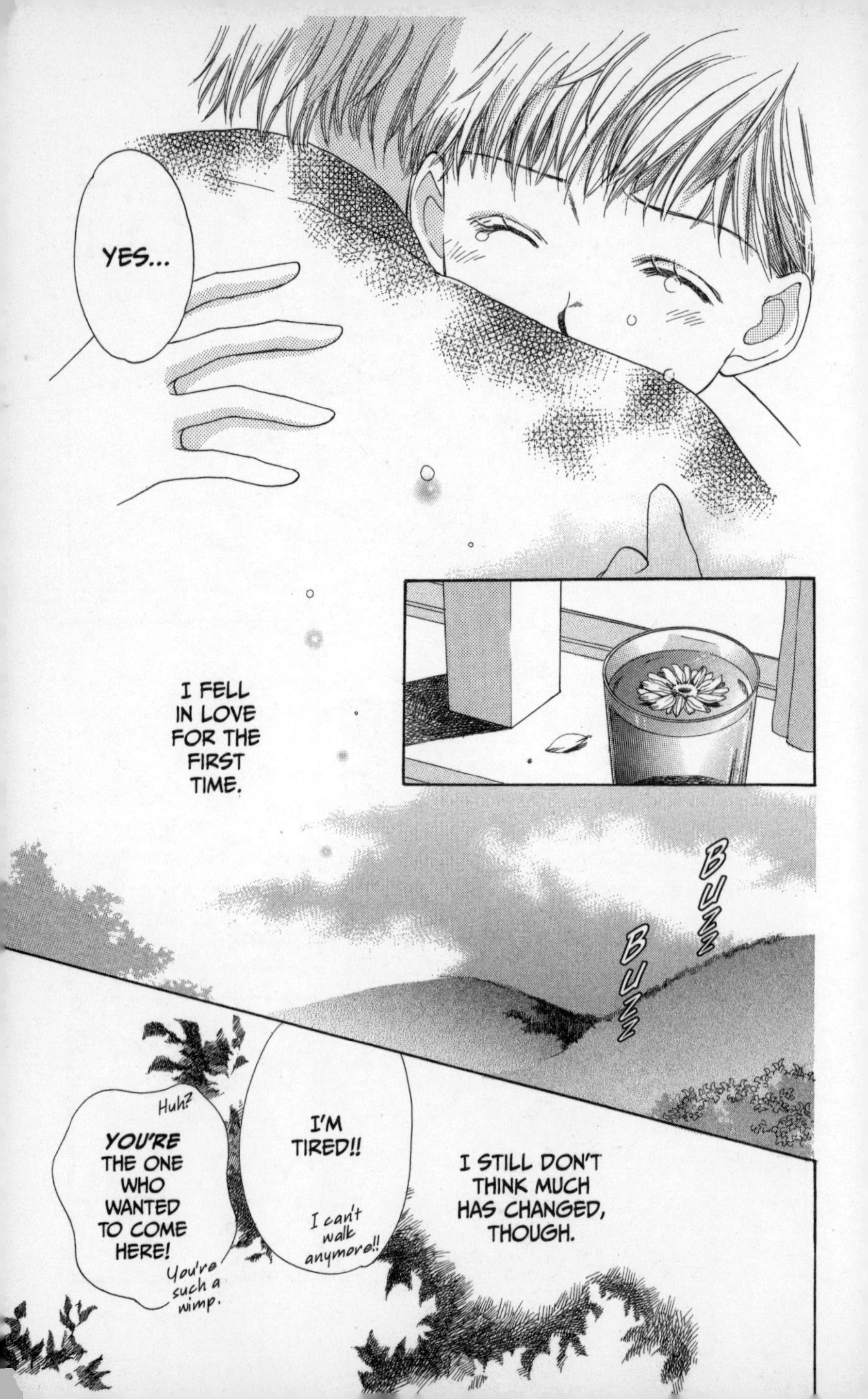
YES...
I FELL IN LOVE FOR THE FIRST TIME.
BUZZ
BUZZ
I STILL DON'T THINK MUCH HAS CHANGED, THOUGH.
I'M TIRED!!
I can't walk anymore!!
Huh?
YOU'RE THE ONE WHO WANTED TO COME HERE!
You're such a wimp.

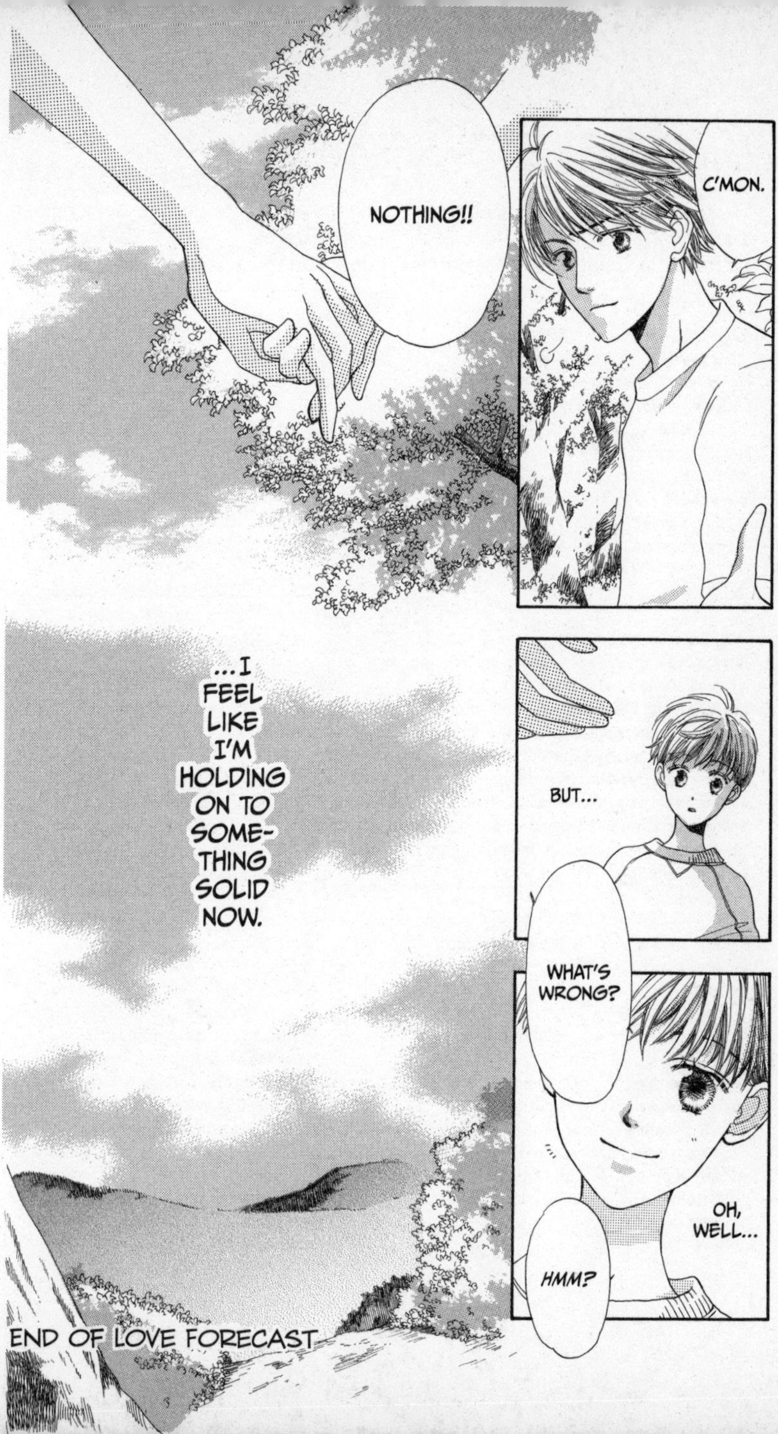
C'MON.
BUT...
WHAT'S WRONG?
OH, WELL...
HMM?
NOTHING!!
...I FEEL LIKE I'M HOLDING ON TO SOME-THING SOLID NOW.
END OF LOVE FORECAST

La Corda d'Oro End Notes

You can appreciate music just by listening to it, but knowing the story behind a piece can help enhance your enjoyment. In that spirit, here is background information about some of the topics mentioned in *La Corda d'Oro*. Enjoy!

Page 57, panel 6: *Ave Maria*
"Hail Mary," a traditional Catholic prayer, has been set to music by many composers, including Antonín Dvořák and Giuseppe Verdi. However, in this case Kahoko is listening to Franz Schubert's well-known 1825 composition *Ellens dritter Gesang*, often called *Ave Maria* because the accompanying chorus opens with those words. Schubert's composition is the piece referred to as *Ave Maria* in the Disney movie *Fantasia*.

Page 86, panel 1: *Tzigane*
The title of this 1924 composition by Maurice Ravel is derived from a word for *gypsy*. Although it doesn't use authentic Gypsy elements, the bold, wild melody is supposed to evoke the spirit of Gypsy music. It was originally written for violin with accompaniment by the luthéal, a piano-like instrument. The luthéal could be used to imitate the sound of the cimbalom, a type of dulcimer often played by Gypsy musicians, fitting with the mood of the piece.

Page 94, panel 2: *From the New World*
Commonly known as the *New World Symphony*, this piece was composed by Antonín Dvořák in 1893 during a visit to America. Dvořák was very interested in traditional Native American and African-American music, saying, "These beautiful and varied themes are the product of the soil. They are the folk songs of America, and your composers must turn to them." He tried to work these elements into *From the New World*, although many critics feel that his "American" melodies have more in common

with the folk music of his native Bohemia. Nonetheless, the *New World Symphony* remains Dvořák's most popular work.

Page 103, panel 2: Tchaikovsky's *Nocturne*
Pyotr Ilyich Tchaikovsky (1840-1893) is one of the most famous Russian composers of the Romantic period. He is perhaps best known for his ballets *Swan Lake*, *The Sleeping Beauty* and *The Nutcracker*, and for orchestral pieces such as the *1812 Overture*. The *Nocturne* referred to here is probably his Opus 19, no. 4, one of a suite of six pieces composed for the piano.

Page 103: *LaLa*; Hakusensha
LaLa is the shojo manga magazine in which *La Corda d'Oro* appears in Japan. Other *LaLa* titles include *MeruPuri*, *Vampire Knight* and *Ouran High School Host Club*. Hakusensha is the Japanese publisher of *La Corda*.

Page 119, panel 6: *Adagio* by Albinoni
The *Adagio in G Minor* is the most famous piece by Baroque composer Tomaso Albinoni (1671-1751), even though it probably isn't his work. It was published in 1958 by music scholar Remo Giazotto, supposedly based on fragments from an unfinished sonata by Albinoni. Giazotto claimed to have found the sonata among the ruins of Dresden, Germany, after it was firebombed by the Allies during World War II. Since no other evidence of the sonata has ever been found, it is widely believed that Giazotto wrote it himself. A popular choice for soundtracks, it can be heard in places as diverse as the movie *Gallipoli*, the anime *Negima!*, and the British sitcom *Butterflies*.

It was also incorporated into the Doors album *An American Prayer*.

Page 124, panel 1: *Serenade* by Schubert

"One Sunday, during the summer of 1826, Schubert with several friends was returning from Potzleinsdorf to the city, and on strolling along through Wahring, he saw his friend Tieze sitting at a table in the garden of the Zum Biersack... Tieze had a book lying open before him, and Schubert soon began to turn over the leaves. Suddenly he stopped, and pointing to a poem, exclaimed, 'Such a delicious melody has just come into my head, if I but had a sheet of music paper with me.' Herr Doppler drew a few music lines on the back of a bill of fare, and in the midst of a genuine Sunday hubbub, with fiddlers, skittle players, and waiters running about in different directions with orders, Schubert wrote that lovely song."
–biographer Kreissle von Hellborn, on Schubert's "Serenade"

Page 128, panel 1: *Après un Rêve* by Fauré

Après un Rêve (After a Dream) is one of the earliest, but also one of the most popular, compositions by Gabriel Fauré (1845-1924), the most renowned and influential French composer of his time. It was originally composed for voice and piano, using the text of an anonymous poem in which a woman and her lover meet in an otherworldly, dreamlike state.

Page 135, panel 1: *Andante*

In music terminology, it's a direction meaning "in a moderately slow tempo."

Page 139, panel 6: *Senpai*

The honorific used to address one's senior in an organization, especially a school. The relationship between upperclassmen (senpai) and underclassmen (kohai) is a major aspect of Japanese school life; upperclassmen are supposed to help and guide the younger students, and underclassmen are supposed to obey and learn from their seniors.

Yuki Kure made her debut in 2000
with the story *Chijo yori Eien ni*
(Forever from the Earth), published
in monthly *LaLa* magazine.
La Corda d' Oro is her first manga
series published. Her hobbies are
watching soccer games and
collecting small goodies.

LA CORDA D'ORO
Vol. 7
The Shojo Beat Manga Edition

STORY AND ART BY
YUKI KURE
ORIGINAL CONCEPT BY
RUBY PARTY

English Translation & Adaptation/Mai Ihara
Touch-up Art & Lettering/Gia Cam Luc
Cover Design/Yukiko Whitley
Interior Design/Izumi Evers
Editor/Shaenon K. Garrity

Editor in Chief, Books/Alvin Lu
Editor in Chief, Magazines/Marc Weidenbaum
VP of Publishing Licensing/Rika Inouye
VP of Sales/Gonzalo Ferreyra
Sr. VP of Marketing/Liza Coppola
Publisher/Hyoe Narita

Printed in Canada

Published by VIZ Media, LLC
P.O. Box 77010
San Francisco, CA 94107

Shojo Beat Manga Edition
10 9 8 7 6 5 4 3 2 1
First printing, April 2008

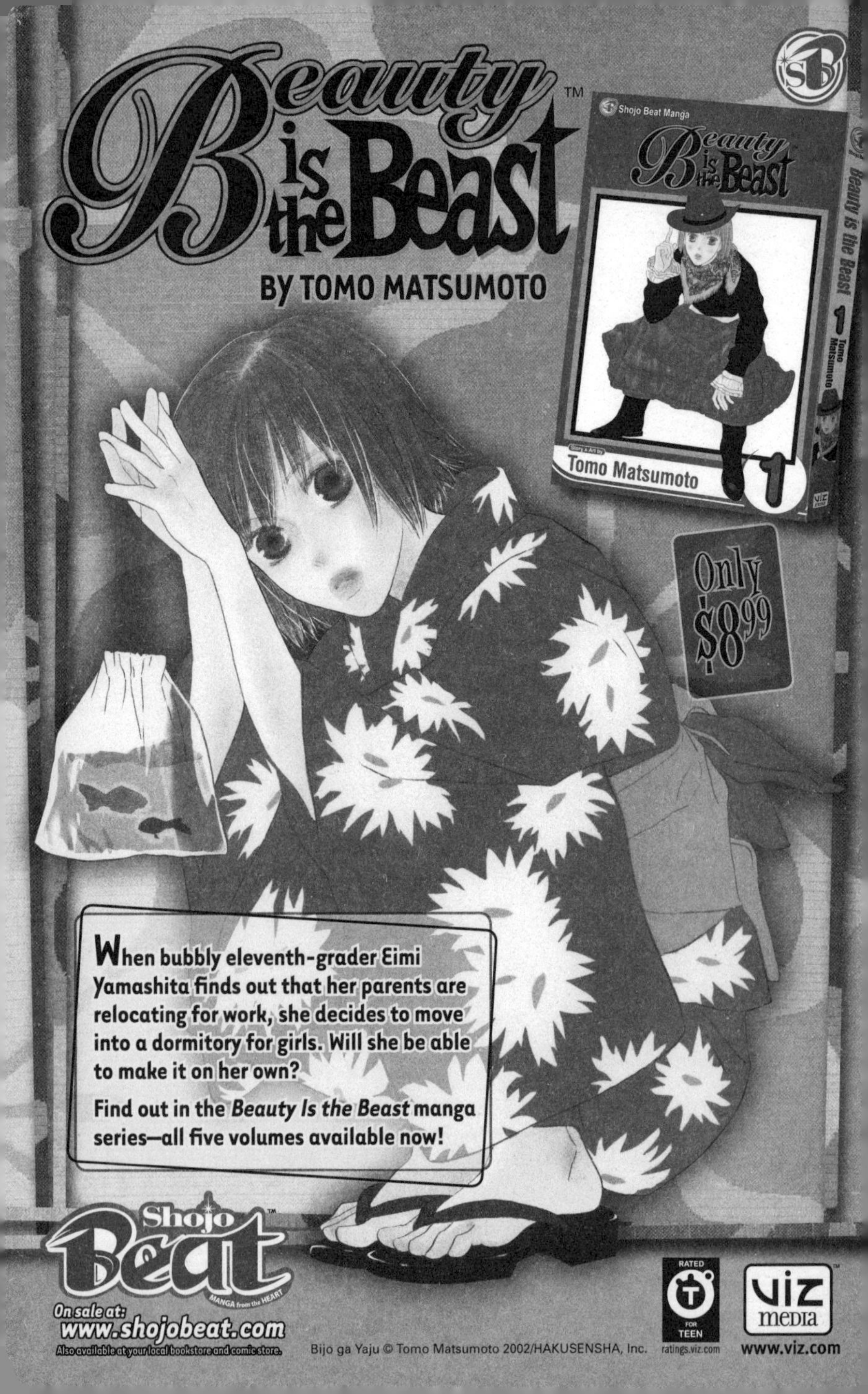

Beauty is the Beast™
BY TOMO MATSUMOTO
Shojo Beat Manga
Beauty is the Beast
Story & Art by
Tomo Matsumoto
1
Only $8.99
When bubbly eleventh-grader Eimi Yamashita finds out that her parents are relocating for work, she decides to move into a dormitory for girls. Will she be able to make it on her own?
Find out in the Beauty Is the Beast manga series—all five volumes available now!
Shojo Beat
MANGA from the HEART
On sale at:
www.shojobeat.com
Also available at your local bookstore and comic store.
Bijo ga Yaju © Tomo Matsumoto 2002/HAKUSENSHA, Inc.
RATED T FOR TEEN
ratings.viz.com
VIZ media
www.viz.com

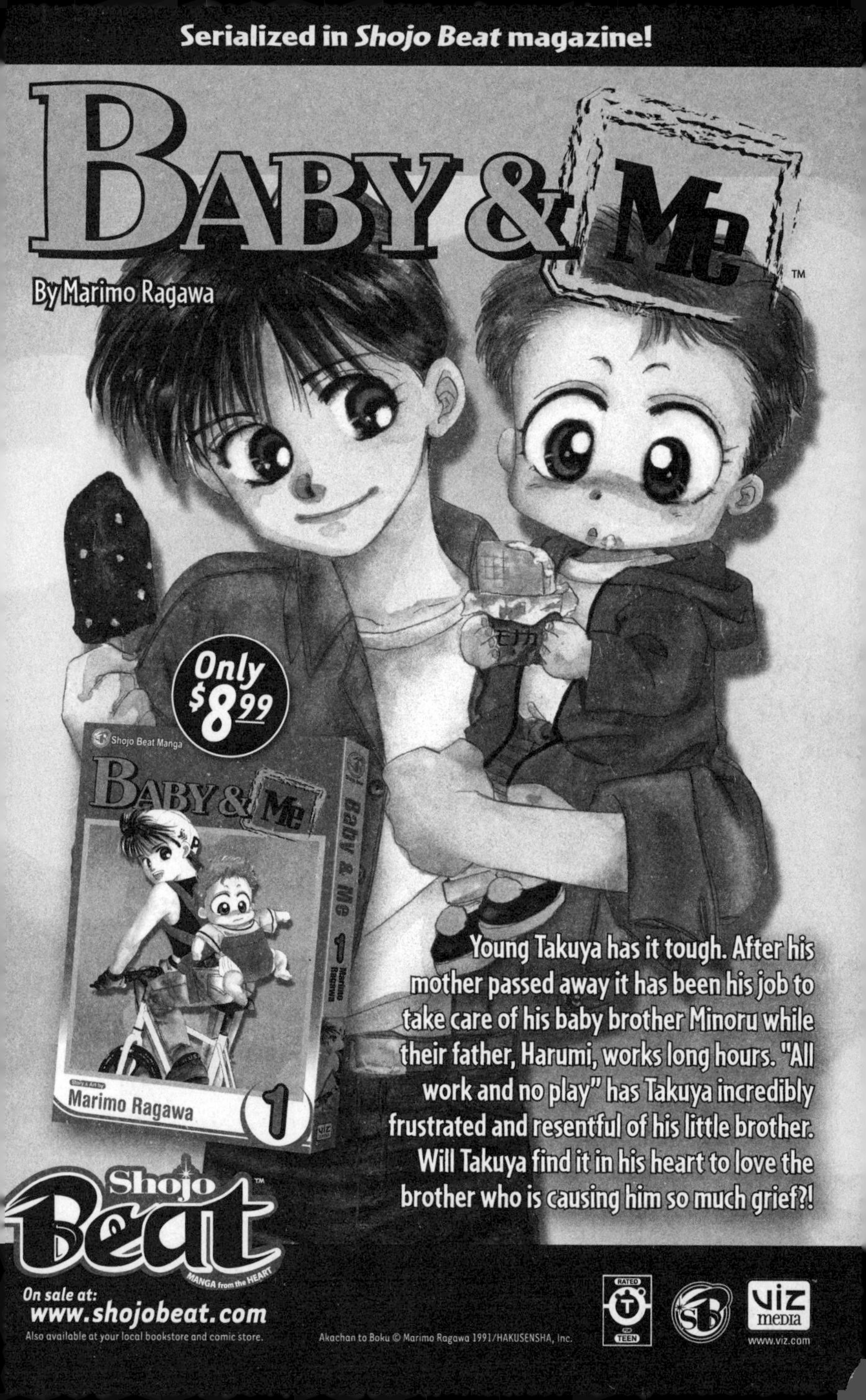
Serialized in Shojo Beat magazine!
BABY & Me™
By Marimo Ragawa
Only $8.99
Shojo Beat Manga
BABY & Me
Baby & Me 1 Marimo Ragawa
Story & Art by
Marimo Ragawa
1
Young Takuya has it tough. After his mother passed away it has been his job to take care of his baby brother Minoru while their father, Harumi, works long hours. "All work and no play" has Takuya incredibly frustrated and resentful of his little brother. Will Takuya find it in his heart to love the brother who is causing him so much grief?!
Shojo Beat™
MANGA from the HEART
On sale at:
www.shojobeat.com
Also available at your local bookstore and comic store.
Akachan to Boku © Marimo Ragawa 1991/HAKUSENSHA, Inc.
RATED T FOR TEEN
viz media
www.viz.com

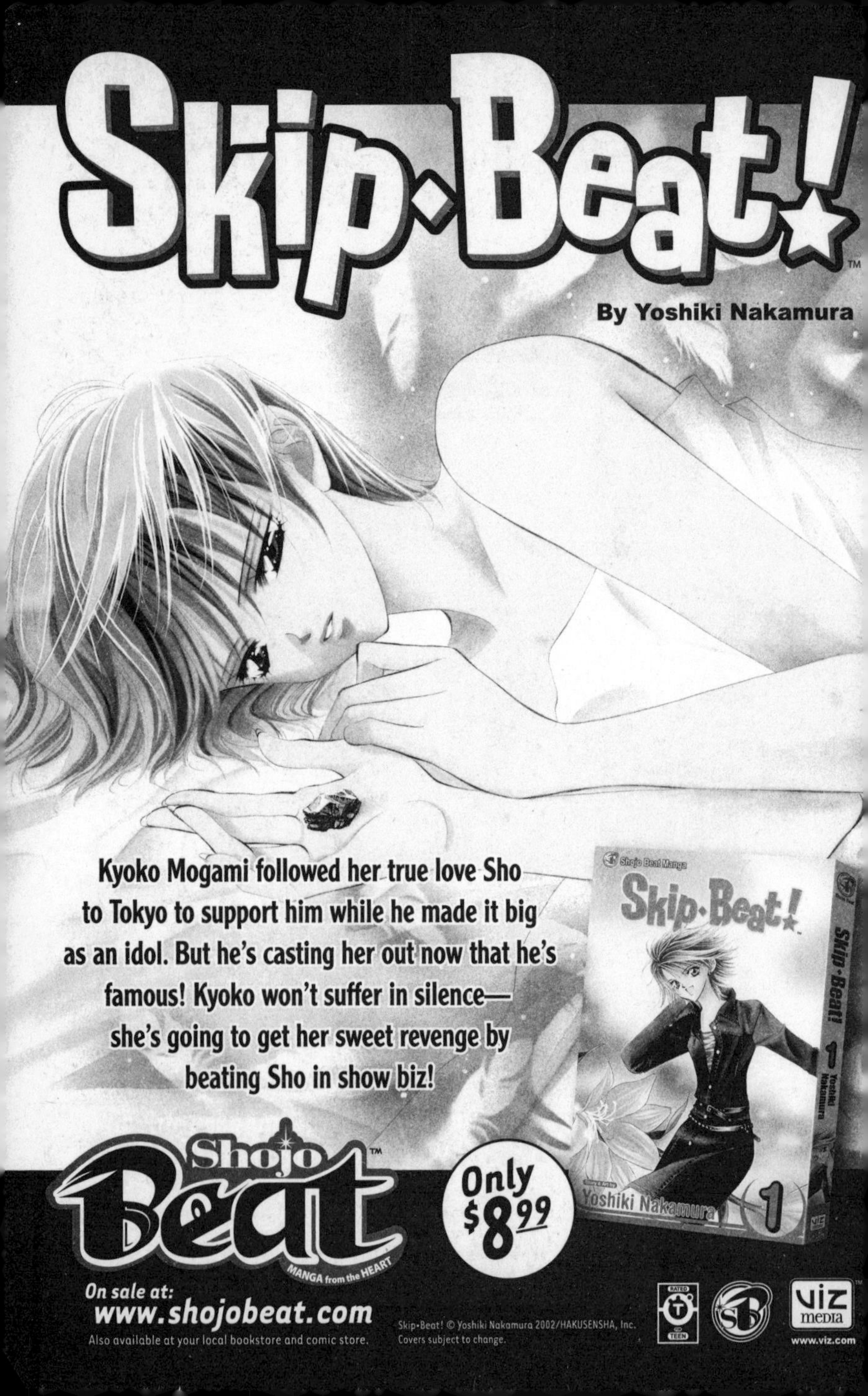
Skip·Beat!™
By Yoshiki Nakamura
Kyoko Mogami followed her true love Sho to Tokyo to support him while he made it big as an idol. But he's casting her out now that he's famous! Kyoko won't suffer in silence— she's going to get her sweet revenge by beating Sho in show biz!
Shojo Beat Manga
Skip·Beat!
Yoshiki Nakamura
1
Shojo Beat™
MANGA from the HEART
Only $8.99
On sale at:
www.shojobeat.com
Also available at your local bookstore and comic store.
Skip·Beat! © Yoshiki Nakamura 2002/HAKUSENSHA, Inc.
Covers subject to change.
RATED T TEEN
VIZ media
www.viz.com

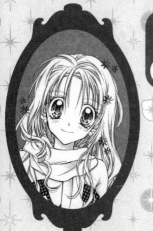
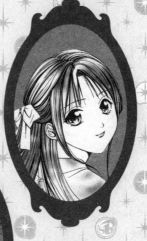

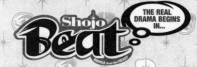

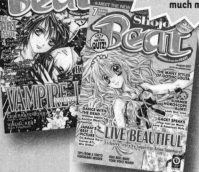
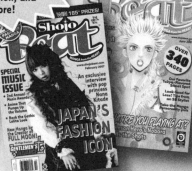